Noel Malcolm was born in 1956, and educated at Eton and Cambridge, where he gained a starred First in English and a Ph.D. in History. Fellow of Gonville and Caius College, Cambridge, from 1981 to 1988, he later became Foreign Editor of *The Spectator* and is now a political columnist on the *Daily Telegraph*. He lives in London and is currently working on a biography of Thomas Hobbes.

NOEL MALCOLM

Bosnia

A Short History

PAPERMAC

First published 1994 by Macmillan London Limited

a division of Pan Macmillan Publishers Limited
Cavaye Place London SW10 9PG
and Basingstoke

and simultaneously in paperback by Papermac

Associated companies throughout the world

ISBN 0-333-61677-4 (hardback)
ISBN 0-333-61678-2 (paperback)

5 7 9 8 6

A CIP catalogue record for this book is available from the British Library

Typeset by CentraCet Limited, Cambridge
Printed by Mackays of Chatham PLC, Kent

For Ahmed and Zdravko

'Bosnia lies at the nodal point of the great historic civilizations and her history is difficult to write, because it needs several languages and a knowledge of very complicated events. In view of the Bosnian disaster today, it also needs an understanding of the world after the Cold War. To combine these qualifications in a book that is accessible is a formidable undertaking, defeating all but the best. Noel Malcolm is the best: here he has triumphed, and there is not a page, from the surveys of archaeological evidence at the start, to the moral condemnation at the end, which is out of place.'

NORMAN STONE

Contents

Acknowledgements

My greatest regret is that I did not have the opportunity to work in the libraries of Sarajevo while it was still possible to do so. I am very grateful to the staffs of those libraries where I have done much of the research for this book: the Bibliothèque Nationale, Paris; the Bodleian Library, Oxford; the British Library, London; the Cambridge University Library; the School of Oriental and African Studies, London; and above all the School of Slavonic and East European Studies, London. For help in supplying or locating hard-to-find publications I am particularly grateful to Anthony Hall, John Laughland, John London, Branka Magaš and George Stamkoski. I am also indebted to Andrew Gwatkin for help with word-processing, and to Mark Willingale and Chris Burke for designing and producing the maps for this volume. My debts to previous writers on Bosnia will be fully apparent from the notes at the end of the book, but I should just like to give special mention here to the lucid scholarship of John Fine, from which I have benefited greatly. I should also like to record a debt of gratitude to John Yarnold, Saba Risaluddin, Ben Cohen, George Stamkoski and Majo Topolovac for all they have done during the last year to provide accurate information to the British media and the world about what was really happening in Bosnia.

Acknowledgments

A Note on names and pronunciations

Readers will notice that I have used the term 'Ragusa' until the early nineteenth century, and 'Dubrovnik' thereafter. For similar reasons, I have referred to Bosnian Orthodox and Bosnian Catholics until the late nineteenth or early twentieth centuries, and Bosnian Serbs and Bosnian Croats thereafter.

The names of territories, such as 'Serbia', are generally used – unless the context indicates otherwise – to refer to their modern (post-1945) geographical areas. Where 'Bosnia' is used as a geographical term, it normally means the whole territory of modern Bosnia and Hercegovina. The only exceptions are when I refer to 'Bosnia proper' (which means: excluding Hercegovina), or where the context clearly shows that I am referring to Bosnia in contradistinction to Hercegovina.

When writing about a multi-lingual and multi-national entity such as the Ottoman Empire, it is necessary to use terms from more than one language. I have tended to use the Turkish forms for general institutions of the Empire (such as *devşirme*), and Serbo-Croat forms for those which were either special to Bosnia, or incorporated in local geographical terms (such as *kapetanija* or *sandžak*). Where standard English forms exist (such as 'spahi'), I have used them. In the case of personal names, I have anglicized a few medieval names which have come down otherwise in a confusing plethora of forms (Stefan, Stepan, Stjepan), and have tried to keep to a standard format for those Ottoman names in which titles are embedded (Husejn-kapetan, Siavuš-paša). The pronunciation of Serbo-Croat is simple and regular; only the following important differences need to be observed.

c	is pronounced	'ts'
č		'tch' (as in 'match')
ć		similar to 'tch', but a thinner sound, more like the thickened 't' in 'future'
dj		roughly like 'j' (as in 'jam')
j		'y' (as in 'Yugoslavia')
š		'sh'
ž		'zh' (as in 'Zhivago')

The pronunciation of Turkish is even simpler:

c	is pronounced	'j' (as in 'jam')
ç		'tch' (as in 'match')
ğ		is silent, but lengthens the preceding vowel
ı		the vowel in French 'deux'
ş		'sh'

POST-1945 YUGOSLAVIA: REPUBLICS, AUTONOMOUS PROVINCES, HISTORIC REGIONS AND CITIES

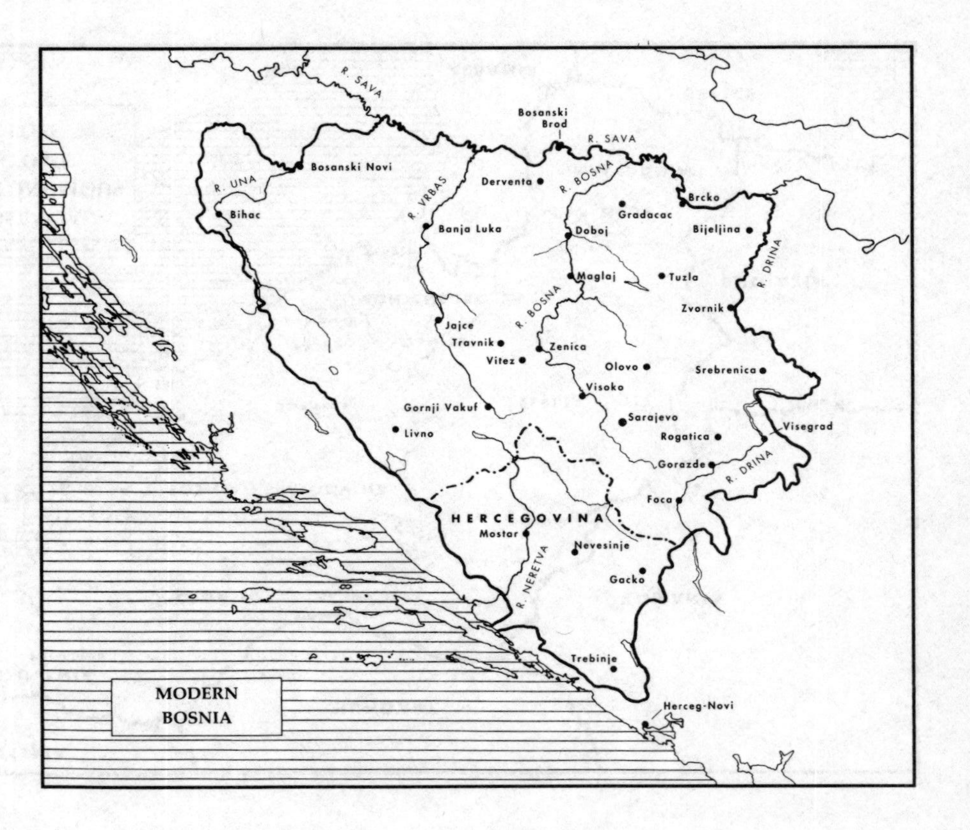
MODERN
BOSNIA
R. SAVA
Bosanski Brod
R. SAVA
Bosanski Novi
R. UNA
Bihac
R. VRBAS
Banja Luka
Derventa
R. BOSNA
Gradacac
Brcko
Bijeljina
Doboj
Maglaj
Tuzla
R. DRINA
Zvornik
R. BOSNA
Jajce
Travnik
Vitez
Zenica
Olovo
Srebrenica
Visoko
Gornji Vakuf
Livno
Sarajevo
Visegrad
Rogatica
Gorazde
R. DRINA
Foca
HERCEGOVINA
Mostar
Nevesinje
R. NERETVA
Gacko
Trebinje
Herceg-Novi

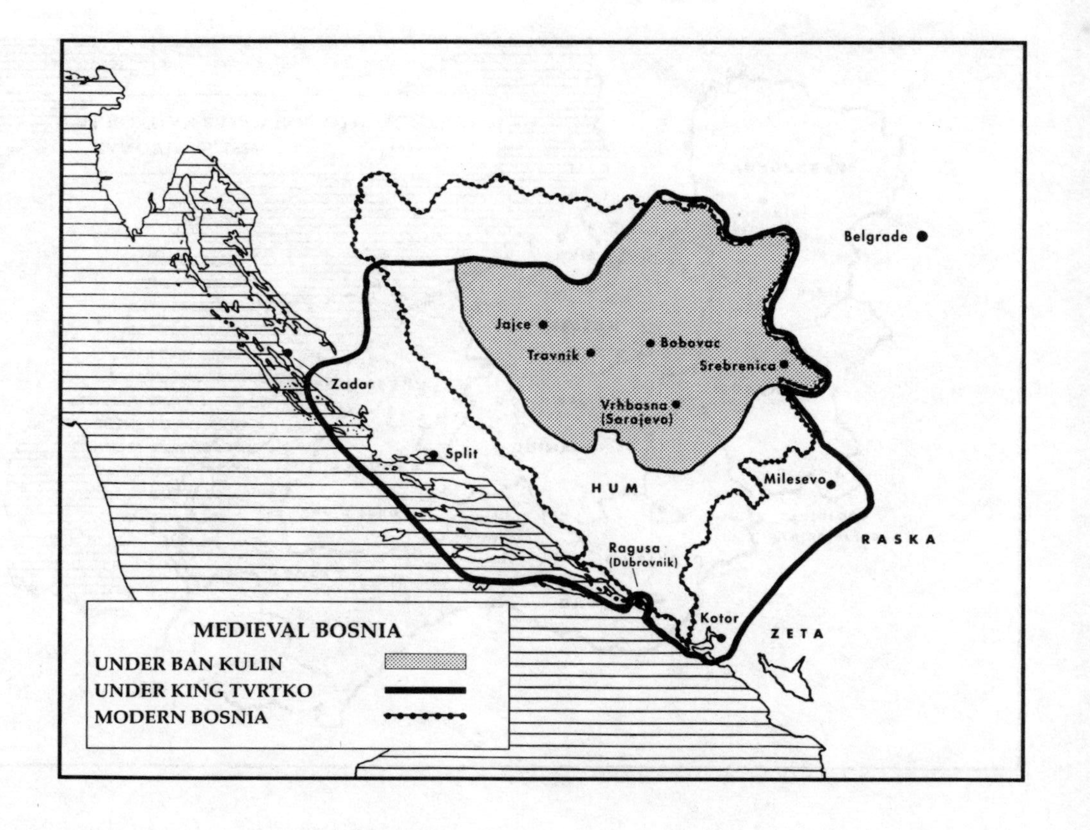
Belgrade
Jajce
Travnik
Bobovac
Srebrenica
Zadar
Vrhbasna
(Sarajevo)
Split
HUM
Milesevo
RASKA
Ragusa
(Dubrovnik)
Kotor
ZETA
MEDIEVAL BOSNIA
UNDER BAN KULIN
UNDER KING TVRTKO
MODERN BOSNIA

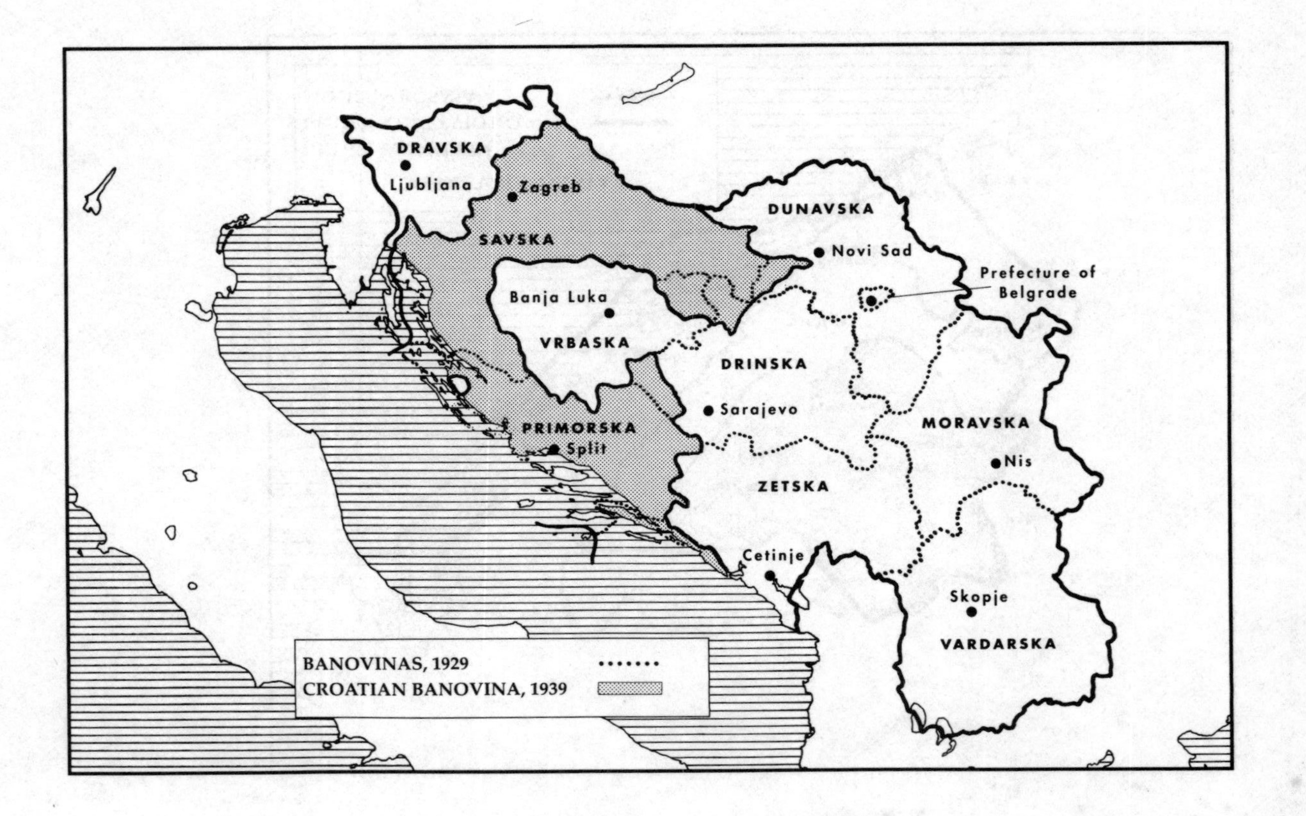
DRAVSKA
Ljubljana
Zagreb
SAVSKA
DUNAVSKA
Novi Sad
Prefecture of
Belgrade
Banja Luka
VRBASKA
DRINSKA
Sarajevo
MORAVSKA
PRIMORSKA
Split
Nis
ZETSKA
Cetinje
Skopje
VARDARSKA
BANOVINAS, 1929
CROATIAN BANOVINA, 1939

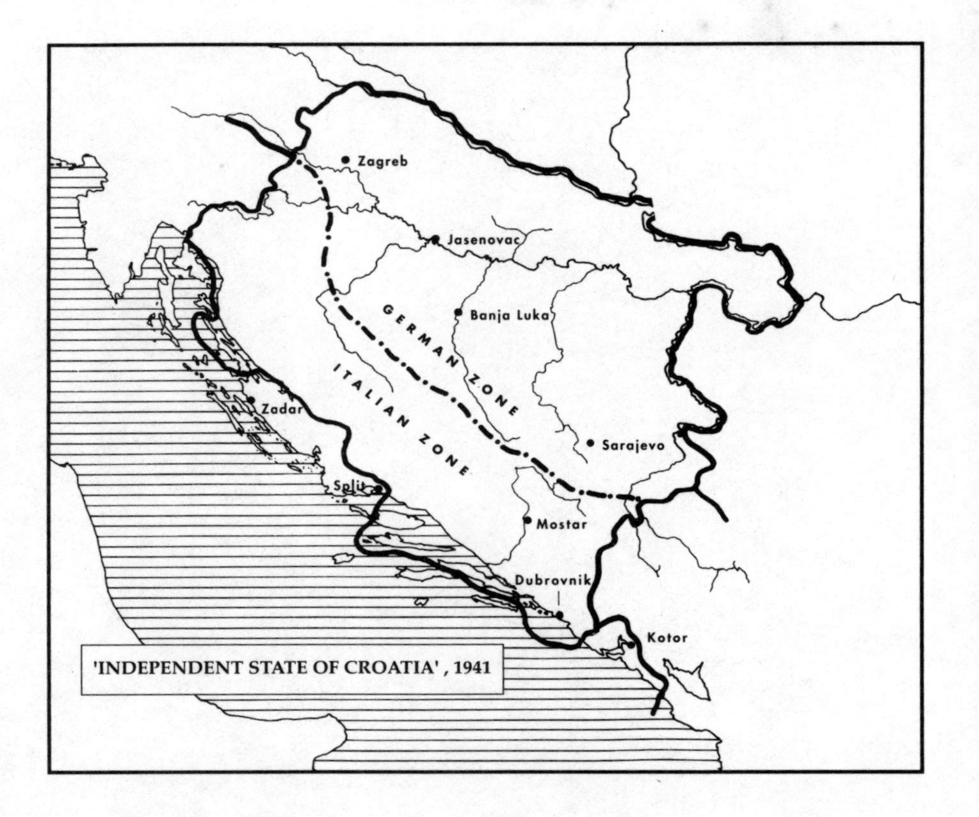

'INDEPENDENT STATE OF CROATIA', 1941

Introduction

The years 1992 and 1993 will be remembered as the years in which a European country was destroyed. It was a land with a political and cultural history unlike that of any other country in Europe. The great religions and great powers of European history had overlapped and combined there: the empires of Rome, Charlemagne, the Ottomans and the Austro-Hungarians, and the faiths of Western Christianity, Eastern Christianity, Judaism and Islam. These facts alone would be sufficient reason for studying the history of Bosnia as an object of unique interest in its own right. But the war which engulfed this country in 1992 has added two melancholy reasons for examining its history more closely: the first is the need to understand the origins of the fighting, and the second is the need to dispel some of the clouds of misunderstanding, deliberate myth-making and sheer ignorance in which all discussion of Bosnia and its history has become shrouded.

Of these two needs, the second is by far the more urgent. Paradoxically, the most important reason for studying Bosnia's history is that it enables one to see that the history of Bosnia in itself does not explain the origins of this war. Of course the war could not have happened if Bosnia had not been the peculiar thing that it was, which made it the object of special ambitions and interests. But those ambitions were directed at Bosnia from outside Bosnia's borders. The biggest obstacle to all understanding of the conflict is the assumption that what has happened in that country is the product – natural, spontaneous and at the same time necessary – of forces lying within Bosnia's own internal history. That is the myth which was carefully propagated by those who caused the conflict, who wanted the world to believe that what they and their gunmen were doing was done not by them, but by impersonal and inevitable historical forces beyond anyone's control.

And the world believed them. It is for future historians to judge which arguments really weighed in the minds of the statesmen of Europe and America, while they reacted to the fighting in Bosnia with policies which not only failed to solve the crisis but actually made it much worse. What is clear is that their minds were already filled with a fog of historical ignorance. Here, for example, is the considered view of the British Prime Minister, John Major, addressing the House of Commons more than one year after the outbreak of the war:

> The biggest single element behind what has happened in Bosnia is the collapse of the Soviet Union and of the discipline that that exerted over the ancient hatreds in the old Yugoslavia. Once that discipline had disappeared, those ancient hatreds reappeared, and we began to see their consequences when the fighting occurred. There were subsidiary elements, but that collapse was by far the greatest (Hansard, 23 June 1993, col. 324).

It is hard to know where to begin in commenting on such a statement. The 'discipline' exerted by the Soviet Union on Yugoslavia came to an abrupt and well-publicized end in 1948, when Stalin expelled Tito from his Cominform organization. Perhaps Mr Major was trying to refer to the decision of Communist leaders such as Serbia's Slobodan Milošević to tap the springs of nationalism for their own political purposes; but this process was well under way in Serbia by the summer of 1989, two years before the 'collapse of the Soviet Union', and in many ways it hardly differed from the exploitation of nationalism by previous political leaders within the Communist system, such as Nicolae Ceauşescu. The idea that Communism in general acted as a valuable 'discipline' to keep nationalism under control is doubly false. Either Communist governments stirred up and manipulated nationalism for their own purposes; or they made it fester and become more virulent by creating a politically frustrated and alienated population; or, frequently, they did both. The double effect is clearly visible in most East European countries today, where the so-called 'extreme right' parties bring together ordinary voters who are roused by religious and historical symbolism from the pre-Communist age, and politicians whose previous careers were in the Communist Party and the state security services. That, more or less, is what has happened in Serbia too.

The other great piece of misinformation expressed by John Major in those remarks, and repeated by most Western leaders in their public comments on the Bosnian war, is the claim that everything which has happened in Bosnia since the spring of 1992 is the expression of 'ancient ethnic hatreds' welling up of their own accord. That hatreds and rivalries existed in Bosnia's past is certainly true; those writers who have reacted in the last two years by portraying Bosnia as a wonderland of permanent inter-religious harmony have over-reacted. But a closer inspection of Bosnia's history will show that the animosities which did exist were not absolute and unchanging. Nor were they inevitable consequences of the mixing together of different religious communities. The main basis of hostility was not ethnic or religious but economic: the resentment felt by the members of a mainly (but not exclusively) Christian peasantry towards their Muslim landowners. This hostility was not some absolute or irreducible force: it varied as economic circumstances changed, and was also subject to political pressures which significantly altered the attitude of the landowning class during the first half of the nineteenth century. And the hostility between the Catholic and Orthodox communities was also subject to changing influences: rivalries between the Church hierarchies, political pressures from neighbouring countries, and so on.

These animosities were not permanently built into the psyches of the people who lived in Bosnia; they were products of history, and could change as history developed. The economic causes of hatred were eroded by changes and reforms in the late nineteenth and early twentieth centuries, until they had largely ceased to exist. The religious causes of hatred were reduced in the second half of the twentieth century by all the processes (some natural, some unnatural) of secularization. For most of the period after 1878, the different religious or ethnic communities in Bosnia lived peacefully together: the two major episodes of violence – in and just after the first world war, and during the four years of the second world war – were exceptions, induced and aggravated by causes outside Bosnia's borders. And since the second of those terrible episodes, two whole generations have grown up, the majority of the Bosnian population, who have no personal memories of the fighting in that war, and no particular desire to revive it.

Of course it is easy to go through the history of a country such as Bosnia picking out instances of regional divisions, violence and ungovernability. The evidence is there, and readers will find plenty of it in the pages of this book. But the political history of late twentieth-century Bosnia has not been determined by what happened in the thirteenth or eighteenth centuries. Commentators who like to give some hastily-assembled historical authority to their writings can always pick out a few bloody episodes from the past and say: 'It was ever thus.' One could perform the same exercise with, for instance, the history of France, picking out the religious wars of the sixteenth century, the barbarity of the St Bartholomew's Day massacre, the frequent regional rebellions, the Fronde, the brutal treatment of the Huguenots in 1685, the appalling violence and mass-murder which followed the French Revolution, the instability of nineteenth-century politics, even the whole history of collaboration and resistance in the second world war. But if a number of foreign-backed politicians and military commanders began bombarding Paris with heavy artillery tomorrow, we would not sit back and say that it was just an inevitable consequence of 'ancient French hatreds'. We would want to look a little more closely at the real nature and origins of this particular crisis. That too has been attempted in this book.

France's great advantage, compared with Bosnia, is that its history is already widely known and studied in depth. In the case of Bosnia so little is generally known that it has been hard, during the last two years, to distinguish between the fog of ignorance and the smokescreen of propaganda. The very existence of Bosnia as an historical entity has been denied by some writers, who have confidently asserted that 'Bosnia has never been a state'. When Lord Owen was appointed to the job of EEC negotiator on Yugoslavia in 1992, one British columnist advised him in all seriousness that the internal borders of Yugoslavia were mere administrative borders as artificial as those imposed on Africa by colonial administrators. It has been a frequent claim of some writers that the borders of Bosnia were invented by Tito; the truth is that Tito simply restored the historic borders of Bosnia as they had been in the late Ottoman and Austro-Hungarian periods. As readers will discover, some parts of those borders had been established by eighteenth-century treaties, and other parts reflected much earlier historic boundaries, such as the division between Bosnia and Serbia along the Drina river which was mentioned by the chronicler Kinnamos in the late twelfth century.

The fragments of historical misinformation which have appeared in the Western media over the last two years have been washed in by tides of national and political mythology from within the old Yugoslavia. For more than a century, Croats have written books claiming to prove that the Bosnians are 'really' Croats; Serbs have argued equally unceasingly that they are all 'really' Serbs. More recently, Croatian propaganda has described all Serbian nationalists as 'Četniks' and has tried to present the leader of the Četniks in the second world war, Draža Mihailović, as a genocidal monster. Serb propaganda has described all Croatian nationalists as 'Ustaša', and has raked up the story of the Muslim SS division in the second world war as a way of suggesting that the Bosnian Muslims are either Nazis or fundamentalists, or both. And those who are caught in the middle of these disputes, the Muslims and/or the believers in a pluralist Bosnia, have been left to nurse what comforting myths they can find: the myth of the Bogomils, the myth of permanent peace and harmony in Bosnia, or the myth of Tito. It is not possible for a commentator or historian to pick his way between all these competing mythologies without causing some ideological offence to almost all parties; nor is it gratifying to do so when one has come to know and love not only Bosnia, but also many of the special qualities of Croatia and Serbia too. At the same time, the fact that there is an almost symmetrical pattern of conflicting claims and justifications does not mean that one can reach an accurate conclusion by treating all claims as equal and merely averaging them out. I have no doubt that the burden of responsibility for the destruction of Bosnia lies predominantly on one side, and I have tried to set out in the final chapters of this book the reasons for thinking so.

One sure way of judging the historical claims of the main perpetrators of violence in Bosnia is to look at what they have done to the physical evidence of history itself. They are not only ruining the future of that country; they are also making systematic efforts to eliminate its past. The state and university library in Sarajevo was destroyed with incendiary shells. The Oriental Institute, with its irreplaceable collection of manuscripts and other materials illustrating the Ottoman history of Bosnia, was also destroyed by concentrated shelling. All over the country, mosques and minarets have been demolished, including some of the finest examples of sixteenth-century Ottoman architecture in the western Balkans. These buildings were not just caught in the cross-fire of military engagements; in towns such as Bijeljina and Banja Luka, the demolitions had nothing to do with fighting at all – the mosques were blown up with explosives in the night, and bulldozed on the following day. The people who have planned and ordered these actions like to say that history is on their side. What they show by their deeds is that they are waging a war against the history of their country. All I have wanted to do in this book is to set out some of the details of that history before the country itself is utterly destroyed.

1

Races, myths and origins: Bosnia to 1180

Racial history is the bane of the Balkans. As anyone who has lived or travelled in that part of Europe will know, there is no such thing as a racially homogeneous province there, let alone a racially homogeneous state. Few individuals in the entire Balkan peninsula could honestly claim a racially pure ancestry for themselves. And yet, at many times during the last two centuries, bogus theories of racial-ethnic identity had dominated the national politics of the Balkan lands. One reason for studying the early history of the region is that it enables us to see that even if it were right to conduct modern politics in terms of ancient racial origins, it would simply not be possible.

Nowhere is this more true than in the history of Bosnia, a country which has often been called the microcosm of the Balkans. There is no such thing as a typical Bosnian face: there are fair-haired and dark-haired Bosnians, olive-skinned and freckled, big-boned and wiry-limbed. The genes of innumerable different peoples have contributed to this human mosaic. The country is heavily mountainous, with terrain ranging from the dense forest and lush upland pastures of north-central Bosnia to the arid and gaunt landscape of western Hercegovina; it is divided by rivers, most of which are non-navigable. An impenetrable mass of land, it stands between two of the main routes through which waves of invading populations entered the western Balkans: the Dalmatian coastal strip, and the lowland thoroughfare which led from Belgrade down through Serbia to Macedonia and Bulgaria. So the direct effect of those invasions on Bosnia was probably much smaller than their impact on the fertile lowlands of Serbia or the eminently plunderable Dalmatian coastal towns. But the indirect effect, in terms of the accumulation of racial types, was probably greater. Mountainous areas act as refuges for populations which, in flatter country, would otherwise be exterminated or driven away. One has only to look at the survival of the Basques in the Pyrenees, or the richly-stocked racial museum which is the Caucasus. In the case of Bosnia, the Slav invasions of the sixth and seventh centuries established a linguistic identity which eventually replaced all others. But the signs of racial diversity are there for anyone with eyes in his head to see.

For reasons of language and culture, and because of more than a thousand years of history, the modern population of Bosnia can properly be called Slav. The arrival of the Slavs in the Balkans is thus the natural starting-point for any history of Bosnia. But no starting-points can be absolute in human history; we need to know something too about the population of Bosnia which the Slavs found on their arrival, and which they later absorbed.

The earliest inhabitants of whom we have any historical details are the Illyrians, a collection of tribes which covered much of modern Yugoslavia and Albania and spoke an Indo-European language related to modern Albanian.[1] The tribe which gave its name to Dalmatia, the Delmatae, was probably named after a word related to the Albanian for 'sheep', *delmë*; its territory covered part of western Bosnia, and the archaeological evidence from several sites in Bosnia shows that the Illyrian tribes were stock-breeders specializing in sheep, pigs and goats.[2] Other tribes, encountered by the Romans as they extended their power inland in the second and first centuries BC, included a mixed Illyrian-Celtic grouping, the Scordisci, on the north-east fringe of Bosnia, and a warlike tribe in central Bosnia, the Daesitates, whose last rebellion against the Roman empire was finally crushed in AD 9. From then on, all the Illyrian lands were firmly under Roman rule, and a network of roads and Roman settlements was gradually established.[3] Several roads ran across Bosnia from the coastal town of Salona (near Split); these were needed not so much for trade as for military operations further to the east, but they also served as delivery routes for the gold, silver and lead which were mined in eastern Bosnia in Roman times.[4] Most of Bosnia was included in the Roman province of Dalmatia, but part of northern Bosnia fell within the province of Pannonia, which included modern north-eastern Croatia and southern Hungary. Christianity came quickly to the Roman towns: the first bishops are mentioned as early as the late first century in Sirmium in Pannonia (Sremska Mitrovica, a few miles beyond the north-eastern corner of modern Bosnia), and at least twenty Roman basilicas have been excavated within the modern Bosnian territory. One of these, near Stolac in Hercegovina, is a burned ruin containing coins from the fourth century: a graphic sign of the fact that this earliest phase of Bosnian Christianity came to an abrupt end with the invasion of the Goths.[5]

The use of Latin must have become widespread in Roman Bosnia. It was the only common language for the settlers from many parts of the Empire who came to live in the province of Dalmatia: from Italy above all, but also from Africa, Spain, Gaul, Germany, Greece, Asia Minor, Syria, Palestine and Egypt. Most of these colonists lived in the coastal towns, but there are records of people with Asian names in the Neretva valley (western Hercegovina) and in the Jajce region of north-western Bosnia.[6] From the mid-second century AD onwards, large numbers of military veterans were also settled as colonists in the Balkans: a telling sign of their importance is the fact that in Romanian, the language which developed out of the Latin spoken in this region, the word for 'old man', *bătrîn*, is derived from *veteranus*. The Illyrians themselves were heavily recruited into the Roman legions, and from the late second century onwards the Illyrian lands were the military power-base for a number of provincial governors and generals who became Roman Emperors. The first of these, Septimius Severus, dismissed the Praetorian Guard when he came to Rome in 193 and replaced it with Illyrian troops: 'a throng', in the words of one Roman historian, 'of motley soldiers most savage in appearance, most terrifying in speech, and most boorish in conversation'.[7]

Other Roman and Greek sources take a similarly superior attitude towards these provincial Balkan tribesmen. As a result, we have no really detailed accounts of their social structure, their religion or their way of life. But one passing comment by the Greek geographer Strabo (63 BC–AD 25) is particularly intriguing: he mentions that tattooing was common among the Illyrians. His testimony has been confirmed by the discovery of tattooing needles in Illyrian burial mounds in Bosnia.[8] Tattooing is not known to have been a Slav custom at any time or in any part of the Slav realms, and yet it has survived well into this century among the Catholics of central Bosnia and the Muslims and Catholics of northern Albania. In the 1920s the English traveller and Balkan scholar Edith Durham made a detailed study of the practice and copied many of the Bosnian designs – simple geometric patterns of circles, crosses and crescents, apparently representing rayed suns and moons. 'Women', she reported, 'are far more elaborately tattooed than men. Their arms and forearms are often covered with patterns . . . The friendly ones said they tattooed "because it is our custom", "because we are Catholics", "because it is pretty", and said my hands would be prettier tattooed.'[9] This practice is striking evidence of cultural continuity in Bosnia stretching all the way back to the Illyrian tribes. Unfortunately, it is the *only* strong piece of evidence; claims about Illyrian origins have been made about other apparently non-Slav practices which survive in Bosnia, such as polyphonic folk-music, but there the corroboration of Roman or Greek writers is lacking.[10]

Given not only the evidence of tattooing, but also what is known about the history of Balkan invasions and settlements, we can be fairly sure that some of the Illyrians survived the later invasions and were absorbed into what became the Slav population. But the romantic theory of some nineteenth-century Yugoslav ideologists, who argued that the Serbs and Croats were 'really' Illyrians (and therefore a single, special, age-old racial unit), tells us more about modern Yugoslav politics than about early Balkan history.[11]

Sometimes it seems as if no population could enter the Balkans without giving rise to some similar theory for later generations to seize on. This is especially true of the next invaders, the Germanic tribes of Goths, who began raiding the Roman Balkans in the third century, inflicted massive defeats on Roman armies in the late fourth century, conquered the fortress of Singidunum (modern Belgrade) in the late fifth century, but mainly withdrew to the kingdom which they established in Italy and Dalmatia soon thereafter. They were finally driven out of the Balkans by the Emperor Justinian in the early sixth century. (After Justinian's campaigns, Bosnia became – notionally, at least – part of the Byzantine Empire; originally it had been on the western side of the dividing-line between the West Roman and East Roman lands.) Any Goths who remained behind were quickly absorbed into the local populations.[12] Although they were settlers as well as raiders, the Goths seem to have left no cultural imprint on the Balkan lands: there is, for example, not a single word in any Balkan language that can be shown to be derived from Gothic.

And yet a curious mythology later developed, in which the Goths were seen as the true ancestors of the Croats and/or the Bosnians. The origin of this myth was a medieval manuscript in Latin, *The Chronicle of the Priest of Dioclea*, which seems to have incorporated an earlier Slav chronicle known by its Latin title as *Libellus Gothorum*, 'The Book of the Goths'; it begins with the migration of the Goths into Pannonia, and treats them as the original ancestors of the Slavs.[13] The *Chronicle* was used by several late Renaissance historians in Ragusa (Dubrovnik). The greatest of these, the Benedictine monk Mauro Orbini, constructed a grandiose theory of racial history in which nearly all the races which did anything interesting in the late classical and early medieval periods were Slavs (including Vandals, Avars, Normans, Finns, Thracians and Illyrians), and all Slavs were Goths: 'All of these belonged to the same Slav nation and spoke the same Slav language; and when at first they left their common homeland, Scandinavia, they were all (except the Illyrians and Thracians) called by the single name of "Goths".'[14] In Orbini's work, this identification with the Goths functioned as part of a kind of pan-Slav ideology, in which the Goth-Slavs were shown to have been the most active and powerful race in European history. But in some later versions of the 'Gothic' theory, people from the western Balkans identified themselves as Goths in order to distinguish themselves from the Slavs. For obvious reasons this theory became especially popular in Bosnia during the second world war, when Bosnians who wanted their country to be given autonomy from the Croatian fascist state tried to establish their Bosnian identity on a separate racial basis. In November 1942 a group of Bosnian Muslim autonomists sent a 'Memorandum' to Hitler, in which they claimed racial superiority over their Slav neighbours: 'By race and blood we are not Slavs; we are of Gothic origin. We Bosnians came south to the Balkans in the third century as a Germanic tribe.'[15] Even Hitler, it seems, found this theory a little hard to believe.

The Goths were not the only race to have visited the western Balkans, and perhaps left some descendants there, between the Romans and the Slavs. Asiatic Huns (a Mongol-Turkic people) and Iranian Alans (ancestors of the modern Ossetians in the Caucasus) also appeared in the fourth and fifth centuries. In the sixth century two new populations entered the Balkans: the Avars (a Turkic tribe who came from the region north of the Caucasus) and the Slavs. Their histories were at first closely intertwined, either as allies or as rivals; the Avars, though less numerous, seem to have had the upper hand in this relationship because of their superior military skills. These Turkic tribesmen were eventually driven out of the Balkans in the early seventh century by Byzantine, Croat and Bulgarian armies. Historians traditionally assumed that the Avars were a rather ephemeral presence in the region, essentially a military force interested only in raiding. However, modern research (in archaeology and the study of place-names) suggests that there were long-term settlements of Avars in many parts of western Bosnia, Hercegovina and Montenegro.[16] In some places, including areas just to the north and north-west of Bosnia, distinct groups of Avar settlers may have lingered for generations: the Slav name for the Avars was *Obri*, and there are many place-names such as Obrovac which record their presence.[17] It is also possible that the word *ban*, which from early times was used as the title of Croatian rulers, is itself of Avar origin.[18]

But it was of course the Slavs who predominated in the end. In the late sixth century they moved in large numbers down the Balkan peninsula; they were colonists and agriculturalists, not just raiders, and they established settlements all the way down to the southern tip of Greece. (There were Slav-speaking villages there well into the fifteenth century.)[19] By the 620s a Slav population was well established in modern Bulgaria and Serbia, and had probably penetrated much of Bosnia too. Then, within a few years, two new Slav tribes arrived on the scene: the Croats and the Serbs. According to the Byzantine historian and Emperor Constantine Porphyrogenitus (writing 300 years later, but making use of the imperial archives), the Croats were invited into the Balkans by the Byzantine Emperor of the day to drive out the troublesome Avars. The Serbs, according to Constantine, were not engaged to fight Avars, but they were connected with the Croats and entered the Balkans in the same period.[20]

Who exactly were the Serbs and the Croats? Scholars have long been aware that the name 'Croat' (*Hrvat* in Serbo-Croat) is not a Slav word. It is thought to be the same as an Iranian name, *Choroatos*, found in inscriptions on tombstones near the Greek town of Tanais on the lower Don, in southern Russia. The whole region north of the Black Sea was inhabited in the early centuries AD by a mixture of tribes which included Slavs and Sarmatians: the latter were Iranian nomads who had passed westwards round the northern side of the Caucasus in the second century BC. The Sarmatians gained political dominance over the other tribes, and it seems likely that some of the Slav tribes thus acquired an Iranian-speaking ruling elite.[21] One theory connects Hrvat and Choroatos with the word *hu-urvatha*, which meant 'friend' in the language of the Alans (who were part of the Sarmatian grouping of Iranian tribes at this time).[22] Another theory proposes that the root of the name 'Serb', *serv*, became *charv* in Iranian, and that together with the suffix *-at* this gave rise to Choroatos and Hrvat.[23] What is clear is that the Serbs and the Croats had a similar and connected history from the earliest times: Ptolemy, writing in the second century AD, also located the *Serboi* among the Sarmatian tribes north of the Caucasus. Most scholars believe either that both Serbs and Croats were Slavic tribes with Iranian ruling castes, or that they were originally Iranian tribes which had acquired Slavic subjects.[24] By the early seventh century both tribes had established kingdoms in central Europe: 'White Croatia', which covered part of modern southern Poland, and 'White Serbia', in the modern Czech lands. It was from there that they came down to the western Balkans.

Once again, modern ideology has had its way with ancient history. There have been Croat nationalist theorists who have selectively accepted the evidence of Iranian ancestry for their own people and rejected it for the Serbs, thus creating an age-old racial divide between the two populations. This theory was also popular during the second world war, when ancient Iranians stood higher in the Nazi racial hierarchy than mere Slavs. On the other hand, there have been South-Slav or Pan-Slav ideologists who have rejected, for their own political reasons, all the evidence of early Iranian connections. But the historical truth is fairly clear: the Serbs and the Croats were, from the earliest times, distinct but closely connected, living and migrating in tandem, and both having some kind of Iranian component. What is also clear is that by the time they came to the Balkans there was already a large Slav population in place – larger than the population of the Serbs and the Croats. That major substratum of Slavs cannot be divided up into separate sub-ethnic groups; so the whole project of inventing ancient ethnic divisions among their descendants is necessarily a futile one. And that Slav substratum itself must have absorbed the remnants of a population whose ancestors may originally have been Illyrians, Celts, Romans, individuals from all parts of the Roman Empire, Goths, Alans, Huns and Avars.

The Serbs settled in an area corresponding to modern south-western Serbia (a territory which later in the middle ages became known as Raška or Rascia), and gradually extended their rule into the territories of Duklje or Dioclea (Montenegro) and Hum or Zachumlje (Hercegovina). The Croats settled in areas roughly corresponding to modern Croatia, and probably also including most of Bosnia proper, apart from the eastern strip of the Drina valley.[25] To begin with, the local Slav populations were organized on a traditional tribal basis: the hierarchy of units started with the family (probably the sort of extended family which has survived in some parts of the Balkans to this day and is known by the Slav term *zadruga*); families were united as clans, and clans as tribes (*plemena*); and the territory of a tribe, called a *župa*, was ruled by a territorial chief called a *župan*.[26] They were pagans, worshipping a variety of gods, some of whose names survive to this day in Yugoslav place-names: the god of horned animals, Veles, for example, or the thunder-god, Pirun or Pir.[27] Attempts were made by Byzantine rulers as early as the seventh century to Christianize the Croats, using Latin priests from the handful of Dalmatian coastal towns which were still under Byzantine control.[28] But it was not until the ninth century that the Croats were mainly Christianized, and we can assume that the remoter and more impenetrable areas of Bosnia were the last to undergo this process, which probably percolated through to them from the coastal lands in the late ninth or early tenth centuries.[29] There are many signs of pagan practices being carried over first into Christianity and later into Islam in Bosnia – for example, the use of mountain-tops as places of worship. The names of pagan gods such as Pir, Oganj and Tur survived in oral tradition until the twentieth century (one researcher recorded a rhyme about them from an old man in Sarajevo in 1933), and they have been preserved also in Bosnian personal names such as Tiro and Pirić.[30]

The political history of the western Balkans from the seventh to the eleventh centuries is patchy and confused, with a succession of conquests and shifting allegiances. The oldest established power in the Balkans, the Byzantine Empire, had little direct control there, but managed to get its authority acknowledged from time to time. Byzantine connections were maintained with the coastal towns and islands of Dalmatia: they were organized as a *theme* (military district) in the ninth century, but Byzantine authority in Dalmatia became increasingly notional – not least because the churches there were placed under the jurisdiction of Rome. The northern Croatian territory, including much of northern and north-west Bosnia, was conquered by Charlemagne's Franks in the late eighth and early ninth centuries, and remained under Frankish rule until the 870s. It was probably during this period that the old tribal system in Bosnia and Croatia began to be remodelled into a form of west European feudalism.[31]

Meanwhile a number of Serb-ruled territories in modern Hercegovina and Montenegro had been established, and the easternmost group of Serb župas in modern south-west Serbia had been gathered together into a kind of Serb princedom (under a 'grand župan') by the mid-ninth century. In the early tenth century Croatia enjoyed a period of power and independence under King Tomislav; again, much of northern and western Bosnia was part of his realm. After his death (probably in 928) the Croatian territory was riven by civil war, and for a brief period (from the 930s to the 960s) much of Bosnia was taken over by a newly restored and temporarily powerful Serb princedom which had agreed to acknowledge the sovereignty of the Byzantine Empire.[32]

These details give us the historical context for the first surviving mention of Bosnia as a territory. It occurs in the politico-geographical handbook written in 958 by the Byzantine Emperor Constantine Porphyrogenitus. In the section of his handbook devoted to the Serbian prince's lands he wrote: 'in baptized Serbia are the inhabited cities of Destinikon [etc.] . . . and in the territory of Bosona, Katera and Desnik'.[33] This makes it clear that Bosnia (an area smaller than modern Bosnia proper, and centred on the river Bosna which flows northwards from near Sarajevo) was considered a separate territory, though at that particular time a dependency of the Serbs. In the 960s it fell once again under Croatian rule, and remained a Croatian territory for roughly half a century.

Then, in 1019, a newly powerful Byzantine Empire under the Emperor Basil II, the 'Bulgar-slayer', forced the Serb and Croat rulers to acknowledge Byzantine sovereignty. The nominal subjection of the Croats gradually turned into something more like an alliance, and during the eleventh century Bosnia was ruled some of the time by a Croatian governor and some of the time by Serbian rulers to the east who were more directly under Byzantine control.[34] There was a little more independence to the south of Bosnia proper, in the territories of Duklje, otherwise known as Zeta (Montenegro) and Hum or Zachumlje (Hercegovina), where the local Serb princes resisted Byzantine rule. These lands were consolidated into a single Serb kingdom, which expanded to include the Serbian territory of Raška in the 1070s. Under King Bodin in the 1080s it expanded still further to take in most of Bosnia; but the kingdom broke up soon after his death in 1101.

The end of the eleventh century is a turning-point in the history of the western Balkans. After Bodin's death, the centre of gravity for Serb political ambitions shifted eastwards to Raška, which became the heartland of the medieval kingdom of Serbia. Meanwhile the Croatian lands had been taken over by Hungary, and in 1102 the Hungarian King Koloman was crowned King of Croatia – thus establishing a relationship between the two states, sometimes of direct subjection, sometimes of personal union and alliance, which would last (with a few interruptions and modifications) until 1918. Hungarian rule was also extended over Bosnia in 1102; but as a more remote and impenetrable territory, it was ruled by a *ban* whose authority became more and more independent as the century progressed.[35] In the 1160s and 1170s Croatia and Bosnia were briefly restored to Byzantine rule after a successful campaign by the expansionist Emperor Manuel Comnenus; but after his death in 1180 his achievements were quickly undone. Croatia resumed its Hungarian connection. Bosnia, however, became virtually free of Hungarian control; and since it was no longer ruled either by the Byzantine Empire or by Croatia, it was able to stand, for the first time, as a more or less independent state. Hence the famous description of Bosnia written by Manuel Comnenus' secretary, the chronicler Kinnamos, who was writing probably in the 1180s: 'Bosnia does not obey the grand *župan* of the Serbs; it is a neighbouring people with its own customs and government.'[36] Kinnamos also noted that Bosnia was separated from Serbia by the river Drina – a dividing-line which remained Bosnia's eastern border for much of its later history.

From the complex history of early Slav Bosnia, between the arrival of the Croats and Serbs in the 620s and the emergence of an independent Bosnian state in the 1180s, no simple conclusions can be drawn. Bosnia proper was under Serb rule at some times: above all, in the mid-tenth century and at the end of the eleventh. It would be misleading, though, to say that Bosnia was ever 'part of Serbia', since the Serb kingdoms which included Bosnia at those times did not include most of what we now call Serbia. For most of this early medieval period Hercegovina was indeed a Serb territory, but Bosnia proper was linked much more closely to the Croat lands; and by the twelfth century, even as it gained independence, it seems to have been increasingly aligned towards the Croat-Hungarian cultural and political realm.[37] In its religious organization, early medieval Bosnia was linked to Croatia, not to the Serb lands: the bishopric of Bosnia is mentioned as a Roman Catholic see in the eleventh century (after the division between Rome and Constantinople in 1054), and seems to have come under the jurisdiction of the Archbishop of Split, before being transferred to the diocese of Ragusa (Dubrovnik) in the twelfth century.[38] (However, as we shall see, there were some distinctive features of the Church in Bosnia which must have set it apart from the Latin Churches of the Dalmatian coast from an early stage.) One symbol of Bosnia's political links with the Croatian world is the fact that its rulers were called by the Croatian title *ban* from the earliest times; the chief ruler of the Serbs was always called a 'grand župan', and never a *ban*.[39]

As for the question of whether the inhabitants of Bosnia were really Croat or really Serb in 1180, it cannot be answered, for two reasons: first, because we lack evidence, and secondly, because the question lacks meaning. We can say that the majority of the Bosnian territory was probably occupied by Croats – or at least, by Slavs under Croat rule – in the seventh century; but that is a tribal label which has little or no meaning five centuries later. The Bosnians were generally closer to the Croats in their religious and political history; but to apply the modern notion of Croat identity (something constructed in recent centuries out of religion, history and language) to anyone in this period would be an anachronism. All that one can sensibly say about the ethnic identity of the Bosnians is this: they were the Slavs who lived in Bosnia.

2

The medieval Bosnian state, 1180–1463

The history of Bosnia in the high middle ages is frequently confused and confusing. But three powerful rulers stand out: Ban Kulin (who ruled from 1180 to 1204), Ban Stephen Kotromanić (1322–53) and King Stephen Tvrtko (1353–91). Under the second of these, Bosnia expanded to include the principality of Hum (Hercegovina); and under the third it expanded further to the south and also acquired a large part of the Dalmatian coast. Indeed, during the second half of Tvrtko's reign Bosnia was the most powerful state within the western Balkans. The only part of modern Bosnia not included in Tvrtko's realm was a strip of land in the north-west, including the modern town Bihać, which was part of the Croatian-Hungarian territory throughout this period.

Those were the high points of medieval Bosnian power and independence. At various times in between the reigns of those three rulers, Bosnia was divided, either officially or *de facto* as a result of the frequent contests for power between the local noble families. Although the social and political system in Bosnia was basically feudal, it was not the strict form of feudalism in which nobles' estates would revert to the crown if they failed to perform their military duties: the nobles were independent landowners, and were often able to dictate the succession to the Bosnian crown from their position of territorial power.[1] Hence the persistent instability of medieval Bosnian politics.

Hungary was the dominant neighbouring country throughout this period. In the thirteenth and early fourteenth centuries the Serbian kingdom also grew into a militarily powerful state; surprisingly, however, there was never any large-scale attempt by the Serbian kings to conquer Bosnia.[2] As the kings of Hungary were frequently to discover, the impenetrability of the Bosnian terrain made it a troublesome prize to obtain, and its fractious noble landowners made it, once obtained, an asset of dubious value.

The remoteness of Bosnia was also the underlying reason for the most distinctive and most puzzling feature of its medieval history: the schismatic Bosnian Church. This Church seems to have fallen away from the Catholic Church in the thirteenth century, and to have operated on its own in Bosnia until the coming of the Franciscans, who tried to reassert the authority of Rome, in the 1340s. Thereafter the Bosnian Church competed against the Roman Catholic Church for a century, until its functionaries were either expelled or forcibly converted to Catholicism on the eve of the Turkish conquest. Throughout the lifetime of this Church, papal writers accused the Bosnians of heresy; and some of these sources identify the heresy as dualist or Manichaean. Because of these accusations, the Bosnian Church has traditionally been identified as a late embodiment of an earlier Balkan Manichaean sect, the Bogomils of Bulgaria. However, modern scholarship has raised powerful objections to this traditional theory. The subject is so complex that it will be dealt with separately in the next chapter.

Ban Kulin has acquired legendary status in Bosnian history. 'Even today,' wrote the historian William Miller in 1921, 'the people regard him as a favourite of the fairies, and his reign as a golden age, and to "talk of Ban Kulin" is a popular expression for one who speaks of the remote past, when the Bosnian plum-trees always groaned with fruit and the yellow corn-fields never ceased to wave in the fertile plains.'[3] The experience of twenty-four years of peace must have been a welcome change for ordinary Bosnians of the time. The fragments of evidence which survive suggest that Kulin gave special attention to the economic development of his country: he made a commercial treaty with Ragusa (Dubrovnik) in 1189, and encouraged Ragusan merchants to exploit the rich Bosnian mines.[4] He also established good relations both with the ruler of Hum (Hercegovina), who married Kulin's sister, and with the Serbian grand župan, Stephen Nemanja, the founder of the Nemanjid dynasty which was to turn Serbia into a great power during the next two centuries. But relations were less amicable with two other states: Hungary, which still regarded itself as holding ultimate sovereignty over Bosnia, and Zeta (formerly called Duklje or Dioclea: modern Montenegro), which allied itself with Hungary for tactical political reasons.

Church politics, not war, was the form the conflict took. Bosnia (unlike Orthodox Hum) was a Catholic country, and came under the authority of the Archbishop of Ragusa. Because of its remoteness, the Catholic Church in Bosnia was little interfered with by the Ragusan hierarchy: it was virtually allowed to appoint its own bishop (whose diocese extended northwards into the Hungarian-Croatian lands). Hungary wanted closer control over the Bosnian bishopric, and campaigned at Rome in the early 1190s to have it transferred to the jurisdiction of the more pro-Hungarian Archbishop of Split. Then the ruler of Zeta, who was keen to discredit both Bosnia and Ragusa, started sending letters to the Pope complaining that Ban Kulin, his wife and thousands of his subjects had become heretics.[5] These complaints may have been a way of requesting papal permission to invade some Bosnian territory. But Ban Kulin eventually defused the crisis by holding a council of the Bosnian Catholic Church (the so-called council of Bolino Polje) in 1203, where a series of errors were officially renounced. These errors seem to have related to lax religious practices rather than any serious doctrinal heresies; but the tradition of stigmatizing Bosnia with accusations of heresy had now been established.[6] Ban Kulin himself, who had always maintained that he was a good Catholic, died in the following year.

During the half-century which followed, Bosnia was under constant pressure from its more powerful Hungarian neighbour. The Hungarians had not given up their plan to gain control over the bishopric of Bosnia. The papacy sent a constant stream of requests to the Hungarian rulers and bishops during the 1230s to drive out heresy from the diocese of Bosnia.[7] This was partly a response to the extremely low quality of the Bosnian clergy: one papal letter of 1232 described the Catholic Bishop of Bosnia as illiterate, ignorant even of the formula for baptism and, needless to say, acting in collusion with heretics. But it may also have reflected concerns artificially stimulated by the Hungarian rulers, who wanted a religious justification for an invasion of Bosnia. The invasion duly took place in the later 1230s; by 1238 the Hungarians had captured the south-central region of Bosnia, Vrhbosna, and were busily attempting to instal the Dominican order of friars.[8] The Bosnian Ban, Ninoslav, retained some territory, however; and when the Hungarian army was suddenly withdrawn northwards in 1241 to meet the threat of a Mongol invasion of Hungary, he was able to regain power in Bosnia. The Mongols crushed the Hungarian army, and proceeded on a trail of plunder and destruction through northern Croatia to Dalmatia. But on hearing of the death of the Great Khan they returned eastwards, via Zeta (Montenegro) and Serbia. They thus managed to circumnavigate Bosnia, leaving it largely unscathed.

In the second half of the thirteenth century Bosnia seems to have led a more isolated existence. Hungary persuaded the Pope in 1252 to place the bishopric of Bosnia under the authority of an archbishopric inside Hungary; however, the main effect of this change was that henceforth the Bosnian bishop lived outside Bosnia (in Hungarian-controlled Slavonia), and the leverage which any outside authority could exert over the Catholic Church inside Bosnia was reduced almost to nothing.[9] Hungary made one more attempt to invade Bosnia in 1253, but thereafter the original Banate of Bosnia – the successor to Ban Kulin's state – seems to have been left to its own devices for the rest of the century.[10] Several northern regions of modern Bosnia, however, such as the Soli or 'salt' region round Tuzla, were assigned to members of the Hungarian royal family. The north-eastern section of these lands was combined with territory in northern Serbia to form a Hungarian duchy known as Mačva.[11]

It was from these northern lands that the next ruling family of Bosnia emerged. Stephen Kotroman succeeded his father in the 1280s as ruler of one of the northern Bosnian territories, and married the daughter of the ruler of Mačva. He then conducted a prolonged struggle for power, the details of which are very unclear, against another Bosnian noble family, the Šubićes, who were from south-western Bosnia. The Šubićes appear to have ruled the old Banate of Bosnia for most of the first two decades of the fourteenth century, and to have had friendly relations with Kotroman's son,

Stephen Kotromanić, for some of that time.[12] But in the early 1320s Kotromanić gained the upper hand: a Šubić was Ban of Bosnia in 1318, but Kotromanić had replaced him by 1322. Once in power, he began building up a larger Bosnian state which united the old Banate with some of the northern territories. To this he then added, by conquest, areas to the west of the Banate which had previously been part of Croatia and would henceforth remain as Bosnian territory. He further extended this conquest to take in a couple of hundred miles of the Dalmatian coast between Ragusa and Split. In 1326 he annexed most of Hum (Hercegovina), thus making a single political entity out of Bosnia and Hercegovina for the first time. Hitherto Hum had led a fairly separate existence under its own succession of local ruling families; and its religious history had been separate too, with a largely Orthodox population.[13]

Kotromanić took care to cultivate friendly relations with foreign powers. It was his great good fortune that the Serbian kingdom, which was undergoing an extraordinary growth in power under its ruler Stephen Dušan, was preoccupied with expanding southwards into Macedonia, Albania and northern Greece. Kotromanić signed treaties with Ragusa (1334) and Venice (1335), and cooperated willingly with the Hungarian king, sending Bosnian troops to assist him in his campaigns against troublesome nobles in Croatia. Yet so long as Kotromanić accepted and supported the existence of the schismatical Bosnian Church (which he did, even though he himself was probably Orthodox), his relations with the papacy could only be fragile. In 1340, to improve relations with the Pope, he agreed to let the Franciscans set up a mission in Bosnia: they were already well established on the Dalmatian coast, but had made only the most tentative efforts to penetrate into Bosnia up until then.[14] And at some time before 1347, Kotromanić himself seems to have converted to Roman Catholicism: in April of that year he wrote personally to the Pope, asking him to help increase the supply of trained priests for Bosnia who would be 'skilled in the teaching of the faith and not ignorant of the Slav language'.[15] All subsequent rulers of Bosnia, with one possible exception, would also be Catholic.[16]

The Franciscans quickly formed a 'Vicariate of Bosnia', an administrative unit which later expanded to include a much larger area of south-eastern Europe, stretching all the way to Romania. (This has added another complication to the arguments about Bosnian heresies, since the term 'Bosnia' could be used in Franciscan documents to cover, so to speak, a multitude of sins.) By 1385 the Vicariate contained thirty-five Franciscan monasteries, though only four of these were in Bosnia itself: at Visoko, Lašva, Sutjeska and Olovo. Twelve more would be built within the Bosnian state before 1463. But each monastery was allowed a maximum of only twelve friars, and the average number per monastery may in fact have been as low as four. And since three of the first four (not Olovo) were close together in the central part of Bosnia, the Franciscans' drive to regain souls for Rome can have had only minimal effects in most parts of the country during this early phase of their campaign.[17] The Bosnian Church, as we shall see, also lacked proper territorial organization; so it seems likely that much of the population in the countryside practised only the lowest form of largely priestless folk-Christianity.

When Stephen Kotromanić was buried in the Franciscan monastery at Visoko in 1353, he left behind him a Bosnian state which was independent, prosperous and powerful. But its stability still depended on the cooperation of noble families who had their own power-bases in different parts of the country. The nephew who succeeded Kotromanić, Stephen Tvrtko, was aged only fifteen, and did not have the authority or the military power to keep these centrifugal forces together. At the same time the Hungarian king was keen to exploit divisions in Bosnia in order to regain territories for himself. For the first fourteen years of his reign Tvrtko had to contend with Bosnian revolts and seizures of land by Hungary; in 1366 he was even forced to seek refuge at the Hungarian court, when a group of Bosnian nobles set up his brother Vuk in his place. But by 1367 – apparently with the assistance of the King of Hungary, who realized that he had been stirring up troubles from which neither Tvrtko nor he himself would benefit – Tvrtko was back in power in Bosnia.[18] Thereafter he had little trouble from the Hungarian king, who became more concerned with events on Hungary's northern borders.

Tvrtko now turned his attention southwards. The huge Serbian empire had broken up very quickly after the death of its creator,

Stephen Dušan, in 1355. One of the Serbian noblemen who were now trying to carve out territory from its remains was Lazar Hrebljanović, who was engaged in a complex struggle for power with other nobles in the region of south-west Serbia, Hum (Hercegovina) and Zeta (Montenegro). Tvrtko gave Lazar the assistance he needed, and was rewarded in the subsequent share-out of the spoils with a large strip of territory adjoining Bosnia to the south and south-east: parts of Hum, Zeta and southern Dalmatia (including a section of the coast between Ragusa and the Bay of Kotor) and what later became the Sandžak of Novi Pazar. This last component included the monastery of Mileševo, which contained the relics of Saint Sava, one of the most sacred figures in the history of the Serbian Orthodox Church. In 1377 Tvrtko celebrated this improvement in his position by having himself crowned as King at Mileševo – not only King of Bosnia, but King of Serbia too. However, this last detail was simply a piece of rather pompous dynastic self-aggrandizement, of a piece with the imposing Byzantine-style court which he now set up for himself in the royal stronghold of Bobovac; Tvrtko was indeed descended from the founder of the Serbian Nemanja dynasty, but he never seriously attempted to exercise political power over Serbia.[19]

King Tvrtko's political and territorial ambitions lay elsewhere. First he tried to develop a new trading port of his own on the northern side of the Bay of Kotor: he called it Novi (meaning 'New': modern Herceg-Novi, previously also known as Castelnuovo). But this angered the traders of Ragusa, and Bosnia was too dependent on Ragusans in its own internal economic life for it to be wise to defy them; so the plan to divert trade from Ragusa to Novi was quietly dropped. Meanwhile a civil war had broken out in the Croatian lands after the death of the King of Hungary in 1382, and there were richer pickings to be had. Allying himself with one of the most powerful of the competing Croatian families, Tvrtko sent his troops into Dalmatia and took control of the entire coastline (including even some of the islands), with the exception of Ragusa, which retained its independence, and Zadar, which was under Venetian suzerainty. Venice had strong ambitions in this region, and would eventually gain most of the Dalmatian coast after Tvrtko's death. But for the time being Tvrtko was the master of a greatly expanded Bosnian kingdom which had also taken in parts of northern Croatia and Slavonia: in the last year or two before his death in 1391 he was calling himself 'King of Croatia and Dalmatia' too.[20]

With the late 1380s and early 1390s we have reached another of the great turning-points in western Balkan history. Ottoman Turkish armies had been moving westwards across Thrace and Bulgaria since the 1350s, and in 1371 a large contingent of Serbian forces had met them in Bulgaria, and had been heavily defeated. In the 1380s the Turks began raiding Serbia itself; and in 1388 a Turkish raiding party crossed into Bosnian-ruled Hum (Hercegovina), where it was wiped out by forces commanded by a local nobleman, Vlatko Vuković. In 1389 Tvrtko's old Serbian ally Lazar (who had modestly taken the title 'Prince' when Tvrtko had proclaimed himself King) refused to accept Turkish suzerainty, and called on his neighbours and allies for help. King Tvrtko sent a large Bosnian force under Vlatko Vuković, which fought alongside Prince Lazar's army at the battle of Kosovo Polje in June 1389. Though Serbian myth and poetry have presented this battle as a cataclysmic defeat in which the flower of Balkan chivalry perished on the field and the Turks swept on through the rest of Serbia, the truth is a little less dramatic. Losses were heavy on both sides, and Prince Lazar was captured and executed; but the remnants of both sides withdrew after the battle, and for a while the Serb and Bosnian forces believed that they had won. It was not the battle itself which brought about the fall of Serbia to the Turks, but the fact that while the Serbs had needed all the forces they could muster to hold the Turks to an expensive and temporary draw, the Turks were able to return, year after year, in ever increasing strength.[21] By 1392 all the Serbian Orthodox lands, apart from Bosnian-ruled Hum, had submitted to Ottoman suzerainty.

After Tvrtko's death in 1391 Bosnia entered a long period of weak rule and political confusion. One account of Bosnia written during this period, compiled from the accounts of other travellers by the French pilgrim Gilles Le Bouvier, paints a miserable picture of the place: 'They live purely on wild beasts, fish from the rivers, figs and honey, of which they have a sufficient supply, and they go in gangs from forest to forest to rob people who are travelling from one country to another.'[22]

The Bosnian state did not split up after Tvrtko's death, as it had after the death of Stephen Kotromanić, but noblemen with strong regional power-bases reasserted themselves, and the rulers of Bosnia were at the mercy of shifting patterns of rivalry among the leading noble families. The Hungarian king also took an interest again in Bosnian affairs, though a heavy defeat of the Hungarian army by the Turks in 1396 limited Hungary's capacity to intervene militarily in Bosnia for several years. In 1404, however, when the Bosnian King Ostoja was driven out by the nobles and replaced by an illegitimate son of King Tvrtko (Tvrtko II), he returned with a Hungarian army and reconquered part of the country. Over the next ten years, with Hungarian backing, Ostoja reasserted his rule and helped to mend relations between Hungary and the most powerful of the Bosnian noblemen, Hrvoje.

Then, in 1414, a new factor entered to disrupt the balance of power, both militarily and politically: the Ottoman Turks proclaimed the exiled Tvrtko II as rightful King of Bosnia, and sent a large raiding force into Bosnian territory. When a much larger Turkish army returned to Bosnia in the following year, there was a new alignment of forces: on the one side King Ostoja and a Hungarian army, and on the other side the Turks and the Bosnian nobleman Hrvoje. The Hungarian army was heavily defeated in central Bosnia, and although Ostoja made some sort of deal in which it was agreed that he, not Tvrtko II, would be confirmed as King, it was clear that from now on the Ottoman Empire would have an influence rivalling that of Hungary over Bosnian affairs.[23] With the eventual Turkish conquest of Bosnia in mind, some modern historians, especially Serbian ones, have felt instinctively hostile towards those Bosnian rulers and noblemen who collaborated in this way with the Turks. But their actions at the time were no different from those of previous players in the Bosnian political game who had appealed to Hungary for support; the main difference in their minds would probably have been that the Turks seemed a more remote and perhaps ephemeral presence, less likely to impose any kind of direct rule.

Ostoja held power for a few more years, and actually enlarged the territory he controlled. But after his death in 1418 his son faced the same problems of competing noble families and Turkish intervention. He was driven out in 1420, and this time the Turks' support ensured that Tvrtko II was fully installed as Bosnian king once more. Bosnia enjoyed a few years of peace in the early 1420s; but then the pattern of allegiances shifted again, with Tvrtko II turning to Hungary for help against the Turks, and also engaging in a territorial war against Serbian forces over the rich mining district of Srebrenica in eastern Bosnia. By the early 1430s his main rivals inside Bosnia, the nobleman Sandalj and King Ostoja's son, Radivoj, were receiving help and encouragement from both Serb noblemen and the Turks, and had gained control over a large part of Bosnia. Between 1433 and 1435 parts of south-central Bosnia, including the region of Vrhbosna (round modern Sarajevo), were conquered and reconquered by Hungarian and Turkish armies. With the help of Sandalj's nephew, Stephen Vukčić, the powerful lord of Hum, the Ottoman forces pushed back the Hungarians. At this stage the Turks were more interested in plunder than in the direct annexation of territory. Most historians have assumed that the Vrhbosna region, with its important fortress of Hodidjed, not only fell to the Turks but remained under direct Turkish rule from 1435 or 1436; but there is evidence which suggests that this did not happen before 1448.[24]

Tvrtko II held on to power in Bosnia until his death in 1443: these final years of his reign were marked by further Turkish raids (including the seizure of Srebrenica in 1440), and the continuing growth in power of Stephen Vukčić, the lord of Hum. At first Vukčić refused to recognize Tvrtko's successor, Stephen Tomaš, and several years of civil war ensued. In 1446 they came to an agreement, but Vukčić continued to give support to a Serb ruler, George Branković, who, as a semi-independent vassal of the Turks, was still warring against the Bosnian king for control over the Srebrenica region of eastern Bosnia. To emphasize his own independent status, Vukčić gave himself a new title in 1448: 'Herceg of Hum and the Coast'. He later changed this to 'Herceg of St Sava', after the saint buried at Mileševo, in his territory. The word 'Herceg' was a version of the German *Herzog* (Duke), and the name

'Hercegovina' derives from this title.[25] Stephen Vukčić enjoyed a few more years of power and prosperity, but in the early 1450s he was embroiled not only in a war against Ragusa but also in a civil war with his own eldest son. This family dispute flared up again in 1462, when the son sought help from the Turks and encouraged them to include Hercegovina, along with Bosnia, in their plans for a massive assault in 1463.

The final years of Christian Bosnia were inevitably overshadowed by the Turkish threat. King Stephen Tomaš, desperate to secure promises of outside help, turned in the 1450s to the papacy. Rome had taken an increasing interest in Bosnia in recent years, particularly since the Franciscans had enjoyed a period of energetic activity there under a zealous Vicar of Bosnia, Jacob de Marchia, in the 1430s. But the papal authorities had also become obsessed with the question of Bosnian heresy, and poured out a stream of documents in the 1440s accusing the Bosnian Church of a whole range of pernicious doctrinal errors, including Manichaeism. Renewed efforts were made by the Franciscans in the 1450s: one report by a papal legate in Bosnia in 1451 stated that 'in places inhabited by the heretics, as soon as the friars arrive, the heretics melt away like wax before a fire'.[26] Then, in 1459, King Stephen Tomaš agreed to change to a policy of direct persecution. He summoned the clergy of the schismatical Bosnian Church and offered them the choice: conversion to Catholicism, or expulsion from Bosnia. According to one later papal source, two thousand chose conversion, and only forty fled, taking refuge in Hercegovina.[27] The back of the Bosnian Church was thus broken by the Bosnian king himself, just four years before the destruction of the Bosnian kingdom.

When Stephen Tomaš died in 1461 and was succeeded by his son, Stephen Tomašević, the end of Bosnia was clearly in sight. Tomašević wrote to the Pope in 1461, predicting a large-scale Turkish invasion and begging for help; he wrote again in early 1463 to Venice, warning that the Turks were planning to occupy the whole of Bosnia and Hercegovina that summer, and that they would then move on to threaten the Venetian lands in Dalmatia.[28] But no help came. A large Turkish army under Mehmet II assembled in the spring of 1463 at Adrianople (Edirne), and marched on Bosnia.

The first Bosnian fortress to fall (on 20 May) was the old royal stronghold of Bobovac; King Stephen Tomašević then fled north-westwards to Jajce, and took refuge in the nearby fortress of Ključ. Besieged by the Turks there, he surrendered himself on a promise of safety. Various elaborate stories of his betrayal and his subsequent execution later grew up. But as it happens we have an eye-witness account in the memoirs of a Serbian-born Turkish janissary, whose description is chillingly matter-of-fact: 'When the King's servants, who were in the fortress, saw that their lord had been taken, they gave themselves up. The Sultan took possession of the fortress, and ordered that the King and his companions should be beheaded. And he took his entire country into his possession.'[29]

Despite its intermittent civil wars and invasions, Bosnia had achieved real prosperity during the high middle ages. The key to its wealth was mining: copper and silver at Kreševo and Fojnica; lead at Olovo; gold, silver and lead at Zvornik; and, above all, silver at Srebrenica. A Roman gold-mine at Krupa (north-east of Gornji Vakuf) may also have functioned through the middle ages. In the late thirteenth or early fourteenth century the first German miners from Hungary and Transylvania, known as 'Saxons' (*Sasi*), had arrived in Bosnia and begun to exploit its mineral wealth.[30] More Saxons arrived in the fourteenth century, when Stephen Kotromanić and King Tvrtko encouraged the development of mining. The mines were privately owned by the local landowner, and managed by the Saxons, who were allowed by law to cut wood in the forests and make mining settlements wherever there was ore. Some of the Saxons became important figures: one whose name appears frequently in the records, Hans Sasinović (Sasinović = 'son of the Saxon'), was granted a large land-holding 'in perpetuity' and was sent several times to Ragusa as a representative of King Tvrtko.[31] Gold was being exported as early as 1339. Lead from Bosnia was shipped to Venice and Sicily; many of the finest medieval and renaissance Italian churches must have had Bosnian lead on their roofs. There was also some extraction of copper. But the greatest source of wealth was silver, and Srebrenica (which means 'Silver' – its Latin name was 'Argentaria') became the most important mining and trading town in the whole region west of Serbia. When it first appears in the records in 1376, it was already a major commercial centre, with a prominent Ragusan colony. Ragusans had a special monopoly of the trade in silver within Bosnia, and all exports of metals via the coast went through Ragusa anyway. In return the Ragusans imported finished goods such as high-quality textiles into Bosnia; and since by 1422 Bosnia and Serbia together were yielding more than a fifth of Europe's entire production of silver, there were plenty of rich Bosnians who could afford to buy.[32]

The Ragusan colonies dominated not only (with the Saxons) the mining towns mentioned above, but also important trading towns such as Foča. There was also a Ragusan colony in Visoko, which was the political capital of the Banate of Bosnia for much of the middle ages. These major towns, with their communities of Catholic Saxons, Ragusans and other Dalmatians, naturally attracted the Franciscans when they began to establish monasteries in Bosnia: the towns thus developed a strongly Catholic character. Other medieval towns on trading routes included Jajce, Travnik, Goražde and Livno. Apart from these major centres there were many small fortified towns (roughly 350 in the whole of medieval Bosnia).[33] These included Vrhbosna, which in the late middle ages consisted of little more than a fortress and a village, and which was quickly developed into the city of Sarajevo by the Turks after 1448.

Out in the countryside the majority of the people were *kmets* (serfs), who did military and agricultural service for their lords and paid a tithe to (in theory at least) the king.[34] There were also slaves, mainly prisoners of war, some of whom were bought or sold at the large slave market in Ragusa; many Bosnians were also sold as slaves there, and were exported to Venice, Florence, Genoa, Sicily, southern France and Catalonia.[35] Higher up in the Bosnian mountains there were pastoral herdsmen, some of them Vlachs (see chapter 6), who were less easily absorbed by the feudal system. The distinction between the ordinary people and the nobles was the essential division in Bosnian society; but there were also differences between the upper and lower nobles, even though these were not properly formalized into the west European system of hereditary rank. Though real power was of course dependent on land, rank was more dependent on office: those who held major offices of state were called *veomože* (magnates), and lower office-holders were given the title of *knez* (roughly equivalent to baron). While the old Slav title for a regional chief, župan, survived, it was somewhere between those two levels.[36] The senior nobles wielded, as we have seen, great political power, and could make or unmake bans and kings. Towards the end of the middle ages, from the 1390s to the 1420s, they met in a more or less formal 'state council' to discuss the succession and other weighty matters of domestic and foreign policy.[37]

Some of the greater nobles kept up courts almost on a par with the court of the king himself; and to these there came, often at considerable expense from Ragusa or beyond, pipers, lutenists, trumpeters, jongleurs, 'buffones' and other performers.[38] The royal courts also had well-organized chancelleries, frequently manned, after the 1340s, by Franciscans; documents were written in Slav or Latin, and a specifically Bosnian variety of script, differing from Cyrillic and known as 'Bosančica', was developed.[39] Artists and craftsmen from Ragusa and Venice also came to work in Bosnia; little of their handiwork, alas, remains, but carving of good quality can be seen in the fragments of sculpture which have survived from King Tvrtko's court at Bobovac, together with the capital of a column decorated with the Bosnian royal symbol, the fleur-de-lys.[40] Of course Bosnia was not an important centre of European culture in the middle ages. But its provincialism should not be exaggerated. The noble and ruling families were well connected with a wider world of central European nobility: at the medieval Bosnian courts there were princesses from Hungary, Prussia, Bulgaria, Poland, Serbia, Italy and Greece.[41] Bosnia may have been a backwater by west European standards, but it was a backwater into which some of the tides of European culture did flow.

3

The Bosnian Church

No topic in Bosnian history has been more argued over than the schismatic Bosnian Church of the middle ages.[1] It is impossible to discuss this subject without also touching on the modern myths and ideologies which it has served or spawned. Medieval heresy, rather like the history of peasant revolts, is a subject which naturally attracts a kind of subconscious romantic identification on the part of the historian: heretics so often seem more brave, more original, more interesting than the merely orthodox. But a national heretical (or allegedly heretical) Church arouses a more special sense of identification; for many historians of Bosnia, this peculiarly Bosnian phenomenon lies at the heart of Bosnian nationhood. It is not surprising if, from time to time, writers on this subject have behaved as if something more important than mere scholarly accuracy were at stake.

The founder of all modern studies of the Bosnian Church certainly was a scholarly man: Franjo Rački, the most important Croatian historian in the nineteenth century. In a sequence of articles published in 1869–70, he gathered together the available evidence and attempted to prove that the Bosnian Church was an offshoot of the Bogomils.[2] This was a Bulgarian heretical movement, founded in the tenth century by a priest called 'Bogumil' ('beloved by God'), which spread in subsequent centuries into Constantinople and other areas of the Balkans, including Macedonia and parts of Serbia. It preached a Manichaean 'dualist' theology, according to which Satan had a power almost equal to that of God; the visible world was Satan's creation, and men could free themselves from the taint of the material world only by following an ascetic way of life, renouncing meat, wine and sexual intercourse. The identification of matter with Satan's realm had some far-reaching theological implications: Christ's incarnation had to be regarded as a kind of illusion, and his physical death on the Cross could not have happened;

various ceremonies involving material substances, such as baptism with water, had to be rejected, and the Cross itself became a hated symbol of false belief. Also rejected were the use of church buildings, and indeed the entire organizational structure of the traditional Church, especially its wealthy monasteries. Two essential ranks of Bogomils were established: ordinary believers, and the purified 'elect'.[3] A similar structure developed among the Cathars of southern France in the twelfth and thirteenth centuries, whose heresy was directly influenced by Bogomil teachings.[4] Rački argued that the same division took place in Bosnia, and that the mysterious terms *gost*, *starac* and *strojnik*, which survive in Bosnian documents as titles for senior members of the Bosnian Church, were special terms for the initiated adepts, the 'elect' or 'perfect', of the Bogomil tradition.

This interpretation had a profound effect on the way in which Bosnian historians, and other South Slavs, thought about the history of Bosnia. Rački was not the first writer to link the Bosnian Church with the Bogomils; and there were of course many earlier Catholic writers who, following fifteenth- and sixteenth-century sources, had described it as embracing a dualist or 'Manichaean' heresy.[5] But with his painstaking work in the archives of Dubrovnik and Venice, and his method of using known facts about non-Bosnian Bogomil beliefs and practices to fill gaps in the Bosnian evidence, Rački produced a much fuller and more rounded picture of the Bosnian Church as a body utterly distinct from the Churches of Croatia or Serbia, with its own principles of organization and theology. The only rival interpretation at the time, that of Božidar Petranović, argued that the Bosnian Church was just an Eastern Orthodox Church, probably Serbian, which had broken away and acquired some heretical beliefs.[6] This theory remained popular among Serb writers who were keen to show that Bosnia was in all essential respects an adjunct to Serbia, and it was still being propagated in the first half of this century; but it then lost most of its scholarly support, at least outside Serbia.[7] Rački's theory, on the other hand, has never been generally abandoned, and in the last fifty years it has been strongly supported by leading scholars in Bosnia such as Aleksandr Solovjev and Dragutin Kniewald.[8] The main rival theory, which has grown in support in the post-war period, argues that the Bosnian Church was essentially a branch of the Catholic Church, probably a monastic order, which receded into schism and acquired some heretical tendencies; this theory, not surprisingly, has been especially popular among Catholic writers.[9] The most convincing explanation, as we shall see, contains important elements of both the Eastern Orthodox and the Catholic theory. But the theory which has been most widely accepted for over a century, Rački's identification of the Bosnian Church as Bogomil, turns out to consist mainly of wishful thinking.

Franjo Rački's Bogomil theory was popular for many reasons. Not only did it explain mysterious features of the Bosnian Church, it also offered a key to explaining two of the other great mysteries in Bosnian history. One of these was the conversion to Islam of a large part of the Bosnian population under the Turks – a much larger proportion than in any other Balkan country except Albania. It seemed natural to interpret this as a mass-conversion of Bogomils who, having held out for centuries against the competition and/or persecution of the Catholic and Orthodox Churches, finally preferred to transfer their allegiance to Islam. In this way the 'Bogomil' theory became especially attractive to twentieth-century Bosnian Muslims. Instead of being seen as mere renegades from Catholicism or Orthodoxy (to which, at various times, Croats and Serbs have suggested that they should 'return'), they could now be regarded as descendants of the membership of an authentically and peculiarly Bosnian Church; and their turning to Islam could be described not as an act of weakness, but as a final gesture of defiance against their Christian persecutors. Unfortunately, however, modern scholarship has comprehensively demolished the claim that the Islamicization of Bosnia consisted essentially of a mass-conversion of the members of the Bosnian Church. Some members of that Church may indeed have been more inclined to convert to Islam because of their alienation from the mainstream Catholic or Orthodox Churches; this seems psychologically possible, but particular evidence is lacking. What is now understood is that many factors were involved in the spread of Islam in Bosnia, and that if the special attitude of the Bosnian Church was a factor at all, it was not one of the most important ones.[10]

The second great mystery which the 'Bogomil' theory seemed to solve was that of the medieval gravestones which are found in many parts of Bosnia. Known as *stećci* (the plural of *stećak*), they come in two forms: slabs, a form common to many parts of Europe, and standing blocks, which are more or less peculiar to the Bosnian region. More than 58,000 have been recorded in modern surveys, and of these nearly 6000 are decorated with carvings, often of human figures. The decorated ones, many of which can be dated to the fourteenth and fifteenth centuries, are found mainly in Hercegovina, southern Bosnia and neighbouring parts of Dalmatia, though some have also been found in districts further afield in Croatia, Serbia and Montenegro.[11] Since this area does at least centre on the known area of activities of the Bosnian Church, it was natural to connect the two phenomena; and a few of the decorated and inscribed stećci actually state that they are monuments to 'Gosti' (the title of senior members of the Bosnian Church). Once the Bosnian Church was identified as Bogomil, historians could begin to interpret the designs on the decorated stećci as expressions of Bogomil theological beliefs. The first attempt at this was made by the Hungarian writer János Asbóth in the 1880s, and in the middle decades of this century the 'Bogomil' interpretation of the stones was pursued in a succession of studies by Aleksandr Solovjev.[12]

Once again, modern scholarship – together with simple logic – has raised a mass of objections to the 'Bogomil' theory. That some members of the Bosnian Church were commemorated in stećci is not in doubt; but what has become increasingly hard to believe is the idea that the whole phenomenon of the stećci as such was an expression of that Church's beliefs. We know that during the late fourteenth and early fifteenth centuries, when many of these stones were made, a significant part of the population of Bosnia proper was Catholic, and a large part of the population of Hercegovina was Orthodox. In all other Catholic and Orthodox lands gravestones were commonly made, at least for the richer sort of people; to identify all stećci as such with Bogomilism is to replace one mystery with another – the mystery of non-existent Catholic or Orthodox gravestones.[13] And on the other hand, if stećci are peculiar to Bogomilism, it is curious that there is no evidence of Bogomils making them in Bulgaria, Thrace or other well-attested areas of Bogomil activity.[14] The determination of some writers to identify this entire phenomenon with Bogomilism has led to strange contortions of argument: the presence of crosses (a symbol hated by Bogomils) on many of the stećci has always been an obstacle to the theory, but János Asbóth showed how to circumvent it when he insisted that these were not *really* crosses in the Christian sense but mere 'patterns' similar to the geometrical crosses in Egyptian or Babylonian art.[15]

Gradually, the 'Bogomil' theory of the stećci has been dismantled and discarded. Most scholars now do not believe that the motifs on these stones all belong to a single doctrinal-pictorial language. Some may reflect survivals of local pagan myths and rituals; others may be simple armorial designs expressing the status of local Slav nobility; and others may depict activities of the people commemorated, such as the pictures of horsemen on the tombs of prominent Vlachs in Hercegovina who had grown rich as caravan-leaders and horse-traders.[16] And of course – though this is normally the last possibility to be considered by historians – it may be that the purpose of some of the decorations on these stones was simply to be decorative.

The failure of the 'Bogomil' theory to explain Islamicization or the stećci does not disprove the theory itself. But it forces historians, instead of making leaps of the imagination into iconography or subsequent history, to look more closely at the written evidence concerning the Bosnian Church itself. Here the fundamental problem is that most of the evidence comes from outside Bosnia itself. Where Catholics in Dalmatia or Bosnia wrote to Rome, it is usually only the papal half of the correspondence that survives. There are papal documents, denunciations of Bosnian 'heresies' penned most probably by people who had never set foot in Bosnia; and there are documents prepared by or for Franciscans in Italy, whose grounding in first-hand knowledge is similarly uncertain.[17] Unfortunately there is no proper description, coming from inside Bosnia, of the organization, ceremonies or theology of the Bosnian Church.

Even the names used in the early documents have been a source of controversy and confusion. The one fact which has become quite clear is that the Bosnian Church was not identified as 'Bogomil' at the time. No Bosnian or Catholic source ever uses that term about the Bosnians; and the only apparent instance of a medieval source referring to 'Bogomils' in Bosnia was almost certainly a forgery.[18]

On the other hand, when some late fourteenth-century Serbian Orthodox documents pronounce curses on the Bosnian heretics, they also curse 'Babuny' (a term which is known to have been used about Bogomils in Serbia), and make it clear that these are two different groups.[19] Fifteenth-century Catholic authors did sometimes refer to the 'Manichaeans' in Bosnia, but that term seems to have been a self-consciously archaizing label used by historically-minded writers who wanted to dignify their works with the terms used in early Christian history.[20]

The word normally used in Ragusan sources and in some Italian documents too – but never in Bosnia itself – was 'Patareni' or 'Patarini' (in English, 'Patarins').[21] This term also has a rather puzzling history. First used in eleventh-century Milan to describe a fiercely puritanical reformist movement in the Catholic Church, it had become transferred by the end of that century to other campaigners, including heretical ones, against the established Church. In the late twelfth century it was being used as a virtual synonym for heresies which aimed at a superior kind of purity or spiritual illumination, such as the Waldensians and Cathars, and in the thirteenth century 'Patarin' was the usual word for the Cathars of northern Italy. But its meaning was never clearly defined in theological terms.[22] It first appears in connection with Bosnia in a letter from the Archbishop of Split to the Pope in 1200: he said that when he recently expelled some 'Patarin' heretics from Split and from the nearby coastal town of Trogir, they had found refuge in Bosnia, where they had been welcomed by Ban Kulin.[23] Another source (a chronicle written in Split in the mid-thirteenth century) says that two brothers from Zadar (another coastal town) who visited Bosnia as artists and goldsmiths in the 1190s had taught heresy wherever they went; after punishment by the Archbishop they had recanted and returned to Catholicism.[24] There are a few references in twelfth- and thirteenth-century Catholic sources to the existence of a centre of dualist heresy in 'Sclavonia'; the term could apply to any of the South Slav lands, but there are reasons for thinking that the heresy was based somewhere on the Dalmatian coast.[25] It is quite possible that either or both of the episodes of heresy just mentioned were connected with this dualist movement, and that there was thus some dualist contact with Bosnia in the late twelfth century.

The term used by the Bosnians themselves was not 'Patarin' but simply 'Christian': *christianus* in Latin and *krstjanin* in Serbo-Croat. And this term surfaces immediately in the first document to come out of Bosnia itself. Following other complaints about heresies in Bosnia (some of them probably stirred up, as we have seen in chapter 2, by political rivalry), the Pope sent a legate to Bosnia in 1203. His task was to find out whether, as Ban Kulin insisted, the people in his country were 'not heretics but Catholics'. The result was the meeting of Bosnian ecclesiastics at Bolino Polje in April of that year, at which they signed a declaration promising to reform their behaviour. They undertook to acknowledge the full supremacy of Rome, accept Catholic priests in their monasteries, restore altars and crosses to places of worship, adopt the confessional and penance, follow the Roman calendar of feasts and fasts, receive communion at least seven times a year, keep the sexes apart in monasteries, and give no shelter to heretics. They also promised not to arrogate to themselves alone the name of 'christianus', but to refer to themselves as *fratres*, 'brothers', instead.[26]

The most striking thing about this declaration is that it is not an abjuration of heresies. Some of the clauses might imply heretical behaviour, such as the lack of altars and crosses, but they might just imply inefficiency and neglect. The only specific mention of heresy is the promise not to give shelter to heretics, which rather suggests that these Bosnian ecclesiastics were not themselves viewed as heretics by the legate. Given the special mention here of the use of the word 'christianus', and given the use of the term 'krstjanin' during the following centuries (when the Bosnian Church was certainly regarded as heretical by Rome), many historians have been tempted to read back into this declaration the whole system of 'Bogomil' belief and organization which they associate with the *krstjani* of the fully-fledged schismatical Bosnian Church. This is a method of inquiry which ensures that the historians will only find what they think they already know. The best solution to the mystery of the Bosnian Church comes from working in the opposite direction: first looking at what the term 'christianus' could have meant at the time, and then seeing what implications can be carried forward into its later history.

As many writers have noticed, the basic structure of the Church which met at Bolino Polje was monastic. The leaders who gathered there were described as 'priors', who were there to represent their 'brotherhoods', and they promised to call themselves 'brothers' in future. Some of their promises related specifically to practices in monasteries. But what kind of monasteries were these? The basic monastic rule of Western Christendom was the rule of St Benedict, and some scholars (especially Catholic ones) have assumed that these Bosnian monks were some sort of rustic Benedictines; yet there is otherwise no evidence of any Benedictine activity in Bosnia.[27] The solution was found by a modern historian, Maja Miletić, who realized that the mingling of the two sexes referred to in the declaration was a survival of the early Christian practice of 'double monasteries', which was permitted under the rule of St Basil, the founder of the monastic tradition in Eastern Christianity. (The declaration is not the only evidence of this practice: some of the early literature, starting with the writings of the fifteenth-century Pope Pius II, also mentions remote monasteries in Bosnia where women, who served the holy men, also lived.)[28] Such monasteries existed in the early Celtic church, and their members were often called *christiani*. Whole families might join them, and this led to some blurring of the distinction between monastic and lay life. (The signers of the Bolino Polje declaration also promised to wear a proper monastic habit to distinguish themselves from laymen.) And such monasteries frequently played a role in lay society by acting as *hospitia* – either inns for travellers or hospitals for the sick. (The declaration also included a promise to establish proper graveyards for travellers who died at the monasteries.) The keeper of a hospitium was a *hospitalarius*, or, more simply, a *hospes*: a host. And this is the literal meaning of the title *Gost* which we later find used by prominent members of the Bosnian Church.[29]

At a stroke, much that is puzzling about the Bosnian Church during its subsequent history now falls into place. As several later references indicate, the basic meaning of 'krstjanin' was 'monk': in the mid-fifteenth century, for example, the Herceg Stephen Vukčić referred to one famous member of the Bosnian Church, Gost Radin, as one of his 'monks'.[30] It is simply not necessary to fit the structure of the Bosnian Church, as Rački tried to do, on to the Procrustean bed of a Bogomil or Cathar hierarchy. The special titles which have survived in the records fit a monastic structure perfectly well. The head of the whole Church was known as the *djed* (literally, 'grandfather'): *nonnus*, the Latin word with the same meaning, was used in both Eastern and Western monasticism to refer to senior priors or abbots.[31] The other two titles used in the records referred to senior members or officials of the monasteries: *starac* ('elder') and *strojnik* ('steward'). These titles, and the term 'Gost', were not mutually exclusive; the records of missions to Ragusa in the fifteenth century include references to 'twelve strojniki, including Gost Radin', and to 'our strojniki, Starac Mišljen and Starac Bilko'.[32]

The term 'strojnik' has strong overtones of the steward who attends guests; once again, this is probably a reminder of the social role of the monastic hospitia. We even find an allusion to this in the inscription on a Bosnian tomb, which says: 'Here lies the good man Gost Mišljen, for whom Abraham had prepared, according to the rule, his great hospitality.'[33] The reference to Abraham is perhaps an allusion to two passages in the New Testament which imply that the righteous, after death, will sit as Abraham's guests in heaven.[34] And the reference to the 'rule' indicates that hospitality was regarded as an essential duty of the monastic Bosnian Church. That the Bosnian monasteries continued to play an important role as staging-posts for travellers and merchants is clear from many references in the archives at Dubrovnik: Vlach merchants would sometimes leave their goods there, and some monasteries may have acted as customs-posts.[35] The term used for 'monastery' in the records is *hiža*, which can mean an ordinary house as well as a monastic house. In many of the locations of these hižas, surviving place-names suggest that there was also a church building attached.[36] The hižas were probably modest buildings, with laymen also living in them, so the distinction may have become partly blurred; but it is not necessary to suppose that these were ordinary lay houses of the sort which acted as centres of Cathar activity in France.[37]

Finally, one other feature of the Bosnian Church also falls into place if we recognize that it was a monastic organization based on the rule of St Basil: its closeness in some ways to Eastern Orthodox practice. These Basilian monasteries, although absorbed into the Roman Catholic Church and (until the Bosnian Church broke away) acknowledging the authority of Rome, must have been founded by people from the Eastern tradition. It is not impossible that the contact had been made via Dalmatia; the link between the Dalmatian cities and Constantinople, which was strong in the ninth century, bequeathed many Byzantine religious traditions to those cities in the middle ages, including the cult of some Eastern saints.[38] One theory is that followers of Saints Cyril and Methodius, returning from Moravia in the late ninth century, had percolated through into Bosnia and introduced the monastic system there.[39] Though we have no direct evidence from the tenth or eleventh centuries, we can assume that some contacts were kept up with the monastic world in lands further to the east. It is clear from the declaration of 1203 that, while Bosnia had been part of the Roman Church since the schism between East and West one and a half centuries earlier, some Eastern practices had survived in the Bosnian monasteries. They were not observing the Roman calendar of feasts and fasts; this probably means that they used an Eastern calendar (rather than no calendar at all). Indeed, as late as 1466, in the testament of Gost Radin, we find clear evidence that the Bosnian Church celebrated saints' days from the Eastern calendar which were not recognized by the West.[40] Whether Rome permitted (as it may have done) the use of the Eastern liturgy in early medieval Bosnia, we do not know; but we do know that the liturgy was in the Slav language, as it was in much of Catholic Croatia, where the 'glagolitic' version of the Roman liturgy was used.[41] One of the mysteries in medieval Bosnian history is the story of what happened to the non-monastic Catholic clergy; they may have faded out altogether, though one historian believes that he can find traces of a 'glagolitic' clergy continuing through the medieval period.[42] Slav-speaking priests in the cities of Dalmatia would have known Italian too, and would have enjoyed a proper theological training in Latin. But most of the clergy (both monastic and secular) who were born and bred in Bosnia were probably monoglot Slavs with minimal access to the standard works of Roman Catholic theology. At times when Bosnia was cut off from the rest of the Roman Church, it must have been very isolated indeed.

As we have seen, Bosnia was in fact cut off from the rest of the Church from the mid-thirteenth century, when the seat of the Bosnian bishopric was moved to Hungarian-ruled Slavonia, to the mid-fourteenth century, when the Franciscans arrived. The Bosnian Church was probably isolated from Catholic jurisdiction from as early as the 1230s; and as it gradually asserted its autonomy, it must sooner or later have reached a point where it was in *de facto* schism with Rome.[43] For most of this period of more than a century we have very little information at all about the Bosnian Church. There are some sporadic references, in non-Bosnian sources, to Bosnian 'heretics' from the 1280s onwards. Since there was never any formal schism, this term could have been used loosely to mean 'schismatics', without implying large-scale doctrinal differences. (When Catholic sources actually mention 'schismatics', they are referring to members of the Eastern Orthodox Church, which was in formal schism with Rome.) Or it could have referred to genuine heretics, such as followers of the dualist heresy on the Dalmatian coast, who may well have become more active in Bosnia once it was beyond the reach of the Dalmatian Catholic bishops.

It is of course possible that some dualists were active in Bosnia. The question is, what effect did they have on the Bosnian Church? There is just one piece of evidence from within Bosnia which appears to show that they exerted a major influence. It is a Bosnian manuscript text, in Slavic (two short sequences of responses, the Lord's Prayer and a reading from St John's Gospel) which corresponds closely to the text of a Cathar ritual known to have been used in Lyon in the thirteenth century.[44] But we can only call this a heretical ritual if we assume that it had a heretical provenance. Its contents are not heretical at all: it contains nothing contrary to mainstream Catholic or Eastern Orthodox theology. As Dragoljub Dragojlović has noted, it does in fact consist of passages from the liturgy of the Eastern Orthodox Church, and the section of St John's Gospel which is read in the Eastern Church in the service for Easter day. He has also deduced, from internal linguistic evidence, that it must have been composed originally in the Orthodox archdiocese of Ohrid (in Macedonia) not later than the early eleventh century – a period when Cathars as such did not yet exist.[45] Instead of saying that the Bosnian text came from Lyon, it makes much more sense to suppose that the Lyon text was itself derived from an earlier Eastern Orthodox original. The same scholarly approach has also overturned the idea that the Bosnian Church practised a 'Cathar' ritual of blessing, breaking and distributing bread – a sort of heretical communion. We know that the Cathars did this in their houses before a meal; and some early sources describe the 'priests' of the Bosnian Church as having done something similar.[46] But it was also normal practice in Eastern monastic houses for common meals to begin with the Lord's Prayer and the blessing, breaking and distributing of bread.[47] When Catholics outside Bosnia heard reports of this, they may indeed have assumed that this was a heretical ritual. But it was almost certainly the Cathars who had copied (albeit in a lay setting, and with genuinely heretical beliefs) an older and non-heretical Eastern practice.

It remains possible to suppose that some dualist-influenced heretics in the region may have had some passing influence on the Bosnian Church during its long years of ecclesiastical isolation. But from that modest assumption it would require a huge leap of the imagination to arrive at the claim that the dualists took over the Bosnian Church, transformed its monastic hierarchy into the lay structure of the Cathars and replaced its rustic but essentially mainstream Christian theology with a radically heretical system of beliefs.

Much of the evidence which has survived is in direct conflict with such a claim. Cathars and Bogomils abhorred the sign of the cross; the cross appears at the head of several Bosnian Church documents. Cathars and Bogomils rejected the Old Testament; one of the surviving biblical manuscripts of the Bosnian Church includes the Book of Psalms. Cathars and Bogomils rejected the Mass; the testament of Gost Radin specifically asks for Masses to be said for his soul. Cathars and Bogomils condemned the use of church buildings; there is strong evidence that the Bosnian Church continued to use monastic buildings with churches attached to them. Cathars and Bogomils rejected wine and ate no meat; early Ottoman land registers in Bosnia record that some krstjani were owners of vineyards, and there is no reason to think that they were ever vegetarian. (The only piece of evidence which seemed to indicate this has turned out to be a misreading of a word in Gost Radin's will: the correct reading is not *mrsni*, 'meat-eating', but *mrski*, 'unsightly'.) Cathars and Bogomils rejected the calendar of saints; Bosnian Church documents, including Gost Radin's will, refer to the celebration of several saint's-days. And so on.[48]

The general character of the Bosnian Church was also very different from what we associate with the Bogomils or the Cathars. Those heretical sects were ascetic and puritanical; they were opposed to the wealth and secular power of the established Churches, and renounced earthly goods. The Bosnian Church in its heyday (the fourteenth and early fifteenth centuries) enjoyed considerable power, and its dignitaries were used to sign charters and carry out diplomatic missions. Kings such as Stephen Kotromanić and Tvrtko, though not members of the Bosnian Church, had friendly relations with it; some of the great noble families seem to have belonged to it.[49] The best-known Bosnian Churchman, Gost Radin, was a senior counsellor to the Herceg Stephen Vukčić, and clearly a magnate in his own right: in his will he left more than 5000 ducats in cash, together with horses, silver or gold plate, a 'fur-trimmed gown with gold' and a 'red fur-trimmed gown of six-stranded silk, trimmed with sable, which the Lord King Matijaš gave me'.[50] This is a far cry from those humble early Cathars who described themselves as *pauperes Christi* – Christ's paupers.

Once the Franciscans got to work in Bosnia in the mid-fourteenth century, the Roman Catholic Church was in direct competition with the Bosnian Church. We have some accounts of hostility towards the Franciscans on the part of the 'heretics': one popular story about the energetic Franciscan Vicar Jacob de Marchia, cited during his canonization proceedings in 1609, has it that the 'heretics' sawed the feet off the pulpit of the monastery church at Visoko while he was preaching in it. (In return he cursed the people responsible, and all their descendants were born with defective feet.)[51] Unfortunately, no Franciscan reports on the beliefs of the Bosnians have survived; one request for instructions by a Franciscan Vicar of Bosnia prompted a detailed papal reply which refers to heretics, schismatics and improperly ordained clergy, but makes no reference to dualist beliefs.[52] Still, for Catholics in Italy, Bosnia was back in the news; and it became known as a place filled with 'heretics' of a rather unspecified kind. The term 'Patarin', which would have been used as a general label for the Bosnian Church in reports coming via Ragusa and the rest of Dalmatia, must have evoked memories of the Cathar heretics of northern Italy. And the rapid expansion of the Franciscan Vicariate of Bosnia meant that, as we have seen, all kinds of East European heretics could be described as 'Bosnian'. One document issued by Gregory XI in 1372 urges the conversion of 'infidels' in Bosnia, especially the ones living in Transylvania; another Catholic document lists the errors of the Hussites living in 'Moldavia' [Moravia?], and concludes: 'here ends the brief summary written against the errors and heretical tenets of the Kingdom of Bosnia'.[53]

It is against this background that we must look at the Italian documents of this period which refer to Catharism or dualism in Bosnia. One puzzling piece of evidence is an inquisition report from Turin in 1387, giving the confession (made after torture) of Giacomo Bech, who claimed to have joined a Cathar sect in the mountains west of Turin. One member of the sect, he said, was from 'Sclavonia', and some of the Italian members had travelled to 'Bosnia' to perfect their knowledge of Cathar doctrine there. Bech claimed that he himself had been given money to go there, but could not cross the sea because of bad weather.[54] The reference to 'Sclavonia' suggests a link with the dualist tradition on the Dalmatian coast. It is possible to imagine Italians going there (where Italian was widely spoken) for instruction, and it is worth remembering that a large stretch of the coastline was at this time incorporated into the Bosnian kingdom; but it is more difficult to believe that they would have travelled to the remote and monoglot Bosnian hinterland. And on the other hand Bech's story about nearly going there, but not quite succeeding, has a familiar ring of untruth about it. It sounds like the sort of confession people make at witch trials, when they insist that witches' covens take place, claim that they were invited to attend one, but then say that they were prevented, as chance would have it, from going – thus saving themselves from the risk of over-extending their imaginations.

Also open to doubt are the lists of 'errors of the Bosnian heretics', drawn up by Franciscans in Italy in the late fourteenth century, which portray the Bosnians as hard-line dualists of the Cathar or Bogomil type. One begins: 'First, that there are two gods, and that the greater god created all spiritual and invisible things, and the lesser, which is Lucifer, all bodily and visible things.' It goes on to include the rejection of the Old Testament, the Mass, material churches and images, 'especially the cross'.[55] This may have been true of some small sect of 'Slavonian' or 'Dalmatian' heretics, but, as we have seen, there are good reasons for thinking that it cannot have been an accurate account of the Bosnian Church. In fact the lists of 'errors' conform so closely to the Cathar model that a rather obvious explanation suggests itself: asked to produce analyses or refutations of 'Patarin' errors, the Italian clerics who composed these documents simply searched through their libraries for tracts against 'Patarins' (in other words, Italian Cathars), and eventually came up with a summary of Cathar beliefs.[56] Similar doubts must arise over the systematic list of 'Manichee' errors which three Bosnian noblemen were asked to renounce by the Inquisitor, Juan de Torquemada, in Rome in 1461; and the whole basis of the sudden upsurge in papal invective against 'Manichees' in Bosnia in the 1440s and 1450s is also open to question.[57]

By the 1450s the Franciscan offensive was (as we have seen in the previous chapter) in full swing. Some time before the spring of 1453 the djed or head of the Bosnian Church left the territory of Bosnia proper and took refuge with the Herceg Stephen Vukčić. Later that year, according to a letter written by Patriarch Gennadios II at Constantinople, the djed joined the Orthodox Church.[58] If this evidence is reliable, we must assume that the Bosnian Church was already severely weakened by the djed's action, even before the official persecution of the Bosnian Church by King Tomaš in 1459. There was strong competition between the Catholic and Orthodox Churches to see which could mop up the remainder of the adherents of the Bosnian Church. One Franciscan reported that many of the 'heretics' were joining the Catholic Church, but that the bishop of the Serbs ('Rascianorum': inhabitants of Raška) would not allow them to be reconciled to Rome.[59] Perhaps, having acquired the Bosnian djed, he thought he had a right to his flock as well. The action King Tomaš took in 1459 was thus probably meant to preempt any further drift to Orthodoxy. The forced conversion of 2000 krstjani and the withdrawal of forty irreconcilables to Hercegovina must have broken the Church's back; though we lack any proper figures for the number of monasteries, this would surely have represented the bulk of the Bosnian monastic churchmen. When Gost Radin wrote to Venice in 1466 requesting permission to migrate there if the Turks forced him to flee, he asked whether he might bring fifty or sixty members of his sect with him: this probably represents the main remnant of the Church, including the forty irreconcilables.[60]

As for the ordinary lay members, it is possible that the Bosnian Church had never had a huge membership, since as a purely monastic organization it lacked the necessary territorial structure of parishes. And whatever the number of lay adherents in its heyday, the figure must have fallen during more than a century of state-supported Catholic proselytism. So it seems that by the time the Turks took over, the Bosnian Church was already broken and virtually defunct. In the Ottoman land-registers of Bosnia for the fifteenth and sixteenth centuries, which categorized people by religion, a few are listed as *kristian* (as opposed to the usual word for Christians, *gebr* or *kâfir*, meaning 'unbeliever', under which both Catholics and Orthodox were listed). A few entire villages are given as kristian in the earliest registers, but the total numbers are very small: fewer than 700 individuals appear in these registers over the entire period.[61] The historian who has studied this material (and who follows the 'Bogomil' theory) suggests that these *kristianlar* were just the 'elect' of the Church, and that ordinary members were being listed under *gebr* or *kâfir*; but this is surely wrong. The Turks were simply using religious categories: Muslim, Jew, unbeliever and kristian.[62] In the whole period from 1468 (the first register) to the late sixteenth century, just two names appear bearing the title 'Gost'. It appears that some tiny remnant of the tradition was thus preserved, perpetuating itself with a do-it-yourself succession of ordinations. One Catholic priest, the Albanian Peter Masarechi, who visited Bosnia in the 1620s, referred in his report to 'Patarins' who live without proper priests and sacraments, 'with their Priest chosen from among the people, without any ordination'.[63] But even this remnant was at last swallowed up, leaving nothing behind but unreliable collective memory, folk history and myth.

4

War and the Ottoman system, 1463–1606

The kingdom of Bosnia was conquered with great speed by the Turkish army in the early summer of 1463. From then on, the heartlands of the old Banate of Bosnia, together with the foothold which the Turks had already established in the Sarajevo region, remained under permanent Turkish control, even though the Turks withdrew their main military force in the autumn. But the gains which the Turkish army had made in the northern half of Bosnia were quickly overturned by King Matthias of Hungary. The Serbian-born janissary whose autobiography has come down to us was left behind with a force of only eighty men to hold the fortress of Zvečaj, near Jajce; as soon as the Sultan had gone, both Zvečaj and Jajce were besieged by Hungarian troops, and they eventually surrendered.[1] King Matthias established a new Hungarian-ruled 'banate' of Bosnia in these northern territories, and in 1471 he promoted the Ban to the title of 'King of Bosnia'. Although the area of this 'kingdom' was quickly whittled down by Turkish campaigns, the rump which survived held out for more than eighty years. By the 1520s, however, the city of Jajce was under almost permanent siege, receiving deliveries of food from Hungarian Slavonia by armed convoy barely four times a year.[2] It was finally conquered by the Turks in 1527, after they had smashed the Hungarian army at the fateful battle of Mohács in the previous year.

A diminishing rump of Hercegovina also held out against the Turks after 1463. The Herceg Stephen Vukčić was able to regain his territory at the end of that year, but most of it was conquered two years later by the Turks: the Herceg had to take refuge in the fortified port of Novi (renamed Herceg-Novi, after him), where he died in 1466.[3] His second son, Vlatko, who succeeded to the title of Herceg, did what he could to bring in Hungarian and Venetian help to defend his remaining territories. But this only embroiled him in further conflicts between those third parties, Ragusa and local noblemen; by the 1470s he was paying tribute to the Ottomans, and in 1481 or 1482 the last fortress on Hercegovinan territory was taken by the Turkish army.[4]

As these events illustrate, the Ottoman Empire was a formidable and highly active military machine. The reign of Mehmet II (1451–81) saw an extraordinary succession of conquests and challenges to the neighbouring powers: after taking Constantinople in 1453, he went on to conquer the north of Serbia, parts of Anatolia, Wallachia, Bosnia and Hercegovina, destroyed the Venetian army in Greece, raided Moldavia and Hungary, besieged the island of Rhodes and was on the point of mounting a full-scale invasion of Italy when he died. His successor, Bayezit II (1481–1512), gave more attention to consolidating the Empire, but still managed to conduct wars against Moldavia, Poland, Hungary and Venice. Süleyman the Magnificent (1520–66) turned again to the northwest: in the first thirteen years of his reign he reduced most of Hungary to the status of a vassal territory and came within an ace of capturing Vienna. The peace treaty which he agreed with Austria in 1533 marks the beginning of a long period of sometimes bloody but mainly static confrontation between the Ottoman and Habsburg Empires; during the rest of the century each side built up a military frontier-zone facing the other, guarded by a network of fortresses and a semi-controlled population of martial peasants.[5] Sporadic raiding became the normal state of affairs, but military activity on the Bosnian border grew more intense at times when the Sultan was waging full-scale war against the Habsburgs – as in Süleyman's final Hungarian campaign of 1566. The next major Ottoman-Habsburg war, which lasted from 1593 to 1606, was actually sparked off by fighting undertaken by local forces on Bosnia's north-eastern border: the Turks had captured the important fortress at Bihać from the Habsburgs in 1592, but in the following year the Pasha of Bosnia was taken by surprise, while besieging the stronghold of Sisak (on the river Sava, below Zagreb), and heavily defeated. In the first major campaign of the subsequent war, the Turks inflicted a serious defeat on the Habsburg army at Mezökeresztes (1596); after that, they were able to strengthen their control over much of Hungary for the next eighty years.[6]

Until it stagnated and declined – a process which began in the mid-sixteenth century – the Ottoman Empire was, in its very essence, a military enterprise. It aimed at plunder and tribute, and its administrative system was designed to supply two things: men to fight wars, and money to pay for them. The military forces fell into two main categories. There were regular soldiers paid directly by the Ottoman government: these consisted of janissaries (the regular infantry) and salaried cavalry known as 'the spahis of the Porte'. ('The Porte' was the traditional phrase for the imperial government in Istanbul.) And on the other hand there was the feudal cavalry: mounted soldiers who performed their military obligations in return for the estates which they had been given. (The term 'spahi' on its own refers always to this feudal type.) These two categories of soldiery together formed the huge armies which conducted the set-piece campaigns from early spring to late autumn. The fact that the army had to gather each time outside Istanbul and march to the periphery of the Empire began to put a kind of natural geographical limit (as Süleyman the Magnificent's Hungarian campaigns showed) on the expansion of the Empire. But there were also various auxiliary forces, which had a more important role in border areas, such as Bosnia, where all-year-round activity was needed. These included *azap* soldiers, a kind of town militia which garrisoned fortresses and functioned as border infantry, and *deli* or *akıncı* horsemen, a type of irregular light cavalry used for raiding. All the forces so far mentioned were Muslim: as a general rule, the subject peoples could not bear arms. For some special purposes, however, which applied especially in the border regions of Bosnia, local Christian forces were used: as guards of roads and passes, as organizers of the supply of horses, and, above all, as the fearsome kind of territorial free-booter infantry soldier known as a *vojnuk* or *martolos*.[7] These will be described more fully in the chapter on Bosnian Serbs (below, chapter 6).

The janissary army, together with the system of boy-tribute (known as *devşirme*: 'collection') which supplied its membership, was the most important method for drawing people from Christian

Europe into the machinery of the Ottoman state. During the fifteenth and sixteenth centuries, when the devşirme system was fully operative, boys from the villages of Christian Europe were gathered at variable but frequent intervals and taken off to Istanbul. There they were converted to Islam and trained as janissary troops, or as personal servants of the Sultan, or as officials in the various departments of state.[8] (All departments of state were essentially branches of the Imperial household.) The senior figures in the Ottoman administration also had large numbers of such people in their own households: one who died in Istanbul in 1557 had 156 slaves, including 52 Bosnians, and it has been suggested that they were the consequence of a sort of private devşirme, perhaps even on a voluntary basis.[9] Although the seizing of children was an intrinsically brutal procedure, it could have obvious benefits not only for the boys themselves (many of whom went on to become senior pashas and viziers) but also for their families, with whom they could later restore contacts. The Sokollu (Sokolović) dynasty in Istanbul, which supplied a succession of grand viziers, did not lose contact with its Bosnian Serb family, and used its influence to protect the interests of the Serbian Orthodox Church. Altogether, there were nine grand viziers of Bosnian origin in the sixteenth and seventeenth centuries, and Bosnians were being sent back to govern Bosnia from as early as 1488.[10] While Christian parents sometimes bribed Muslim neighbours to substitute their not-yet-circumcised children for Christian boys, there were also cases of parents of both faiths bribing officials to take their own children. Certainly the benefits of the system were apparent to the Bosnian Muslims, who made a special arrangement in 1515 to have 1000 of their children sent off to the training schools of the Imperial palace.[11]

The system of regular devşirme ceased to operate some time in the first half of the seventeenth century. By the 1660s, when the English diplomat Paul Rycaut wrote his classic account of the Ottoman Empire, it was 'wholly forgotten'.[12] But its impact had been enormous. At least 200,000 children from the Balkans had passed through the system in its two centuries of operation.[13] Since the great majority of these were Slavs, the Serbo-Croat language (with its almost mutually intelligible neighbour, Bulgarian) was implanted into the heart of the Ottoman state. One Western commentator noted in 1595 that 'Slavonic' was the third language of the Empire (after Turkish and Arabic), because it was the language of the janissaries; and another observed in 1660 that 'the Turkish language is hardly ever heard at the Sultan's court', because 'the whole court and a majority of the magnates' were 'renegades' from Slav-speaking lands.[14] The system also had an important social and political effect: it created a class of powerful state officials and their descendants which came into conflict with the feudal-military spahis and gradually encroached upon their land, hastening the movement away from feudal tenure towards private estates and tax-farms. 'Essentially', Stanford Shaw has written, 'it was the triumph of the Balkan element in the Ottoman ruling class through the devşirme system which led to the breakdown of the financial and administrative system of the Ottomans and caused the subsequent decline of the empire.'[15]

The Ottoman feudal system had been imposed on Bosnia from the outset. There were two main types of estate which a spahi could receive: the larger type was a *zaim*, and the smaller was a *tımar*, held by a *tımarlı* or timariot. (The third and largest type, known as a *hass*, was granted only to the most important provincial governors and members of the Sultan's family.) The system, known in general as the timar system, was strictly military-feudal: tenure was dependent on military service, the land was the property of the Sultan, and the timariot's heirs had no legal right to inherit it (though inheritance was in practice the norm). Holders of these estates had to appear with arms and horses when summoned for military duty; they also had to bring and pay for other soldiers, in direct proportion to their income.[16] They gathered for war according to the military district where they lived (*sancak*, meaning literally 'banner', in Turkish; *sandžak* in Serbo-Croat), and were commanded by the sandžak-beg, who was the most junior rank of official to enjoy the title of pasha.

Since the timariots were often away on military duty for six or nine months of the year, their tenure need not have weighed too heavily on the peasants (Christian or Muslim) who worked their lands. The peasants had to pay a tithe in kind, varying between a tenth and a quarter of their produce, and pay a few other smaller dues; they also did some obligatory labour for the timariot, though this was much less onerous than in most other European feudal systems. They also paid an annual land tax (the *haraç*, which later merged with a poll-tax called the *cizye*) to the Sultan. Their basic legal position was that of leaseholders, having a right, which their children could inherit, not in the land itself but in the use of it. They could sell this right, and were in theory free to move elsewhere, even though the timariots naturally tried to prevent this.[17] In general, a timariot had no further legal interest in his peasants beyond the requirement that they pay their tithe and other dues and obey him when he acted as a functionary of the state: he had no judicial powers of the sort practised in manorial courts in western Europe.

These conditions would later change, of course, as the feudal system decayed. But to begin with, life as a peasant on a timar estate may well have been preferable to life in feudal pre-Ottoman Bosnia – especially in the final years before the Turkish conquest, when the population bore the extra financial burdens of both defending Bosnia against the Turks and raising tribute to placate them. In one of his last appeals for help before the conquest, King Stephen Tomašević had written: 'The Turks . . . are showing a kindly disposition towards the peasants. They promise that all who desert to them shall be free and they welcome them graciously . . . The people will be easily induced by such tricks to desert me.'[18] The 'trick' was in some respects no deception. And for those peasants who converted to Islam, a more secure form of tenure was possible, in which the peasant could have full ownership of a smallholding or *çift*, commonly of five to ten hectares in size.[19]

Being a Muslim was certainly an advantage for anyone in the Ottoman state. But we misunderstand the Ottoman Empire of this period if we assume – as many standard works still do – that it was strictly organized on religious lines, with an absolute division between on the one hand a ruling class of Muslims, and on the other a subject class of unbelievers who were categorized by the *millet* (religious unit) to which they belonged. The Empire became like that in its later centuries; in the first period of its rule in the Balkans, however, the picture was more fluid. The original distinction was not between Muslims and unbelievers, but between Ottomans (meaning the entire military-administrative class, which people could join if they acquired an Ottoman outlook and Ottoman behaviour) and *raya*. The Koranic term 'raya' ('flock' or 'herd') was a general word for subject people: Muslims could be raya too, especially if, like the Arabs, they exhibited a non-Ottoman culture. The basic Ottoman legal system was not dependent on Islamic holy law: it flowed from the will of the Sultan, often taking the form of confirming by his authority local laws and privileges, and was merely presumed not to be in conflict with the holy law or *şeriat* (shariat). Only gradually, during the sixteenth and seventeenth centuries, did Islam and the principles of Ottoman-hood become more closely merged. When the Turks conquered Bosnia, and for several generations to come, it was still possible for a Christian to become a spahi and be granted a timar estate, without renouncing his Christianity: proven loyalty to the Ottoman state and an acceptance of its ways were the only essential requirements.[20]

Although Bosnia was ruled by Muslims, one could hardly call it an Islamic state. It was not state policy to convert people to Islam or make them behave like Muslims; the only state policy was to keep the country under control and extract from it money, men and feudal incomes to supply the needs of the Empire further afield. This meant that Ottoman rule in this period could in some ways be quite light, in that there were areas of life with which it was simply not concerned. The Christian and Jewish religions were still allowed to function, albeit under various restrictions, and they were also permitted to apply their own religious law to their people, in their own courts – at least in civil matters. But at the same time the limited nature of the Ottoman government's interest in the territories it ruled was obviously conducive to corruption and oppression. So long as a provincial governor supplied men and revenues and kept his territory under control, no one in the Imperial administration would look too closely at how he conducted himself there. A brutal or corrupt pasha enjoyed wide freedom of action; governors might be recalled for incompetence or rebellion, but never for mere corruption. And the fact that provincial governors and military commanders were circulated frequently from place to place, usually spending only a few years in charge of any one province, was almost an invitation to them to extract riches from their territories as quickly as they could. There were several types of civil law in the Ottoman Empire, and there was also the sacred law of Islam, which grew increasingly important; but one would hesitate to describe the Ottoman Empire as having enjoyed the rule of law.

Ottoman law was dispensed locally by a *kadi* or judge. He was the most important administrator at the local level, and the area he was responsible for was a *kaza* or *kadiluk*.[21] A number of these would be contained in a sancak, the military-administrative district. Each sancak was a large and important region; but it was itself a sub-division of an *eyalet* or province, the largest constituent unit of the Empire. The first sandžak (to use the Serbo-Croat form of the word) set up by the Turks after their conquest of Bosnia was the sandžak of Bosnia itself, with its administrative seat first at Sarajevo (till 1553), then at Banja Luka (till 1639), then Sarajevo again (till the 1690s), and then Travnik. The sandžak of Zvornik, to the north-east, was set up a little later, and the sandžak of Hercegovina in 1470. Five more neighbouring sandžaks were established in the sixteenth century, partly out of land conquered from Croatia and Slavonia. Until 1580 all of them formed part of the eyalet of Rumelia, the province which covered most of the Balkans.[22] But in that year the decision was made to create a new eyalet out of them: the eyalet of Bosnia. This meant that it was ruled by the highest rank of pasha, a *beylerbeyi* (Turkish) or *beglerbeg* (Serbo-Croat): a 'lord of lords'. There was now a Bosnian entity which included the whole of modern Bosnia and Hercegovina, plus some neighbouring parts of Slavonia, Croatia, Dalmatia and Serbia.[23] While the old kingdom of Serbia, for example, was to remain divided into a number of smaller units, each of which was just one of the many components of the eyalet of Buda or Rumelia, Bosnia was to enjoy this special status as a distinct entity for the rest of the Ottoman period.

5

The Islamicization of Bosnia

The arrival of the Turks in the fifteenth century was probably not the first contact between Bosnia and Islam. The early Arab expansion in the Mediterranean, which by the ninth century had established Muslim rule in Crete, Sicily, southern Italy and Spain, must have brought Muslim merchants and raiders frequently to the coast of Dalmatia. The slave trade from that coast, which, as we have seen, spread Bosnian slaves round the western Mediterranean throughout the later middle ages, was certainly operating during this earlier period: enslaved Slavs from the Mediterranean region were present in early Muslim Spain, and the Saracen rulers of Andalusia are known to have had a Slav army of 13,750 men in the tenth century.[1] But we can only speculate about whether any Bosnians converted to Islam, obtained their freedom and returned to their homeland. Speculation too is all that is possible on the relations between Bosnia and the Muslims of medieval Hungary – Arab merchants, descendants of Islamicized Turkic tribes and other immigrants. They are known to have lived in many parts of the Hungarian lands, including Srem, the area adjoining north-eastern Bosnia, until their eventual expulsion from Hungary, along with the Jews, in the fourteenth century.[2] It is understandable that some Bosnian Muslim scholars have been particularly eager to establish that Islam was an ancient presence in Bosnia, perhaps older than the Bosnian state itself. But the historical significance of these early possible contacts is slight. Contact is one thing; mass conversion is another.

The Islamicization of a large part of the population under the Turks remains the most distinctive and important feature of modern Bosnian history. Many myths have arisen about how and why it happened; some of them still percolate from the earlier scholarly literature (and from not-so-scholarly modern works) into the minds of ordinary Bosnians. Until historians began the serious analysis of Ottoman administrative records in the 1940s, much of the essential evidence was unavailable. But over the last few decades a much fuller picture has been built up, and some of the commonest myths and legends about the Islamicization of Bosnia are at last being laid to rest.

The best source of information is the Ottoman 'defters', tax-registers which recorded property-ownership and categorized people by their religion. From these quite a detailed picture can be formed of the spread of Islam in Bosnia. The earliest defters, from 1468/9, show that Islam had established only a toehold in the first few years after the conquest: in the area of east and central Bosnia which they cover, 37,125 households were Christian and only 332 were Muslim. Assuming an average of five people per household, this gives a figure of 185,625 Christians; separately listed were also nearly 9000 individual Christian bachelors and widows. Half of the Christian households, and two-thirds (234) of the Muslim, were simple raya living on ordinary timar estates: the others lived on the larger hass estates, or in towns, or on their own land. The scholar who first analysed these documents, Nedim Filipović, also noted that Islamicization was very slight in Hercegovina, and that it was most advanced, not surprisingly, in the small area round Sarajevo which had been held by the Turks since the 1440s.[3] Some of the holders of the timars are specifically described in these earliest defters as 'new Muslim'; others have a Muslim name, and are listed as 'son of . . .', with the father bearing a Christian name.[4]

The next defter to have been fully analysed covers the sandžak of Bosnia for 1485; it shows that Islam was now beginning to make significant progress. There were 30,552 Christian households, 2491 individual Christian bachelors and widows, 4134 Muslim households and 1064 Muslim bachelors.[5] Again assuming five people per household, this gives a total of 155,251 Christians and 21,734 Muslims. Compared with the figure for 1468–9, the decline in total numbers (which was even greater in real terms, if one allows for the normal rate of population growth) is striking; during this period there was a steady flow of people out of Bosnia, and a large number of abandoned villages are mentioned in the registers. Naturally it was the non-Islamicized who fled, and the Islamicized who stayed behind. But over the next four decades, while the total population remained static, the proportion of Muslims grew much larger: the defters of the 1520s yield total figures for the sandžak of Bosnia of 98,095 Christians and 84,675 Muslims.[6] Since we know that there was no large-scale Muslim immigration into Bosnia during that period, the figure must represent conversions of Bosnian Christians to Islam.

The process of Islamicization speeded up gradually in Hercegovina; one comment survives from an Orthodox monk in Hercegovina in 1509, noting that many Orthodox people had voluntarily embraced Islam.[7] In northern and north-eastern Bosnia the spread of Islam could only take place slowly as the territories were captured from Hungary. After the process of conquest was completed in the 1520s, Islamicization proceeded a little faster. The Dominican historian Father Mandić claims that there was – for the first time – a deliberate campaign of persecution against Catholics, forcing them to convert to Islam, in the period 1516–24.[8] The most detailed study of north-eastern Bosnia during this period, by Adem Handžić, does not support Mandić's claim, however – though it does show that many Catholics emigrated from the area, and that five out of the ten Franciscan monasteries there ceased to operate. Handžić also demonstrates that Catholics were more likely, understandably enough, to convert to Islam the further away they lived from Catholic churches. The most resistant place was Srebrenica, home to a large Catholic German and Ragusan population, which was still two-thirds Catholic in the mid-sixteenth century. Towns were usually more Islamicized than the countryside; the whole area of north-eastern Bosnia was roughly one-third Muslim by 1533, and 40 per cent Muslim by 1548.[9]

More precise figures are lacking for the rest of the sixteenth century, and thereafter the practice of keeping defters was abandoned. Yet it seems clear that at some time in the late sixteenth or early seventeenth century the Muslims became an absolute majority in the territory of modern Bosnia and Hercegovina. From the early seventeenth century we do have some accounts by visiting Catholic priests who compiled detailed reports for Rome; but their figures must have been based largely on hearsay, their use of the term

'Bosnia' was elastic, and they were evidently keen to emphasize either the numerical strength of the Catholic Church or the degree of oppression it suffered. One such visitor gave a total of 250,000 Catholics for the whole of Bosnia in 1626, and added that the number of Muslims was larger than the total number of Christians.[10] Another, the Albanian priest and apostolic visitor Peter Masarechi, sent a more carefully researched report in 1624; unfortunately, the figures he gave for Bosnia have been misconstrued by almost all the historians who have cited them. What he actually reported was that there were 150,000 Catholics, roughly 75,000 Eastern Orthodox, and 450,000 Muslims.[11]

The process by which Bosnia gained a majority population of Muslims thus took the best part of 150 years. In the light of the evidence accumulated so far, it is clear that some of the oldest myths about the Islamicization of Bosnia can be rejected. The idea that there was any sort of mass settlement during this period of Muslims from outside Bosnia must be dismissed: though the Ottomans did settle some Turkic peoples in other parts of the Balkans, the defters confirm that no such policy was ever applied to Bosnia. A few of the most superficial foreign visitors to Bosnia during the Ottoman period may have been confused by the fact that the Bosnian Muslims came to describe themselves as 'Turks'; but this did not mean that even they thought they were Turkish. On the contrary, they always used a different term for Ottoman Turks: either *Osmanli* or *Turkuš*.[12] Individual Muslims – merchants, artisans, spahis – certainly came to settle in Bosnia from other parts of the Empire; some of these, probably a large proportion in the late fifteenth and early sixteenth centuries, were Muslim Slavs from the other Slav lands. Of the many non-Slavs who served with Bosnian forces during the sixteenth and seventeenth centuries, hardly any settled on Bosnian soil.[13]

Similarly, the idea that there was a massive forcible conversion of Bosnians in the early years after the conquest is obviously false: the process of conversion was slow at the outset and took many generations. Although we lack the sort of personal testimony which would tell us how and why individuals decided to convert, we do have occasional comments, such as that of the monk mentioned above, indicating that people made the change of religion voluntarily. The evidence of the defters also suggests a rather untroubled approach to the persistence of unconverted Christians in their faith: it was normal for people to become Muslims and take Islamic names, but continue to live with the rest of their Christian family.[14] This practice helps to explain why the Muslims of Bosnia retained the Slav system of patronymic names: there are many entries in the early defters of the sort 'Ferhad, son of Ivan' or 'Hasan, son of Mihailo'. By the time these patronymics were later stabilized as surnames, most Muslims had Muslim fathers; but they continued to form these family names in the Slav way, yielding surnames such as Hasanović and Sulejmanović.[15]

To say that there was no general policy of coercing individuals does not mean that no obstruction or oppression was used against the Christian Churches. The Orthodox Church suffered least in this early Ottoman period, for two reasons: first, because Ottoman policy preferred the Orthodox to the Catholic Church (the Church of the Austrian enemy); and secondly, because in much of Bosnia, excluding Hercegovina, there was very little Orthodox presence before the Turkish invasion. Indeed, an Orthodox population was introduced to large parts of Bosnia as a direct result of Ottoman policy. (This subject will be dealt with in chapter 6.) The Orthodox Church was an accepted institution of the Empire.[16]

The Catholic Church, on the other hand, although it was granted the essential legal status necessary to continue its activities, was regarded with deep suspicion.[17] Its priests were seen as potential spies for foreign powers, and with good reason: one Venetian government official recorded in 1500 a report from 'certain Franciscan friars who have been in Bosnia' analysing the military intentions of the Turks.[18] Many Catholics fled to the neighbouring Catholic lands during the first half-century of Ottoman rule – especially, it may be presumed, those who had cooperated with the Hungarians in their attempt to hold the northern part of Bosnia. As we have seen, five out of the ten Franciscan monasteries in the north-eastern region studied by Adem Handžić disappeared during the process of Turkish conquest. Before the Turks entered Bosnia, there were thirty-five Franciscan monasteries in Bosnia proper, and four in Hercegovina. Most of these are absent from the defters; some were destroyed in war, and others (in Foča, Jajce, Zvornik, Srebrenica and Bihać) were turned into mosques. In the 1580s a visiting

Franciscan general found only ten in the whole of Bosnia; the same figure (for the territory of modern Bosnia) is given by another Catholic, Bishop Maravić, in his report of 1655.[19] The Franciscans were the only Catholic clergy functioning in Bosnia; the Catholic administrative unit of Bosnia was divided in 1514 into two provinces, Croatian Bosnia (i.e. non-Ottoman Croatia) and 'Silver Bosnia', 'Bosnia Argentina' (i.e. Bosnia), and the latter was impoverished as well as isolated. Though the Church in Bosnia had no source of income other than money from abroad and gifts of the faithful, local Ottoman governors found many opportunities for extracting large payments from it. Under the more capricious governors, any pretext could be used for demanding money; one plaintive report from Bosnia to Rome in 1603 described how Franciscans were being held and maltreated in prison and told to pay 3000 aspers for permission to stay in their monasteries.[20] Obviously, conditions were hard for Catholic churchmen, and coercion of various kinds was a frequent occurrence. But it was used to gain money, not converts.

Another popular theory about the Islamicization of Bosnia is that it resulted from the mass conversion of members of the Bosnian Church – which, in all versions of this theory, is assumed to have been Bogomil. At first glance, there is something plausible about this claim: the Bosnian Church and the development of a large Islamic population are the two most distinctive things about Bosnian history, and the first ends almost exactly when the second begins. What could be more natural than to suppose that the one explains the other? But in its simplest form the theory is clearly false. Some connection can be made between the two phenomena, but it is only an indirect one. As we have seen, the process of Islamicization took many generations. If the main source of Muslim converts throughout that period had been the membership of the Bosnian Church, one would expect to find evidence of that continuing membership – large at first, and gradually diminishing – in the defters; but the defters show fewer than 700 individual members in Bosnia over nearly 150 years. We have already seen that there is good reason to believe that the Bosnian Church was largely defunct even before the Turkish conquest, and that the numbers of its lay adherents in the years before its collapse may not have been very large anyway. Some of these people may, as a few contemporary reports suggest, have welcomed the Turks to spite their Catholic persecutors.[21] But welcoming the Turks was quite a different matter from welcoming Islam; those individuals whose politics were guided in this way by the strength of their devotion to the Bosnian Church would surely have been the least likely people to abandon their religion. Attempts have been made by some writers to find deep spiritual affinities between the theology of the Bosnian 'Bogomils' and the mystic tradition in Islam, especially in the Sufism of the dervish orders.[22] If we reject, as we must, the 'Bogomil' theory about the Bosnian Church, this argument must also fall.

The only connection which can be drawn between the Bosnian Church and Islamicization is indirect and rather negative. What the story of the Bosnian Church shows is that Bosnia had a peculiarly weak and fractured ecclesiastical history during the period leading up to the Turkish conquest. In some areas (Hercegovina and the Serbian fringe of eastern Bosnia) there had been three different Churches acting in competition. In most of Bosnia proper there had been two: the Bosnian Church and the Catholic Church. Neither, until the final decades of the Bosnian kingdom, was exclusively supported by state policy, and neither had a proper territorial system of parish churches and parish priests. Many villages must have been out of reach of both Franciscan monasteries and Bosnian Church hižas, at best seeing a friar or krstjanin on an annual visit. If we compare this state of affairs with conditions in Serbia or Bulgaria, where there was a single, strong and properly organized national Church, we can see one major reason for the greater success of Islam in Bosnia. The fractious competition between Catholic and Orthodox continued throughout the period of Islamicization; while members of both Churches were becoming Muslims, some Catholics were also being converted to Orthodoxy, and vice-versa.[23] It is significant that the only other Balkan country (outside Turkish-inhabited Thrace) to acquire a Muslim majority was Albania, which had also been an area of competition between Christian Churches (Catholic and Orthodox). But the Albanian case is different again; that country seems to have been Islamicized as a matter of deliberate Ottoman policy to help suppress resistance after the Turkish-Venetian war in the seventeenth century.[24]

If we recognize that Christianity was quite weakly supported by any Church organization in many parts of Bosnia, we can understand the psychology of conversion to Islam a little more clearly. There is no point in talking about these conversions in the terms one would use for, say, Martin Luther or Cardinal Newman. In country areas poorly served by priests, Christianity (in whatever form) had probably become little more than a set of folk practices and ceremonies, some of them concerned with birth, marriage and death, and others aimed at warding off evil fortune, curing illnesses, securing good harvests, and so on. The shift from folk Christianity to folk Islam was not very great; many of the same practices could continue, albeit with slightly different words or names. Without the controlling presence of a Church, warning of danger to one's immortal soul, the shift could be made quite easily. Earnest Protestant visitors to the Balkans were frequently shocked by the insouciance with which people made the transition. The English doctor George Wheler, visiting Corinth in the 1670s, observed that 'the Christians here, for want of good Instruction, and able and faithful Pastors to teach them, run daily into Apostasie, and renounce their Religion for the Turkish Superstition, upon every small Calamity, and Discontent that happens to them'.[25]

Some of the folk-religion practices mentioned in early sources have had a long history in both the Christian and the Islamic traditions. Belief in the protective powers of tablets or pieces of paper with religious inscriptions – either as an amulet or as something to bury in a field to protect the crops – was current in the middle ages and has survived to the present day, among both Christians and Muslims.[26] One traveller in 1904 was struck by the fact that Muslims and Christians shared 'the same superstitious belief in the power of amulets, which the Muslims often have blessed by the Franciscans, and which are worn by children round the neck, on their clothes or on their fez: snakes, fishes, eagle's claws, stag's antlers, and so on'.[27] Many of the same festivals and holy days were celebrated by both religions: these included Jurjevo (St George's Day), and Ilinden (St Elias's day), which was known to the Muslims as Alidjun. As one popular saying put it: 'Up to mid-day Ilija; after mid-day Ali'.[28] And where the basic attitude to religion is practical-magical, even the most important ceremonial elements of one religion can be borrowed by another – or rather, *especially* the most important, since these are thought to be the most powerful. Thus we not only find Muslims kissing the most venerated Christian icons, such as the one at Olovo, or entering Christian churches to pray; we also find them, in the early nineteenth century, having Catholic Masses said for them in front of images of the Virgin in order to cure a serious illness.[29] The cult of the Virgin Mary seems to have been particularly popular. One Franciscan, the 'guardian' of the monastery at Olovo, wrote in 1695 that the church there was 'held in the highest veneration by the Muslims, because of the continual succession of prodigious miracles which God works there by the intercession of the Holy Virgin'.[30] Conversely, there are also records of Christians inviting Muslim dervishes to read the Koran over them to cure them of a dangerous illness. As one wide-ranging study of this subject throughout the Ottoman Empire has put it: 'The tendency to participation is of course strongest . . . where all sects meet on a common basis of secular superstition.'[31]

It is against this background that we should look at the one other mysterious element in Bosnian religious history which, according to some writers, indicates a link between Islam and the medieval Bosnian Church: the Poturs. The original meaning of this name is obscure. It was generally used to refer to Islamicized or Turkicized Bosnian Slavs of a rather rustic and provincial kind, who may have retained some Christian practices. (Discussion of the Poturs has been dominated by one late source, a description by the English diplomat Paul Rycaut, which appears to give them the attributes of members of a religious sect; but this, as we shall see, is misleading.) Some writers have argued that 'Potur' is derived from 'Patarin'.[32] This derivation must be rejected, for the simple reason that 'Patarin' was an Italian or Ragusan term, and was never used by the Bosnians themselves. 'Potur', on the other hand, was a term used from the sixteenth century to the eighteenth by Bosnians and Turks. Folk-etymology explains it as a condensed version of the Serbo-Croat *polu-turk*, meaning 'half-Turk', and this does have some connection with the way it was used in that period. Another similar derivation is from the Serbo-Croat verb *poturčiti se*, meaning 'to Turkify oneself', to turn Turk.

However, the earliest surviving uses of this word are in Turkish, not Serbo-Croat. After the Bosnian Muslims had made their special arrangement in 1515 to send their sons to be trained in Istanbul, the children were grouped together by the Ottoman administrators under the name 'potur' when they were sent to the Imperial palace.[33] A number of Imperial decrees of the period 1565–89 give the poturs the privilege of sending their sons to become *acemi oğlanı*, members of the elite chosen from the devşirme intake: the term 'potur' is used in these decrees as a general word for the Islamicized Bosnian Slavs. The earliest written source which uses the term is the set of laws for Bosnia issued by the Sultan in 1539: it too uses 'potur' simply to mean the Bosnian Muslim population. Another Turkish source, the record of a court case in Sarajevo in 1566, distinguishes poturs, who are clearly local Bosnian inhabitants, from other Muslims, who may be Ottomans. And a Turkish-Bosnian (i.e. Turkish-Serbo-Croat) dictionary of 1631 translates 'potur' simply as 'villager'.[34] Given this evidence, it is curious that none of the scholars who have puzzled over this question has ever put forward the most obvious explanation, which is that the name 'potur' came from the Turkish word *potur*. This is a word for a type of baggy pleated trousers (Turkish *pot* = 'pleat') worn by peasants, of a sort that was common in the western Balkans; the word passed also into Albanian as *poture*, and is defined in the Albanian Academy dictionary as 'wide trousers for men, worn in some parts of Albania, made of coarse white felt or cloth'.[35] The Turkish word *poturlu*, for someone who wears a potur, also has the general meaning 'peasant'. So it seems likely that this was originally just a contemptuous term used for those Bosnian Slavs who, despite having converted to Islam, remained evidently primitive and provincial when seen through Ottoman eyes.

Against this background, and in view of what we know about the mixture of Christian and Islamic practices in Bosnian religion, some of the later references to Poturs in Bosnia begin to look altogether less mysterious. One Catholic writer reported to the Habsburg court in 1599 that there were many Poturs in the border areas of Bosnia who had kept their Christian names and remained Christians 'at heart'; he said that they would, if liberated from the Turks, willingly undergo baptism.[36] This is not a surprising thing for people to have said if they hoped that the neighbouring Christian power would liberate them; and we should remember that the report was written in the middle of a long Ottoman-Habsburg war when the burden of taxation and military duties on the Bosnian Muslims was heavily increased. It is simply not necessary to read into this evidence any sign of an esoteric crypto-Bogomil religious tradition. Another Catholic, visiting in the 1620s, made similar comments: 'few of the "Turks" who work on the land [i.e. the Bosnian Muslim raya] can speak Turkish; and if they did not fear the fire, almost all of them would become Christians, knowing well that their ancestors were Christians'.[37] This writer too was compiling a report for the Habsburgs, and was eager to persuade them to reconquer Bosnia for Catholicism. A number of such reports seem to have convinced the Austrians that if they ever made a large-scale invasion of Bosnia, they would be welcomed by the entire population; they were to be sorely disappointed when they eventually made the attempt in 1697. It is of course possible that there were in Bosnia, as there were in other parts of the Ottoman world, cases of genuine crypto-Christianity – that is, an outward show of Islam concealing private adherence to Christian beliefs and practices.[38] But this is a much rarer phenomenon, quite different from the sort of mingling of Christianity and Islam which has been described above. It arises only when there has been a determined policy of forcible conversion – and no such policy, as we have seen, was generally applied in Bosnia.

Finally, there is the puzzling statement about the Poturs supplied by Paul Rycaut in 1668. His reference to them comes in a section of his book discussing the *Kadizâdeler*, a puritanical and ultra-orthodox Islamic movement which acquired great influence in Istanbul in the early seventeenth century, before being crushed by the authorities in 1656. Rycaut notes the extreme orthodoxy of the movement ('they are exact and most punctual in the observation of the rules of Religion'), but adds that they introduced special prayers for the dead. For this reason, he says, they were joined by many of 'the *Russians* and other sort of Renegado Christians, who amongst their confused, and almost forgotten notions of the Christian Religion, retain a certain Memory of the particulars of Purgatory, and prayers for the dead'. He continues:

> But those of this Sect who strangely mix Christianity and *Mahometanism* together, are many of the Souldiers who live on the

> confines of *Hungary* and *Bosnia*; reading the Gospel in the *Sclavonian* tongue . . .; besides which, they are curious to learn the Mysteries of the *Alchoran*, and the Law of *Arabick* tongue; and not to be accounted rude and illiterate they affect the Courtly *Persian*. They drink wine in the month of Fast called the *Ramazan* . . . They have a Charity and Affection for Christians, and are ready to protect them from Injuries and Violences of the *Turks*: They believe yet that *Mahomet* was the Holy Ghost promised by Christ . . . The *Potures* of *Bosna* are of this Sect, but pay Taxes as Christians do; they abhor Images and the sign of the Cross; they circumcise, bringing the Authority of Christ's example for it.[39]

The leading modern proponent of the 'Bogomil' theory, Aleksandr Solovjev, seized on this passage as proof of the identity of Poturs and Bogomils.[40] The only correspondence with Bogomil practice, however, is the phrase 'they abhor Images and the sign of the Cross'; and the plain significance of this is that the Poturs were following Muslim practice on this point (or at least claiming to do so, when speaking to Rycaut's Muslim informants).

It is evident that Rycaut has lumped together three very different sets of people here, linking them rather spuriously through the connection he originally made with 'Renegado Christians'. One group is the ultra-orthodox Kadizâdeler. Another consists of soldiers in Hungary and Bosnia doing things which no ultra-orthodox Muslim could possibly countenance, such as drinking wine in Ramadan. In view of their literacy and their Arabic and Persian studies, these must have been janissaries who had received a thorough education in Istanbul. Some of them were no doubt, by origin, Poturs in the ordinary sense. Their laxity and their interest in Christian theology make them sound much closer to the Bektashi order of dervishes, the most open-minded and syncretist of the Sufi movements, which was especially popular among janissaries. As Rycaut noted elsewhere, this order was fiercely condemned by the Kadizâdeler because of its lax behaviour.[41] And thirdly, there are the Poturs: Rycaut's reason for putting them in here seems to be either by geographical association with the soldiers 'on the confines of . . . *Bosnia*', or because they too are 'Renegado Christians' who retain some folk-connection with Christianity. Rycaut had never been to

Bosnia, and must have depended on others for this information; not every detail can be relied on.[42] But as it happens his claim that they 'pay Taxes as Christians do' (i.e. the cizye or haraç, the poll-tax on non-Muslims) may have been correct; one official Bosnian document of 1644–5 states that the Poturs paid the cizye, and it is known that Muslims could be required to pay these taxes at times when there was an exceptional need for revenues to support a war.[43]

Rycaut's account has nothing to do with Bogomilism; and while it is statistically possible that a few Poturs had originally been members of the Bosnian Church, no identification can be made between that Church and the entire rural population of Bosnian Muslims. Nor is there any necessary connection between the remnants of that Church and the remote groups of nominal or vestigial Christians who were sometimes encountered by Catholic visitors: people 'of miserable quality, so blind in religious matters that only the fact that they are not circumcised allows them to call themselves "Christians".'[44] Such people could have been the remnants of a Christian community of any denomination which had been without the services of a priest or church for generations. Whatever they were, they were not Poturs – who were simply the ordinary Slav Muslim peasants of Bosnia.

One other false theory about the Islamicization of Bosnia must also be mentioned; it is still widely believed, even though it was demolished by historical research in the 1930s. This is the claim that when the Turks conquered Bosnia, the local Christian nobility converted to Islam *en bloc* in order to retain its feudal estates. The theory was popularized by the nineteenth-century Franciscan and Slav nationalist Ivan Franjo Jukić, who published a history of Bosnia in 1851 under the pseudonym 'Slavoljub Bošnjak' ('Slavophile Bosnian'). Of the Muslim aristocracy in Bosnia, he asserted: 'They sprang from the bad Christians who turned Muslim because only thus could they protect their land . . . The new faith secured to them their property and wealth, freed them of all taxes and assessments, and gave them carte blanche to indulge in any vice, any evil dealing, all for the sake of living as great lords without toil and effort.'[45] We have already seen that this could hardly be an accurate description of the position of any Bosnian nobleman who did retain his property: with his land converted to a timar estate, he was required to spend much of the year on active service as a soldier. (The non-timar freehold or *mülk* property was a form of tenure mainly confined either to smallholdings or to larger grants of land to Ottomans.) In the 1930s the historian Vaso Čubrilović noted that a minority of the old Bosnian land-holders did become spahis and retain some of their estates; but, as he also noted, it was not necessary for them to become Muslims in order to do so.[46] Christian spahis were quite common in the early years of Ottoman Bosnia; one famous one who became *cerrah başı* (chief surgeon) in the household of the governor of Bosnia in Sarajevo in the 1470s was called Vlah Svinjarević – 'Vlach the swineherd's son', a memorably un-Muslim name.[47]

One of the errors committed by Ivan Franjo Jukić was his assumption that there was an unbroken line of succession from the pre-Ottoman Bosnian nobility, through Islamicization, to the Muslim land-owning aristocracy of his own time. As Čubrilović and other scholars have shown, there were so many interruptions and alterations in the history of land-holding in Ottoman Bosnia that this theory could not possibly account for the large estates of Jukić's day. Those were the products of later social and political developments, and were formed mainly in the seventeenth and eighteenth centuries. But even if we go back to the sixteenth century, we find that Jukić's theory is more false than true. One modern historian has made a detailed study of the origins of forty-eight families who belonged to the Muslim land-holding aristocracy of sixteenth-century Bosnia. She concludes that five came certainly, and two probably, from the old (pre-Ottoman) high nobility; seven came certainly, and seven probably, from the old lower nobility; seven had ordinary Bosnian origins; four or five had non-Bosnian Slav origins; four or five had non-Slav origins; and in eleven cases the origins could not be established.[48] Many members of the Bosnian nobility had been killed or had fled during the Turkish conquest; some of the lower nobility were taken into slavery. There was no pact between 'great lords' and Turks to exchange Christianity for a life of easeful 'evil dealing'.

The general idea that people turned to Islam in order to improve their economic or social position is hard to gainsay, because it is so very general. There must have been very many cases which could be described under this heading. But the economic motivation cannot be confined – as it is in one popular theory about the Islamicization of Bosnia – to the single issue of avoiding the tax on non-Muslims, the cizye or haraç. This was an annual tax which had become a kind of graduated poll-tax: in the sixteenth century the rate was four ducats for the rich, two for the middling sort and one for the poor.[49] (At this time, the Venetian ducat would buy roughly twenty kilograms of wheat in Venice, the Austrian ducat slightly more.)[50] In times of war the rate might be increased; many of the most gloomy reports of Christians suffering from Ottoman oppression in Bosnia come from periods when heavy tax increases were made to pay for campaigns against Venice or the Habsburgs. But at some times, as noted above, the tax might even be extended to Muslims. The avoidance of this tax cannot have been an overwhelming reason for conversion; and we should not forget that Muslims, unlike Christians, also paid the *zakat* (*zekjat* in Serbo-Croat), the alms-tax which was one of the basic obligations of Islam. (As a rough counterpart to this, Orthodox Christians might have to pay dues to the Orthodox Church; the Franciscans relied more on voluntary contributions.) Some Muslims might also find themselves called up for military duties, either in the town militias or as part of the contingent furnished by a spahi. Outside the border areas, Christians were generally exempt from such duties.

It is not true that one had to be a Muslim in order to become rich in the Ottoman Empire. There were many successful merchants – Greeks, Vlachs, Armenians – who never abandoned Christianity. But it is true that, after the early sixteenth century at least, it was necessary to be a Muslim in order to have a career in the structure of the Ottoman state itself. As we have seen, the devşirme system of child tribute poured a huge stream of Balkan youths into the army and the Imperial administration. Bosnians were said to be particularly prized: one Austrian-Slovenian writer observed in 1530 that the Sultan preferred to recruit Bosnians because he believed them to be 'the best, most pious and most loyal people', differing from other 'Turks' in that they were 'much bigger, more handsome and more able'.[51] Although janissaries and administrators might end up anywhere in the Empire, and janissaries remained unmarried during their active career, there were some who returned eventually to their homeland and were given large grants of land. After twenty years as a janissary it was not too late to take a wife and start a family. The devşirme system was one of the main engines of Islamicization throughout the Balkans, and its effect was particularly strong in Bosnia.[52]

Another social factor promoting the spread of Islam was the privileged legal status of the Muslims. Much attention has been given to the *kanun-i raya*, the traditional discriminatory laws which were applied to non-Muslim subjects: among other prohibitions, they were not allowed to ride horses, carry weapons or wear the same style of clothes as Muslims. Seventeenth-century sources show that Christian priests and merchants in Bosnia dressed almost exactly like Muslims, did ride horses and did carry arms. Some classes of Christian, such as the martial Vlachs, were formally exempted; and other prohibitions in the kanun-i raya, such as that forbidding Christians to build or repair churches, were in fact overruled – either by special permission, or by the general privilege awarded originally to the Franciscans and confirmed by each successive Sultan.[53] Nevertheless, there was a definite sense that the Christian raya owed deference and submission to their Muslim superiors, not just because they were of higher social rank, but also because they were Muslim. And perhaps the most important privilege was not one contained in the kanun-i raya; it was the principle that Christians could not bring law-suits against Muslims, and that their testimony could not be used against a Muslim in court. This was a serious form of legal discrimination, and must have been most keenly felt when the Christians and Muslims concerned were in fact social equals – townsmen or villagers.

Two other important socio-economic factors contributing to the spread of Islam in Bosnia remain to be mentioned: slavery and the growth of Muslim towns. The taking of slaves in war – not just enemy soldiers, but the local inhabitants too – was standard Ottoman practice. On a smaller scale it was practised by Christian states as well. Large numbers of slaves were seized by the Turks in their campaigns against the Habsburgs: 7000 were taken from Croatia in 1494, for example, and 200,000 (reportedly) in Hungary and Slavonia in 1526.[54] Slaves who converted to Islam could apply for freedom; and those slaves who were brought to Bosnia, mainly from the surrounding Slav lands of Dalmatia, Croatia and Slavonia, must have made a significant contribution to the growth in the Muslim population. Converted and freed slaves were especially likely to end up in the expanding towns, which offered fresh opportunities for work. In 1528 these freed slaves made up nearly 8 per cent of the entire population of Sarajevo.[55]

Most of the large towns which grew up in the Ottoman Balkans were predominantly Muslim. They were filled with Muslim institutions and Muslim buildings. The old Catholic towns in Bosnia, such as Srebrenica, Fojnica and Olovo, with their Ragusan merchants and German miners, held out against Islamicization for a long time, but even they were mainly Islamicized in the end. (Their economic importance was declining, though the mining of precious metals did continue, despite a Ragusan ban on the import of silver from Turkish lands.)[56] Towns which became the seats of sandžak-begs, such as Banja Luka, Travnik and Livno, acquired a Muslim character more rapidly. In towns such as Mostar and Sarajevo, however, which only began to be properly developed in the mid-fifteenth century, Islam was an overwhelming presence from the moment the Turks arrived. The speed of development was impressive. In the fifteen years of Ottoman control of Sarajevo (formerly known as Vrhbosna) before 1463, the Turks had built a mosque, a *tekke* (*tekija* in Serbo-Croat: the lodge of a dervish order), a *musafirhan* (inn for travellers), a *hamam* (Turkish baths), a bridge across the river Miljacka, a system of piped water, and the *serai*, or governor's court, which gave the town its new name. The large market in the heart of the town was also established at the outset.[57] Although much of the town was burnt by a Hungarian raiding party in 1480, it was rapidly rebuilt and extended. Its population was almost entirely Muslim; it was an important garrison town, and in its early decades it was filled with the kinds of artisans and traders who were needed to support military operations. Later in the sixteenth century its inhabitants would be divided into two classes, merchants and soldiers, each with its own *kadi* or judge.

The flowering of Sarajevo came under the rule of Gazi Husrev-beg, who was governor of the Bosnian sandžak for several periods between 1521 and 1541. A man of extraordinary energy and philanthropy, he was the son of a convert from the Trebinje region of Hercegovina.[58] He built the fine mosque which bears his title ('Begova džamija', 'the Beg's mosque'), a *medresa* (theological school), a library, a hamam, two hans (inns), and an important *bezistan* (cloth-market). It was normal for rich men to set aside lands in permanent trust to provide an income for institutions of this kind (not only mosques and schools, but also inns, baths and bridges); this type of religious-charitable foundation, known as *vakıf (vakuf* in Serbo-Croat) was vital to the development of all Ottoman towns, and helped to interlock the institutions of the town with those of Islam. Gazi Husrev-beg's vakuf was the richest of them all, and survived until the twentieth century.[59] By 1530 the city had an entirely Muslim population. The spread of its influence into the area around it can be seen from the fact that forty-six per cent of the local administrative district was Muslim too.[60] Sarajevo grew in population mainly by drawing in people from the surrounding countryside; many of the early street-names are names of nearby villages. By the end of the sixteenth century it also included a number of Christians, including a colony of Ragusan merchants, and a small community of Jews. Out of ninety-three *mahalas* (quarters – probably of fewer than forty households each), two were Christian and ninety-one Muslim. There were also six bridges, six hamams, three bezistans, several libraries, six tekkes, five medresas, more than ninety mektebs (primary schools) and more than a hundred mosques. The inhabitants enjoyed various privileges and exemptions from taxes; some historians regard it as having become a virtual free city or city-republic.[61] Life in Sarajevo during this period was good, by Balkan standards or indeed by any standards of the time. It is understandable that many Bosnians should happily have embraced Islam to take part in it.

Finally, one other factor also played a part in the Islamicization of Bosnia: the influx of already Islamicized Slavs from outside Bosnia's borders. That some Muslim Slavs arrived in the early years as spahis from Serbia, Macedonia and Bulgaria has already been mentioned. But the biggest influx came at the end of the seventeenth century, when the retreat of the Ottomans from areas which they had long occupied in Dalmatia, Croatia, Slavonia and Hungary brought in its wake many of the Muslim inhabitants of those regions. Some of these families, no doubt, were themselves of

Bosnian origin, their ancestors having settled as spahis after the Ottoman conquests. Such influxes added large numbers of Slav Muslims to the population of Bosnia; this movement in the 1680s and 1690s was not the only influx of its kind, though it was certainly the largest. Its circumstances will be described more fully in chapter 7.

6

Serbs and Vlachs

There has been little mention so far of the Serbian Orthodox Church. This is for the simple reason that, until the Ottoman period, the Orthodox Church was barely active in the territory of Bosnia proper; only in Hercegovina was it an important presence. In its early medieval history, Hercegovina (Hum) had been part of the cultural and political world of the Serb župe and princedoms, with Zeta (Montenegro) and Raška (south-west Serbia). Most of the nobility of Hercegovina was Orthodox during the fourteenth and fifteenth centuries, and so, probably, was the majority of its population.[1] During the century of Catholic activity before the Turkish conquest, significant gains were made there by the Catholic Church, which set up four Franciscan monasteries on Hercegovinan soil: but some of these gains were lost, especially in the eastern part of Hercegovina, in the sixteenth and seventeenth centuries. By 1624 there were still fourteen Catholic parish churches in eastern Hercegovina; fifteen years later the total had sunk to eleven, of which four were said to be almost in ruins.[2]

The Banate or Kingdom of Bosnia, on the other hand, seems to have contained no organized activity by the Serbian Orthodox Church until its territory was extended by King Tvrtko in the 1370s to include the upper Drina valley (south-east of Sarajevo) and parts of modern Montenegro and Serbia, including the Orthodox monastery at Mileševo. Although Tvrtko had himself crowned at Mileševo, he was and remained a Catholic, like all the Bosnian kings after him (with the possible exception of Ostoja, who may have been a member of the Bosnian Church). Away from the upper Drina valley, there are no clear signs of Orthodox church buildings in pre-Ottoman Bosnia. One Serbian art-historian has claimed that some of the Orthodox monasteries in northern Bosnia go back to before the Turkish conquest, but his dating is very unsure.[3] Of course individual members of the Orthodox Church may have settled in Bosnia; some of the aristocracy married women from Serbian noble families, and there is one mention of an Orthodox family in the Vrhbosna region (round modern Sarajevo) in the 1420s.[4] There was no doubt a gradual percolation of Orthodox believers from Hercegovina into the neighbouring parts of Bosnia. Some Catholic reports of the 1450s indicate direct competition for souls between the two Churches, but this was a reflection of two things: the inroads made by the Franciscans into Hercegovina, and competing attempts to mop up the remnants of the Bosnian Church.[5] In terms of Church organization, the Serbian Orthodox Church remains virtually invisible on the territory of modern Bosnia proper in the pre-Ottoman period.

After the arrival of the Turks, however, the picture begins to change quite rapidly. From the 1480s onwards, Orthodox priests and believers are mentioned in many parts of Bosnia where they were never mentioned before. Several Orthodox monasteries are known to have been built in the sixteenth century (Tavna, Lomnica, Paprača, Ozren and Gostović), and the important monastery of Rmanj, in north-west Bosnia, is first mentioned in 1515. These new foundations are particularly striking when one considers that the kanun-i raya forbade the construction of any new church buildings: clearly, specific permission had been given each time by the Ottoman authorities.[6] Although the Orthodox suffered a fair share of indignities and oppressions, it is no exaggeration to say that the Orthodox Church was favoured by the Ottoman regime. Orthodox believers looked inside the Ottoman Empire for their sources of religious authority; Catholics looked outside, and would be more likely to regard the reconquest of Bosnia by a Catholic power as a liberation. A Metropolitan (Orthodox bishop) of Bosnia is first mentioned in 1532, and the first Orthodox church in Sarajevo was probably built in the mid-sixteenth century.[7]

But although there are many recorded cases of Catholics being converted to Orthodoxy in sixteenth- and seventeenth-century Bosnia, it is clear that this spread of the Orthodox Church did not happen by conversion alone.[8] In the areas where Orthodoxy made its most striking gains, especially in northern Bosnia, the same period saw a large influx of settlers from Orthodox lands. It was evidently deliberate policy on the part of the Ottomans to fill up territory which had been depopulated, either by war or by plague. There are signs in the earliest defters of groups of Christian herdsmen, identifiable as Vlachs, being settled in devastated areas of eastern Hercegovina. In the defters of the 1470s and 1480s they can be seen spreading into central and north-central Bosnia, in the regions round Visoko and Maglaj: soon after 1476, for example, roughly 800 Vlach families were settled in the Maglaj district, accompanied by two Orthodox priests.[9] The number of Vlachs in north-central and north-east Bosnia continued to grow over the next fifty years, and they began to spread into north-west Bosnia too. During the wars of the early sixteenth century more areas of northern Bosnia became depopulated as Catholics fled into Habsburg territory. Since it was particularly important for the Ottomans not to leave land empty close to the military border, there were large new influxes of Vlach settlers from Hercegovina and Serbia. Further movements into this area took place throughout the sixteenth century; plague, as well as war, left demographic gaps which needed to be filled.[10]

As early as 1530, when the Habsburg official Benedict Kuripešić travelled through Bosnia, he was able to report that the country was inhabited by three peoples. One was the Turks, who ruled 'with great tyranny' over the Christians. Another was 'the old Bosnians, who are of the Roman Catholic faith'. And the third were 'Serbs, who call themselves Vlachs . . . They came from Smederovo and Belgrade'.[11] So important was the Vlach element in the creation of this Bosnian Orthodox population that, three centuries later, the term 'Vlach' was still being used in Bosnia to mean 'member of the Orthodox Church'.[12] Of course, non-Vlach Serbians and Hercegovinans also took part in this process of settlement. The problem of distinguishing them, and of saying what the term 'Vlach' meant during this period, will be discussed below. But it is clear that Vlachs, as a distinctive ethnic and cultural group, played a major role. The Vlachs were particularly suitable for the Ottoman government's purposes, not only because they were mobile (their typical occupations were shepherding, horse-breeding and organizing transport for traders), but also because they had a strong military tradition. Special arrangements were made to induce them to move to the Ottoman-Habsburg border: the tax on sheep was reduced for those living in the border region, and their leaders were granted large timars.[13] Although they received no military salary, they were entitled to carry arms and expected to fulfil a military role; in place of a salary, they were permitted to plunder enemy territory. Known by the terms 'martolos' or 'vojnuk', they became the most feared element in the Ottoman military machine.

At the same time, Vlachs and Serbs who had fled northwards from the Ottoman advance in the fifteenth century, and who had similar military traditions, began to be organized by the Habsburgs on the other side of this fluid and shifting border. Vlachs from inside Bosnia also crossed the border to join them; the three reasons given by Benedict Kuripešić for the depopulation of Bosnia in the early sixteenth century were plague, the devşirme, and the flight of the Serb-Vlach martolosi across the border.[14] In 1527, after his election as King of Hungary and Croatia, Ferdinand I of Austria established a formal system of land-holdings and military duties for them. They were free of feudal obligations, permitted a share of booty, allowed to elect their own captains (*vojvode*) and magistrates (*knezovi*), and free to practise Orthodox Christianity. In this way a special system of land tenure and military organization grew up under the Habsburgs, the so-called *Militärgrenze* or *vojna krajina* (military border), which was eventually to involve a strip of territory twenty to sixty miles wide and a thousand miles long. The borderers or *Grenzer* on the north and north-western frontier of Bosnia, equally renowned for their military prowess and ferocity, were known as 'Vlachs' or 'Morlachs', and in 1630 their privileges were re-established by Ferdinand II in a document known as the 'Law of the Vlachs' – 'Statuta Valachorum'.[15] Apart from the big set-piece campaigns, the military struggle between Ottoman and Habsburg on this border consisted mainly, year in, year out, of Vlachs fighting Vlachs.

Who were the Vlachs, and where, originally, did they come from? This is one of the most vexed questions in Balkan history.[16] Vlachs are found today scattered over many parts of the Balkans; the biggest concentration is in the Pindus mountains of northern Greece, but there are also Vlachs in Bulgaria, Macedonia, Albania and Serbia, as well as the remnants of a Vlach population in the Istrian peninsula. Traditionally they were herdsmen and shepherds practising a form of semi-nomadism called transhumance, in which flocks are moved, sometimes over great distances, between a regular summer pasture in the mountains and a regular winter pasture elsewhere. Some grew rich from the products of their pastoral life: wool, cheese and livestock. Many also became well known in the eighteenth and nineteenth centuries as merchants and international traders. These occupations have changed very little over the centuries; one twelfth-century Byzantine poem refers to Vlach cheese, which was famous in Constantinople, and to a Vlach cloak, the large black sleeveless cape or *tălăgan* which can still be seen on the shoulders of Balkan shepherds. Other Byzantine writers refer to the transhumance of the Vlachs, and medieval Serbian documents refer to them as shepherds and *kjelatori* – a version of the Latin *calator*, 'packhorse-leader', surviving in modern Vlach as *călător*, 'traveller'.[17] Their only other distinctive occupation at that period was fighting: as hardy mountain-dwellers they were valued for their stamina, and their supply of horses made them useful adjuncts to any military campaign. The Byzantine authorities seem not to have trusted them very much, and generally used them as auxiliaries; sometimes they functioned as quite independent irregular troops. But there are also references to an entire regiment of Vlach infantry in an early fourteenth-century Byzantine army.[18]

In the early records the Vlachs are often a rather shadowy, passing presence. They moved from area to area, speaking the local language and merging into the local population: there are references in late Byzantine documents to 'Bulgaro-Albano-Vlachs' and even 'Serbo-Albano-Bulgaro-Vlachs'.[19] Other names for them include the Byzantine Greek 'Mavrovlachos', 'black Vlach', from which 'Morlach' was derived, and the modern Greek 'Koutsovlachos', literally 'limping Vlach', which may be a folk-etymologized version of the Turkish *küçük eflak*, 'little Vlach'. The word 'Vlach' itself comes from a term used by the early Slavs for those peoples they encountered who spoke Latin or Latinate languages: hence also 'Wallachian', 'Walloon' and (by a more roundabout application) 'Welsh'.

There is no definite historical record of the Vlachs before the late tenth century. Before that, the only evidence which can be drawn on is linguistic. The Vlach language is a Latin language, very closely related to Romanian: linguists call it 'Macedo-Romanian', and the Romanian of Romania 'Daco-Romanian'. Obviously it was the product of the Roman colonization of the Balkans, and had a continuous existence there, being encountered by the Slavs on their arrival in the sixth and seventh centuries. But the Roman Empire in the Balkans covered a wide area, and this has given plenty of scope for modern nationalist historians to locate the origins of the Vlachs in whichever area they prefer: thus Greeks claim that the Vlachs are Romanized Greeks, Bulgarians say they are Romanized Thracians, and Romanians insist they are Romanized Dacians (and/or descendants of Roman legionaries in Dacia: it does not matter which, so long as they were there before the arrival of the Hungarians). By far the most picturesque – and preposterous – theory is the one put forward by the distinguished Croat historian Father Mandić, who, investigating the origins of the Vlach-Serbs of Bosnia, has concluded that they were originally from Morocco. This, he thinks, would explain the Byzantine Greek word 'Mavrovlachos' or 'black Vlach': a reference to their dark, Moorish faces. His theory is that they are the descendants of Roman legionaries from Mauretania (modern Morocco) who were stationed in the Balkans. It is true that large numbers of legionaries were settled there by the Romans; but they included, as we have seen, people from all over the Empire. Of the only two military colonies of Mauretanians mentioned by Mandić, one was near the Black Sea in Bessarabia, and the other was on the river Inn, near Vienna. That is hardly a sufficient starting-point for an entire population in the southern Balkans. Though it will of course delight modern anti-Serb nationalists in Bosnia to learn that the Bosnian Serbs are really Africans (and it certainly trumps the modern Serb prejudice towards Albanians, which tends to treat them as if they were dark-faced people from the Third World), the theory cannot possibly be correct.[20]

The true origin of the Vlachs can be worked out, however, from the linguistic evidence. The Vlach-Romanian language (which was a single language until the two main forms of it began to diverge in the early middle ages) has a large number of special features in common with Albanian. These include fundamental matters of grammar and syntax, a number of special idioms, and a core vocabulary of words connected with pastoral life.[21] Albanian, the one survivor of the languages of the Illyrian tribes, also contains a huge number of words borrowed from Latin, indicating close contact with a Latinized population throughout the Roman period.[22] A combination of historical linguistics, the study of place-names and the history of the Roman Empire yields the fairly certain conclusion that the heartland where both these languages developed was an area stretching from northern Albania through Kosovo and south-central Serbia; it may also have included parts of northern Macedonia and western Bulgaria. Most of the Romanized and Latin-speaking population of this area (whose version of Latin was influenced by their own earlier language, Illyrian) was dispersed, destroyed or assimilated by the invasions of the dark ages, especially those of the Slavs. A remnant which practised pastoralism was able to survive in the mountains, unaffected by the Slavs' takeover of settled agriculture; and in the more remote mountains (especially those of northern Albania) it was also in close contact with an even earlier remnant, which still spoke the Illyrian language, albeit a version of Illyrian which had become heavily infused with Latin after centuries of contact. That is the explanation accepted by nearly all the independent scholars who have studied this question; unfortunately the issue has been bedevilled by misplaced national pride on the part of Romanian writers, who cannot accept that the first speakers of Romanian came from south of the Danube.[23]

Since this northern Albanian and southern Serbian region was the original heartland of the Vlachs, it is not surprising that they should have spread out into the nearby uplands of Hercegovina from an early period. From there they moved northwards through the mountainous Dalmatian hinterland, where they are found tending flocks (and bringing them down to the coastal lands in the winter) as early as the twelfth century. There are many references to them in the records of Ragusa and Zadar from the thirteenth to fifteenth centuries.[24] Some of these pastoral Vlachs also penetrated as far as central Bosnia, where medieval place-names in the regions of Sarajevo and Travnik indicate their presence: Vlahinja, Vlaškovo, Vlašić.[25] And many Vlach words connected with pastoral life were absorbed into Bosnian dialects of Serbo-Croat: *trze*, a late-born lamb, from the Vlach *tîrdzîu*, for example, or *zarica*, a type of cheese, from the Vlach *zară*. This last word is in fact a version of the Albanian word *dhallë*, 'buttermilk' – one of many details pointing to the pastoral symbiosis between Vlachs and Albanians, which continued to operate over a long period.[26]

Most of these early Dalmatian and Bosnian Vlachs seem to have led quiet, secluded lives in the mountains.[27] But in Hercegovina itself, where there was a large concentration of Vlachs, a more military and aggressive tradition developed. There are many complaints in Ragusan records of raids by these neighbouring Vlachs during the fourteenth and fifteenth centuries.[28] The Vlachs of Hercegovina were horse-breeders and caravan-leaders who, when they were not engaged in plunder, grew rich out of the trade between Ragusa and the mines of Bosnia; as we have seen, some of them were probably responsible for commissioning the imposing stone tombstones or *stećci* decorated with carvings of horsemen. Their trading links to the east must have brought them more into contact with the Vlach peoples of Serbia and Bulgaria, who had long traditions of military activity in the armies of the Byzantine emperors and Serbian kings.

One of the still unsolved mysteries of this story is the exact significance of the term 'Morlach' ('Mavrovlachos', 'black Vlach'), and how it came to be used in Hercegovina and Dalmatia. The obvious original meaning was a reference to the black cloaks worn by the Vlachs of the central Balkans (Serbia, Bulgaria, Macedonia, northern Greece): they were also known at various times as 'Karagounides' and 'Crnogunjci', which literally mean 'black-cloaks' in Turco-Greek and Serbian.[29] Possibly a distinct wave of these Vlachs entered Hercegovina and Dalmatia, bringing the name (which they must have acquired in a Greek-speaking area) with them.[30] It was quickly altered by Slav folk-etymology into 'Morovlah', meaning 'sea-Vlach' (i.e. coastal Vlach).[31] From its use in Dalmatia the term later spread to the Vlachs in Croatia who filled the military border-zone or 'krajina' round the north-western shoulder of Bosnia. 'Morlacchi' became the standard Venetian name for these people, and the region appears as 'Morlacchia' on many seventeenth- and eighteenth-century maps. Because of their fearsome methods of irregular warfare the Morlachs acquired an evil reputation, and were regarded as primitive and brutal people. But all changed in the late eighteenth century when they were visited by an Italian priest, the Abbé Fortis. Inspired by the poetry of Ossian, and accompanied by another enthusiast for heroic poetry and folklore, the Professor of Modern History at Cambridge, Fortis travelled among the Morlachs of the Dalmatian hinterland in search of poetry and primitive virtue. He found both: 'The sincerity, trust, and honesty of these poor people . . . in all the ordinary actions of their life, would be called simplicity and weakness among us,' he declared. He also heard plenty of poetry, noting that 'A Morlacco travels along the desert mountains singing, especially in the night time, the actions of ancient *Slavi* Kings, and barons, or some tragic event'; and he observed that 'the Bosnian dialect, spoken by the inland Morlacchi, is more harmonious, in my opinion, than the littoral Illyrian'.[32] The poem he printed in translation, *Hasanaganica* ('The Wife of Hasan Aga'), was in fact a Bosnian Muslim song; a short tale of tragic love and misunderstanding, it became one of the most popular specimens of folk poetry in the whole of Europe, and was translated by Goethe, Byron, Sir Walter Scott, Mérimée, Pushkin and Lermontov.[33]

Inside Bosnia, the term Morlach was not so much used for the martial Vlachs who went to fill the border areas under the Ottomans. These Vlachs, who came from both Hercegovina and Serbia, were called either Vlachs or martolosi. The latter word referred to their military status, and so could include non-Vlachs too: it was a version of the Greek word for an armed man, *armatôlos*. The Vlachs of Bosnia and Hercegovina had their own system of social and military organization, which is clearly defined in the early Ottoman documents: at the top of each local community was a magistrate or knez (an old Slav term); under him was a mayor or *primikür* (from the Greek, *primikêrios*); below him was a *lagator* (from the Greek *alagatôr*, the head of a military detachment), and the basic military group was a *gönder* (from the Greek *kontarion*, or lance).[34] As these terms show, the Ottomans simply inherited a system which had been established to serve the armies of the Byzantine Empire. Like the Byzantine and Serbian rulers before them, they gave the Vlachs special tax privileges in return for their military services: the leaders of the Vlachs were given timars and treated virtually as spahis, and their people were freed from the basic tax on non-Muslims, the haraç. The Vlachs did, however, pay a special 'Vlach tax' – *rusum-i eflak* – consisting mainly of a sheep and a lamb from every household on St George's day each year.[35] Since they were taxed differently, they were listed differently in the Turkish defters. This enables us to see that in the late fifteenth century there were at least 35,000 Vlachs in Hercegovina, and in the sixteenth century as many as 82,692 mainly Vlach households (including some non-Vlach martolosi, with similar privileges) in the Smederovo region to the south of Belgrade.[36] (Many of the Vlachs in the eastern part of Hercegovina had themselves been moved there by the Turks to repopulate areas devastated by fighting in the 1460s.)[37] These were the main reservoirs of population from which the depopulated lands of northern Bosnia were filled. And because, living in Hercegovina and Serbia, they had long been members of the Orthodox Church, they established the Orthodox presence in that part of Bosnia which has lasted ever since.

How distinct were these Vlachs from the surrounding Slavs? Clearly they had a different status and a different social-military organization. Those who had moved into northern Bosnia could not practise the tradition of long-distance transhumance, and the evidence of sixteenth-century Ottoman decrees on the Vlachs of Bosnia and Hercegovina indicates that the majority of Vlachs were now sedentary; but their way of life still centred on stock-breeding and shepherding.[38] Giovanni Lovrich noted in the 1770s that the Croatian Morlachs all had flocks of 200, 300 or 600 sheep, and when he asked why they were so reluctant to till the soil, they replied: 'Our ancestors didn't do it, so neither shall we.'[39] Some writers, especially Serbian ones, have argued that the term 'Vlach' was used just to mean 'shepherd' and did not imply any ethnic or linguistic difference – so that most of these people were really just Serbs with sheep.[40] This view is rejected by the leading modern expert on Vlachs in the early Ottoman Balkans, who insists that they were regarded as a distinct population.[41]

Vlachs have always been bilingual, and since they were never the administrators, the language which has survived in the records is never their own one. But we do have some evidence of its use, apart from the appearance in the records of Vlach personal names such as Ursul and Šarban. Vlachs who moved to an Adriatic island in the fifteenth century were still speaking Vlach there four hundred years later. One sixteenth-century Venetian writer described the Vlachs of the Dalmatian hinterland as speaking 'Latin, though in a corrupted form'; shepherds in those mountains were still using Vlach counting-words as recently as 1985.[42] There is other evidence of bilingualism in the seventeenth century, even though the writer Ioannes Lucius (Ivan Lukić) stated that the language had disappeared by then.[43] But of course, having lived for centuries among the Slavs of Hercegovina and Serbia, these Vlachs could be outwardly indistinguishable (in speech and dress) from the ordinary Slavs of those regions. The suggestion that they must have been monoglot Vlachs, because they did not bring the Serbian *ekavian* dialect when they came from Serbia into northern Bosnia, is certainly false.[44] They spoke whatever the Slavs around them spoke, which may have changed over time in an area as subject to demographic flux as northern Bosnia; and the Vlachs from Hercegovina would have spoken *jekavian* anyway.[45]

Some attempts have been made to prove that there was still a Vlach-speaking population in Bosnia as recently as the beginning of the twentieth century. Sixteen 'Romanian-speaking' villages were mentioned in the 1910 census for Bosnia, and in 1906 an enthusiastic Romanian Vlachophile published an entire book about the 'Romanian colonies' which he had found there.[46] When the leading German expert on the Vlachs, Professor Weigand, went to check these claims in the following year, he found that the only Vlach villages consisted of people who had migrated from Macedonia in the eighteenth century and had since lost the use of their language. The 'Romanian-speaking' villagers, known locally as 'Karavlasi' or 'black Vlachs', were indeed speaking Romanian; this was because they were not Vlachs at all, but Romanian gypsies from Transylvania.[47]

Finally, it is necessary to point out that there is little sense today in saying that the Bosnian Serbs are 'really' Vlachs. Over the centuries many ordinary members of the Serbian Orthodox Church would have crossed the Drina into Bosnia or moved north from Hercegovina; a Serb merchant class also became important in Bosnian towns in the eighteenth and nineteenth centuries. Not all the people who were sent to populate northern Bosnia in the fifteenth and sixteenth centuries were Vlach, and since then there have been so many influxes and exoduses in Bosnian history that we cannot possibly calculate precise percentages for the 'Vlach' ancestry of the Bosnian Serbs.[48] Nor did the Vlachs contribute only to the Serb population; some (mainly in Croatia) became Catholics, and quite a few were Islamicized in Bosnia.[49] To call someone a Serb today is to use a concept constructed in the nineteenth and twentieth centuries out of a combination of religion, language, history and the person's own sense of identification: modern Bosnian Serbs can properly describe themselves as such, regardless of Vlach ancestry. But it is still slightly piquant to think, when one hears so-called right-wing Russian politicians talking about the need to defend their ancient Slav brothers in Bosnia, that the one component of the Bosnian population which has a large and identifiable element of non-Slav ancestry is the Bosnian Serbs.

7

War and politics in Ottoman Bosnia, 1606–1815

The history of Bosnia through the seventeenth and eighteenth centuries continued to be punctuated and dominated by major wars. And just as the Ottoman Empire had grown by war, so warfare and the social changes it caused helped to bring about the decline of the Empire. By the seventeenth century the old feudal cavalry was becoming militarily out of date; infantry soldiers equipped with modern firearms, together with artillery, were much more important. A regular salaried army developed, for which recruitment by devşirme was no longer necessary. But what was necessary was money-revenues for the central government to pay for it: and this meant taking over the feudal timar estates as they fell vacant and converting them into a combination of private estates and tax-farms. These changes, as we shall see in chapter 8, transformed the nature of provincial Ottoman society. Taxes were increased by the tax-farmers, and a multitude of new taxes were invented by Istanbul – producing poverty, resentment and frequent unrest. Cash taxes collected by the central government, known as *avarız* (the similarity with 'avarice' is coincidental), had once been emergency measures; they now became the norm. Corruption increased, and law and order deteriorated. Conditions were, admittedly, better organized in Bosnia than in the neighbouring Serbian territory of the Empire, where peasants fled from the estates and turned bandit or *hajduk*. But Bosnia too had its share of discontents in the eighteenth century. By then it was clear to many observers that the Empire was rotting from within.

The major wars happened at least every two generations. After the Habsburg war of 1593–1606, which left Bosnia financially drained and militarily exhausted, there were several decades of recovery, marred only by a bad bout of currency-devaluation and inflation throughout the Ottoman Empire in the period 1615–25.[1] In the 1640s the Turks became embroiled in a long war with Venice, which lasted until 1669. This led to frequent raids mounted from the Venetian territories on the Dalmatian coast, and there were some large clashes between Venice and Bosnian forces: in 1645 an entire Bosnian army marched into Dalmatia, but was unable to make any gains there.[2] This long-drawn-out war put a heavy burden on Bosnia, in addition to the new tax increases and inflation which it caused throughout the Empire. The Catholic Bishop Marijan Maravić reported in 1655 that more than 2000 Catholic families had fled from Bosnia 'during the present war', and another report in 1661 said that four Franciscan monasteries had been burnt down in 'the continual wars occurring in these parts'.[3] In 1663 war was resumed against the Habsburgs, and a large Ottoman army marched into Austria in the following year; after a battle regarded by the Ottomans as a draw and by the Austrians as a victory, a peace treaty was signed in which each side agreed to stop carrying out border raids so long as the other did likewise.[4]

The most important war, from which the Ottoman Empire never really recovered, was the Habsburg war of 1683–99. The year 1683 was disastrous for the Turks. After the failure of their siege of Vienna, they were driven back and defeated in battle by the Austrian and Polish army; the Grand Vizier who had led the campaign was executed by the Turks at Belgrade. In 1684–7 the Austrians gradually conquered the whole of Ottoman-ruled Hungary, sending thousands of spahis and Muslim converts retreating southwards from their abandoned lands and flooding into Bosnia. Meanwhile Venice was mounting direct attacks on Bosnian territory. A major Venetian advance into Bosnia in 1685 was repelled, but Muslims were driven into Bosnia by Habsburg forces out of the Lika area of Croatia, which had been the westernmost part of the Bosnian eyalet; by 1687 roughly 30,000 had fled from there, and the 1700 who remained were forcibly converted to Catholicism.[5] These influxes of refugees had a huge effect on the size and nature of the Bosnian population: it has been estimated that as many as 130,000 in total were transferred to Bosnia as a result of the entire war.[6] The biggest single component was the Slavonian Muslims – either Bosnian Muslim settlers who had originally moved north from Bosnia, or Croat Slavs who had been Islamicized during the long period of Turkish rule. Some of the refugees, especially spahis who had lost everything, were embittered men who probably brought with them a new sense of hostility to Christianity.[7]

Worse was to come for the Ottoman authorities. In 1689 the Habsburg army marched across Bosnia and into Serbia; it penetrated as far as Kosovo, and many Serbs took the opportunity to rise up against Turkish rule. For a while it looked as if the Ottomans would lose control of the Balkans altogether. But with a surprising revival of efficiency and power the Turks drove the Austrians back again in the following year. Led by their Patriarch, a large number of Orthodox Serbs – at least 30,000 – fled northwards with the retreating Austrian army from the Kosovo region. (The Albanian numerical majority in Kosovo, at least in modern times, dates probably from this event.) But on the other hand many Orthodox Serbs welcomed the return of the Turks, having experienced the zeal of Austrian Catholic priests in the meanwhile. A period of virtual stalemate then followed; the Ottomans continued to campaign rather ineffectually across the Danube in Hungarian territory, and they were resisted by an ineffectual Austrian, Field Marshal Caprara. But when Caprara was replaced by the youngest and most brilliant commanding officer in the army, Prince Eugene of Savoy, things quickly began to change. Prince Eugene inflicted a huge defeat on the Turks at the battle of Zenta, in southern Hungary, in September 1697. And then, with extraordinary speed, he set off with a small army of 6000 men into the heart of Bosnia.

On 22 October they arrived at Sarajevo, where they found the Turks completely unprepared for battle. An entry in Prince Eugene's military diary describes the events of the following two days:

> On 23 October I placed the troops in a broad front on a height directly overlooking the city. From there I sent detachments to plunder it. The Turks had already taken the best things to safety, but still a great quantity of all sorts of goods remained behind. Towards evening the city began to burn. The city is very large and quite open; it has 120 fine mosques. On the 24th I remained at

> Sarajevo. We let the city and the whole surrounding area go up in flames. Our raiding party, which pursued the enemy, brought back booty and many women and children, after killing many Turks. The Christians come to us in crowds and ask for permission to come into our camp with their belongings, since they want to leave the country and follow us. I hope too to take all the Christians in this country back across the river Sava.[8]

Most of these Christians were probably Catholic merchants, whose domination of trade in Bosnia seems to have come to an end with this war.[9] As Prince Eugene returned northwards, thousands of other Catholics did join his army on the march to Austria. If the Orthodox population of Bosnia did not already outnumber the Catholics by the second half of the seventeenth century, its numerical superiority was assured by the end of this war.[10] Whether these Catholics were persuaded (as the Serbian Patriarch had been) that they would soon return with an army of liberation remains unclear. There are some signs that the Austrians had been thinking seriously about taking over Bosnia altogether: in 1687–8, through intermediaries in Ragusa, they had inquired whether the Muslims of Sarajevo (who were notoriously independent *vis-à-vis* the Ottoman government) would accept Austrian rule if their freedom of religion were guaranteed; twelve families said yes, but nothing further seems to have come of it.[11] No such matter had been in Prince Eugene's mind, however, when he made his military excursion into Bosnia – the essential purpose of which was nothing more than plunder and destruction.

The Treaty of Karlowitz (Sremski Karlovci, north-west of Belgrade, near Novi Sad) which ended the war in 1699 confirmed that the Ottoman Empire was on the retreat in Europe. Hungary and Transylvania were ceded to the Habsburgs, and large territories in Dalmatia and Greece to Venice: for the next century, the south-western border of Bosnia marched with Venetian land. So great was the psychological blow of these losses that their recovery became an obsessive long-term aim of Ottoman policy. The opportunity came in 1714, after some blatant violations of the treaty by Venice. In the war which followed, Austria resumed its alliance with Venice, and once again (in 1716) Prince Eugene inflicted a huge defeat on the

Turks at Petrovaradin (near Novi Sad). But Bosnian defence forces mainly held their ground. At the Treaty of Passarowitz (Požarevac, in Serbia) in 1718, Austria received a strip of Bosnian territory south of the traditional border, the river Sava; and Venetian-ruled Dalmatia advanced further inland, reaching a line which since then has formed the south-western border of Bosnia.[12]

During this war there had been another wave of Muslim refugees into Bosnia.[13] Conditions were unsettled; taxes were increased again, and tax revolts broke out in Hercegovina in 1727, 1728, 1729 and 1732. Non-Ottoman sources suggest that Christians took part in two of these revolts (1728 and 1729), but the main actors were Muslims.[14] Epidemics were also rife during these years: 20,000 died in Bosnia from plague during the early 1730s.[15] When the Austrians violated the Treaty of Passarowitz in 1736 and invaded Bosnia, they must have thought it would quickly fall. But an unusually energetic and decisive governor, Hekim-oglu Ali-paša, had just been appointed to Bosnia, and he organized the defence with great skill.[16] In the following year he defeated the Austrian army at the battle of Banja Luka; and in the peace agreement which ensued (the Treaty of Belgrade, 1739), the Austrians renounced all the territory south of the river Sava apart from one fortress.[17] The northern border of modern Bosnia dates from this settlement.

It was one of the more lasting peace treaties of the century. Bosnia suffered no foreign invasion for nearly fifty years. But the Bosnian eyalet had to bear the burden of increased taxation to pay for other campaigns elsewhere; in 1745, when Hekim-oglu Ali-paša returned for another stint as governor of Bosnia, the revolt against tax increases was so uncontrollable that he was forced to leave the country again for six months. When he came back in 1747 there were more revolts; he retreated to Greece in the following year.[18] A large uprising in Mostar in 1748, in which even the janissaries took part, was joined by other tax revolts elsewhere in Bosnia during the next few years.[19] Muslim villagers were also protesting about changes to the system of land-tenure. Finally a new governor of Bosnia, Mehmet-paša Kukavica, received a letter from the Sultan consisting of one sentence: 'Bosnia must be conquered again.'[20] He complied with brutal efficiency. Peace was restored in Bosnia, though the city of Mostar continued to be a centre of disaffection and resistance; in 1768 the governor had to send a large army to subdue it. But unlike some of the popular revolts of the 1740s, this urban resistance came from senior Muslims who were trying to defend their tax privileges.[21]

The next Austrian war, which began in 1788, had a more serious political dimension to it than any of its predecessors. There was now a plan, agreed between Joseph II of Austria and Catherine the Great of Russia, to take over the Ottoman lands in the Balkans and share them out between those two Christian empires. This set the pattern of geo-political interest in the Balkans which was to lead eventually to the Austrian occupation of Bosnia in 1878 and to its annexation thirty years later. The Emperor Joseph II showed that he was thinking in terms of rule, not just conquest, when he announced at the start of the war that he would extend freedom of religion to all Muslims who agreed to lay down their arms.[22] Having tried to cultivate the Bosnian Catholics (some of whom had been brought to study in Zagreb), the Habsburgs still hoped for a general uprising of Bosnian Christians.[23] Early in 1788 Austrian forces entered Bosnia, but their dreams of being welcomed as liberators were not fulfilled. A small number of Bosnians did volunteer to join the Austrian army. But Bosnian Christians as well as Muslims kept up a stiff resistance against the Austrians in the frontier region, and the Habsburg army became bogged down in a five-month-long siege of the fortress of Dubica.[24] (The war is thus known as the Dubica War in Bosnian history.) In the following year the Austrians were better organized; this time they overran most of Bosnia and pushed deep into Serbia. But again there was a foreshadowing of the way things would be done in the nineteenth century: what checked the ambitions of Austria and Russia was not the military might of the Ottomans, but the diplomatic and political pressure of the other European powers. In 1791 Austria agreed to give up all the gains it had made in Bosnia and Serbia; in return, the Sultan granted the Austrian Emperor official status as the 'protector' of the Christians under Ottoman rule.[25]

Before the pattern of the nineteenth century could become fully formed, however, there was one prolonged and massive interruption to the international system: the Napoleonic wars. After Napoleon's first victories over Austria, the French took over Venetia, Istria and

Dalmatia (including the Ragusan Republic) in 1805 – thus creating a French-Bosnian border. Most of the European powers were keen to curry favour, for strategic reasons, with the Ottoman Empire. Napoleon sent assistance to the Sultan when he was trying to suppress a rebellion in Serbia, and the French also intervened more directly in a local quarrel in Hercegovina in 1808, when they sent a small expeditionary force to relieve a local pasha, Hadži-beg Rizvan-begović, who was besieged in the fortress of Hutovo as a result of a quarrel over an inheritance with two of his brothers.[26] In 1809 Austria declared war on France again. Napoleon encouraged the Bosnians to raid Slavonia in the early summer of that year; but after the battle of Wagram in July, the Austrians sued for peace. The Habsburgs ceded territory again: the western half of Croatia (bordering the north-west shoulder of Bosnia), and much of modern Slovenia. These were joined with the other gains in the area to form a new French territory, the 'Illyrian Provinces', which were ruled by Marshal Marmont (named 'Duke of Ragusa' for the occasion) for four years.

Like most rulers of the border area before him, the Marshal soon found himself having to deal with raiding parties from Bosnia. In late 1809 a French punitive expedition crossed into Bosnia, where it was met by a small force, mainly irregular cavalry, under the aga (lord) of Bihać. Though they were no match for troops trained in the Grande Armée, the horsemanship of the Bosnian irregulars impressed one French soldier, who described them in his memoirs as 'a cloud of men, none of them wearing uniform, mounted on thin little horses of extraordinary lightness, which obeyed the rider's voice and the pressure of his knees, without the use of bridle or stirrups'. The French drove them back for six leagues, then stopped at a village and set it on fire. 'I ran with some officers', the soldier later remembered, 'to the most imposing house; we decided that the rooms with barred windows looking onto a courtyard were the harem, and set fire to it in honour of the fairer sex.'[27]

When the French withdrew from the 'Illyrian Provinces' in 1813, Austrian rule was resumed there; and so too was the usual pattern of border conflicts and incursions. Things were back to normal. But the biggest long-term threat to Ottoman Bosnia had been forming to the east, in Serbia, where a serious revolt had broken out in 1804. In fact there were two Serbian revolts: the first was that of a group of local janissary leaders who seized power to stop the implementation of reforms which had been granted by Istanbul (allowing the Christian Serbs to raise their own militia, collect their own taxes, and so on), and the second was a large rebellion of the Christian population. Though at first the Sultan sided with the subjects against the janissaries, the scale of the popular revolt became too threatening, and he decided to suppress it. One Ottoman army was trounced by the Serbs in 1805; an army sent from Bosnia was also heavily defeated in 1806. The general anti-Ottoman violence in Serbia included widespread massacres, robberies and forced baptisms of ordinary Slav Muslims as well as Turks; the survivors began to flee to Bosnian territory.[28] There were some risings of people belonging to the Serbian Orthodox Church in Bosnia, and a more serious revolt (arising from more local causes) in Hercegovina. Eventually, in 1815, the Sultan agreed to give the Serbs – or at least those in the sandžak of Smederovo, a slice of north-central Serbia containing Belgrade – a large measure of autonomy, with their own Assembly and their own elected prince. Turkish garrisons remained, and a Turkish pasha still resided in Belgrade; but the foundations had now been laid for the eventual development of Serbia as an independent kingdom – one which would act towards Bosnia either as a beacon of freedom and hope, or as a centre of expansionary territorial ambitions.

The two conflicting revolts which had begun the Serbian move to independence expressed two tendencies which had long been visible in the Balkan provinces of the Ottoman Empire. There was popular unrest against the entire system, and there was the desire of the local representatives of that system to defend their privileges against interference (above all, reform) from Istanbul. The power of the local Muslim notables was more entrenched in Bosnia; this meant that their resistance to central rule, of which we have seen some signs already from the mid-eighteenth century, was strongly based and would take several generations to crush. Special political and social institutions had grown up in Bosnia which, taken together, made up an unusually effective system of local power.

The most important of these was the *kapetanije* or 'captaincies'. To begin with, in the late sixteenth century, a *kapetan* was a military administrator in a frontier region: his task was to raise troops, check travellers who crossed the border, keep roads safe from bandits, and perform various similar police and administrative duties. The territory he governed, a *kapetanija*, could be smaller or larger than a *kadiluk* (the basic administrative unit covered by a *kadi* or judge), but was smaller than a sandžak.[29] During the seventeenth century this system was extended inland; the range of powers of the kapetans was extended too, and some prominent families began to treat the kapetanije as hereditary offices. By the time of the Treaty of Karlowitz (1699), there were twelve kapetanije in Bosnia; by the end of the eighteenth century there were thirty-nine, and the system now covered most of the Bosnian territory. At the turn of the seventeenth and eighteenth centuries, when they also began to collect taxes, the kapetans were at the height of their powers.[30] The kapetanije were peculiar to Bosnia, forming a socio-political structure which set it apart from all the other Balkan lands. When it functioned well, this institution was a great improvement on the original Ottoman system: instead of being at the mercy of predatory sandžak-begs appointed from outside who spent their few years in Bosnia trying to enrich themselves, people now had local rulers with a strong vested interest in the long-term prosperity of their area. Istanbul accepted the growth in power of the kapetans because they were militarily efficient and delivered the taxes. But at the same time they could put a serious check on the power of the governors of Bosnia appointed by the Sultan.

In theory, the governor exercised the supreme power of the Sultan over the whole of Bosnia. As the ruler of an eyalet he had, as we have seen, the title of beglerbeg or vizier; he held the highest of the three ranks of 'pasha', called a 'three-tailed pasha' after the traditional military standard adorned with three horse-tails which would precede him in battle.[31] Below him there were the sandžak-begs (by the end of the seventeenth-century wars Bosnia contained four sandžaks: Bosnia, Hercegovina, Zvornik and Klis), also appointed directly by the Sultan. At district level, in addition to the kapetans, there were also four independent agaluks or lordships; areas could also be governed by musselims, administrators appointed by the vizier himself.[32] But in practice the vizier's power was more and more limited from the early eighteenth century onwards: an energetic vizier such as Hekim-oglu Ali-paša could mobilize Bosnia when it was in the interests of the Bosnians to be mobilized, but could hardly control the country when it turned against him. Only severe force could do that, and its use was not a regular occurrence. By the end of the century most observers agreed that the vizier's real power extended only to the area round the town of Travnik, where he had his residence and court.[33]

The Bosnian viziers had moved out of Sarajevo after the war in the 1690s, and found it almost impossible to return. The growth of Sarajevo and, to a lesser extent, Mostar as cities fiercely guarding their own political independence was another factor limiting central power. Sarajevo had been granted a privilege or *muafname* (involving some tax-exemptions) by Mehmed II in the 1460s as a reward for the help given by Sarajevans during the original conquest of Bosnia. This became the basis of ever more ambitious claims of special status on the part of the Sarajevans – especially by the leaders of the powerful guilds, who acquired the power (reserved elsewhere to the state) to appoint the chief administrator of the city.[34] After the ending of the devşirme system in the seventeenth century, the nature of the janissary corps degenerated throughout the Empire: in Bosnia during the eighteenth century it turned into something rather like a guild or association, concerned as much (or more) with social privileges as with military duties. One French observer in 1807 noted that 'the title "janissary" is held by most of the Muslim townsmen'; he was told that out of 78,000 janissaries in Bosnia, only 16,000 received pay and performed real military service, and the rest were artisans who just enjoyed the rank.[35] Since Sarajevo contained at least 20,000 janissaries, some of whom were military men, its privileges could not be lightly set aside by any vizier. A musselim stayed in Sarajevo as the vizier's representative, but exercised little real authority.

Sarajevo led the way in the resistance to central power: one Bosnian chronicler noted that when a new tax was imposed in 1771, other places waited to see whether the Sarajevans would accept it before paying it themselves.[36] But Mostar was also important. Though it had no written record of any grant of privilege, it tried to assume a similar status; it resisted all attempts at control, and was involved in frequent clashes with the vizier's troops. There were campaigns against Mostar in 1768 and 1796, and in 1814 it took an army of 30,000 men to restore the rule of the vizier there: a musselim was installed, but the people promptly rejected him and put in their own nominee instead.[37] The town officials who led the resistance in Mostar held the rank of *ajan*, and this position too became a bulwark against central power. When the post was first introduced to Bosnia during the 1683–99 war, an ajan was a town official with responsibilities for law and order, chosen from among the spahis, janissary officers and other senior figures. Though the term developed a wider significance elsewhere in the Balkans, where it applied generally to all kinds of local semi-independent Muslim lords, in Bosnia it kept its meaning as an administrative office. In many provincial parts of Bosnia the kapetan also had the function of an ajan. But the special role of the ajans was in the main cities, where they were actually elected, during much of the eighteenth century, by representatives of the citizens – Christian as well as Muslim. The ajans themselves were Muslim, of course, and in both Sarajevo and Mostar the janissary organizations had a strong influence on their nomination. In Sarajevo ordinary townsmen could become ajans; in Mostar the local estate-owning aristocracy took over the post and eventually 'feudalized' it, making the election a mere formality. It was through the exercise of this office that the leaders of Mostar, with the support of other members of the local land-owning class, kept their city in a state of almost permanent resistance to central government from the 1760s to the 1830s.[38]

8

Economic life, culture and society in Ottoman Bosnia, 1606–1815

As the history of the kapetans and ajans helps to show, a social change of huge importance was under way during the seventeenth and eighteenth centuries. The old system of military-feudal tenure was gradually eroded, and in the place of the timar class there arose a new kind of local aristocracy holding large estates in full, hereditary ownership. Some of the reasons for this change have already been outlined: the growth of the devşirme class of imperial officials who competed in seventeenth-century Istanbul for grants of non-military private estates; the shift in military importance from spahis to paid infantry; and the general and insatiable need for revenues, which led to large areas of land being handed over to local lords in return for the collection and delivery of taxes in cash. In Bosnia the flood of displaced spahis, janissaries and officials out of Hungary, Slavonia, Croatia and Dalmatia in 1683–97 increased the pressure to convert timar lands into private estates (known by the general term *čiftlik*): many of these people wanted the security which land-ownership would give them, and it was possible to squeeze more revenue out of a čiftlik, where peasants had fewer legal rights.

Some of the estates which had been converted in this way were known in Bosnia as *agaluks*, and their owners as *agas*: the peasants here retained some rights of utilization, but the burden of tithes and legally obligatory labour was increased. Those estates which were based on unqualified land-ownership were known as *begliks*, and their owners as *begs*, the general term for 'lords'.[1] Many of these were large properties run by estate managers, who exacted as much as they could from the peasants employed on them: they were able to make their own contractual arrangements with the peasants, unregulated by customary law. In general usage the terms 'aga' (which originally applied to janissary officers) and 'beg' just came to mean members of the lower and higher land-owning nobility. Meanwhile the Muslim peasants, who had always been allowed by law to have smallholdings of their own, were moving increasingly into that type of farming as the conditions of work on the large estates deteriorated. And so in this way a long process of social and religious polarization took place: from the fifteenth century, when the feudal estate-holders could be Christian as well as Muslim, and their estates were worked by peasants of both kinds, to the nineteenth, when all the big landowners were Muslims and the great majority of the non-land-owning peasants were Christians.[2] These peasants were still called 'kmets', which is usually translated as 'serfs'; but strictly speaking those who worked on beglik estates no longer had the legal status of serfdom. They were merely peasants disadvantaged in a system which gave them much too little bargaining power.

Conditions of life for the kmets deteriorated. An increasing number drifted off the land and went in search of work in the large towns.[3] In the sixteenth century it had been quite common for peasants in the Ottoman Balkans to retain a surplus after tax, which they could then take to market.[4] This became impossible on the more demanding of the čiftlik estates, where peasants were reduced to little more than subsistence. The French writer Fourcade, on his way to take up his post of consul at Salonica in 1812, spent a night in a kmet's house in Kožarac: it was twenty feet by twelve, with a hearth in the middle but no chimney and no windows (just openings in the walls and a hole in the roof); the floor was earthen and the only furniture were chests; they slept with their feet to the fire, wrapped in sheepskins on bundles of hay, and were devoured by vermin.[5]

Such reports paint a very bleak picture of life in rural Bosnia. Yet one of the striking discoveries of modern historians of the Balkans is that the population was actually growing very strongly during the eighteenth century – especially in Bosnia. There had been an overall decline in numbers during the seventeenth century, for reasons which are not altogether clear: one possible cause is typhus.[6] The influx of Muslim refugees may have only just matched the outflow of Catholics during the whole of the seventeenth century: Catholic sources estimate that more than 50,000 may have left during the 1683–99 war, and the overall exodus during the Venetian war of 1645–69 was probably in tens of thousands too.[7] It was the Muslim population, however, which bore most of the burden of military activity – not only in the defence of Bosnia, but in the almost perpetual warfare of the Ottomans in other corners of their Empire. The importance of Bosnian forces in the Ottoman army is indicated by a list of 1553 Bosnian spahis who served in the campaign against Russia in 1711: each one of these spahis would have brought his own retinue of serving men.[8] Many thousands of Bosnian Muslims perished in these distant campaigns; out of 5200 sent to fight in Persia in the war of 1723–7, for example, only 500 returned home.[9] Other causes of death included plague, which, as we have seen, continued to ravage Bosnia in the early eighteenth century. That the Muslim population grew only sluggishly after the influx of the 1690s is understandable.

The strongest growth was in the Christian population. One set of tax records in the Ottoman archives suggests that it grew by more than 200 per cent during the eighteenth century. This figure must be treated with caution: the starting-point, a tax return for 1700, looks improbably low. But the general trend is clear. If we apply a multiplier of three to the figure for adult males, the rounded totals for the Christian population in these tax returns come to 118,000 in 1718, 190,000 in 1740, 295,000 in 1788 and 312,000 in 1815. (These figures are not properly comparable, however; the administrative areas covered vary.)[10] Figures estimated on a different basis for the whole of Bosnia and Hercegovina suggest that the Christian population grew from 143,000 in 1732 to 400,000 in 1817.[11] We have no records indicating large-scale immigration by Christian peasants into Bosnia, though occasional settlements by people from Serbia or Macedonia undoubtedly took place.[12] Despite the frequent unrest in eighteenth-century Hercegovina, the Bosnian eyalet was in general better governed than neighbouring regions of Serbia and less troubled by marauding bandits; possibly it attracted a steady trickle of settlers from the Serbian lands throughout the century.

But the main cause of the population increase must have been natural growth. This suggests a functioning economy in which, even if most Christians in the countryside lived in poverty, they did not live in extreme want.

A small minority of the Christian population, on the other hand, enjoyed real prosperity in the major towns of Bosnia, where a Christian (and Jewish) merchant class developed. Catholics, with their old Ragusan connections, dominated Bosnian commerce up to the end of the seventeenth century; thereafter Serbs, Vlachs, Greeks and Armenians played a greater role. Some of the artisans too were members of the Serbian Orthodox Church, especially goldsmiths.[13] Muslim townsmen stuck mainly to handicrafts, but from the mid-eighteenth century they also began to engage in trade.[14] Prosperous Sarajevo in the seventeenth century was one of the wonders of the Balkans, and by far the most important inland city west of Salonica. One visitor noted in 1628 that there were merchants whose stock there was worth 200,000 or 300,000 ducats.[15] A glowing description of Sarajevo survives in the journal of the indefatigable Turkish traveller Evliya Čelebi, who visited the city in 1660: he noted that it had 17,000 houses (implying a population of more than 80,000), 104 mosques and a market with 1080 shops, selling goods from India, Arabia, Persia, Poland and Bohemia. He was also impressed by the inhabitants themselves: 'As the climate here is fine, the people have a rosy complexion. There are mountain pastures on all four sides of the town, and much running water. Because of that, the population is strong and healthy. There are even more than a thousand elderly people . . . who have lived more than 70 years.'[16] A French traveller who was there just two years earlier was equally enthusiastic. 'There are very beautiful streets, fine and well-made bridges of stone and wood, and 169 beautiful fountains', he noted. 'The town is full of gardens: most of the houses have their own private gardens, and they are all full of fruit-trees, particularly apple-trees.' He was struck too by the market, with its 'infinite number of people and all kinds of goods', and by the large weekly horse-fair – a Bosnian speciality.[17]

Sarajevo took a long time to recover after its devastation in 1697. There were other fires too, in 1724 and 1788.[18] Its population in 1807 was thought to be 60,000: less than the figure suggested by

Čelebi in 1660, but still impressive if one compares it with the population of Belgrade in 1838 (12,963) or Zagreb in 1851 (14,000).[19] The Balkan lands experienced an important boost to their trade after the Treaty of Passarowitz, which opened up commerce with the Austrian Empire and actually gave a trading advantage to the Ottomans.[20] Soon merchants from Sarajevo were operating in the great trading fairs of Leipzig and Vienna; Bosnia's main exports were agricultural products (hides, furs and fruit, especially dried plums), and the main imports were textiles.[21] The rich mines of Bosnia were by now defunct (apart from some extraction of iron ore at Vareš), and there was very little industry other than that carried out by artisans in the towns: working metal, leather, and so on.[22] The failure to develop large productive enterprises in the Ottoman Empire was commented on by one shrewd eighteenth-century observer, the Muslim convert Mouradgea d'Ohsson, who blamed it on the lack of proper legal protection: 'No one dares to put his wealth on show, for fear of attracting the attention of the Government.'[23]

The corruption inherent in the later Ottoman system was remarked on frequently. 'The policy of every Turkish minister has himself for its first object', wrote the English diplomat Sir James Porter, in 1768.[24] But he also noted that this was a fault of the political-administrative system, not a matter of general moral decay. Even in this period of stagnation, those who described life in Ottoman Europe at first hand – as opposed to those who propagandized from a distance – were impressed by some of its moral and social conventions. Porter recounted the comments of an Ottoman *effendi* (gentleman) 'who was a native of Bosnia, and had lived long in his own country', who told him that 'they scarce knew in a mere Turkish [i.e. Muslim] village, what trick, deceit, or roguery were amongst each other'. In corroboration, Porter noted the lack of theft in Istanbul: 'you may live there with security, and your doors remain almost continually open'.[25] Some might suppose that the reason for this blameless behaviour was that people were living in fear of the ruthless enforcement of Islamic law; but there is plenty of evidence to show that although the general level of piety remained high in the Muslim population, the sacred law was not rigorously enforced. One historical study of attitudes to alcohol in Bosnia has found that views became less strict during the eighteenth and nineteenth centuries: no longer were people liable to be denounced for drinking by their neighbours, as they had been in the sixteenth century.[26]

Porter's informant blamed the Orthodox community for the corruption of morals. There is no real evidence (apart from such anecdotal remarks) to support the idea that the Orthodox population was more corrupt than any of the other religious groups. But there were many reports of corruption among the hierarchy of the Orthodox Church, which, controlled at its highest levels by the Greek-speaking 'Phanariot' families in Istanbul, had adopted some very venal practices. Having gained the highest ecclesiastical offices by payment, the Phanariots then sold the lower ones to recoup the cost. The Orthodox Metropolitan of Bosnia acquired an official residence in Sarajevo in 1699; by the end of the eighteenth century he had four bishops under him, at Sarajevo, Mostar, Zvornik and Novi Pazar (which is in modern Serbia).[27] But there is little record of the pastoral or intellectual activity of these bishops in Bosnia during this period. The sixteenth-century Orthodox 'Old Church' in Sarajevo was rebuilt and repaired at various times, and an Orthodox elementary school was built in the city in 1726.[28] The general level of activity of the ordinary Orthodox clergy was very low; they were poorly educated, and were dependent mainly on printers in Russia or Romania for their tiny supply of Gospels and liturgical books.[29] During the eighteenth century, a period when the Orthodox population in Bosnia was growing at a great rate, some Orthodox monasteries were destroyed by fire or war, and others seem simply to have fallen into disuse. By the end of the century there were twelve monasteries in Hercegovina, but only two in Bosnia proper, at Derventa and Banja Luka.[30]

The Catholic Church, still represented exclusively by Franciscans in Bosnia, had little or no scope for the sale of offices. The friars had long practised the custom of demanding alms or tithes from their flock, but this was defended by visiting churchmen on the grounds that they had no other source of income.[31] One rather poignant report from Olovo in 1695 shows that this practice too was open to abuse. The 'guardian' of the monastery there wrote that unless it received money from Rome it would have to close down: it had received no alms from the parishes for seven years, because the person who collected the alms, Father Stanić, had embezzled them.[32] But the genuine poverty of the Catholic Church in Bosnia emerges from many reports. Bishop Maravić noted in 1655 that 'few of the parishes have churches where the Mass can be said and the holy sacraments administered; the Mass is usually said in cemeteries and in the private houses of Catholics'.[33] To administer the sacraments, the Franciscans would ride out on horseback to outlying villages and stay the night; indistinguishable in their lay clothes from the peasants, they were addressed as 'Ujak' ('uncle'), a practice which has survived to the present day. One observer, the French consular official Chaumette-des-Fossés in 1808, was shocked by the ignorance and superstition of the Franciscan friars and their interference in the lives of the people.[34]

Nevertheless, thanks to their sometimes tenuous link with the wider intellectual world of the Catholic Church, these Bosnian friars did produce some published works: they mainly wrote simple devotional tracts, but there are one or two more original items, including an early eighteenth-century polemical poem declaiming fiercely against the profanity of folk-songs.[35] The most important published writer among them was Filip Laštrić (1700–83), who became the head of the Bosnian Franciscans and defended the rights of their province, 'Bosnia Argentina', against a proposal in Rome to demote its status. The treatise he wrote for that purpose, *Epitome vetustatum bosnensis provinciae* (1765), was the first printed book written about Bosnia by a Bosnian.[36]

It was not only against threats from Rome that the Bosnian Franciscans needed to defend themselves. Competition between the Catholic and Orthodox Churches in Bosnia persisted throughout this period. Letters from Bosnia to the Pope in 1661 said that the Orthodox Patriarch was trying to force all the Catholics there to accept the Orthodox rite, and that he had obtained a decree from the vizier of Bosnia to suppress the Catholics. To resist these moves, the Bosnian Catholics were having to spend 'a large amount of money on litigation'.[37] The Franciscans retained their original *ahdname* or grant of privilege from Mehmet II, which was renewed (thanks to diplomatic intervention by Austrian, French, Ragusan and even English envoys at Istanbul) by every Sultan throughout this period; and other decrees of the seventeenth and eighteenth centuries did guarantee exemption for the Franciscans from various taxes, and protection against take-over attempts by the Orthodox Church.

By the beginning of the nineteenth century some observers were remarking that the Ottoman policy in Bosnia was more favourable to the Catholics than to the Orthodox.[38] This was probably a reflection of a growing identification of the Orthodox with the movement of resistance to Ottoman rule in Serbia; and the Catholics of Bosnia could be trusted not to conspire with the new neighbouring power, the Napoleonic Empire, since their priests regarded it as dangerously atheistic.[39] The rivalry between the Catholic and Orthodox clergy in Bosnia was commented on by many visitors: Chaumette-des-Fossés, who spent seven months in the country, noted that hostility between the two religious communities was 'maintained by the clergy of the two Churches, who make horrible allegations about one another'.[40] Without the urging of these interested parties, it is doubtful whether the Catholic and Orthodox peasants would have found much cause for antipathy between themselves; they spoke the same language, wore the same clothes, went sometimes to the same churches and shared exactly the same conditions of life.

Reading standard accounts of the Ottoman Balkans, it would be easy to come away with the impression that these centuries form a cultural wasteland, with intellectual and spiritual life surviving only in the most rudimentary and stultified forms. That is the picture painted in many works by Yugoslav historians, and offered almost in caricature form by the novelist Ivo Andrić in his bitterly anti-Muslim treatise on Ottoman Bosnian culture. 'The effect of Turkish rule was absolutely negative', he declared. 'The Turks could bring no cultural content or sense of higher mission, even to those South Slavs who accepted Islam.'[41] Such remarks are an expression of blind prejudice – a wilful blindness in the case of the great monuments of Ottoman architecture in Bosnia, and a more understandable blindness in the case of the wide range of literary works written by Bosnian Muslims under Ottoman rule, many of which were unknown when Andrić was writing in 1924. It is still very difficult to form any proper judgement of these Bosnian writings, which are known to only a handful of specialist scholars in the world: few have been translated, and many still exist only in the original manuscripts – assuming that, after the massive and deliberate destruction of the Bosnian Muslim cultural heritage in 1992–3, they still exist at all. Before the bombardment of Sarajevo began in 1992 there were 7500 manuscripts in the Gazi Husrev-beg Library, 5000 in the Oriental Institute, 1762 in the Historical Archives and 478 in the National Library.[42] From these figures alone one can deduce that Ottoman Bosnia was not a cultural desert; and many works by Bosnian writers, in Turkish, Arabic and Persian, survive in collections in Istanbul, Vienna, Cairo and elsewhere.

One type of writing which has gained special attention is the so-called 'Aljamiado' literature. These are works written in the Serbo-Croat language but in the Arabic script. (The name has been borrowed by modern scholars from similar non-Arab materials written in Arabic script in Muslim Spain.) During the first two centuries of Turkish rule the old *bosančica* script, the Bosnian alternative to Cyrillic, continued in use among the begs of Bosnia; the Roman script was used by the Catholic friars, and Cyrillic printed works were also read by the Orthodox clergy in the seventeenth and eighteenth centuries. But the move to write in Arabic script was a natural one for Muslims to make: it was the script in which Arabic, Turkish and Persian were all written, and it was taught in the Muslim mektebs or elementary schools throughout the land.[43] The Aljamiado literature consists mainly of poetry of various kinds, written in Arab classical metres: religious poetry, verses with moral and social themes, and some erotic love poems as well. The poets included dervish sheikhs, soldiers and women.[44] One Aljamiado writer, Mehmed Havaji Uskufi (d. 1651), also compiled a Serbo-Croat-Turkish dictionary in verse – the second oldest dictionary for any south-Slav language. And apart from producing these written works, Muslims also played a large part in the creation and transmission of the rich heritage of folk poetry in Bosnia: ballads and laments (such as the famous *Hasanaganica*, already mentioned), epic poems, and the special genre of love-songs, equally popular among Muslims and Christians, known as *sevdalinke*.[45]

With Serbo-Croat functioning as the third language of the

Ottoman Empire, it is hardly surprising that some Ottoman literature should have been written in it. One eighteenth-century Bosnian writer, the chronicler Mula Mustafa Ševki Bašeskija (who added a collection of Serbo-Croat songs to his chronicle), declared that it was a much richer language than Arabic because it had forty-five different words for 'to go'.[46] Much significance has been attached by modern Bosnian historians to the fact that writers in this period called their language 'Bosnian'. But what they meant by that was simply the language spoken in Bosnia: they were not suggesting that it was quite separate from the language spoken anywhere else. Regional differences in Serbo-Croat were noticed, of course; thus one Franciscan in the early eighteenth century said that the Bosnian language was different from Croatian, Dalmatian and Ragusan.[47] And of all the varieties of Serbo-Croat, Bosnian had long been regarded as the best. In 1601 Mauro Orbini wrote: 'Out of all the Slav-speaking peoples, the Bosnians have the most smooth and elegant language; and they take pride in the fact that they alone nowadays maintain the purity of the Slav tongue.'[48] The great nineteenth-century Serbian writer, folksong-collector and language-reformer Vuk Karadžić also regarded the dialect of central Hercegovina as representing the popular language in its best and purest form.[49]

Most of the literary works of the Bosnian Muslims, however, were written in Turkish, Arabic or Persian. There are obvious reasons for this: some were writing in forms where the language was an inseparable part of the genre, such as the elaborate courtly poetry of the Persian tradition; some were dealing with subjects, such as philosophy, where an entire technical vocabulary was present in Arabic but lacking in Serbo-Croat; and of course many were writing for readers outside the Slav lands. In the prose writings, works on theology, philosophy, history and law predominate; but the range was evidently very wide, and only a few authors can be mentioned here. Major writers include Ahmad Sudi al-Bosnawi (d. 1598), who wrote commentaries on the classic Persian poets; Hasan efendi Pruščak (d. 1616), who wrote a famous 'Mirror for Princes'-style treatise on government and many works on logic, rhetoric and law, as well as compiling a register of learned Bosnian authors; Abdi al-Bosnawi (d. 1644), who composed ecstatic-mystical treatises in the Sufi tradition; Ibrahim Alajbegović, known as 'Pečevi' (d. 1651), who compiled a history, in Turkish, of the period 1520–1640 and drew on west European printed sources; Ahmad al-Mostari Rušdi (d. 1699), one of many poets from Mostar who wrote Turkish poetry on Persian models; Mustafa al-Mostari Ejubović, known as Šejh Jujo (d. 1707), who wrote nearly thirty treatises on logic, grammar and Islamic law; Mustafa al-Aqıhisari (d. 1755), who wrote several moral and religious works and a commendatory treatise on coffee; and Mustafa Ševki Bašeskija (d. 1809), whose chronicle of eighteenth-century Sarajevo, written in rather workaday Turkish, was mentioned above.

Some of these writers pursued careers in teaching or administration outside Bosnia, but there were many learned men occupied in the government of Bosnia itself. Šejh Jujo, for example, was the mufti of Mostar; and one of the governors of Bosnia, Darviš-paša al-Bosnawi (d. 1603), was a talented poet who translated Persian poetry into Turkish.[50] No doubt Bosnia had its fair share of ignorant and boorish administrators too. But the idea that Bosnia was just a cultural desert during the Ottoman period is very evidently absurd. And that is to say nothing of the decorative arts, such as calligraphy and miniature-painting, which were also widely practised by Bosnian Muslims throughout the Ottoman centuries.[51]

Several of the writers mentioned above were members of the Sufi dervish orders, which played an important part in Bosnian Islamic life. Once again it is difficult to write about such a subject, not only because material remains unpublished (such as the 222 manuscripts from one dervish lodge in Sarajevo, the Sinan tekke), but also because the orders have always functioned as a kind of 'unofficial Islam', outside the official structures of the medresas (seminaries) and mosques – so that their role has always been understated in the standard histories of Islam. These orders are societies or fraternities of believers led by spiritual teachers or 'sheikhs', meeting regularly in tekkes (lodges) for fellowship, and for ceremonies which may include ritual movements (the best-known being the 'whirling' of the Mevlevi dervishes) and a type of spontaneous ecstatic religious poetry known as *ilahi*. At different times the dervish orders have been quietist and apolitical, or politically active and militant, as in the famous Muridist movement which resisted the Russian advance into the Muslim northern Caucasus. And their theology, usually inclined towards mysticism, has sometimes been so open-mindedly speculative, absorbing ideas from philosophy, love-poetry and even Christian theology, that it has been regarded by strict Muslims as heretical. This applied especially to the Bektashi order, which operated among the janissaries.[52]

The dervish orders came early to Bosnia and probably played an essential role, as they did elsewhere in the Balkans, in the two interrelated processes of Islamicization and the development of Muslim towns.[53] The first dervish tekke in Sarajevo, the Išakbegova tekija, belonging to the Mevlevi order, was built before 1463; another, the Skender-paša, of the Naqshbandi order, was built in 1500, and two more important tekkes (the Sinan-paša and the Bistrigina) were added in the seventeenth century.[54] A mass of smaller tekkes which have not survived were also built: Evliya Čelebi counted forty-seven altogether in Sarajevo in the mid-seventeenth century.[55] Tekkes could be located in remote parts of the country too: one of the last surviving ones, still functioning in the 1970s, was in an isolated mountain village above Fojnica – the birthplace of the famous eighteenth-century Bosnian dervish leader, Šejh (sheikh) Husejn.[56] As well as being centres of local fellowship and piety, the tekkes were also part of a huge international network; members of the largest order, the Naqshbandi, might travel as far afield as Central Asia to seek out famous sheikhs. The one order which, curiously, never became very popular in Bosnia was the Bektashi order of the janissaries: it did have some tekkes there, but these were supported mainly by visiting Albanians and Turks. It seems that the aura of heterodoxy which hung over the Bektashi order was disapproved of in Bosnia.[57]

Islam in Ottoman Bosnia was, for the most part, orthodox and mainstream. The only seriously heterodox movement was that of the 'Hamzevites', followers of a sheikh Hamza Bali Bošnjak who was executed for heresy in 1573. Little is known about his teachings, though they apparently went far beyond the Bektashi in admitting elements of Christian theology. During the subsequent persecution of the Hamzevites in Bosnia some members of the movement took their revenge by assassinating the Grand Vizier Mehmed-paša

Sokolović; and the Hamzevites seem to have continued as a kind of shadowy opposition movement throughout the seventeenth century.[58]

Most observers regarded the Bosnian Muslims as orthodox and pious. Evliya Čelebi wrote warmly of the Muslims of Sarajevo: 'They are all god-fearing people, of pure, upright and untroubled faith. They are free of envy and hatred, and all of them, old and young, rich and poor, are persistent in their prayers.'[59] But although 'god-fearing', the Bosnians were notably less strict than some other Muslim societies in their adherence to several Islamic practices; they always had a weakness for drinking raki, the use of the veil was disregarded in some areas (especially rural Hercegovina), and the Bosnian practice of courting, even of love-matches, was often commented on by foreign observers.[60] Other Muslims gave descriptions of the moral character of the Bosnians which chime with Çelebi's account. A Syrian writer who compiled a Persian-Turkish dictionary in the late seventeenth century wrote, in his entry for 'Bosnian': 'The Bosnians are known for their gentleness and dignity; erudition, accurate understanding, sound deliberation, loyalty and trustworthiness are their characteristics.'[61] And after two months in Sarajevo in 1658 the French traveller Quiclet exclaimed: 'I received nothing but all kinds of good treatment, favours and courtesies from all the Muslims of this city, where everyone befriended us.'[62]

Such descriptions are worth bearing in mind when one reads accounts of the 'fanaticism' of the Muslims of Bosnia in the nineteenth century. It is too easily assumed that this was a permanent feature of Bosnian Islam. A fanatical attitude certainly developed in the nineteenth century among some of the begs, the Muslim clergy and the lower-class urban Muslims; but there are good reasons for thinking that it was the product of specific political and social causes. Chaumette-des-Fossés, writing after his seven-month stay in Bosnia in 1808, made a perceptive comment on the growth of anti-Christian suspicion among the begs: 'To do justice to the Muslims of this province, one must say that, as the raya [mainly Christian peasants] themselves admit, they were very mild, up until the last few years. But since the beginning of this century, their political situation has made them extremely suspicious.' After the French takeover of Dalmatia and the armed risings of the Serbs and

Montenegrins, he said, they felt surrounded and threatened. 'This situation, by raising their fears, has rendered them ill-disposed towards everyone. It has inspired them with a fear of seeing their raya rebel; and to keep them in check, they have had recourse to barbarity.'[63] The social-religious polarization of land-owners and peasants was nearing completion in this period, and must also have played its part. The rise of Serbia as an armed and quasi-autonomous Christian state, from which those Muslims who were not massacred were brutally expelled, strengthened the fears of the Muslim clergy. And the continuing growth in importance of the Christian merchant community in Sarajevo, which in the early nineteenth century began to enjoy the protection of consular officials from France, Austria and Prussia, intensified the suspicions and the envy of the ordinary Muslim townsmen. By 1822 another French visitor, Charles Pertusier, could write that 'the Muslim takes his faith to the most extreme form of fanaticism'.[64] By then, such a generalization, although improbably sweeping, must have had some truth in it. But it was not always so.

9

The Jews and the Gypsies of Bosnia

Two populations have received little mention so far, although they were present in Bosnia from an early stage: the Gypsies, who were probably there before the Turkish conquest, and the Jews, who came within the first century of Turkish rule. This chapter will give a brief summary of their histories in Bosnia, from their arrival until the early twentieth century. The two peoples have little in common, of course, apart from the fact that each has preserved its identity while scattered through innumerable lands. But in both cases the difference between the treatment they received in the Ottoman Empire, and that which was meted out in northern and western Europe, is striking. Those writers who refer automatically to the cruelty and intolerance of Ottoman rule should look a little more closely at the history of these minorities. Prejudice against both Jews and Gypsies certainly existed in Balkan society; but local prejudice on its own would not have swept so many thousands of them to their deaths in the twentieth century. Only an ideology developed in the more advanced and 'Christian' parts of Europe could do that.

As with Islam, it is possible to speculate about very early contacts between Judaism and the Bosnian territory. From archaeological evidence we know that many Jews must have settled in neighbouring parts of Roman-ruled Yugoslavia: the remains of third- and fourth-century synagogues and Jewish tombs have been found at places in Macedonia, Dalmatia and Montenegro, and at Osijek, thirty miles from the north-eastern Bosnian border. The most intriguing find is an eighth- or ninth-century Avar graveyard near Novi Sad (east of Osijek, and a similar distance from Bosnia), which contains a large number of tombs with Jewish symbols and Hebrew inscriptions – suggesting that these Avars had absorbed members of the Crimean Khazar tribe which converted to Judaism in the eighth century.[1]

A Jewish population continued in Macedonia throughout the Byzantine period; and because of the importance of the overland trade route to Salonica it attracted new members from Jewish communities in other parts of Europe, who joined the descendants of the Jews of Roman Salonica. One famous Macedonian Jew, Leon Mung, who converted to Christianity and became Archbishop of Ohrid in 1120, had probably fled from persecution in Germany. Other refugees must have gone to Macedonia after the expulsion of the Jews from Hungary in the fourteenth century. At that time there were also Jewish communities in Ragusa, Split and Belgrade.[2] But the largest influx was at the end of the fifteenth century, when Jews expelled from Spain were welcomed and well treated by the Ottoman Empire. Many of these Sephardic Jews settled in Salonica, and some moved north to the city of Skopje, which they rapidly developed into an important trading centre.

Bosnia was not on the main north-south trade route (which went through Serbia), but an important east-west route ran from Ragusa, through Foča (south of Sarajevo) to Novi Pazar and on down to Skopje. Jewish traders from Skopje and Ragusa must have had frequent dealings with Bosnian intermediaries. But it seems to have been the development of Sarajevo as a trading city in its own right which first brought Jews to settle on Bosnian soil. Their date of arrival is not known, but three court records of 1565 refer to Jewish merchants who were apparently fully established in Sarajevo.[3] Probably the decisive factor was the building of the Bursa Bezistan ('Bursa' cloth-market) by Gazi Husrev-beg in the 1530s: the silk trade with Bursa was largely in the hands of Anatolian Jews.[4] Whether it was Jews coming all the way from Bursa who first settled in Sarajevo is not known; the Sarajevan community's main links through the next two centuries were with Skopje and Salonica, and it can be assumed that most of the Jewish settlers were from those cities. The cloth trade, which dominated imports into Bosnia throughout the Ottoman period, was to remain in Jewish hands until the destruction of the Jewish community in the second world war.[5]

The Jews of Sarajevo lived at first in a Muslim mahala or quarter, but in 1577, as a reward for assistance against the Habsburgs, they were allowed a quarter of their own.[6] The word 'quarter' is a rather misleading translation of 'mahala'; as noted in chapter 5, these were small subdivisions of a town, of perhaps no more than forty houses. The word 'ghetto', sometimes also used for this Jewish mahala, is also a misnomer: there was complete freedom of movement, without gates, curfews or any other discriminatory measures. A story given in an eighteenth-century manuscript says that the Muslims had complained about the noise the Jews made and about the danger of fire. The significance of this story – assuming that there is some truth in it – is that it indicates that the Jews of Sarajevo were already engaged in industry, probably operating a metal-foundry (which is known to have been one of their occupations in later years). And if they were helping to make the kinds of metal weaponry and equipment needed for a military campaign, this might explain the gratitude of the Turkish authorities. A seventeenth-century Jewish writer in Salonica recorded, however, that the move was made at the Jews' request.[7] Whatever the reason, the richer Jews moved into houses grouped together in an area near the central market, and others moved into a special building erected there by a beneficent governor of Bosnia in 1580–1, known as the *Siavuš-pašina Daire*, 'the bequest of Siavuš-paša'. It consisted of a large house with forty-six rooms and an inner courtyard: the poorer Jewish families lived there, each inhabiting one or two small rooms. The Jews called it *Il Cortijo* – 'the Courtyard'; the Muslims called it *velika avlija*, 'the great courtyard', or *čivuthana*, 'the Jews' house'. (Such communal houses were built in other parts of the Balkans too: the one known as the *Türkischer Judenhof* in Belgrade contained 103 rooms, 49 kitchens and 27 cellars.)[8] At the same time, the first synagogue was built in Sarajevo, alongside the Cortijo.[9]

There are few traces of the Jewish community in Sarajevo in the seventeenth century. We know that it had a continuous existence, but it cannot have been very prominent, as there is hardly any mention of it in other Jewish literature of the period. Its first known rabbi, Samuel Baruh, came from Salonica in the early seventeenth century, and his grave is traditionally said to be the oldest in the Sarajevo Jewish cemetery.[10] When Evliya Čelebi visited in 1660 he noted that the Jews now had two mahalas in the city.[11] The legal position of the Jews was similar to that of the Christians: subject to the kanun-i raya, they were not allowed to build new places of worship without special permission. This, like most other legal dispensations, was obtained by making suitable payments. Like the Christians, the Jews lacked legal equality with Muslims in the Ottoman courts, but were allowed to use courts of their own to judge civil suits within the Jewish community. The Jews also paid the haraç, and they were subject as well to the rules of the kanun-i raya on dress, including some additional stipulations made by Sultan Murat IV in 1574, which decreed that Jews should not wear turbans, silk clothes, or anything green; the practice later grew up of allowing rabbis to wear turbans, so long as they were yellow.[12] But in general the treatment of the Jews was much less discriminatory in the Ottoman Empire than in any of the Christian lands to the north and west in the late medieval and early modern periods.

In 1665 the Jews of the Ottoman Empire were shaken by an extraordinary piece of news: a charismatic young rabbi from Smyrna, Sabbatai Ṣevi, had declared himself the Messiah. News of this announcement swept through Europe, and the mystical writings of Sabbatai's followers, especially his chief disciple and promoter, Nathan of Gaza, were read with great eagerness: one report mentions that the Jews of Vienna received copies of Nathan's devotional works in 1666 from Sarajevo.[13] The doctrines of Sabbatai and his followers (the 'Sabbatians') were based on the tradition of cabbalism, a method of extracting hidden prophecies and theological truths from the words and letters of sacred Hebrew texts. The great mystery and scandal of the whole Sabbatian story occurred in 1666, when Sabbatai Ṣevi, having been arrested and brought before the Sultan, agreed to become a Muslim. Many of his followers did likewise; others who remained in the Jewish faith preserved his teachings, and developed an extreme, paradoxical theology in which this estrangement from Judaism had been a necessary and mystical act (comparable perhaps to the nature of Christ's death in Christian theology). One of the leading Sabbatians of the next generation was Nehemiah Ḥayyon or Chajon, who was born in Sarajevo in 1650; his family (spelt Kajon, Gajon or Gaon in Serbo-Croat) was one of the old Jewish families in the city, where it has remained until the late twentieth century. Ḥayyon travelled in Palestine, Greece, Italy and Germany. In Berlin in 1713 he published a book, *Oz l'Elohim*, 'The Power of God', which has been described as the only document of Sabbatian cabbalism ever printed; it included a treatise attributed to Sabbatai himself, and caused a great uproar in Jewish circles. Ḥayyon was subsequently denounced as a heretic by one of the rabbis of Amsterdam, Ṣevi Ashkenazi, who had himself lived in Sarajevo from 1686 to 1697, when he fled northwards with Prince Eugene's army.[14] (This rabbi was possibly the only Jew to feel grateful for the Austrian invasion; the Jewish mahala in Sarajevo was badly damaged by Prince Eugene's artillery. In return for a reduction in tax, the Sarajevan Jews agreed to help pay for the rebuilding of the whole area.)[15]

The earliest records of the Sarajevo community to have survived in any form were from the 1720s and 1730s; extracts from them were printed by the historian Moritz Levy, but the documents themselves were later destroyed along with all the Jewish archives in Sarajevo in the second world war.[16] Sixty-six family names are mentioned from that early period, and a name-list of 1779 gives 214 heads of households – equivalent, perhaps, to a population of just over a thousand. A small Talmud Torah (Jewish primary school) is also mentioned. The Jews of Sarajevo practised a variety of professions: apart from traders there were physicians, pharmacists, tailors, shoemakers, butchers, wood and metal-workers, and makers of glass and dyes.[17] They were served for most of this period by rabbis brought in from elsewhere. The most famous of these, David Pardo, a Venetian Jew who was Chief Rabbi of Sarajevo in the 1760s and 1770s, was a distinguished scholar and writer; he founded a yeshivah (rabbinical training college) there during his term of office. Until then, Sarajevo had been subordinate to the Jewish community of Salonica, but now it was able to produce its own rabbis.[18] However, the dominant neighbouring community by this time, both in trade and in culture, was at Belgrade. The future Serbian capital had a mixed community of Sephardic and Ashkenazi Jews; it seems likely that some Ashkenazi also came to Sarajevo, but if they settled there they must have been absorbed by the Ladino-speaking Sephardic community, since there was no Ashkenazi synagogue in Sarajevo until the late nineteenth century. Ladino, the version of fifteenth-century Spanish spoken by the descendants of the Jews expelled from Spain in 1492, is still spoken by some of the surviving Sarajevan Jews today. And one special token of Sarajevo's Spanish heritage is the 'Sarajevo Haggadah', a fourteenth-century Spanish illuminated manuscript of the service for the first nights of the Passover, which belonged to one of the city's Jewish families until 1894 and is one of the finest works of art of its kind in the world.[19]

In the first few decades of the nineteenth century the Jewish population of Bosnia was 2000 or more. In one detailed report the French consul in Salonica, who went to Bosnia to gather information about trading conditions in 1813, said that there were 2000 Jews in Sarajevo, and noted that out of the most important trading businesses in the city two were Jewish, one was Greek, one Austrian and one French.[20] There was also by now a small Jewish community, of roughly sixty people, in Travnik: this town had gained importance as the seat of the governor of Bosnia, and now had a predominantly Muslim population of 7000.[21] And by the 1860s there were a few Jewish families living in Mostar too.[22]

One intriguing story from the early nineteenth century involves the fate of a Jew from Travnik, Moses Chavijo, who converted to Islam, took the name of Dervish Ahmed, and began to rouse the local Muslims against the Jews. In 1817 the leaders of the Bosnian Jews complained of his attacks, and had him tried and executed. Some of his followers later complained to the next governor of Bosnia, Ruždi paša, who seized the opportunity to squeeze some money out of the Jews: he demanded that they pay a recompense of 500,000 groschen, and seized ten leading Sarajevo Jews, including the rabbi, threatening to kill them if the payment were not made. The end of the story, however, is that a crowd of 3000 Muslims took up arms and demanded the Jews' release – which was promptly done.[23] Relations generally between Jews and Muslims seem to have been good, and frequently better than between Muslims and Christians. In many parts of the Ottoman Empire the Jews were regarded by Christians with resentment. This was partly because anti-semitism grew more easily in the soil of Christian theology; but it was also because some of the Ottoman governors relied on Jewish physicians and merchants as personal and diplomatic advisers, so that the

Jewish presence seemed to Christian eyes more like an adjunct to Turkish power. (The fact that Jews dressed like the Turks may have been an extra factor in some other Balkan countries – but not in Bosnia, where Christians dressed just like the Muslims, apart from a few tiny distinctive details arising from the kanun-i raya.)

The reforming Sultans of the 1830s and 1850s issued laws granting equal civil rights to subjects of all religious faiths; but these remained a matter of theory rather than practice. The biggest change to the status of the Jews came with the Austro-Hungarian occupation in 1878: four years later a 'Sephardic Israelite Religious Community' was set up in Sarajevo, a *Cultusgemeinde* (religious community) on the Austrian model, which elected its own governing body, kept a register of all Sephardic Jews in the city and was entitled to levy taxes on them, up to an amount equivalent to twenty per cent of direct state taxes. Many Ashkenazi Jews from Hungary, Galicia, Poland, the Czech lands and elsewhere came to settle in Bosnia under Austro-Hungarian rule, and a separate community was set up for them too.[24] They were looked down on by the Ladino-speaking Jews, and the two communities led separate lives; one observer in 1908 described them as 'sharply distinguished' from each other.[25] This influx helps to explain the rapid growth of the Jewish population in the city: having stayed at around 2000 for most of the century, it rose to 2618 in 1885, 4058 in 1895 and 6397 in 1910.[26]

The population of Jews in other parts of Bosnia was also swelled by immigration: by 1900 there were 9311 in the whole of the country.[27] The economic policies of the Austrians gave new opportunities to the Jews of Bosnia; unlike the Muslims, they took quickly to industrial enterprise, and the three leading Bosnian factory-owners who emerged were all Sephardic Jews. Austrian policy also had the effect of integrating the Jews more fully into the rest of Bosnian society: Serbo-Croat was introduced into the curriculum of the Jewish primary school, and some Jews sent their children to receive, for the first time in the history of this Jewish community, a secular education at secondary school level.[28] Up until 1941 the Jews of Bosnia played an essential role in the economic life of their homeland: there were Jewish communities in Sarajevo, Travnik, Mostar, Banja Luka, Zenica, Bugojno, Bijeljina, Brčko, Rogatica,

Vlasenica and Tuzla.[29] Most of this Jewish world was swept away in a flood of barbarism in 1941.

The Gypsies of the Balkans have a much more shadowy history than the Jews; their society produced very few buildings, written records, writers or indeed literate people. And yet their population was larger, and their presence in Bosnia was probably much older. Though the date of their original exodus from India is unknown, they were on Byzantine territory by the year 835, and there is firm evidence that Gypsies had crossed into the European part of the Byzantine Empire by the eleventh century. In the fourteenth and fifteenth centuries the main centre of Gypsy settlement was in southern Greece, and they were also well established on the island of Corfu. Some probably continued up the Adriatic coast; others had already spread overland. Gypsy villages in western Bulgaria are mentioned in a grant of land in 1378; this suggests that they had already been established for quite a long period in that area. Like the Vlachs, they also had some military traditions: a kind of military grouping is recorded among the Gypsies in fifteenth-century Greece. So it is interesting to note that the first definite record of Gypsies on the territory of modern Yugoslavia is a legal document from Ragusa in 1362, referring to a petition by two 'Egyptians' (i.e. Gypsies) called 'Vlach' and 'Vitanus'.[30]

It is tempting to speculate, on the slender basis of this solitary Gypsy called 'Vlach', that there was some symbiosis between Gypsies and Vlachs in these regions during the late middle ages. The types of nomadism they engaged in were utterly different; but if Gypsies were already engaged in metal-working and similar crafts, they might have been useful to a horse-breeding and trading population. There is some linguistic evidence too to support the notion of Vlach-Gypsy contact in the western and central Balkans. The vocabularies of most of the west European Gypsy dialects not only show a heavy debt to Greek and the southern Slav languages, but also contain some traces of the Romanian or Vlach language. We know that these tribes of Gypsies moved out of south-eastern Europe in the early fifteenth century; they could have spent some time in Romania, but not long, and there is no trace of any early

Hungarian influence on their vocabulary. The evidence points to a more prolonged contact with Vlach-speakers to the south of the Danube.[31]

If this speculation about the Ragusan document has any truth in it, Gypsies were present in Hercegovina long before the Turkish conquest. We know nothing about their activities in Bosnia during the early Ottoman years, but some were probably Islamicized at an early stage: a law issued in 1530 by Süleyman the Magnificent for the eyalet of Rumelia (which included Bosnia at the time) distinguished sharply between Muslim and non-Muslim Gypsies. The former had to pay a tax of twenty-two aspers per household, the latter twenty-five; and Muslim Gypsies were forbidden to lodge with non-Muslim ones.[32] The first specific reference to Gypsies in Bosnia comes from 1574, when Selim II issued a decree awarding tax privileges to Gypsies who worked in the mines: it mentioned those working in an iron ore mine near Banja Luka, as well as other Gypsies in mines 'beyond Novi Pazar' – probably meaning the mines of northern Kosovo. And in addition the Gypsy miners were allowed to elect a leader for each group of fifty men.[33] Whether these were local Gypsies who had taken to mining, or whether they had come down – like the Saxon miners – from the Hungarian-Romanian lands, can only be guessed at. Gypsies were established north of the Danube by the late fourteenth century, and the traditional categories of Transylvanian Gypsies included *rudarĭ* or *băieşĭ*, miners, and *aurarĭ*, gold-washers.[34] Perhaps some of the gold-washers noticed by Benedict Kuripešić in a river near Jajce in 1530 were Gypsies of this kind.[35]

For most of the early Ottoman period the Gypsies were well treated by the Turkish administration. A decree of 1604 on the Gypsies of southern Albania and north-western Greece refers to both Christian and Muslim Gypsies, and says: 'Let no one harass and oppress the race in question.'[36] This was a more humane attitude than that shown by any government in Christian Europe at the time; only eight years earlier, for example, 106 Gypsies had been convicted at York and nine of them beheaded, under an Elizabethan Act of Parliament aimed at the 'further Punishment of Vagabonds, calling themselves Egyptians'.[37] Of course most Gypsies remained at the bottom of the social heap in Ottoman life, as they did elsewhere.

City administrations preferred to leave them living outside the city boundary, instead of assigning them a mahala of their own, unless they could persuade them to settle down as craftsmen. One record from Bulgaria in 1610 shows that the cizye or poll-tax was set at 250 aspers for non-Muslim Gypsies and 180 for Muslim ones; despite the discount, this looks as if it must have been a form of discrimination, since Muslims generally were not meant to pay the cizye at all.[38] At the end of the seventeenth century attitudes seem to have hardened in the Ottoman administration. A campaign started in which Gypsies were accused of being prostitutes and pimps, and their taxes were heavily increased.[39]

Nevertheless, the basic legal rights of the Gypsies were the same as those of their fellow-Christians or fellow-Muslims. The great majority of the Bosnian Gypsies were Muslim. They seem to have been mainly nomadic until the end of the Ottoman period, and numerous: Bishop Maravić reported from Bosnia in 1655 that 'one finds Gypsies everywhere'.[40] When the Austrians invaded Bosnia in 1788, a 'large number' of Gypsies joined Bosnian forces to fight against them.[41] How large the total population was in Bosnia is very unclear: Chaumette-des-Fossés estimated 30,000 in 1808, but Pertusier, who was there four years later, put it at only 8000.[42] To judge by the other statistics they gave, Pertusier was the more reliable of the two. Ottoman statistics for 1865 give a total of 9630 Gypsies for Bosnia and Hercegovina; a German observer in the late 1860s estimated a total of 11,500; the 1870 census put it at only 5139, but this was a survey of households which probably missed many of the ones who were still nomadic.[43] Efforts had been made to persuade the Gypsies to settle, and in the nineteenth century there were Gypsy mahalas at Sarajevo, Travnik (where Chaumette-des-Fossés noted 300 Gypsies), Banja Luka and Visoko.[44]

By this time there were three distinct categories of Gypsies in Bosnia. The oldest population, known as 'White Gypsies', was more settled, and its members were gradually losing the Romany language. Most had lost it altogether by the twentieth century. These Gypsies were Muslim inside Bosnia, but similar 'White Gypsies' in Serbia and Macedonia were Orthodox. Their dialect of Romany indicated a long residence in the South Slav lands. The 'Black Gypsies', on the other hand, kept up a more nomadic life, and worked mainly as tinkers; they were known as *čergaši*, from the Turkish word *çergi*, meaning 'tent'. They were also Islamicized (though sometimes excluded from mosques on the grounds that they were unclean), but their version of the Gypsy language contained more Romanian elements, which suggests that they had come down from Transylvania or the Banat during the early Ottoman period. (It is possible, as suggested above, that the Gypsy miners of the sixteenth century had such an origin.) Both of these groups referred to themselves as 'Turks', meaning 'Muslims'.

The third group called themselves 'Karavlasi', which means 'Black Vlachs'; they resented being described as Gypsies, and claimed that they were Romanians. They did indeed speak Romanian, and one patriotic Romanian writer spent nearly a hundred pages in 1906 trying to prove that they were not Gypsy at all. But any informed observer could see that they were in fact Gypsies who came originally from Romania; apart from Romanian itself, they also spoke a version of the Gypsy language deeply imbued with Romanian vocabulary. The local population called them, confusingly, 'Serbian Gypsies', either because they had previously lived for some time in Serbia, or because they were members of the Eastern Orthodox Church.[45]

These self-styled 'Black Vlachs' had, of course, nothing to do with the Morlach 'Black Vlachs' of earlier history. They formed part of that population of Gypsies, speaking so-called Vlach (i.e. Romanian-influenced) dialects of Romany, which spread out into western Europe in a new wave of emigration in the nineteenth century and forms the basis of the American Gypsy population. Some of them were bear-leaders (an old Romanian Gypsy occupation, its members known as *ursari*); Bosnian bear-leaders could be found trudging through France in the 1870s.[46] One English traveller in Bosnia in the 1890s noted that they 'wander all over Europe with performing bears, and Captain von Roth [an Austrian officer in Bosnia] told me he had seen one of them in London'. The same writer also described them as 'a singular people who live in holes in the ground'.[47] A reader's first reaction to this may be to assume that the author was just repeating the prejudiced comments of his Bosnian or Austrian informants. But in fact the nomadic Gypsies of the Romanian lands had long practised a system of travelling with tents during the summer and digging underground shelters in the forests for the winter.[48]

There were no doubt many other smaller movements of Gypsy populations into Bosnia. The most successful group came in the early nineteenth century from the Novi Pazar sandžak (then part of the Bosnian eyalet) and settled in the village of Pogledala, near Rogatica, to the east of Sarajevo. Rade Uhlik, an expert on the Bosnian Gypsies, visited Pogledala before the second world war and described it then as 'unquestionably the most interesting and vital Gypsy settlement in Bosnia'.

> The people are very industrious, able, thrifty, honest tinkers who show a solid capacity for organization. They are not nomads; they live in rather poor houses. They travel during the warm season from spring to autumn over the whole of Bosnia, in various directions, by railway, seeking work every year. . . . Most of them can write, and they preserve their Gypsy speech very carefully.[49]

When Uhlik returned to Pogledala after the second world war he found the village deserted: 'Today it is utterly derelict, and the Gypsy survivors have fled to North-West Bosnia.' Altogether, 28,000 Gypsies had been exterminated within the Ustaša state; but the Muslim Gypsies fared better than the Orthodox 'Karavlachs'. 'Thanks to the intervention of the higher Muslim priests', wrote Rade Uhlik, 'a greater slaughter of the Bosnian Gypsies was prevented.'[50] What had caused those Gypsies of Pogledala to flee from south-eastern Bosnia, however, was the killing of Muslims by Serbs. The Muslim Gypsy quarters of many towns in south-eastern, eastern and northern Bosnia were to witness similar episodes of murder and destruction in 1992 and 1993.

10

Resistance and reform, 1815–1878

By the end of the Napoleonic period, it was clear to the authorities in Istanbul that there were weaknesses in the structure of the Ottoman Empire which had to be dealt with vigorously if it were not to break up altogether. The many successes of the Serbian rebels had struck a blow at Turkish military pride; and the Napoleonic wars themselves had displayed a new level of military efficiency in western Europe which made the Ottoman army look ramshackle and old-fashioned – which indeed it was. Serbia's new semi-autonomous status set a precedent for other parts of the Empire, and there were rumblings of revolt in Greece. The tendency of other European powers, notably Russia and Austria, to act as patrons and protectors of the Christian populations in the Balkans put added pressure on the Sultans to reform the legal status of the raya; and other legal and administrative reforms were needed simply to modernize the system and make it less grindingly inefficient. But the most important political problem in the short term was the growth of power and autonomy in the hands not of Christian subjects but of local semi-independent Muslim lords. The most ambitious were Ali Pasha of Ioannina in north-western Greece, who was besieged there by Ottoman forces in 1820 and eventually killed in 1822, and Muhammad Ali Pasha of Egypt, a far more formidable figure who had built up his power by copying military and administrative methods from western Europe: an attempt to dislodge him by force in the early 1830s ended in miserable failure. Many other local rulers of lesser stature were also asserting themselves; of these, few understood the need for reform in the way that Muhammad Ali Pasha did, and there were certainly no would-be reformers among the rebellious begs, kapetans and ajans of Bosnia.

The first trouble came in a familiar form, a clash between an assertive governor of Bosnia and the civic pride and privilege of Sarajevo. Siliktar Ali-paša, appointed governor of Bosnia in 1813, was a hot-headed military man who was determined to curb Bosnian independence. On his arrival at Sarajevo he announced that he was not going to spend just the three days there which were all that was allowed by custom; instead, he would alternate between Sarajevo and Travnik at six-monthly intervals. This proposal was rejected, and he had to send in his troops (mainly Turkish and Albanian) to subdue the city.[1] Mostar, as we have seen, was also attacked by a large army in 1814. Similar action was taken in 1820, when the Sultan wanted to make sure that Bosnia would give no trouble while the Ottoman army was engaged in crushing Ali Pasha in north-western Greece: a punitive force under Djelaludin-paša attacked Mostar and Srebrenica, and killed the rebellious kapetans of Banja Luka and Derventa.[2]

Such clashes were just a matter of meeting resistance with force. But a more systematic attack on local power was under way in the 1820s, which involved reforming the military and political system from which those local lords drew their support. The starting-point, as in all previous attempts at Ottoman reform, was the army; and the fact that the Sultan had had to depend on Muhammad Ali's French-trained army from Egypt to crush the revolt in Greece was a sign that radical military reform was needed. When Sultan Mahmut II announced the creation of a new army corps in the summer of 1826, the janissaries gathered in their drill-square to march on the Imperial palace and carry out the traditional janissary coup. But Mahmut had stationed loyal soldiers with cannons round the square, and after half an hour of bombardment with grape-shot the entire janissary corps in Istanbul was exterminated. This event (referred to rather delicately in Ottoman history as the 'Auspicious Incident') enabled Mahmut to abolish the institution of the janissaries, creating a new regular army based in Istanbul and new units in the provinces for which soldiers would be recruited for twelve-year stints.[3] The reaction in Bosnia – where the janissaries formed a privileged social institution to which most Muslim townsmen belonged – was understandably enraged. A new vizier, Hadži Mustafa-paša, was despatched with six commissaries to impose the reform there, but the Bosnians sent him packing. The Sultan then sent a force under

Abdurahman-paša from Belgrade in 1827; he entered Sarajevo, crushed the janissaries there and executed seven of their leaders. But in 1828 the resistance flared up again, and after three days of fighting in Sarajevo Abdurahman-paša was forced to abandon the city and resume the old practice of residing at Travnik.[4]

The changes to the army, which involved new west European-style training methods and uniforms, caused continuing resistance in Bosnia, and the local lords harnessed this popular resentment among the Muslims for their own political purposes. In 1831 a charismatic young kapetan called Husejn, from Gradačac in northern Bosnia, arrived at Travnik with a small force and occupied the town. In an act of public humiliation he made the vizier take off his modern uniform and, after a ritual purification, put on traditional dress. He wanted to keep the vizier captive there, but his prisoner escaped and fled to Austria. (This set a precedent for future cooperation between the Austrian and Ottoman authorities on this border: the Austrians were tired of continuing raiding carried out on the initiative of the rebellious local kapetans.)[5] Meanwhile a similar but more serious revolt had broken out in northern Albania, and the rebel army there was moving eastwards to engage with Ottoman forces under the Grand Vizier. Seizing his opportunity, Husejn-kapetan led an army of 25,000 Bosnians down into Kosovo, ostensibly to help the Ottoman forces. Once there, they presented their demands: administrative autonomy and an end to the reforms in Bosnia, a promise that the vizier of Bosnia would henceforth always be a Bosnian beg or kapetan, and the immediate appointment of Husejn-kapetan to that office.

The Grand Vizier agreed; but he had no intention of carrying out these promises, and was soon at work stirring up rivalries among the various Bosnian begs. Eventually he managed to detach the kapetans of Hercegovina, led by Ali-aga Rizvanbegović, from Husejn's revolt; then, in 1832, he sent an army of 30,000 men to Bosnia. Husejn-kapetan tried to mount a defence of Sarajevo, but his support melted away, and in the end he too had to seek refuge in Austria. He was later given a conditional pardon by the Sultan, and sent into internal exile in Trebizond. Ali-aga Rizvanbegović's reward was that Hercegovina was separated from the Bosnian eyalet as a separate territory under his rule.[6] There was some further resistance in Bosnia, but the new governor, Mehmed Salih-paša Vedžihija, dealt with it with ruthless efficiency. A persistently troublesome ajan from Banja Luka was tricked into coming to Sarajevo, and garotted.[7]

While Husejn-kapetan had been grasping at his dream of an autonomous Bosnia within the Ottoman Empire, the gradual transformation of that Empire had continued. The system of timar estates was abolished in 1831. This caused no great upset in Bosnia: many spahis simply ignored it, and other land-holders were merely encouraged to speed up the process of converting timars into agaluks and begliks.[8] The revolts of peasants again landowners in several parts of Bosnia in 1834 and 1835 would no doubt have happened anyway; the second of these was remarkable only for the cooperation shown between Catholic and Orthodox kmets.[9] A reform which was peculiar to Bosnia and Hercegovina, however, was the abolition of the system of kapetans in 1835. It is not known how this was received by most of the kapetans themselves, but it seems to have caused less of a convulsion than might have been expected. In place of kapetans, the country was to be governed by musselims (officials representing the governor and appointed by him). Many former kapetans, ajans and spahis were appointed as musselims, which must have salved their pride, even though they no longer commanded their own local forces and could not treat the office of musselim as hereditary. A few kapetans in western Bosnia did revolt in 1836, and were destroyed by troops from Anatolia. Some agas rose up again in the following year. Another revolt in 1840 temporarily drove the governor out of Travnik, but was then suppressed by regular troops. The remaining disaffected kapetans who had not been appointed musselims would eventually rise up in 1849–50 and meet a similar fate.[10]

Most other Imperial reforms of the 1830s impinged less on Bosnia: the introduction of a postal service and an official newspaper, the development of new schools and reformed ministries. But in 1839 Mahmut was succeeded by his son, Abdulmecit I, who in November of that year decreed a much more sweeping set of reforms in a document known as the *Hatt-i Şerif* of Gülhane. (This literally means the noble signed decree of the rose-garden courtyard, so called after the courtyard at the Topkapı palace where it was proclaimed.) It announced that all subjects, regardless of their religion, would be guaranteed equal security of life, honour and property – thus in effect abolishing the kanun-i raya; it set out a new basis for conscription to the army; and it decreed new methods of tax assessment and collection, ending the notorious system of tax-farming. These principles were to be elaborated in a series of later measures, and repeated in a similar decree of 1856, the *Hatt-i Humayun*. The whole body of reform measures during this period is known collectively as the Tanzimat, the 'reorganization' of the Empire – or, to use a late twentieth-century word with suitable overtones of ill success, *perestroika*.[11] The principles set out in the Hatt-i Şerif were noble and well thought-out. Unfortunately, they had little or no effect in outlying areas of the Empire such as Bosnia, where they were simply ignored.

By now Bosnia was in a poor condition. Parts of the country may not have suffered too badly from the fighting and unrest, and we should hesitate before assuming that the whole population of Bosnia was sunk in misery: one Orthodox woman told an English visitor in the mid-1870s that 'thirty years ago, the common people were much better off than they are now, for then there were no taxes but the *haratch* . . . They were rich, and had horses, oxen, swine, sheep, and poultry . . . Although there was no liberty, yet the Begs and Agas, lords of the land, protected and defended their own kmets.'[12] But then, things always seem to have been better thirty years ago, and things were particularly bad in the mid-1870s. The general condition of Bosnia was certainly not good in the 1840s. Its infrastructure and economy had been weakened by years of fighting. The great French geographer and historian Ami Boué produced a classification of Balkan roads in 1840, in which the lowest category, reserved for Bosnia and Albania, was 'execrable': he described these roads as 'escaliers de rochers', staircases of stones.[13] The Austrian consular official Demeter Atanasković reported to Metternich after a visit to Bosnia in 1844: 'The impressions I brought with me on my departure from Bosnia were, if possible, even worse than those I formed on my arrival.'[14] Regularly crushed at the level of national politics, an embittered land-owning class was devoting its energies instead to trying to squeeze more income out of the peasantry. There was, as Boué noted, an increasing suspicion on the part of the begs against Christians, who they feared would invite their foreign co-religionists to invade; the essential problems were economic and political, not religious.[15] Muslim peasants were, when possible, squeezed just as hard as Christian ones. A heartfelt petition to the governor of Bosnia in 1842, complaining of intolerably high tithes and taxes, began: 'We, the humble Muslim citizens and miserable Christians of the whole region of Tešanj . . .'[16]

The new governor who arrived in 1847, Tahir-paša, tried to reform the customary system of tithes and other peasant dues for the agaluk estates: he abolished the *corvée* (obligatory labour on the landowner's estate) and, in compensation, raised the proportion of the peasant's grain crop which had to be handed over to the landowner from one-quarter to one-third. Unfortunately, many landlords carried out the second of these changes but not the first.[17] When Tahir-paša also tried to implement the army reforms which had still not been properly carried out in Bosnia, a rebellion of the begs and agas broke out again. The country was engulfed in fighting in 1849, and the revolt was still in full swing when Tahir-paša died in 1850.[18]

The Sultan now sent to Bosnia one of the most effective and intelligent governors it ever had in this last century of Ottoman rule: Omer-paša Latas. Born Michael Lattas, he was a Slav from the Lika area who had served as a sergeant in the Austrian army on the military border. He spoke good German, understood how things were done in a West European army and had real political as well as military skills. Having thoroughly crushed the rebellion in 1850–1, he sent many of the begs and agas into exile in Anatolia; he also abolished the separate pašaluk of Hercegovina and made a new administrative division of Bosnia and Hercegovina into nine districts, each under the command of a 'kajmak' (a representative of the governor, like a more military version of a musselim).[19] Demeter Atanasković, now back in Bosnia as Austrian Consul-General, met him in August 1850 and reported his comments: 'He said that, for political reasons, the Ottoman government could proceed only slowly and cautiously with the improvement of the condition of the Christians, so as not to upset the Muslims, on whom the state depends for its main support and strength.'[20] Some of his own reforming measures were not popular with the Christian peasantry:

his policy of disarming the entire population made them feel more vulnerable, and some of his new kajmaks, of non-Bosnian origin, were guilty of abuses. 'Dissatisfaction is universal', wrote Atanasković in July 1851.[21] But the political power of the old land-owning class had been decisively broken, and from now on an attempt could be made to introduce the reforms of the Ottoman Tanzimat.

How badly those reforms were wanted can be seen from a petition sent by the Christians of Bosnia to the Sultan in 1851. Among other things they asked to be treated as Turkish subjects, not as raya; they demanded equality before the law; they wanted an equal number of Christian and Muslim judges; and they asked for the removal of the poll-tax or haraç.[22] The first two demands were for things which had been theirs of right since the Gülhane Hatt-i Şerif of 1839, and the third was only an extension of the same principles. (In fact there were already two Christian judges in the municipal court in Travnik; but this was an exceptional arrangement.)[23] The abolition of the haraç was to come in 1855, when the traditional ban on Christians serving as regular soldiers was also lifted. However, since the haraç was replaced by a tax in lieu of military service which was levied in the same way, and since most Christian subjects continued their traditional abstention from the army, this change made little difference to the Christians in practice. The only real difference was that non-serving Muslims now had an additional tax to pay.[24]

As has already been suggested, the attitude of Bosnian Muslims towards Christianity had hardened during the first half of the nineteenth century. Consular reports from this period offer several examples. When the small Orthodox community at Travnik got permission to build a church in 1853, the Muslim citizens insisted that it be built outside the town. In the same year the Catholics were refused permission to build a church in Sarajevo (though this was in fact granted soon thereafter, partly as a result of pressure from the foreign consular corps). And Catholic priests in Livno complained that a Christian could not get a favourable judgement in a court one time in a hundred.[25] But when reading these complaints we should also remember that quite a number of new churches, presbyteries and schools were being built in various parts of Bosnia between the 1820s and the 1850s. In addition to the elementary school in Sarajevo which they had had since the early eighteenth century, the Orthodox community built a secondary school there in 1851; they already had elementary schools in ten other Bosnian towns, and by 1870 they would have at least twenty-eight of them, and possibly as many as fifty-seven schools altogether. In the 1860s the Catholics had secondary schools in some of the main towns, and twenty-seven elementary schools; several new Catholic churches were built in the 1850s.[26]

In quantitative terms, both Churches underwent a revival in late Ottoman Bosnia: by the 1860s there were roughly 380 Catholic priests and more than 400 Orthodox.[27] Qualitatively, the record is less impressive. Most foreign observers commented on the generally low calibre of the Franciscans, and nearly all observers were shocked by the avaricious behaviour of the Orthodox clergy: one German visitor noted that they bought their parishes for between twenty and 200 ducats, and described them as 'the scum of humanity'.[28] Another observed that the Orthodox bishops bought their sees for large sums of money, which they then tried to recoup from their flocks; this led them into 'an extremely intimate friendship with the local Muslim authorities'.[29] But in amongst the Christian clergy and schoolteachers of both denominations there were a few energetic individuals. Some were genuinely religious men, such as Grgo Martić, the leader of the Franciscans in Sarajevo from the 1850s to the 1870s. But there were others whose activities were not merely religious, but political too. These were men such as the Franciscan Ivan Franjo Jukić, whose historical observations on the conversion of the medieval nobility to Islam we have already encountered; Teofil Petranović, a teacher at the Orthodox school in Sarajevo in the 1860s, who formed a group of people to go out into the villages and tell the Orthodox peasants that they must stop calling themselves 'hrišćani' (the local term for 'Orthodox') and start calling themselves 'Serbs'; and Vaso Pelagić, director of the Orthodox school in Banja Luka, who agitated for the Serbian nationalist cause.[30] Pelagić was eventually arrested and sentenced to prison, though permitted to stay in the Orthodox Metropolitan's residence in Sarajevo instead of going to gaol.

But in general it is the tolerance of the Bosnian authorities towards such activities which is striking. They were of course aware that nationalists on both of Bosnia's flanks, in Croatia and in Serbia, were campaigning for the eventual annexation of the Bosnian lands. One *Grenzer* officer in Croatia, Major Antunje Orešković, even tried to organize a revolutionary network in Bosnia in the early 1860s with a view to a general uprising and the creation of a new South Slav state; however, since his plans involved throwing off Austrian rule too, it was the Austrian authorities who eventually cracked down on him and his friends.[31] As for the semi-autonomous Serbian state, its ambitions for Bosnia were obvious. The leading Serbian intellectual Vuk Karadžić published an article in 1849 under the title 'Serbs All and Everywhere', in which he claimed, on the basis of a thoroughly question-begging historical argument, a Serb ethnic identity for the people of Bosnia and Dalmatia too.[32] And in 1844 the Serbian Minister of the Interior, Ilija Garašanin, had written a secret memorandum in which methods of stimulating pro-Serbian sentiment in Bosnia, with a view to an eventual annexation, were set out in detail: these included training young Bosnians in the Serbian administration, and cultivating senior Franciscan friars.[33] It is a little anachronistic, however, to view these endeavours simply in terms of 'Greater Serbian' expansionism. At the time, Serbia was the only state that could possibly play the role which Piedmont had played in the unification of Italy. Any Serb who wanted an independent South Slav state to develop would naturally see it in terms of the enlargement of Serbia. And on the other hand there were plenty of Croatian intellectuals, such as Ante Starčević and Eugen Kvaternik, who had a similar but opposite ideology in which all Bosnians were proclaimed to be Croats.[34] The Muslim authorities in Bosnia would not, of course, have followed these intellectual debates in any detail. But they were perfectly well aware that Bosnia was a prize for which both Orthodox and Catholic neighbours were keen to compete.

While these agitations were going on in the 1860s, Bosnia was enjoying a comparatively golden decade under one of its most benign rulers, Topal Osman-paša. It is impossible not to admire this man – partly because much of what we know about him comes from the memoirs of a Turcophile Swiss doctor, Josef Koetschet, who settled in Sarajevo in 1861, opened a pharmacy there and became a confidant and adviser to a succession of Bosnian governors, among whom Topal Osman-paša was clearly his favourite. (Not everything was golden in this period, however: Koetschet's reason for coming to Bosnia in the first place was that he was personal physician to Omer-paša Latas, who had been sent back there in 1861 as a military commander to crush another revolt, fomented by neighbouring Montenegro, in Hercegovina.)[35] But Topal Osman-paša – the nickname 'Topal' ('lame') referred to his limp from a war-wound – was clearly the best sort of civilized Turkish administrator. A former admiral and civil governor of Belgrade, he was learned in Turkish, Arabic and Persian literature, wrote good Turkish poetry, and spoke French and Greek. He built new Muslim schools in Sarajevo, permitted the Christian communities to build more schools of their own, started a library of Arabic, Persian and Turkish works at the Begova mosque, and set up a printing-press which produced school textbooks and a weekly gazette, *Bosna*, in Serbo-Croat and Turkish. He also embarked on an energetic road-building programme, completing a main road from Sarajevo northwards to Bosanski Brod in a year, and he even had a stretch of railway constructed, from Banja Luka to the Croatian border. He also set up a hospital in Sarajevo, the first public hospital in Bosnia, with forty beds for patients of all religions.[36]

There were some major political reforms too. The new system of military conscription for Muslims was finally introduced into Bosnia in 1865; Topal Osman-paša was cautious, promised they would not be used outside Bosnia, and drew the sting of the reform by enlisting more than 1000 volunteers. In the following year he put into effect the far-reaching changes required by the Provincial Reform Law of 1864. This involved reorganizing the structure of the whole eyalet of Bosnia (now to be called a *vilayet*), setting up new courts (with a joint Muslim-Christian Court of Appeal), and dividing the whole Bosnian-Hercegovinan territory into seven sandžaks. Each of these now sent representatives (two Muslim, one Christian) to a consultative assembly, which met for a period of up to forty days once a year to advise the governor on economic and financial matters: agriculture, taxation, road-building and so on. And there was in addition a small executive council, consisting of three Muslims, two Christians and one Jew, which met under the governor twice a week. Though both councils had only consultative status, this was a huge advance on the way things had been done in Bosnia for the previous 400 years.[37]

One of the biggest problems, as always in this final period of Ottoman Bosnia, was that of the relations between peasants and landowners. Here the main reform measure had been decreed in 1859, just before Topal Osman-paša's arrival, so that he just had the more difficult task of trying to get it implemented. The decree was an attempt to codify the customary law on the duties of peasants who worked on the agaluk estates, the type of ex-timar estates where there was still a legal basis to peasant-landlord relations. It fixed the tithe paid to the landlord at one-third of the crop (known as the *tretina*, meaning 'third'). Since the state tithe, a money payment equivalent to one-tenth of the crop, was deducted first, and the tretina was calculated on the remainder, this meant that these two basic dues accounted for forty per cent of the peasant's total product; and there were other state taxes of various kinds, such as the new tax in lieu of military service, on top of that. When modern historians describe the tax levels in Bosnia as 'exorbitant' because they 'absorbed over forty per cent of the peasant's income', it is tempting to point out that this is similar to the proportion of gross national product taken through all forms of taxation in many late-twentieth century states.[38] But it is difficult to make real comparisons. Modern workers expect most of their tax payments to return to them in the form of health care, education and so on; this was not the case for Bosnian peasants. On the other hand, these peasants did not have to buy their houses or invest any money in the land. Another principle codified in the 1859 decree was the rule that landlords should provide housing for the peasants and help in its upkeep and repair. The peasants were free to leave the landlord; the landlord was allowed to evict them, but only on grounds of unsatisfactory work or non-payment of dues, and with the approval of government officials.[39] Unfortunately these rules applied only to the agaluks and did not affect the begliks, where landlords could set whatever contractual relations they wanted. Their main effect was therefore to encourage landlords to convert their tenure from the one form to the other.

Josef Koetschet, looking back on this period, thought that the landowners' exactions and maltreatments had been overstated.

> Most kmets lived on tolerably friendly terms with their landlords; indeed, in bad years the landlords – I mean the rich and respected ones – gave every possible kind of assistance to their kmets. It is true that there were also some brutal agas, whose armed fist lay heavily on the defenceless peasants. However, the antagonism which grew up in such cases arose much more from economic interests than from any religious or political motivation.[40]

The picture Koetschet paints of life in Sarajevo at this time is certainly a rosy one. He recalls the Sunday afternoons in the summer when Catholic and Orthodox families would picnic on the hillside by the road to Ilidže. 'Muslim, Christian and Jews went peacefully on their way . . . enjoying in equal measure that peaceful, blessed time, and there was no thought of any religious hatred.'[41] It was only at the end of the 1860s, according to Koetschet, that the atmosphere soured, after Topal Osman-paša's nine years of office were at an end. In 1869 there were urgent orders from Istanbul to search for Russian-backed Slav agitators, and Koetschet himself, to his embarrassment, was asked by the new governor to hunt for Serbian propaganda in the Orthodox monastery of Žitomislić, near Mostar.[42] There was more public discontent in the late 1860s too, directed not against landowners but against the state tax-collectors, whose common practice of assessing the peasants' crops (and demanding payment) before they were harvested was particularly hated. In 1868 1000 Orthodox and Muslim peasants protested in the Posavina region of northern Bosnia; in 1869 a group of a hundred Muslim and Orthodox people made a similar protest at Foča.[43] These examples of inter-religious cooperation do indeed bear out Koetschet's view that the basic causes of anger and unrest were economic rather than religious. But at the same time there was definitely a new sense of anti-Christian hostility growing among the Muslim clergy and hodžas (religious teachers) in Sarajevo. It was in the period 1871–2, according to Koetschet, that 'we first began to see a picture of religious hatred'.[44]

One cause célèbre was the building of the Orthodox cathedral. This was a symbol of the changing status of the Bosnian Christians, whose interests were now being promoted by the foreign consular corps and the governments of the would-be 'protector' powers –

Russia for the Orthodox and Austria-Hungary for the Catholics. Indeed, the intrusion of foreign-sponsored Christian organizations into Bosnia was one of the most striking features of this period: in 1869 a group of Catholic monks from the Rhineland was allowed to build a convent near Banja Luka; in 1870 Miss Pauline Irby opened a girls' school in Sarajevo, funded by an English Christian organization and staffed by Protestant deaconesses from Germany; and in the following year a group of Austrian nuns, the Sisters of Charity, arrived to build a convent and engage in primary teaching.[45] When permission was granted in 1863 for an Orthodox cathedral in Sarajevo, money was raised from all over the Orthodox world; an emissary from the Metropolitan of Bosnia travelled through Russia with a holy relic, the hand of Saint Tekla, to collect donations.[46]

As the building neared completion in 1872, a bitter dispute broke out between the Orthodox community and the Muslim clergy, with the latter insisting that the cathedral's belfry should not exceed the height of the Begova mosque's minaret.[47] The ringing of bells was itself a novelty; by long-established custom, no Christian bell-ringing had been allowed in Ottoman cities. Some of the more demagogic hodžas and imams (prayer-leaders) began rousing the Muslim population on these issues. One was a big uncouth man called Hadži Lojo; having been on the haj (the pilgrimage to Mecca) he was treated as a hodža or teacher, although he was utterly unlearned.[48] Another was the fanatical imam of the Begova mosque. However, when the latter led a deputation to complain about the bell-ringing, he met his match in the new governor, a no-nonsense Albanian called Mehmed Akif-paša. The imam began by quoting a verse of the Koran. 'Silence, you donkey!' cried the governor. 'You're not going to teach me the Koran! So you can't bear the sound of bells, can you, you dog? And the rest of you, are you such block-heads that you can't see that this scoundrel would ring the bells himself, so long as he were paid fifty groschen a month to do it?'[49]

In the summer of 1873, twenty-four Bosnian Christian merchants fled to Croatia; they said that 'many' Christians had been condemned to death in Bosnia for fraternizing with the Austrian consul.[50] Such incidents were given great prominence in later Austrian writings on the events of the 1870s, since they seemed to put a moral or religious obligation on the Austrians to intervene. But the real causes which led to the breakdown of Ottoman rule and the intervention of the Austrian army were economic and political, not religious. It was in the summer of 1875 that news first came of Christian peasants in the Nevesinje district of Hercegovina (east of Mostar) fleeing into the mountains to avoid paying the state tithe of one-tenth or one-eighth of their crop; the harvest had failed completely in 1874, but the local tax-collectors (two Muslim and one Christian) resorted to violent measures to force them to pay. By the end of July all the peasants in the region had taken to the mountains and were making armed resistance.[51] This was a politically sensitive area because of its closeness to the Montenegrin border: there had been several previous episodes of conflict between Ottoman and Montenegrin forces, such as Omer-paša's expedition in 1860–1, and the prince of Montenegro, a client of the Russians, was suspected of sending arms and men to destabilize Hercegovina.[52]

Soon other peasant risings were taking place in northern Bosnia, and large numbers of people fled into Croatia and Montenegro – from either the violence, or the taxes, or both.[53] The basic cause of popular discontent was agrarian; but this discontent was harnessed in some parts of Bosnia by members of the Orthodox population who had been in contact with Serbia, and who now publicly declared their loyalty to the Serbian state.[54] Volunteers from Serbia, Slavonia, Croatia, Slovenia and even Russia (plus some Italian Garibaldists, and a Dutch adventuress called Johanna Paulus) were flooding into the country, convinced that the great awakening of the South Slavs was at hand.[55] The Bosnian governor assembled an army in Hercegovina, which acted with ineffective brutality during the autumn and harsh winter of 1875–6. The fiercer begs raised their own 'bashi-bazouks' (irregular troops) and, fearing a general overthrow in Bosnia, began terrorizing the peasant population. During 1876, hundreds of villages were burnt down and at least 5000 peasants killed; by the end of the year, the number of refugees from Bosnia was probably 100,000 at least, and possibly 250,000.[56]

By mid-1876, this large but local crisis had become an international one. Not only was news spreading across Europe of a similar uprising in Bulgaria, and of its brutal repression (the famous

'Bulgarian atrocities' which so horrified the elderly Gladstone); but also in July 1876 Serbia and Montenegro declared war on the Ottoman Empire. They had agreed between them that the former would annex Bosnia and the latter Hercegovina. Montenegro had some military success, but Serbia performed miserably and was only saved from Ottoman re-conquest by the intervention of the Russian government, which forced the Turks to agree to an armistice in November. Serbia's actions hardened the already hostile attitude of the Bosnian authorities towards their own Orthodox population; one refugee heard reports in early 1877 that 'there is a complete clearing out of the Serb people of Bosnia, for the Turkish authorities themselves hunt them down, and give full licence to the Bashi-Bazouks and Gipsies, also to the Catholics and the Jews'.[57] (This remark about the Catholics and the Jews, however, suggests that the refugee was both Orthodox and biased; Arthur Evans noted that 'one of the most curious features of the present insurrection has been the way in which the two Christian sects have fought side by side'.)[58]

In 1877 Russia declared war on the Ottoman Empire. There had already been much behind-the-scenes negotiation between the Russians and the Austrians to plan a share-out of the Balkan lands. By early 1878, however, with Russian troops almost at the gates of Istanbul, Russia was able to dictate a settlement which satisfied its own interests much more than Austria's. Under this agreement (the Treaty of San Stefano) Russia's chief client in the Balkans, Bulgaria, was hugely expanded and granted almost full autonomy. Bosnia was to remain Ottoman territory, but various reforms were to be introduced there, and under article fourteen of the treaty Bosnia's own revenues were to be used only for Bosnian purposes (the compensation of refugees and inhabitants) for the next three years.[59]

This reawakened the old ambitions of the Bosnian begs to manage an autonomous Bosnia within the Ottoman Empire. After all, as Arthur Evans had noted in 1877, the Ottoman governors and officials were 'detested alike by the Bosnian Mahometans and the Bosnian Christians'.[60] Unfortunately, after the events of the last three years the Bosnian Muslims and Christians so detested one another that a Bosnia left to its own devices would have been a hotbed of unrest for a long time to come. This was one of the considerations which weighed on the great powers of Europe when they met at the Congress of Berlin in July 1878 to rewrite the settlement made at San Stefano and redraw the map. The desire to counterbalance Russia's new influence in the Balkans and block its drive to the Mediterranean was even more important. And so it was that the Congress of Berlin not only cut Bulgaria down to size, but also announced that Bosnia and Hercegovina, while still in theory under Ottoman suzerainty, would be occupied and administered by Austria-Hungary.

Once more the Austrians made the mistake which they had made in the seventeenth and eighteenth centuries: they assumed that they would be welcomed by most of the Bosnian population. Otherwise they would never have sent the news of the Congress's decision to Sarajevo by telegram on 3 July, ten days before the European newspapers had it. On 5 July a large public meeting of Muslims was held at the Begova mosque; the old agitator Hadži Lojo appeared, unfurled a green flag (the symbolic colour of Islam), and led them to the governor's residence.[61] The governor agreed to appoint a new military commander and prepare to resist the coming of the Austrians; but his heart was obviously not in this policy, which would involve open defiance of the Sultan's treaty obligations. On 20 July the Sarajevo gazette warned of an imminent Austrian invasion; and four days later the first Austrian troops did indeed cross the river Sava. Hadži Lojo led another mob to the governor's residence on 27 July, encouraged the garrison to mutiny, and obtained from the governor the dismissal of several officials and the formation of a 'national government'. The military commander fled the city with a hundred horsemen, but was captured, brought back and persuaded to help organize the defence against the Austrians.[62]

Meanwhile Hadži Lojo obtained the enthusiastic support of the leading Orthodox priests, who were happy to think that Bosnia had thrown off Ottoman rule and had no wish to see it replaced by the rule of Austria. A general Muslim-Orthodox celebration was held: as Joseph Koetschet later recalled, 'Archimandrite Sava Kosanović and Pop [priest] Risto Kanta-Novaković, both dressed like robber chiefs, with pistols and scimitars in their belts, placed themselves at the head of the crowd of singing Serb youths.' On 2 August a parade of Muslim volunteers was held, together with 'the Christian legion, consisting overwhelmingly of Orthodox, with only a very few Catholics'. Lojo's credit fell not long thereafter, when he shot a young Christian peasant. But his actions had succeeded in rousing the Muslims in other parts of Bosnia too, and their somewhat ill-organized forces in different parts of the country amounted to roughly 40,000 men.[63]

The Austrians, on the other hand, had 82,000. Some 9400 of these were 'occupation troops' whose role was to move in from Dalmatia and hold places taken by the main fighting force. That principal force, under a Croatian commander, Baron Josip Filipović, moved swiftly down through northern Bosnia, seizing Banja Luka, Maglaj and Jajce. The Austrians were well equipped, and well informed about the towns, roads and bridges of Bosnia, thanks to an Austrian military surveyor whom the Bosnian authorities, in their innocence, had permitted to travel round the country in 1871–3.[64] On 16 August they heavily defeated a Bosnian force at the battle of Klokoti, near Vitez. On 18 August the Austrians reached the outskirts of Sarajevo. They began the attack on the following morning with an artillery bombardment at 6.30; then infantry entered the city, where they were fired at 'from every house, from every window, from every doorway . . . even women were taking part'. But the battle was won by 1.30 p.m., with Austrian losses of fifty-seven dead and 314 injured. The army moved on through Hercegovina and the sandžak of Novi Pazar in the rest of August and September, and by 20 October the entire occupation of Bosnia and Hercegovina was complete. It had taken less than three months. There had been some fierce resistance, and frequent guerrilla attacks: altogether there were fifty-three battles, many of them involving the taking of defended towns. The Austrians' total losses came to 946 dead and 3980 wounded. But no town had taken more than two days to capture; given the appalling state of most of the roads, it is barely an exaggeration to say that the Austrian army conquered Bosnia in the time it took to walk through the country.[65]

11

Bosnia under Austro-Hungarian rule, 1878–1914

Austria-Hungary had made the decision to take over Bosnia only with hesitation and reluctance. Of course, commentators had long argued that Bosnia had rich resources (agriculture, forestry, minerals), and that it would make sense for them to be developed as part of an economic unit with the coast – which was Austrian territory. Military men in Austria were also keen on gaining the strategic hinterland to the vulnerable Dalmatian coastline.[1] But when the idea of taking over Bosnia was discussed in 1869, two of the leading policy-makers were against it: Gyula Andrássy, the Foreign Minister, and Benjámin Kállay, the expert on South Slav history (and author, subsequently, of a respected history of the Serbs) who was then Austrian Consul in Belgrade. Neither of them wanted Austria-Hungary to be weighed down with another million or so Slavs.[2]

There were political problems which would flow from the peculiar in-tandem constitution of the Dual Monarchy: would Bosnia be ruled by Austria, or by Hungary, or by a joint commission? Or would it be united to Croatia, which since 1868 enjoyed a kind of home rule with a governor nominated by Hungary, a Croatian parliament of its own and a set of Croatian MPs in the Hungarian parliament? Worries about Croatia were the strongest reason for not wanting to take on Bosnia as well: adding a large extra component of South Slavs would strengthen the arguments of those Croats who demanded greater status for their country. Some wanted Croatia to be elevated to equal partnership with Austria and Hungary (the so-called 'Trialist' idea); others aimed at full independence for Croatia and the development of a South Slav state.

Neither plan was welcome in Vienna or Budapest. But there was something the Austro-Hungarian authorities were even more keen to avoid. For Croatia to expand into a South Slav state would be bad enough; but for Serbia to do it, first absorbing Bosnia and then undermining Austro-Hungarian rule in Croatia, would be far worse. It was Serbia's declaration of war against the Ottomans in 1876 that had finally made the Austrians think seriously about taking Bosnia; had they been sure that the Sultan could retain power indefinitely over Bosnia, they would not have bothered.

Once they were committed to ruling Bosnia, however, there could be no half-measures. A set of pious statements about what would happen in Bosnia was agreed with the Ottoman government in April 1879; but some of these were half-truths, and some were no truths at all. It was agreed that 'the fact of annexation' would not 'prejudice the rights of sovereignty of His Imperial Majesty the Sultan'; that Turkish money would continue to circulate; that the revenues of Bosnia would be used locally; that the administration would employ Turkish officials and Bosnian natives; that the Muslims would enjoy freedom of religion; and that the name of the Caliph-Sultan would continue to be recited in Friday prayers.[3] Of these promises, only the last two were properly kept. Turkish money was excluded, Bosnia was brought within the Austro-Hungarian customs union (which meant that revenues from customs collected at the Bosnian border might be spent anywhere in the Empire), and the administration was largely taken over by Austro-Hungarian citizens. As for the Sultan's sovereignty, any idea that these occupied provinces might one day be returned to Turkish rule was abandoned from the start: the only change envisaged was from occupation to full annexation. When the Austrian Emperor joined the Three Emperors' League with Russia and Germany in 1881, one of the confidential clauses stated that 'Austria-Hungary reserves the right to annex the provinces at whatever moment she shall deem opportune'.[4]

The problem of whether to assign Bosnia to Austria or Hungary was solved by making it a Crown land, which meant that it was ruled by neither and at the same time by both. A joint commission was set up under the Common (i.e. Austrian and Hungarian) Ministry of Finance; in theory the chief authority in Bosnia was the military governor, responsible directly to the Crown, but it was the Common Minister of Finance who made the policy decisions. In theory too Bosnia was under military law; but a proclamation at the end of 1878 announced that all Ottoman laws in Bosnia would remain in force until further notice, and these were only gradually replaced or supplemented by Austro-Hungarian laws and by new laws specially designed for Bosnia. The shariat courts of Islamic sacred law also remained in place to judge a range of civil matters for Muslims. Generally, where the Ottoman administrative structure was considered workable it was kept in place and merely Austro-Hungarianized in name and personnel: the sandžaks were renamed 'Kreise' (regions), and their subdivisions, the kazas or kadiluks, 'Bezirke' (districts), with a 'Bezirksvorsteher' ('district superintendent' – the equivalent of a Deputy Commissioner in British India) in charge of each. But whereas the Ottomans had governed the whole territory with 120 officials, the number of Austro-Hungarian administrators, through a combination of bureaucratic thoroughness and Parkinson's Law, had risen by 1908 to 9533.[5]

The first few years were the hardest for the new administration. There were huge problems at the outset, such as the need to return more than 200,000 refugees to their homes. Sporadic violence flared up in some areas, particularly in those parts of Hercegovina for which Montenegro still harboured territorial ambitions: there was insurgency in the Nevesinje region again in 1879, and a serious attack on army personnel near Gacko (close to the Montenegrin border) in 1881.[6] To build confidence among the population in Hercegovina, and to encourage refugees to return, the Austrians set up a special local militia force there, the 'Pandurs'; but many of these militia men became rebellious themselves, and some took to brigandage.[7] By November 1881 there were 12,840 Austro-Hungarian troops in Bosnia proper and 4000 in Hercegovina. This would have been sufficient to keep the peace, had the authorities not announced a new measure which was to be intensely unpopular: an army law making all Bosnian males liable for conscription into the Austro-Hungarian armed services. A revolt quickly sprang up in Hercegovina, and by mid-January 1883 several large bands of insurgents were operating in the area.[8]

These insurgents are referred to as 'robbers' in the official

Austrian reports; no doubt some of them were, but they were joined by Pandur leaders and village headmen too, and their main activity was not robbing but attacking gendarme posts and army positions. An infantry column sent to deal with them was ambushed on a hill-road and forced to retreat to Mostar. Larger forces were now deployed, and there was fighting throughout February in the region round Foča, including some of the mountains between Foča and Sarajevo. The insurgents were estimated to have up to 1000 men, divided into one mainly Orthodox band (under a Pandur officer, Pero Tunguz), one Muslim (under a prominent landowner, Omer Šačić) and two mixed.[9] Gradually the Austrian-Hungarian forces regained control of the area. In the words of the official report: 'The whole region was covered with a thick but constantly changing network of mobile columns, which hemmed in the individual bands ever more closely; finally it made their conditions of life so difficult that, albeit after dogged attempts at resistance, they had completely given up by July.'[10] Banditry of various kinds would continue in Hercegovina for more than a decade, but this was the last serious revolt against Austrian rule.

One reason why resistance was not greater was that a large number of irreconcilables had left the country altogether. They were mainly Muslims who had fled to Turkey – some who were unwilling on religious grounds to live under infidel rule, and others, no doubt, who feared justice or reprisals for the terrible things they had done against the Christians during the last three years of Ottoman rule. The great majority of these émigrés were peasants, but there were also some landowners, who formed a group in Istanbul to lobby for greater Turkish political pressure on the Austro-Hungarian government in Bosnia.[11] How many emigrated altogether is a question hotly debated among modern historians. The Austro-Hungarian authorities issued official figures stating that between 1883 and 1905 32,625 left and 4042 returned.[12] Another 24,000 left between 1906 and 1918. But these figures are only of those who got official permits to leave the country – a requirement imposed in 1883 when the authorities became alarmed at the number of people leaving to avoid conscription. They do not include those who left illegally, or any of those who fled in the first four years. A total emigration of 300,000 has been claimed by some Muslim historians, but this seems improbably high. One geographer who has studied the émigré population and their descendants has reckoned that there are now 350,000 'Bosniaks' in Turkey; however, the term is used in that country to mean people whose families came from Serbia and Montenegro as well as Bosnia – and the total today includes large numbers who moved in the inter-war years.[13] Serb historians, on the other hand, put the total emigration at roughly 60,000, a figure which means accepting the official statistics as accurate and allowing barely 8000 for the period 1878–83.[14] Something in the region of 100,000 seems much more likely as a figure for net emigration, but this is only a guess. And we should not forget that not all of these were Muslims; many hundreds of Orthodox peasants were leaving Hercegovina every year around the turn of the century.[15] Edith Durham, one of the most perceptive of foreign observers and not pro-Austrian in her sympathies, described one simple cause of emigration in the 1900s: 'Wages were low. The peasant was very poor. Very high wages were obtainable in America, and thousands emigrated thither. They ascribed this to Austrian rule, but the same thing was happening in Montenegro . . . It was simply an economic question of supply and demand.'[16]

The main cause for resentment against Austria-Hungary among these Christian peasants was that the great land reform which they expected never took place. This was the most striking example of the Austro-Hungarian policy of continuity and gradualism. At an early stage it was decided that the last major Ottoman reform, the decree of 1859, would remain in force, and that no radical changes would be made thereafter. Some minor things were done to improve the lot of the peasants: the assessment of their crops was entrusted to proper tax commissioners and assessors, a land registry was set up to prevent encroachments by landlords, and a system of 'tithe-averaging' was introduced. (This meant that tithes were calculated on an average of the previous ten years' produce; so a peasant whose production was increasing would pay less than the actual tithe-proportion of his current year's crop.) The right of serfs to free themselves by paying an indemnity – something introduced in a Turkish law of 1876 – was confirmed, and some extra measures were introduced to make it easier for them to do so. Altogether 41,500 serfs freed themselves in this way in the period 1879–1913;

but in early 1914 it was calculated that there were still 93,368 serf families working on agaluk estates, which represented roughly one-third of all arable land.[17] Calling them serfs does not mean, however, that they were all sunk in misery and oppression. The British historian William Miller noted when he visited Bosnia in the 1890s that 'the Bosnian *kmet* is better off than the Dalmatian or Sicilian peasant'; he also observed that the frequent division of estates under Ottoman laws of inheritance had left many agas as little more than peasant smallholders themselves.[18]

While the Austro-Hungarian administrators were cautious about doing anything that would create big social changes, they were extremely energetic in their efforts to develop the Bosnian economy. The only hindrance to their plans was a law passed in Vienna in 1880 which decreed, in an inverted version of the promise made to the Sultan, that the expenses of the Bosnian administration must be covered by Bosnian revenues. This made it difficult to fund the large-scale infrastructure projects which the development of Bosnia required; but special government credits were devised to cover the gap. In the first two years a railway from the Croatian border to Zenica (190 kilometres) was built at a cost of 8 million florins; three years later it was extended to Sarajevo (another eighty kilometres), at a cost of another 4 million.[19] The scale of public investment was colossal: by 1907 the government had built 111 kilometres of broad-gauge railway, 911 of narrow-gauge, more than 1000 kilometres of main roads and the same again of local roads, together with 121 bridges.[20] 'The mountain roads', commented Edith Durham in 1906, 'are second to none in Europe.'[21]

Some of these roads and railways had military purposes, of course; but they were also part of a huge drive for economic improvement. Forestry and coal-mining were strongly developed; other minerals, such as copper and chrome, were also extracted; iron ore was mined at Prijedor, iron and steel works were built, and several chemical factories too. By 1912–13 Bosnia had exports of $28 million and an industrial labour force of more than 65,000.[22] The factory workers in many of the towns were women (mainly Christian, but with some Muslims too); in Sarajevo, for example, they made cigarettes and carpets. The tobacco factory workers even organized a strike for shorter hours and higher pay in 1906. It was settled within five days, but some similar strikes took place in other towns, and at a demonstration of steel-workers in Zenica several people were shot. This strike had no major effect on the politics of the country, though it did encourage the formation of trade unions in many trades and industries in the following year.[23] However, since socialist countries have always hunted through their pre-socialist pasts for heroic episodes of this kind, the 'General Strike' of 1906 looms unnaturally large in modern Yugoslav histories of the period.[24]

Agriculture, the mainstay of the economy, was not neglected by the Austro-Hungarian authorities. Model farms were set up, including a model vineyard near Mostar, and even a model fish-farm; training in modern methods was given to country schoolmasters, and an agricultural college was established at Ilidže near Sarajevo.[25] Stud-farms were established, and, to encourage pride in horse-breeding, race-courses were made at Ilidže and Prijedor. (The races, which became very popular, were not at first conducted by Jockey Club rules: 'They rode barebacked, and as they neared the winning-post they threw themselves off in order to lighten their horses, which raced in by themselves.')[26] Not all of these developments were so fully appreciated by the Bosnian peasantry. One Austro-Hungarian gendarme officer told Edith Durham in 1906 that 'the changes were too quick for the people; they preferred the old Turkish tracks and pack beasts to carts and the new roads, and they suspected everything new'. In his part of Hercegovina, the peasants had refused to use even the iron ploughs which the government supplied at less than cost price. 'We have spent no end of money', he said, 'trying to improve the livestock: bulls, stallions, rams, boars of the finest breed. We sent a splendid boar last year to a village in the charge of a man who was supposed to be reliable. And when Christmas came he killed it, roasted it and asked all the village to a feast.'[27]

One of the most controversial aspects of the agricultural policy was the encouragement of foreign settlers. The first of these colonists had in fact come on the initiative of a German priest, who put an advertisement in a religious magazine in Germany appealing for pious farmers to come and settle in Bosnia. Families from Silesia and the Rhineland arrived, bought land near the Croatian border and built a settlement which was officially recognized under the name of 'Windhorst'. An offshoot of it was named 'Rudolfstal' after Crown Prince Rudolf's visit to Bosnia in 1888, and another settlement, by Protestant ethnic Germans from Hungary, was called 'Franzjosefsfeld'. The government looked favourably on these farmers and gave them tax concessions; and in 1890 it passed a special law on 'agrarian colonies', offering up to twelve hectares per family, rent-free for the first three years and then on a low mortgage which would end after ten years if they took Bosnian citizenship. Altogether fifty-four such colonies were established, with a population of nearly 10,000. Fewer than 2000 of these were ethnic Germans; the majority were Slavs (Poles, Czechs and Ruthenians), whose descendants have merged with the Bosnian Slav population. But whatever the origins of the settlers, the policy was resented at the time, and when the Bosnians first acquired a parliament in 1910 one of their earliest demands was that it be stopped.[28] By then, the perpetual increase in the foreign population of Bosnia was beginning to worry local political leaders. In 1880 there were only 4500 Austrian and 12,000 Hungarian citizens in Bosnia; in 1910 there were 47,000 of the former and 61,000 of the latter. But the figures are not quite as alarming as they seem. Many of these people were administrators or businessmen who were not intending to settle there permanently. Some were soldiers: as a general rule, Austro-Hungarian soldiers were stationed in Bosnia and Bosnian soldiers in Austria-Hungary. And of the Hungarian citizens, the majority were Croats and only a small minority were Magyars.[29] Apart from the promotion of 'agrarian colonies', the main purpose of which was agricultural rather than demographic, there was never any serious policy of mass colonization; but there was enough of an influx to remind the people of Bosnia that they were indeed under a kind of colonial rule.

On the whole, the Austro-Hungarian administrators understood such sensitivities and tried to allow for them. Each community continued to have its own schools, which were now subsidized by the state; and a shariat school, to train judges for the Muslim courts, was built by the authorities in 1887. In the system of free state schools which the administration set up, members of each religious community were given instruction separately by their own clergy.

Modern Yugoslav writers have poured scorn on the educational efforts of the Austro-Hungarian government, pointing out that only a minority of children attended school. But no government which builds nearly 200 primary schools, three high schools, a technical school and a teacher-training college can be described as utterly negligent in its education policy. Peasants who refused to use iron ploughs were unlikely to rush to send their children to acquire an education which they themselves had never received. Compulsory education was introduced in 1909; until then the policy was the one aptly summarized by William Miller: 'A parent is not compelled to send his children to school at all, but arguments are used by the local authorities to persuade him of the advantages of education should he desire to keep his offspring ignorant.'[30]

The handling of the three main religious communities was by far the most delicate task facing the Austro-Hungarian administration. Subsidizing their schools was partly, of course, a way of gaining their cooperation and exercising a degree of control. Efforts were made to ensure that the Austro-Hungarian authorities would also control the appointment of the senior figures in each religious group: the Emperor was granted by the Orthodox Patriarch the right to appoint the bishops in Bosnia, and a similar right to nominate Catholic bishops was obtained from the Pope. The Muslims themselves suggested the creation of a religious hierarchy in Bosnia independent of Istanbul, and in 1882 this was done with the appointment by the Emperor of a *Reis ul-ulema* ('head of the religious community'), who presided over a four-man *medžlis* or council of advisers.

Of the three religious organizations, the Catholic Church was the one most visibly growing and changing. The Franciscans lost their monopoly and the Jesuits were brought into the country; two seminaries were established for the Jesuits to teach in; and a Catholic cathedral was built in Sarajevo, followed by a new church of St Anthony of Padua. The influx of people from Austria-Hungary swelled the Catholic population (which grew in Sarajevo itself from 800 in 1878 to 3876 only six years later), and with four bishops and a particularly determined archbishop (Monsignor Stadler, who served in Sarajevo for the whole period from 1882 to 1918), the Catholic Church was more active than it had ever been in the previous thousand-odd years of Bosnian history.[31] But the authorities were conscious of the danger of turning the Bosnian Catholics into a privileged community. William Miller, writing in 1898, was impressed by the circumspection of their policy:

> The Roman Catholics . . . who had long looked to Austria for aid and naturally welcomed her advent as that of a great Catholic Power, have felt somewhat disappointed that they, who form little more than a fifth of the population, have not been allowed to act as 'the predominant partner' in the Bosnian firm. To my mind there can be no better proof of the even-handed treatment which these various confessions have received from the Government, than that such disappointments should be felt.[32]

And the American journalist W. E. Curtis, who visited Bosnia in 1902, formed a similar impression of even-handedness: 'Members of the different religious faiths mix with each other on amicable terms and show mutual respect and mutual toleration; the courts are wisely and honestly administered, justice is awarded to every citizen, regardless of his religion or social position.'[33] But from time to time religious concerns could still throw a spanner in the works of the most carefully constructed state machinery.

The most disruptive problem was that of conversions. These cases usually involved Muslim girls being converted to Catholicism by their husbands-to-be, and thereby causing great scandal and shame to their own families. Although the Catholic priests did not go out openly proselytizing among the Muslims, they did everything in their power to assist those who came to them – hiding girls in convents or in Archbishop Stadler's residence, for example, and refusing to reveal their whereabouts to the police. After several incidents of this kind the authorities gave in to Muslim pressure in 1891 and enacted a 'Conversion Statute', which laid down a procedure for disputed cases: a two-month waiting period, a government commission to investigate any charge of coercion, and so on. This calmed the fears of the Muslims; but twelve years later, when Archbishop Stadler was involved in another controversial case involving a Muslim widow and her two children, he revealed that the government had made a covert agreement with the Pope in 1895 which granted the Catholic clergy the right to communicate with potential converts – thus secretly undermining the Conversion Statute. Once again there was great anger among the Muslims, whose leaders campaigned vigorously, presenting petitions and lists of other grievances too. However, they were pacified when the widow in this latest case was located by the government in a convent, seized by gendarmes and returned to her village, where she agreed to become a Muslim again.[34]

Popular feelings were certainly aroused by such events; but the way in which these incidents were taken up by leading Muslims and associated with other concerns (complaints about taxes, etc.) indicates an increasingly sophisticated political strategy on their part, something very different from blind fanaticism. As one detailed modern study of these events says: 'The Muslim activists were careful to cloak their goals in the garb of religious devotion, but their real objective was to preserve or increase their own power.'[35] An elaborate contest for power went on during the first two decades of Austro-Hungarian rule, with the Muslim élite of Sarajevo acquiring power and influence by cooperating with the government, and the more hard-line Muslim leaders of Travnik and Mostar taking up uncompromising positions in order to discredit their Sarajevan rivals and take over some of their power. (In the 1890s the pattern became further complicated, with strong rivalries developing among the Mostar Muslims as well.)

The most important issue was control of the charitable-religious foundations. As mentioned in chapter 5, these foundations, known as vakufs, played an essential role in Islamic society, funding the upkeep of mosques, schools, tekkes and even inns and bridges. Their special fiscal status had been an invitation to massive abuse over the centuries: all the donor had to do was appoint his descendants as salaried administrators of the incomes in perpetuity, and he had in effect created an almost tax-free family trust. By 1878 it was estimated that nearly one-third of all usable land in Bosnia was owned by vakufs; and it was a basic principle of Islamic law that once a property had become vakuf land it could never revert to ordinary ownership. One of the first things the Austro-Hungarians did was to collect and repromulgate all the Ottoman laws which had tried to regulate the vakuf administrations, requiring proper accounting, and so on. They then set up a Vakuf Commission in

1883, with a membership of senior Muslims nominated by the government: it placed local family-administered vakufs under central control, drew up proper budgets and planned a Bosnia-wide policy for the funding of mosques and schools. Although this was widely accepted as a useful reform, the Commission was dominated by the more cooperative of the Sarajevo Muslims, and therefore became an object of jealousy and resentment on the part of senior Muslims elsewhere. And even when the Vakuf Commission was expanded in 1894 to take in representatives of all the regions of Bosnia, those representatives were still appointed by the government.[36]

It was the Muslims of Mostar, under their determined leader Mula Mustafa Džabić, who turned the question of vakuf administration into a large-scale political issue. Riding high on a wave of petitioning and other activities stimulated by the conversion scandals, they presented a draft statute in 1899 for an autonomous 'Vakuf Assembly' for Hercegovina. Instead of being organized by government appointment from the top down, the structure they proposed would be based on local associations: those associations would appoint the members of district assemblies, and the district assemblies would send deputies to the provincial assembly.[37] The government's first reaction was to treat these Muslims as dangerous agitators and close down the club which was the focus of their activities. Immediately, the Mostar leaders began organizing support throughout Hercegovina and Bosnia too. Using the moral authority of Džabić and the energies of younger activists such as Šerif Arnautović, they formed a country-wide organization – in effect, an embryonic political party – within a year, and held an assembly of Bosnian Muslim leaders in a Budapest hotel in the summer of 1900. And so began a long process of agitation and negotiation, with the authorities trying alternately to woo, conciliate, divide and suppress the campaigners.[38]

This growth of Muslim activism was especially unwelcome to the man in charge of Bosnia at the time, Benjámin Kállay, the historian and former diplomat who was Common Minister of Finance from 1882 to 1903. Kállay's whole Bosnian policy had aimed at insulating the country from the nationalist political movements in Serbia and Croatia, and developing the idea of Bosnian nationhood as a separate and unifying factor. The Turks had in fact used a word meaning 'Bosnians' (*bosnaklar*) to refer to all those who lived in Bosnia; but in Serbo-Croat the only people who had traditionally called themselves 'Bosnians' (*Bošnjaci*) were the Bosnian Muslims.[39] (The Catholics had referred to themselves as *latinci*, 'Latins', or *krisčjani*, a word for 'Christians' – not to be confused with the medieval *krstjani* – and the Orthodox had called themselves *Vlasi*, 'Vlachs', or *hrisčjani*, another word for 'Christians'.) Kállay hoped to extend the term 'Bosnian' to people of all religious communities; and it was essential for his purposes that the idea of Bosnian nationhood should be taken up first by the Muslims. He knew that his best chance lay with them, since unlike the Catholics and the Orthodox they had no sponsor-nation to look to outside Bosnia's borders, and it was clear that if they developed their own separate identity instead, his whole project would fail.

Kállay had some success with the more cooperative Muslims of Sarajevo, who saw this line of thought as a natural continuation of the tradition of seeking Bosnian autonomy under the Ottomans. Their leader, a prominent former mayor of Sarajevo, Mehmed-beg Kapetanović, founded a journal in 1891 entitled *Bošnjak* – 'The Bosnian'. Though addressed to readers of all kinds, it was essentially a Muslim journal which attacked conservative attitudes in the Muslim clergy and tried to fend off the attempts of both Croat and Serb nationalists to argue that the Muslims of Bosnia were 'really' Croats or Serbs. 'Whereas the Croats argue that the Orthodox are our greatest enemies and that Serbdom is the same as Orthodoxy, the Serbs wear themselves out calling our attention to some bogus history, by which they have Serbianized the whole world', declared the *Bošnjak*. And again: 'We shall never deny that we belong to the South Slav family; but we shall remain Bosnians, like our forefathers, and nothing else.'[40]

Kállay's project would not have seemed absurd to anyone who looked only at the history of Bosnia up to a generation or so before the Austro-Hungarian occupation. As we have seen, the Catholics and Orthodox of Bosnia had long maintained their religious links with the Croats and the Serbs. During the Ottoman centuries there were separate religious identities in Bosnia, and those identities could indeed have political implications: many Bosnian Catholics had looked to the lands beyond the Croatian and Dalmatian border for support or even liberation. But that was a matter of religion, not nationhood. Those Catholics were looking to Catholic Austria, or Catholic Venice, or to other Catholics who happened to be Croats; they were not looking to the nation of Croats as such. Only in the mid-nineteenth century at the earliest did the modern idea of nationhood begin to spread from Croatia and Serbia to the Catholics and Orthodox of Bosnia. Of the three basic criteria by which the Croat and Serb nations established and distinguished themselves during this period – history, language and religion – only religion could apply in Bosnia, a country which had its own separate history and in which the contours of the linguistic map cut across all religious boundaries. There had never been any purely economic or social reasons for Catholic-Orthodox hostility in Bosnia; and the reasons which had existed for hostility to the Muslims were partly eliminated by Austro-Hungarian rule. One English writer in 1897 commented on the attitude of the Christians to the Muslims in Bosnia as follows:

> It is strange that they should bear so little hatred to their former oppressors, and the explanation lies probably in the fact that they are all of the same race. Whatever the reason may be it fully bears out the contention of all who have studied the country in Turkish times, that . . . the deplorable condition of the people was due to agrarian rather than to religious causes, and that if these causes could be removed, the ill-feeling engendered by them would gradually die out.[41]

Had Kállay somehow been able to isolate Bosnia's Orthodox and Catholics utterly from the religious, cultural and political developments in neighbouring lands, his policy might have stood a chance; but such total isolation would have been quite impossible. As Croat and Serb nationalism spread among the Catholic and Orthodox Bosnians through the very networks of priests, schoolteachers and educated newspaper-readers which Austro-Hungarian policy had helped to bring into being, Kállay's 'Bošnjak' project became more and more obviously doomed to failure. By 1908 a clear-eyed observer such as the Austrian MP Joseph Baernreither could pronounce it dead.[42]

Outside Bosnia's borders, meanwhile, the crassness of Austro-

Hungarian policy was inflaming Croatian and Serbian nationalism with every year that passed. The Hungarian governor of Croatia pursued a deliberate policy of setting Croats against Serbs, and resentment was stirred up by absurdly unnecessary measures such as a decree that all railway officials in Croatia should speak Magyar. Relations between the Dual Monarchy and Serbia deteriorated, and the fact that Serbia's commerce was overwhelmingly dependent on Austria-Hungary only made the Serbs chafe more impatiently at Habsburg dominance of the region. When Serbia tried to find outlets for trade elsewhere in 1906, the Austro-Hungarians retaliated by imposing punitive duties on the main Serbian export, pigs. (This so-called 'pig-war', like so many sanctions operations in modern history, actually encouraged the development of more trading outlets.) Relations were now exceptionally bitter between the two states. The Austro-Hungarian Foreign Minister, Baron von Aehrenthal, began to consider seriously an eventual take-over of Serbia, and Austro-Hungarian opinion in Bosnia favoured the idea of extending the Empire to Salonica too: travelling through Bosnia in 1906, Edith Durham noted that 'the Austrians . . . were anxious to consolidate their position in Bosnia as far as possible, so as to be ready for a forward move. "Nach Salonik" was a favourite topic of conversation.'[43]

It was in this context that the decision was made to change Bosnia's status from an occupied Ottoman territory to a land fully annexed by the Austro-Hungarian Empire. What finally prompted the move was the revolution of the Young Turks in 1908. This looked as if it would create a regime in Istanbul which might plausibly reclaim Turkey's rights over Bosnia, by offering a more democratic constitution to the Bosnians than the one they enjoyed under Austro-Hungarian rule. Baron von Aehrenthal acted swiftly, announcing the full annexation of Bosnia on 5 October 1908. The effect on public opinion in Serbia was explosive: nationalists there felt that the potential prize of Bosnian territory had been snatched unfairly from their grasp. Mass meetings were held in Belgrade, and soon afterwards two secret societies were formed to campaign for pan-Serb unification: 'Narodna Odbrana' ('National Defence') and 'Ujedjenje ili Smrt' ('Unification or Death' – also known as 'Crna Ruka', 'The Black Hand'). By the end of 1908 there were already several branches of Narodna Odbrana in Bosnia.[44] Serbia was restrained from declaring war on Austria-Hungary by the Russian Foreign Minister, Izvolsky, who, though he himself was smarting at the way he had been wrong-footed by von Aehrenthal, still advised Belgrade: 'Serbia must remain quiet, and should do nothing which could provoke Austria and provide an opportunity for annihilating Serbia.'[45] The Austro-Hungarian and Turkish governments eventually signed an agreement in February 1909, under which the former would acquire full rights over Bosnia, withdraw from the Sandžak of Novi Pazar, guarantee full freedom of religion for Bosnian Muslims and pay 2,500,000 Turkish pounds to Istanbul; but still the diplomatic crisis rumbled on for months.[46] The interaction of great power rivalry and Balkan small-state nationalism which this incident displayed was an ominous foreshadowing of the events of August 1914.

But the main effect of the annexation on Bosnia's internal life was actually beneficial. The authorities in Vienna and Budapest felt that they now held Bosnia more securely, and became more willing to allow political life within it. Under the liberal-minded Common Minister of Finance Baron Burián (who held the post from 1903 to 1912), some large concessions were made: first, in 1909, the Muslims were granted the system of vakuf administration for which they had so persistently campaigned, and then, in the following year, a Bosnian parliament was elected. True, it was based on a limited franchise and had no direct legislative power. But it did enable the various organizations which the local communities had set up in recent years – the Muslim National Organization (1906), the Serbian National Organization (1907) and the Croatian National Society (1908) – to begin to function as real political parties.[47]

Only members of the more educated or more prosperous elites of each community played any active role in these parties, of course. This fact helps to explain why the two main Christian parties did not campaign fiercely for land reform, even though most of the people they claimed to represent were peasants. Sheer parliamentary arithmetic also mattered: with the number of MPs reflecting quite closely the general proportions in the population (37 Orthodox, 29 Muslim, 23 Catholic, 1 Jewish), neither of the two Christian groups could dominate on its own, and they soon found themselves competing for Muslim cooperation.[48] In 1911 the Catholics won the competition and formed an agreement with the Muslim leaders, who regarded them as less likely to support any agrarian reforms.

This courting of the Muslims was merely the political counterpart of a process of intellectual and cultural courtship which had been going on for at least a decade, as each side tried to establish that Bosnian Muslims were 'really' Croats or 'really' Serbs. During most of that period the Croats had had more success in terms of cultural identification, especially with Muslim intellectuals who had spent time in Zagreb or at other Austro-Hungarian universities frequented by Croats. The leading Muslim cultural association in Sarajevo, 'Gajret' (founded in 1903), was dominated in its early years by Croatian-inclined writers such as the poet and historian Safvet-beg Bašagić.[49] But at the same time there had been more political cooperation, though of a loose and informal kind, between Muslim leaders and Serbs in the years before the formation of the parliament. The Serbs had had their own campaign, led by another Mostar activist, Vojislav Šola, for a more autonomous religious organization; they had sent their own delegation to lobby alongside the Muslims in Budapest in 1900, and had even held a joint conference with them in the following year.[50] All three sides were playing a delicate game of political opportunism, and the alignments were always fluid. Though some prominent Muslim intellectuals 'declared' themselves as Croats or Serbs, such individual acts never undermined the general position of the Muslims, who were now firmly established as a distinct political entity. As Robert Donia, the leading expert on this period, has put it: 'the declarations were mostly tactical and political in character; some Muslims changed from one camp to another on several occasions. Simply stated, a separate Muslim identity was too advanced to be easily renounced by any significant number of Muslims.'[51]

We can only speculate about how effective and how stable these inter-faith, inter-party arrangements would have been, had they been allowed to develop unhindered over a decade or two. But it was not to be. The ferment of Serbian nationalism, stirred up after the annexation, was spreading among parts of the Bosnian Orthodox population – or at least, among a few hundred schoolboys and students. Anti-Austro-Hungarian feeling was growing stronger in Croatia too, and in the period 1907–10 it increasingly took the form of cooperation with Serbs in the project of establishing a common South Slav state. One marvellously cumbersome expression of this new attitude was the name of a students' organization which operated in universities outside Bosnia, presided over by the young Bosnian writer Ivo Andrić: it called itself 'The Croat-Serb or Serb-Croat or Yugoslav Progressive Youth Movement'.[52] Inside Bosnia, the Serb students began soon after 1910 to change their position from a narrow Serb nationalism to a broader, pro-Yugoslav campaign. One loose grouping of schoolboys and students, 'Mlada Bosna' ('Young Bosnia'), adopted this stance, which was the simplest common position on which all anti-Habsburgs could unite; and their membership could thus include Croats and even some Muslims as well.[53] As the most famous member of Mlada Bosna, Gavrilo Princip, put it at his trial in 1914: 'I am a Yugoslav nationalist, aiming for the unification of all Yugoslavs, and I do not care what form of state, but it must be free from Austria.'[54]

Much has been written about the political philosophy of these young activists – perhaps too much, as there is a limit to the amount of philosophically interesting material to be found in the heads of a loose assortment of idealistic but ill-educated teenagers. They were fiercely anti-clerical; they wanted social revolution just as much as national liberation; they were especially keen on the writings of anarchists or anarcho-socialists such as Bakunin, Herzen and Kropotkin; and above all they wanted to be heroes. The first in a succession of hero-martyr-assassins was a depressive student from Hercegovina called Bogdan Žerajić, who went to Sarajevo on the opening day of the new Bosnian parliament in 1910, fired five shots at the military governor as he left the ceremony, missed with every one of them and then used the sixth bullet to kill himself.[55] In the summer of 1912 a Bosnian Croat, Luka Jukić, tried to assassinate the governor of Croatia in Zagreb. Earlier that year Jukić had helped to organize protest demonstrations of schoolboys in Sarajevo, together with Gavrilo Princip and several other youths who would later be involved in Princip's assassination plans in 1914. On this occasion, as one boy noted in his diary, 'Princip went from class to class, threatening with his knuckle-duster all the boys who wavered in coming to the new demonstrations.'[56]

What brought people onto the streets later in 1912 was not Princip's knuckle-duster but the dramatic events happening to the east and south of Bosnia. In October Montenegro and Serbia declared war on Turkey, and with the help of Bulgaria and Greece they drove the Turkish forces out of the Sandžak of Novi Pazar, Kosovo and Macedonia. The speed and scale of the Serbian and Montenegrin victories in this First Balkan War caused a great upsurge of feeling among the anti-Habsburg activists in Bosnia and Croatia. Many members of Mlada Bosna rushed off to serve as volunteers with the Serbian forces; their numbers even included some Muslim boys.[57] They either did not know or did not care that the Serbs and their allies were slaughtering Muslim Albanian villagers, causing tens of thousands of Slav Muslims to flee from Macedonia and subjecting Bulgarian-speaking Muslims to forced conversions.[58]

By the spring of 1913 relations between Austria-Hungary and Serbia were extremely tense. Serbia's conquests had already almost doubled the size of its territories, and if it acquired part of the Albanian coastland too (as indeed it intended) it might pose a strategic threat to the Austro-Hungarians in the Adriatic. With a war between the two powers now seen as imminent, the military governor of Bosnia, General Potiorek, imposed a security clamp-down. He declared a state of emergency on 2 May, dissolved parliament and suspended the civil courts, closed down many Serb associations and took the administration of all Bosnian schools into his own hands.[59] The immediate crisis passed when the First Balkan War was ended by the Treaty of London on 30 May; and the victorious allies then fought among themselves in the Second Balkan War in June and July. But General Potiorek's hard-line policy was now entrenched in Bosnia; the Common Minister of Finance, Leon von Bilinski (who had replaced Burián in 1912) favoured a more subtle policy of playing different Bosnian groups off against one another and cultivating the Serb merchant and professional classes, but Potiorek's more crudely anti-Serb policy prevailed.[60]

And so the stage was set for the great summer manoeuvres of

the Austro-Hungarian army in Bosnia in 1914, and the trip to observe them by Archduke Franz Ferdinand, heir to the Habsburg throne and Inspector General of the Armed Forces of the Empire. With overwhelming stupidity his visit to Sarajevo was fixed for 28 June, the anniversary of the Battle of Kosovo and therefore the most sacred day in the mystical calendar of Serb nationalism. Following an itinerary which had been published the previous day in the *Bosnische Post*, his convoy of limousines drove past no fewer than six Mlada Bosna assassins armed with bombs and pistols. Five failed to act; one, Nedeljko Čabrinović, threw a bomb which bounced off the back of the Archduke's car and wounded the people in the car behind. Gavrilo Princip took up a new position further down the official itinerary for the day, on the corner of Franz Josef Street. Meanwhile the Archduke decided to change the route, because he wanted to go straight to the hospital to visit the wounded officers; but no one told his driver, who turned into Franz Josef Street as planned. General Potiorek told him to stop and go back. And so he reversed slowly past the exact spot at which Princip was standing. 'Where I aimed I do not know,' Princip told the investigating magistrate. 'But I know that I aimed at the Heir Apparent. I believe that I fired twice, perhaps more, because I was so excited. Whether I hit the victims or not, I cannot tell, because instantly people started to hit me.'[61] Both the Archduke and his wife, the Duchess of Hohenberg, died slowly from their wounds. Exactly one month later, Austria-Hungary declared war on Serbia.

12

War and the kingdom: Bosnia 1914–1941

Historians still argue over whether it was Serb nationalism or Yugoslavism, Serbian secret societies or sheer local initiative that had caused the assassination to happen. Many Bosnians made up their minds very quickly about who was to blame: on the evening of 28 June 1914 there were anti-Serb demonstrations and riots in Sarajevo, with the destruction of Serb-owned shops and houses. The new Reis ul-ulema, Džemaludin Čaušević, spoke out publicly against this pogrom and took some Serbs into his protection.[1] Some leading Bosnian Serbs also felt there was a burden of Serb guilt to be absolved, and when the war began they petitioned the authorities to let them go straight to the front line against Serbia and display their loyalty to the Emperor.[2] The fact that most of the conspirators were Bosnian Serbs seemed significant; and when it emerged that the chief perpetrators, Princip and Čabrinović, had been studying in Belgrade, had acquired their bombs there and had crossed with them into Bosnia, the evidence seemed damning. It is clear that they did receive some help from an agent of the Narodna Odbrana organization who also worked for Colonel Apis, the head of Serbian Military Intelligence.[3] Many theories still circulate about Apis's involvement and his possible political motives; but the idea that the Serbian government itself had planned the assassination can be firmly rejected.

Even the Austro-Hungarian government did not accuse Serbia of direct responsibility for what had happened. Their ultimatum of 23 July complained merely that the Serbian government had 'tolerated the machinations of various societies and associations directed against the monarchy, unrestrained language on the part of the press, glorification of the perpetrators of outrages, participation of officers and officials in subversive agitation' – all of which was essentially true. Of the ten demands made for the suppression of these activities by Austria-Hungary, Serbia accepted all but one, which would have involved the presence of Austro-Hungarian magistrates or policemen conducting their investigation on Serbian soil.[4] This demurral on one point was sufficient for those in Budapest, Vienna and Berlin – above all, Berlin – who wanted a war. Historians used to write as if the war had been caused by an impersonal thing called 'the international system'; but it is now widely agreed that Germany was pushing hard for a war, in order to put some decisive check on the growing power of Russia.[5] The Austro-Hungarians were more hesitant, fearing Russia's involvement (as the protector of Serbia) as much as the Germans hoped for it. Although there were ministers in the Austro-Hungarian government who wanted to take punitive action against Serbia, they had no serious plan of territorial advancement in the Balkans: on the contrary, the Hungarian minister Tisza insisted (because of the traditional Hungarian fears of acquiring too many Slavs) that no Serbian territory should be annexed. Even when Austria-Hungary had contemplated war with Serbia in 1906 and 1913, it had never really known what it would do with the country if it conquered it. And while Serbia itself obviously did want to acquire the territory of Bosnia, it had never supposed that it could win an all-out war against the Austro-Hungarian Empire. Within this local Balkan context, therefore, there were strong reasons for hostility but not sufficient reasons for war. Without German pressure, the assassination at Sarajevo would probably not have caused even a serious Balkan war – and certainly not a war in which all the great powers of the world became engulfed.

The Serbs fought heroically. Many of the Austro-Hungarian troops who were sent into Serbia under the command of the military governor of Bosnia, General Potiorek, were also Serbs, from Bosnia itself and the former military frontier districts of Croatia. Orthodox fighting against Orthodox: it was a return to the old days of Habsburg-Ottoman warfare. But among the Austro-Hungarian soldiers there were many Muslims and Catholics too, the latter including a young half-Croat, half-Slovenian called Josip Broz – later better known as Tito. During 1914 the Austro-Hungarian army was twice repulsed on Serbian soil, with huge losses on both sides. Serbia held out until the late summer of 1915; then, with a new offensive against it under the German General von Mackensen and the entry of Bulgaria into the war on the German and Austrian side, the Serbian army conducted its epic retreat, with massive loss of life, through the mountains of northern Albania to the Adriatic coast. The survivors of that retreat were eventually to join the allied army which fought at Salonica; from there they worked their way up through Macedonia and Serbia in the autumn of 1918, reconquering Belgrade on 1 November and then moving into Bosnia and the Vojvodina.

Within the Serbian army there were many volunteers from Bosnia and the other Slav territories of Austria-Hungary. Nearly 5000 Bosnians were known to have joined the 'First Serbian Volunteer Division', and there were also three battalions of volunteers from Hercegovina in the Montenegrin army.[6] So it is not altogether surprising that the authorities in Bosnia, first under Potiorek and then under his successor, Baron Sarkotić, took some heavy-handed actions against Serb nationalists, political activists and other potential sympathizers with the Serbian cause. Serbs from the eastern border region of Bosnia were resettled in the west of the country, for fear of fifth-column activities, and roughly 5000 Serb families were driven across the border into Serbia or Montenegro.[7] There were arrests and internments too; the future novelist Ivo Andrić, for example, who had returned to Bosnia the moment he heard of the assassination, was arrested on 29 July and held in a succession of prisons in Dalmatia and Slovenia. (He was eventually kept in a kind of internal exile at a village near his home town of Travnik, until the general amnesty for such cases in 1917.)[8] At least 3300 and possibly as many as 5500 Bosnian suspects, mainly Serbs, were held in internment camps in Bosnia and Hungary; between 700 and 2200 are thought to have died there. The crackdown on Mlada Bosna and other groupings of schoolboys and students was severe: 142 such individuals were put on trial in 1915. And at the most famous of these proceedings, a trial of people associated with the Narodna Odbrana movement, held in Banja Luka in 1916, 156 were accused, of whom sixteen were sentenced to death and eighty-six to hard labour.[9] Such actions, as might have been expected, achieved little for the Austro-Hungarian war effort but a great deal for the Serbian and/or Yugoslav nationalist cause.

The majority of Bosnians, whatever their misgivings, remained loyal to the Austro-Hungarian state. Though some Muslims did serve as volunteers in the Serbian army, most had no wish to see their country swallowed up in some post-war expansion of Serbia; their leaders had been happy to make tactical alliances with the Bosnian Serbs in the fifteen years before the war in order to gain particular concessions from the government, but that had been a different matter.[10] The Bosnian Croats were more divided, reflecting the divergence of opinion within Croatia itself. An interesting analysis of the Bosnian Croats' position comes in a letter from the director of the Catholic seminary in Travnik to the Austrian government. Some, he said, wanted to join Serbia, while others were absolutely against it. Those who wanted unconditional unification with Serbia were mainly among the intelligentsia, and some of these were even willing to give up their Catholicism: 'their "Freedom from Rome" tendencies chime with their political "Freedom from Austria" tendencies'.[11]

Among the leading politicians from Croatia itself, some of whom now joined a 'Yugoslav Committee' in exile, no one envisaged conversion to Orthodoxy as the price of union with Serbia; they wanted to preserve the distinct identity of Croatia within a future Yugoslav state, and were suspicious of any plans that would amount to the creation of a 'Greater Serbia'. Their suspicions were strongly reinforced in 1915 when the Serbian government accepted an arrangement under which large parts of Dalmatia, Istria and Slovenia would be carved off and given to Italy, as a reward for Italy's entry into the war on the side of the allies. Such moves strengthened the arguments of those politicians still active inside the Austro-Hungarian territories who preferred an expanded version of the old 'Trialist' solution: a unified Yugoslav entity as an equal partner with Austria and Hungary within a continuing Habsburg Empire. That was the position taken by the leading representative of the Slovenians in the Austrian parliament, Monsignor Korošec.[12]

On 30 May 1917 Korošec and some of his colleagues issued a declaration calling for the unification of 'all the lands in the

Monarchy inhabited by Slovenes, Croats, and Serbs'. This 'May Declaration' had a powerful effect in Bosnia, and many of the Bosnian Serb and Croat politicians were won over to it. The Serbs welcomed the explicit inclusion of Serbs in the proposal (an advance on all previous versions of Trialism), and naturally saw it as the closest thing to a Yugoslav state that could be achieved under Austro-Hungarian rule. Moderate Bosnian Croats were in favour of such a plan; the conservative Catholics, led by Archbishop Stadler, preferred a more limited version of the same idea, in which the entity in question would include Bosnia but have the character of a Greater Croatia. The Muslims were more divided, however. When two of the leading Muslim politicians, Šerif Arnautović and Safvet-beg Bašagić, went to see the Emperor in August 1917, they asked instead for Bosnian autonomy within Hungary.[13] This idea, presented as a stronger, more independent version of the status which Croatia already enjoyed, was really a revival of the old dream of autonomy which had preoccupied leading Bosnian Muslims since the days of Husejn-kapetan in the 1830s. Its main appeal was that it would prevent the swallowing up of Bosnia into a Croatian-dominated state; most Muslims were keen to avoid that, though Safvet-beg Bašagić himself was so pro-Croat in his general outlook that he was able to shift a little later to a 'Greater Croatia' position.[14] But there were many Muslims who regarded even autonomy under Hungary as an unsatisfactory compromise, and were willing to take the plunge into a separate Yugoslav state. These included the Reis ul-ulema, Čaušević, who told Monsignor Korošec in 1917 that he had had enough of being ruled by Turks or Germans.[15]

The Austro-Hungarian authorities dithered over these various proposals and did nothing. By the time they began to take them seriously, in the spring of 1918, it was already too late. In February of that year there was a mutiny in the Austro-Hungarian fleet in Montenegro; desertions and strikes were increasing daily, and overall defeat now had to be contemplated. The governor of Bosnia, Baron Sarkotić, began a series of meetings and discussions to try to thrash out some political rearrangement which might offer a way of preserving Habsburg rule. First he recommended to the Emperor in March that Bosnia be joined to Croatia; then in May he suggested that Bosnia might either join Croatia, or have autonomy as a 'corpus separatum' under the Hungarian crown; then, when these issues were discussed at the Imperial council at the end of May, he came down in favour of union with Croatia again.[16] In August, as the Austro-Hungarian war effort was faltering day by day, Monsignor Korošec organized a new meeting of politicians which abandoned the idea of Austro-Hungarian sovereignty altogether, proclaiming a 'National Council' for the purpose of 'uniting the Yugoslav people within an independent state'. With the end now in sight, the Emperor sent the Hungarian minister Count Tisza to visit Zagreb and Sarajevo in September, in a final doomed attempt to persuade the local politicians to accept a new constitutional arrangement under the Hungarian crown.

The replies Tisza received in Sarajevo give an interesting picture of the attitudes of the leading Bosnian politicians. The Serbs and Croats (led by the Serb politician Vojislav Šola) presented a joint memorandum in which they said they were all one people and wished to form a Yugoslav state with all the Serbs, Croats and Slovenes. They complained bitterly of wartime measures such as the suppression of local government, requisitions and political trials. Their demands included a full amnesty for political prisoners and the restoration of constitutional rule, with free elections for a new parliament. Among the Muslim leaders, Arnautović was still in favour of autonomy under Hungary, and Bašagić was willing to make that his second preference, after unification with Croatia. But the dominant attitude was expressed by a man who was then secretary of the Chamber of Commerce, but would become the leading Bosnian politician of the inter-war years: Mehmed Spaho. He too complained bitterly of the treatment of the people of Bosnia during the war, especially the requisitions of supplies and the conscription of old men and teenagers into the army. He said that divisions between the Muslims and the other religious communities had been softened by the misery of war; partly as a result of this experience, he declared, most of the Muslims of Bosnia were now in favour of the creation of a Yugoslav state.[17]

The end came quickly. In October a general meeting of the 'National Council' was held in Zagreb; Bosnian delegates who attended it returned to Sarajevo and set up their own National Council for Bosnia. On 29 October the Croatian parliament formally renounced the rule of the Habsburgs and handed over power to the National Council, declaring that a new sovereign state of Slovenes, Croats and Serbs was now in existence. This announcement, although applying only to the former Austro-Hungarian lands, clearly signalled the imminent creation of a Yugoslav state. With unification with the Kingdom of Serbia just days away, and with the Serbian army now close to Bosnian territory, it was the Serbs who felt most like victors among the people of Bosnia. Baron Sarkotić reported on 29 October: 'In Sarajevo the exaggerated joy of the Serbs seems to have had, to a certain extent, a calming effect on the Croats and Muslims.'[18] The leaders of the Bosnian National Council came to see him on the following day; they had various requests, such as stopping the requisitioning of livestock, but curiously they did not ask him to hand over power. It was the Ministry of War in Vienna that told him, by telegraph that evening, that all military forces in Bosnia should be put at the disposal of the National Council. On 1 November Sarkotić invited the army commanders and the leaders of the National Council to see him and told them that he was stepping down. One of the politicians, the Bosnian Croat leader Josip Sunarić, asked him to free the political prisoners. His reply was simple: 'You are in power now.' Two days later the 'First National Government of Bosnia and Hercegovina' was formed.[19]

The first consequence of the collapse of Austro-Hungarian power was a general outbreak of anarchy and peasant *jacqueries* in the countryside. The worst cases were in northern Croatia, where many of the big estates were ransacked and their livestock stolen. When this also happened in Bosnia it tended to be Muslims who were the victims of these attacks, since they owned most of the larger estates. But there was also an element of Serb triumphalism against Muslims as such, especially after the arrival of Serbian and Montenegrin soldiers in early November. In March 1919 the Reis ul-ulema, Džemaludin Čaušević, told a French journalist that 1000 Muslim men had been killed, seventy-six women had been burnt to death and 270 villages had been pillaged with the assistance, passive or active, of the Serbian troops. When the journalist published this statement in *Le Temps*, the new government in Belgrade put pressure on the Reis ul-ulema to withdraw it.[20] These atrocities can scarcely be seen, however, as evidence of ancient ethnic-religious hatred among Bosnian Serbs and Muslims. They happened in extreme and unusual circumstances, at the very end of a war in which people had suffered severe privations. (How many died altogether in Bosnia, from military action and typhus, is hard to calculate: there was a demographic loss of more than 300,000, nearly one-sixth of the population, between 1910 and 1921, but this loss also includes Muslims who fled in a second wave of emigration to Turkey after 1918.)[21] Throughout the war, Muslims in Bosnia had generally been regarded as loyal to the government which was making war on Serbia. Muslims had also served (along with Croats, and some Serbs too) in the *Schutzkorps*, the local defence units which had executed the government's anti-Serb policies in eastern Bosnia, sometimes with real brutality.[22] That there were some embittered individuals among the local Serbs is understandable. And some age-old hatred of Muslims no doubt did exist among the soldiers who came from Serbia; most of them had no experience of living among Muslims, and had been brought up to think of Muslims as such almost as mythical symbols of the enemies of Serbia. But that was not true of Bosnian Serb villagers, who had lived at peace with their Muslim neighbours for forty years or more.

Still, it was clear that the Bosnian Muslims needed a powerful political organization to protect their interests. Several groupings were formed in these early months: a 'Muslim Organization' and a 'Yugoslav Muslim Democracy' party in December, and a 'Muslim Union' in Banja Luka early in 1919.[23] But the main party, which quickly acquired a near-monopoly of Muslim support, was the 'Yugoslav Muslim Organization', founded in Sarajevo in February 1919. Mehmed Spaho joined its leadership, and soon found himself embroiled in arguments over the fundamental principles of the new Yugoslav state. One group within the party, led by its president, Ibrahim Maglajlić, was in favour of a unified and centralized Yugoslavia of the kind urged by the Serbian political leader, Nikola Pašić. Many of these Muslims were intellectuals whose views had been formed in the 'Gajret' Muslim cultural society: since 1909 Gajret had been strongly pro-Serb (so strongly that it had been banned by the authorities during the war), arguing that to establish their independence from Austria-Hungary it was necessary for

Muslims to identify with the Serbs.[24] But support for this attitude declined in the face of the anti-Muslim violence by Serb peasants and Serbian soldiers in the aftermath of the war. Had the Bosnian Muslims known of the private views of one minister in the Serbian government, Stojan Protić, who had recommended in 1917 'solving' the problem of the Bosnian Muslims through a programme of forced conversions and massacres, it would no doubt have declined more steeply.[25]

Mehmed Spaho's argument, which eventually carried the day within the Yugoslav Muslim Organization, was that Bosnia should seek to preserve its identity as an autonomous unit within the Yugoslav state. In general terms, this placed him on the side of Croatia in the long battle between Serbian centralism and Croatian regionalism which was to dominate the politics of the inter-war period. It certainly placed him closer to the position of the Bosnian Croats, whose leader, Josip Sunarić, was a fierce critic of the centralists in Belgrade and argued for a confederal Yugoslavia. The main Bosnian Serb party, the Radical Democrats, was in favour of a centralized Yugoslav state, and it also remained true to its origins in the pre-war Mlada Bosna movement by demanding far-reaching social reforms. There was also a more violently pan-Serb organization, publishing a journal called *Srpska Zora* ('Serbian Dawn'), which demanded the total absorption of Bosnia into Serbia.[26]

When Yugoslav-wide elections were held in November 1920 for a constituent assembly which would decide the future structure of the Yugoslav state, Spaho's party won nearly all the Muslim votes in Bosnia, acquiring twenty-four seats.[27] Because the votes of these deputies, together with those of six Muslims elected in Macedonia, were able to tip the balance in the assembly, they were courted assiduously by the other Yugoslav politicians. One concession which Spaho was keen to obtain was a softening of the blow of land reforms against the Muslim landowners. Decrees had been issued by the Yugoslav government in 1919 abolishing serfdom and ordering that serf families should be given legal title to the land they worked. Spaho fought hard to ensure that the landowners would be properly compensated by the state; millions of dinars were eventually paid out, but the general level of compensation was below the market value of the land. Roughly 4000 Muslim landowning families were affected by this reform, and some were reduced to poverty.[28] Spaho's concerns on this issue led to him and his party being denounced by their critics as representatives of the old feudal classes; but in fact only six out of the seventy-eight candidates put forward by his party in 1920 were landlords, while fifty-two were lawyers, teachers and other professionals.[29] The landowners were in any case only a small minority of the Muslim population, the great majority being peasant smallholders.

Spaho's other concern in the constituent assembly was to preserve the regional-administrative identity of Bosnia. In this he had some success, though the paradoxical price he paid was that he had to support the thoroughly centralist constitution put forward by the Serbian leaders. (This became known as the 'Vidovdan' (St Vitus' day) constitution, because it was adopted in 1921 on the saint's day which was also the anniversary of the Battle of Kosovo, 28 June.) There was little alternative, however, since the leader of the main Croatian party had foolishly withdrawn his deputies altogether from the assembly. And so it was that when the whole of the Yugoslav territory was reorganized as thirty-three 'oblasts' or provinces, the outline of Croatia disappeared from the map, but the outline of Bosnia was preserved – indeed, the six Bosnian oblasts corresponded precisely to the six 'Kreise' of the Austro-Hungarians, which had in turn been based on the sandžaks of the final period of Ottoman rule.[30] Thanks to Spaho's efforts, Bosnia was the only constituent element of Yugoslavia which retained its identity in this way.

These political manoeuvrings, which continued through the 1920s as tensions grew stronger between Zagreb and Belgrade, help to explain why it was that some prominent Muslims publicly identified themselves as 'Muslim Croats' or 'Muslim Serbs'. We have already seen that some had done this in the pre-war years out of a sense of cultural identification – especially writers such as Safvet-beg Bašagić who had become absorbed in Croatian literary culture. But the main basis of all such declarations was political. Just as the trend in the first decade of the century had been to side with the Serbs as natural allies against Vienna, so the trend now was to side with the Croats as natural allies against Belgrade. In the Yugoslav parliament of 1924, all the Bosnian Muslim deputies identified themselves as

Croats, except for Spaho himself, who insisted on being called a Yugoslav.[31] Of Spaho's two brothers, however, one called himself a Croat and the other a Serb. An editorial in the Yugoslav Muslim Organization's journal in 1920 openly recommended that Muslims should identify with whichever nation offered them the fairest chance of 'economic development'.[32] The whole idea of making a choice of 'national identity' on the basis of rival economic policies was self-evidently superficial, not to say absurd. There was actually less reason for the Muslims to identify as Croats or Serbs in Bosnia than there would have been for similar identifications of, say, Macedonian Muslims with Macedonians or Muslims in Serbia with Serbs. As we have already seen, the only real basis for the Bosnian Orthodox and Catholics calling themselves Serbs and Croats was their religious identity, and this was of course the one thing which the Bosnian Muslims could not share. What the superficial and largely tactical self-identifications of Muslims with Serbs or Croats during this period show is that there was still a theoretical reluctance to use the word 'Muslim' as a cultural-historical label of equal rank; but in practical terms the Muslims were already operating as a community on a par with the others, a community which defended its own identity and actually did so more effectively than any other grouping in Bosnian politics.

While the term 'Muslim' was acquiring political significance in this way, so too the strictly religious basis of the term was being gradually eroded by the secularizing influences of the twentieth century. Islamic observance in Bosnia had never been generally 'fanatical', though casual visitors had sometimes described it as such; there had indeed been some fiercely orthodox Muslim clergy, but the population at large was more relaxed in its practices. As Arthur Evans had noted in 1875: 'What about the prohibition of the Prophet against the portrayal of living things? Actually it is observed about as rigorously in Bosnia as the prohibition against drinking wine.'[33] Since 1878 a slow process of secularization had been under way; increasing numbers of Muslims had acquired a Western education at state schools, and some had gone on to study subjects such as medicine or engineering at Vienna or Budapest. As the old advantages of economic power from land-owning declined, the upper stratum of Muslim society naturally began to move into the professions, for which a Western education was required. One observer in 1920 was struck by the number of young Muslims studying at universities and technical colleges.[34] Meanwhile ordinary Muslim women had been encouraged to go to work in factories in Sarajevo – something unthinkable in strict Muslim societies at the time.

All these tendencies were strongly encouraged by the Reis ul-ulema, Čaušević, who had studied at Istanbul, had read the works of the great Muslim modernists and reformers al Afghani and Abduh, and had visited Atatürk's Turkey. In 1927 he caused a scandal among the more conservative Bosnian Muslim clergy, first by suggesting that vakuf land in town centres which had been used for graveyards could be put to more beneficial use by building schools on it, and then by giving a press interview in which he argued against the veiling of women. 'I had rather see a Muslim girl unveiled and honourably earning her living, than a girl who walks round the streets veiled in the daytime and spends the evening in a café.'[35] He insisted that veiling was just a custom, not a religious duty, and he also recommended replacing the fez with an ordinary hat *à la* Atatürk. (The fez had itself been imposed by the Sultan as a Westernizing measure in 1828, and had been fiercely resisted as an infidel symbol at the time; but no one was aware of that ninety-nine years later.)[36] These remarks by Čaušević caused a storm of protest: speeches were made, pamphlets were written and an official judgement condemning his views was issued by the Islamic council in Sarajevo. Čaušević was in a minority among the Muslim clergy, and the Westernizing process still had a long way to go before it would touch ordinary Bosnian Muslim villagers. But at a time when there was already a Muslim prima donna, Bahrija Nuri Hadžić, singing in the Belgrade Opera House, it was clear that social changes were under way which no amount of judgements by the Muslim clergy could stop.[37]

To the casual visitor during these inter-war years there may have seemed to be more of a differentiation between Muslims and Christians in Bosnia than before, for the simple reason that the Christians much more rapidly abandoned 'oriental' dress. As recently as 1903 one observer had written: 'Strangers find great difficulty in distinguishing between the Christians and the Turks in Bosnia, for both wear turbans, embroidered waistcoats, loose open jackets, zouave trousers gathered at the knee, and heel-less shoes with toes that turn up.'[38] Now that the Catholics and Orthodox identified themselves as Croats and Serbs, they put aside – in the towns at least – their old Bosnian clothes. The journalist John Gibbons commented in 1930 that the Muslims stood out in the streets of Sarajevo because of their traditional dress; 'the oddest thing of all, though,' he added, 'seemed to me the way in which they all fitted in so perfectly happily with each other'.[39] Three years earlier an American writer had formed a similar impression: 'Here one sees the Bosnian peasant of Orthodox faith drop his contribution into the cup of a blind Mussulman who squats, playing his *goussle*, at the entrance of a mosque. Glancing at the peaceful little stalls where Christians, Mussulmans and Jews mingle in business, while each goes his own way to cathedral, mosque or synagogue, I wondered if tolerance is not one of the greatest of virtues.'[40]

The main threat to tolerance came, as so often in Bosnia's history, from outside Bosnia's borders. The unresolved political tensions between the centralists and their opponents grew more and more severe during the 1920s. Mehmed Spaho was involved in several of the unstable governments which were formed in those years; frequently he found himself operating alongside the Slovene leader, Monsignor Korošec, as a kind of third force to mediate between the anti-centralist Croats and the centralist Serbs. The two of them helped to bring down the government of the high-handed Nikola Pašić in 1924; both were included as ministers in another Serb-led government in February 1928. By now, the atmosphere in Yugoslav politics was exceptionally acrid. The Croat leader Stjepan Radić was suspended from parliament in March 1928 for telling the Minister of Social Policy: 'You are a crybaby with that pumpkin instead of a head! You ignoramus! You are a thief in a ministerial chair!'[41] Three months later a Montenegrin deputy, irritated by interruptions to his speech, pulled out a gun and shot several deputies, Radić among them. King Alexander tried at first to defuse the crisis and to set up a new government under Korošec. But then, in January 1929, the King took more drastic action, suspending the constitution, and imposing a far more unitary political system than anything the Serbian politicians had hitherto attempted.

The first symbolic change was the announcement that the state would now be called 'Yugoslavia' – a more unitary term than 'the Kingdom of the Serbs, Croats and Slovenes'. Alexander wanted to erase the old regional identities from the map; so he imposed a completely new division of the Yugoslav territory into nine *banovine* ('banates' – the use of this old Croatian term was almost the only sop to Croat pride), and arranged for each banovina to cut across the old borders of the constituent elements of the Yugoslav state. The banovinas were named where possible after rivers. Bosnia was divided between four: Vrbaska, which included some Croatian territory, Drinska, which included a large part of Serbia, Zetska, which consisted mainly of Montenegro, and Primorska, which extended to the Dalmatian coast. For the first time in more than four hundred years, Bosnia had been partitioned.

The 'bans' were governors appointed by the King, and they in turn appointed commissioners in place of the elected local government officials. One Bosnian Serb priest, Simo Begović, a respected figure who had been given a death sentence by the Austro-Hungarians at the Banja Luka political trials in 1916, led a deputation of peasants from Pale to the ban's residence in Sarajevo to complain about these changes. He asked the ban to give him 4000 dinars. 'Why do you want 4000 dinars?' inquired the ban. 'I want to buy a ticket to Vienna,' replied Begović, 'to visit the grave of Franz Joseph, so I can tell him, "Well, Franz, if only I had known what a mess Bosnia would be in after your death, I would never have worked to depose you."'[42] If an Orthodox Serb priest could feel like that, we can imagine how ordinary Croats felt, who regarded this new unitary Yugoslavia as nothing less, in essence, than the realization of Serbia's dreams. No one was happy with these changes, not even the Serbian politicians, who resented the way their wings had been clipped by a royal coup. The Bosnian Muslims were deeply unhappy: they were a minority in each of the four ex-Bosnian banovinas, and Muslim officials were allotted the lowest positions in the ministries and departments of the new royal government. But the Croats were the least happy of all. The most radical Croatian politician, Ante Pavelić, left the country and began organizing, with Mussolini's support, the 'Ustaša' movement which would campaign for Croatian independence.[43] The leader of the main Croatian party,

Vladko Maček (successor to the assassinated Stjepan Radić) issued a 'Resolution' in November 1932 calling for a return to democracy and the ending of Serbian hegemony; similar statements were then issued by Korošec in Slovenia and Spaho in Bosnia, and all three were arrested. The Slovenian and Bosnian Muslim leaders were released soon afterwards, but Maček was sentenced to three years in gaol.[44]

One of the lesser centralizing measures brought in during this period of personal rule by the King was a reorganization of the Muslim community in Yugoslavia. Hitherto there had been two separate organizations, one for Bosnia and the other for the Muslims of Macedonia and Kosovo (based in Skopje). By royal decree in 1930, all Yugoslav Muslims were placed under a single Reis ul-ulema and a single council, and the seat of the Reis ul-ulema was moved to Belgrade. Čaušević, who objected to this plan, resigned, and the new Reis ul-ulema appointed for the whole of Yugoslavia was Ibrahim Maglajlić, the pro-Serb former president of the Yugoslav Muslim Organization.[45] Other smaller changes which went through at the same time included introducing a more general, Western syllabus into the medresas (Muslim seminaries); this was part of a policy of standardizing school curricula throughout the country.[46] The 1930 law gave the King a large degree of control over the Muslim community; however, after King Alexander's death new laws were brought in and a more democratic structure was provided for, with the assemblies of local vakuf commissions choosing three candidates for Reis ul-ulema, of whom the King would choose one.[47]

There had been a cautious relaxation of the system of royal autocracy after the assassination of King Alexander in 1934. The new regent, Prince Paul (acting on behalf of the eleven-year-old successor to the throne, King Peter), released Maček from prison, held new elections in 1935 and appointed a young Serbian politician, Milan Stojadinović, to form a compromise government. The only well-known politicians he included in his administration were Korošec and Spaho. With their support, as he later recalled, the government was 'strong among the people, but weak in the parliament': Korošec's party had boycotted the elections, and Spaho's Yugoslav Muslim Organization had fought the elections as part of the opposition list headed by Maček (which had suffered under an electoral system which gave a disproportionate number of seats to the winning 'list').[48] Later in 1935 Stojadinović formed a new government party, the 'Yugoslav Radical Union', uniting his own party (the Serbian Radical Party) with the parties of Korošec and Spaho. In the following spring, however, the committee of the Radical Party renounced this arrangement and declared their opposition to the government: so Stojadinović found himself in the strange position of governing Yugoslavia without the support of mainstream Croatian or Serbian parties, merely on the basis of the Slovenians, the Bosnian Muslims and his own remaining personal supporters.

Stojadinović's governments lasted four years, during which time he made some gradual progress towards democratization, allowed discussions to proceed with Maček about the eventual reorganizing of Yugoslavia into a federal system, and developed a conciliatory foreign policy aimed at trade and friendly relations with Italy and Germany. The most disruptive force in Yugoslav politics during these years was Serbian nationalism: whipped up by the Orthodox Church, violent demonstrations by the Serbs succeeded in stopping a 'Concordat' between Yugoslavia and the Vatican in 1937. On 3 February 1939 one of Stojadinović's Serbian ministers made a speech in parliament in which he asserted the superiority of Serbs over Croats and Slovenes: 'Serb policies will always be the policies of this house and this government', he declared. Mehmed Spaho asked Stojadinović to disavow this statement, but Stojadinović remained silent. That evening, Korošec organized the resignation of five ministers in protest, including Spaho, the Serbian minister Dragiša Cvetković and Džafer Kulenović, who was Spaho's deputy in the Yugoslav Muslim Organization. This action enabled Prince Paul to dismiss Stojadinović from power and instal Cvetković in his place.[49]

With Hitler now advancing into Czechoslovakia, and his admirer Ante Pavelić in Italy becoming more outspoken in his demands for the break-up of Yugoslavia, it was clear that the problem of finding a federal solution acceptable to the Croats could not be put off any longer. Discussions began in April between Cvetković and Maček aimed at re-forming a national territory of

Croatia and giving it some political powers of its own. Their first agreed position was that the two main Croatian banovinas, Savska and Primorska (which included parts of Bosnia), should be united, together with the district of Dubrovnik, and that the inhabitants of the rest of Bosnia should 'decide by plebiscite whether they would join Croatia or Serbia' – the final aim being a tripartite federal state of Serbia, Croatia and Slovenia.[50] But Prince Paul refused to accept such a constitutional structure, and another round of discussions was held. This time, extra portions of Bosnian territory were simply carved off the map and added to Croatia: they included Brčko, Gradačac, Derventa, Travnik and Fojnica. Instead of a tripartite state, the new system would just treat Croatia as a special banovina with its own parliament: so the remains of Bosnia would continue to be divided between the two existing but reduced banovinas of Vrbaska and Drinska. This was the plan finally adopted in the 'Sporazum' (Agreement) of August 1939.[51]

Mehmed Spaho died in June 1939, while these negotiations were in their most critical phase. He was a shrewd politician who had managed to give the Bosnian Muslims a degree of political leverage in the inter-war period out of all proportion to their numerical strength; but even his vehement opposition could not halt the carve-up now in progress. His successor, Džafer Kulenović, called for the creation of a special banovina for Bosnia. His requests were ignored, not least because the remaining areas of Bosnia had a majority of Serbs, who did not want to be separated from the Serb-dominated cluster of remaining banovinas.[52] Kulenović remained in the government, but became increasingly isolated and morose. When Korošec went to see him in early 1940 to ask why he was boycotting meetings of the cabinet, he issued a stream of complaints. His party received only the crumbs of political patronage, he said; and he could not tolerate the continuing discussions about creating Slovenian and Serbian banovinas of equal status to Croatia, without any mention of the idea of giving similar status to Bosnia. He demanded a new banovina made up of the remaining Bosnian territories and the largely Muslim-inhabited Sandžak of Novi Pazar.[53] Once again his wishes were ignored. Kulenović was an embittered man, and nursed a strong hostility towards the Serbs, whose desire to absorb Bosnia altogether into Serbia was increasingly apparent.

While these issues were debated inconclusively during the rest of 1940, the pressure exerted on Yugoslavia by the Axis powers grew ever stronger. Public opinion was shocked by the collapse of France and angered by the Italian attack on Greece; nevertheless, with the German Reich bordering Yugoslavia (since the annexation of Austria), and with the obvious inability of Britain to offer any effective protection in the Balkans, the Yugoslav politicians felt obliged to adopt a policy of appeasement. Prince Paul and his government held out for many months against German pressure to join the Axis pact, but after Bulgaria had done so at the beginning of March 1941 they decided they could resist no longer. The Yugoslav leaders signed the pact in Vienna on 25 March 1941. On the day after their return, they and Prince Paul were ejected in a bloodless and immensely popular coup mounted by the army and the old Serbian political parties. A new government of national unity was installed, including the Croat leader Vladko Maček as well as some of the previous ministers. It called for peace and calm, and tried to continue with a conciliatory policy towards Germany. Ten days later, on 6 April, came the first of a series of massive bombing raids on Belgrade by the Luftwaffe. Yugoslavia was invaded by German, Italian, Bulgarian and Hungarian forces. After a campaign lasting eleven days, the Yugoslav army capitulated to the German High Command.[54]

13

Bosnia and the second world war, 1941–1945

The history of the second world war in Yugoslavia is the story of many wars piled one on top of another. First, of course, there was the initial war conducted by Germany and Italy against Yugoslavia itself. Some territory was annexed: half of Slovenia by Germany, the other half of Slovenia and several parts of Dalmatia by Italy, and other areas by Hungary, Bulgaria and Italian-controlled Albania. The truncation of Serbia was punitive, but the main aim was merely subjection and control. Then there was the continuing Axis war effort against the Allies: for this purpose Yugoslavia was important for communications, and for the supply of raw materials and labour. There was also the war of the Axis occupiers against Yugoslav resistance movements; this war was always subsidiary to the wider aims of Axis strategy against the Allies. And then there were at least two civil wars. One was a war conducted by Croatian extremists against the Serb population of Croatia and Bosnia, a war of aggression on one side and sometimes indiscriminate retaliation on the other. And finally there was a war between the two main resistance organizations in which the Serbs from those areas enlisted: the Četniks and the Communist Partisans. Both movements, as time went on, gathered in members of other ethnic groups as well. It is not possible to disentangle all these strands when looking at the total number of deaths in Yugoslavia during those terrible four years. But it is clear that at least one million people died, and it is probable that the majority of them were Yugoslavs killed by Yugoslavs.[1]

On 10 April 1941, even before their blitzkrieg had ended, the Germans proclaimed a new 'Independent State of Croatia' (known by its Serbo-Croat initials as the NDH), incorporating the whole of Bosnia and Hercegovina. It was not independent, of course, and was divided into two zones of German and Italian military occupation, with the dividing-line running diagonally through Bosnia from the north-west to the south-east. At Mussolini's suggestion the Germans invited Ante Pavelić to govern the NDH as its 'Poglavnik' or Führer. His 'Ustaša' organization had not been a proper mass-movement until then (it may have had no more than 12,000 members in the whole of Croatia), but it quickly became one once it was established in power. After two decades of political resistance to the centralism of Belgrade, the great majority of Croats regarded the setting up of any 'Independent State of Croatia' as something to celebrate, whatever the circumstances of its birth and however spurious its 'independent' status. However, the responsible politicians of the inter-war period, such as Vladko Maček, remained passive and inert while the state was taken over by fanatics and turned into an instrument of terror and genocide.

The first anti-Jewish law in the NDH was issued on 18 April 1941. Twelve days later three fundamental laws of the state were promulgated: on citizenship, on racial identity and on 'the protection of Aryan blood and the honour of the Croatian people'.[2] But the persecution of the Jews had begun even before these legal formalities were completed. On 16 April, the day after the arrival of the Germans in Sarajevo, the old synagogue there was attacked by German soldiers. In the course of a two-day rampage, the contents of all the synagogues in the city were completely destroyed.[3] An unusually well-informed German officer also called immediately at the National Museum to confiscate the priceless Sarajevo Haggadah; but thanks to the 'brilliant improvisations' of the Museum's director the manuscript was saved and hidden for the duration of the war in a mountain village.[4] When it was decreed, in the following month, that all shops, factories and other enterprises must have Ustaša 'commissars' appointed to supervise them, the most brutal ones were appointed to Jewish businesses, and a succession of expropriations and murders now began. Mass internment of the Jews started in the NDH in June; in Serbia, which in August was placed under a non-fanatical but cooperative quisling administrator, General Nedić, the round-up of the Jews began a little later, but by the end of 1941 the majority of Jews in both territories had been taken to concentration camps. Local personnel cooperated in these round-ups in Serbia as well as in the NDH: no territory was guiltless. All the synagogues in Bosnia were looted, and many were destroyed altogether. By the end of the war it was calculated that out of 14,000 Jews in Bosnia nearly 12,000 had been killed.[5]

Anti-semitism was of only secondary concern to Ustaša ideologists, however. The main aim was to 'solve' the problem of the large Serb minority (1.9 million out of a total of 6.3 million) in the territory of the NDH.[6] Widespread acts of terror against the Serbs began in May. In June there was a mass arrest of Serbs in Mostar; hundreds were shot and thrown into the river Neretva. Similar atrocities were carried out in many other places in the NDH, including Bosnian towns such as Bihać, Brčko and Doboj, while entire Serb villages in the Sarajevo region were destroyed. By July even the Germans were complaining about the brutality of these attacks.[7] The reaction of the Serb peasants – especially in Hercegovina, the heartland of peasant armed resistance in 1875 and 1882 – was predictable: in the Nevesinje region they rose up in June 1941, drove out the Ustaša militia and established, for a while, a 'liberated area', joined to a similar area of resistance in neighbouring Montenegro. They then turned against local Croat and Muslim villagers, whose acquiescence in NDH rule they regarded as collaboration; more than 600 Muslims were killed in the district of Bileća, in the southern corner of Hercegovina, and in July and August roughly 500 were killed in the area round Višegrad.[8] By mid-August one Communist organizer was writing from Sarajevo that in the Mostar region 'the insurgents had plundered Muslim villages and thereby turned the entire Muslim population against themselves'.[9]

The genocidal policies of the NDH caused thousands of Bosnian Serbs to enlist, where they could, in one of the organized resistance movements. There were two of these organizations operating on Bosnian soil, with different characteristics and very different aims – so different that an incipient civil war between them was clearly visible by October 1941. The first was formed by a Yugoslav Army colonel, Draža Mihailović, a royalist, Anglophile and expert on guerrilla warfare, who was in Bosnia when the German invasion took place. With the remnants of the men under his command he travelled eastwards into the hill country of Ravna Gora in west-central Serbia, and set up his resistance headquarters there. As an army officer he represented a survival of royal authority (the Yugoslav royal government-in-exile was later to make him a General and declare him Minister of War); and as a patriotic Serb he commanded the loyalty of many ordinary Serb citizens. His men became known as Četniks, the traditional term for the much-heroicized bandit fighters of earlier Serbian history. The name was a source of endless confusions, since there was already an official 'Četnik' organization, based on a first world war veterans' movement, which became an arm of the Serbian quisling regime. Many local Serb groupings sprang up elsewhere which called themselves 'Četniks' but had little or no connection with Mihailović's men; and the great weakness of his own organization was that his regional commanders operated for long periods in independence – or disregard – of any orders from him.[10] Mihailović's Četniks began active resistance to the Germans in May, but the overall policy he adopted, as requested by the government-in-exile in July and September, was to lie low, build up an organization, infiltrate the forces of the Nedić quisling régime and prepare for an uprising which would eventually come when the Allies had turned the war against Germany.[11]

The other organization, the Communist 'Partisans', had very different aims. The Communist Party had played an almost invisible role in inter-war Yugoslav politics, being officially banned for most of that period. By 1940 it had just over 6000 members in the entire country.[12] Its leader, Tito (the former Austro-Hungarian army corporal, Josip Broz), was a Stalin loyalist who had survived the purges in Moscow; during the period between the Molotov-Ribbentrop pact and Hitler's invasion of Russia, he followed the official Comintern line of complaining about British aggression against Germany. But he was a resourceful man and a natural organizer, and within days of the invasion of Russia in June 1941 he was planning a resistance operation which would not only try to drive out the Germans (while, as he assumed, Germany was quickly defeated by Russia), but also engage in a social revolution, seizing power for a post-war Communist state. This last aim meant that his tactics could be quite different from those of the Četnik leader.

Mihailović wanted to preserve not only the population but also the entire social order, and was thus very reluctant to invite German reprisals or the devastation of whole areas. On the other hand, the destruction of society and the creation of an uprooted, radicalized population were grist to Tito's mill. Areas liberated by his forces were ostentatiously 'sovietized'; many local 'bourgeois' were executed; and even within the ranks of the Partisans, Tito's security chief, Aleksandar Ranković, carried out purges of his own. Social revolution was the higher priority: as one of Tito's right-hand men, Milovan Djilas, later explained, 'The military operations . . . were motivated by our revolutionary ideology. A revolution was not feasible without a simultaneous struggle against the occupation forces.'[13] So it is not surprising that, although a rough-and-ready cooperation between local peasants, Četniks and Partisans had temporarily liberated large areas of Montenegro, Bosnia and western Serbia in the late summer and autumn of 1941, long-term cooperation between the two organizations was impossible. Some clashes between them had already occurred before a German offensive, in the winter of that year, dispersed Mihailović's forces in Serbia and obliged the Partisans to move to the highlands of south-eastern Bosnia.

One other aspect of the rival Četnik and Communist policies also needs to be mentioned here: their attitude towards the Muslims and the status of Bosnia. Among the leading Četniks there were several rabid Serb nationalists whose desire it was to absorb not only Bosnia but Dalmatia, Montenegro, parts of Croatia and Slavonia, and even northern Albania, into the territory of Serbia.[14] Such aims were nurtured by two dominant intellectuals in the Četnik movement: the Serbian lawyer and politician Dragiša Vasić and the Bosnian Serb lawyer (from Banja Luka) Stevan Moljević. In June 1941 the latter drew up a memorandum entitled 'Homogeneous Serbia', in which he demanded the inclusion in Serbia of the territories mentioned above, and explained that the 'fundamental duty' of all Serbs was 'to create and organize a homogeneous Serbia, which must include all the ethnic territory inhabited by Serbs'.[15] In a letter to Vasić in February 1942 Moljević wrote that Serbian land should be extended all the way to Dalmatia, and that there should then follow 'the cleansing (*čišćenje*) of the land of all non-Serb elements. The thing to do would be to send the offenders on their way: Croats to Croatia, and Muslims to Turkey or Albania.'[16] With people like this influencing the policy of the Četniks (Moljević became political director of the movement in early 1943), there was clearly a theoretical basis for a virulently anti-Muslim policy.

But on the other hand there is no definite evidence that Draža Mihailović himself ever called for ethnic cleansing. The one document which has frequently been cited as evidence of this, a set of instructions addressed to two regional commanders in December 1941, is probably a forgery – though it must be pointed out that it was forged not by enemies wanting to discredit Mihailović but by the commanders themselves, who hoped it would be taken for a genuine Četnik document.[17] Mihailović was certainly capable of using the rhetoric of Serbian nationalism. In one proclamation attributed to him there is a declaration: 'I am from the Serbian Šumadija [district of central Serbia], from Serbian land and of Serbian blood. As such, I shall fight for the most sublime ideals which a Serb can have: for the liberation and unification for ever of all Serbian lands . . . Wherever Serbian graves are found, there is Serbian land.'[18] Nevertheless, he remained a loyal servant of the King and the government-in-exile, whose policy was to save and rebuild the whole kingdom of Yugoslavia. 'The Serbs would have the right to say: "We no longer want Yugoslavia",' Mihailović once commented; 'but there are higher interests which compel us to remake this country.'[19] Initially he regarded himself as fighting for the restoration of Yugoslavia, including the Croatian semi-autonomous banovina, exactly as it had been before the war. After he became aware of the extent of the Ustaša massacres, however, he agreed that some territories should be removed from Croatia: its eastern tip (Srem and Baranja) should be joined to Serbia, southern Dalmatia should join Bosnia, and Serbia should take eastern Hercegovina. Bosnia itself would be entitled to decide by plebiscite whether it wanted to join Serbia or not.[20] Since the rump Bosnia had a majority population of Serbs, this territorial adjustment would have produced a result quite similar to that planned by his more ideological advisers; the main difference between him and them was that he personally had no plans to expel the Muslims. But in any case, unlike Tito, he was not expecting to run the country himself.

All such decisions, if he were successful, would be in the hands of the politicians and the King.

Given that Tito was indeed hoping to run the country after the war, it is at first sight curious how little clear information he provided about how the country would be arranged or divided. But there is a simple reason for that. At this stage he was still a loyal servant of Stalin, and would create whatever Moscow required: a strongly centralized state, a Yugoslav union of socialist federal republics, or even a Balkan federation including Bulgaria and Albania. The combination of head-in-clouds theorizing and ruthless opportunism which had marked Stalin's own policy on the 'nationalities question' was evident in the Yugoslav Communist Party too. Up until the mid-1930s the Comintern policy had been to regard Yugoslavia as part of the wall of unfriendly states erected against the Soviet Union at Versailles: Comintern called for the dissolution of Yugoslavia in 1924, and the Yugoslav Communists were encouraged to incite disaffected nationalities against Belgrade as a means to that end. In 1935 the line changed completely: Communists were now meant to preserve Yugoslavia and work in the spirit of a 'popular front' against international fascism.[21] There can be little doubt that if Stalin had denounced all forms of national identity as bourgeois and demanded that they be abolished, Tito would have jumped through that hoop too. Only as the war progressed did he learn some lessons from the experience of trying to weld his army together out of members of Yugoslavia's different and competing nationalities.

So it is not surprising to find that the Yugoslav Communist Party had no clear ideas about what the status of the Bosnian Muslims should be. In its earliest phase of operation, from 1919 to the mid-1930s, it paid little or no attention to the matter, partly because the Communist Party in Bosnia itself was an isolated splinter group which as late as 1939 had only 170 members.[22] Generally, it rejected at this stage the idea that any set of people defined by their religion could have a political or national identity. But after the change-around of 1935, the Communists began to put forward quasi-federal proposals for a country formed out of seven distinct territorial units, of which Bosnia was to be one; this meant having to counter the rival claims that Bosnia was 'really' Croatian or 'really'

Serbian, and obliged the Communists to pay more attention to the special identity of the Muslims.[23] In 1936 one Communist intellectual, the Slovenian Edvard Kardelj, wrote: 'We cannot speak of the Muslims as a nation, but . . . as a special ethnic group.'[24] An 'open letter' written by Communists in Bosnia in 1939 said that the Muslims had always been a *posebna cjelina*, a special whole or entity. But the classification remained deliberately vague; at the Party congress in 1940 the man in charge of nationalities policy, Milovan Djilas, described the Muslims as an 'ethnic group' yet excluded them from the list of Yugoslav nations.[25]

During the war the pronouncements of the Party chiefs continued to be ambiguous or contradictory. One document issued by the 'Anti-Fascist National Council of Bosnia' (the Communist regional assembly) in 1943 referred to 'representatives of the Serb, Croat and Muslim peoples'; but in the same year the meeting of the general 'Anti-Fascist Council', which laid the foundations of post-war federal Yugoslavia, rejected the idea that the Muslims were a nation. The plan put forward by Djilas was based on the Soviet model: five 'national republics' for the five 'nations' of Yugoslavia (Serbs, Croats, Slovenes, Montenegrins and Macedonians). Bosnia was to be a distinct unit, but only an autonomous province, not a national republic. There was then a tug-of-war between Serb delegates, who wanted Bosnia to be absorbed into Serbia, and Bosnian ones, who wanted it to have equal status as a republic; the final compromise was to give it republican status but to describe it as a republic inhabited 'by parts of the Serb and Croat nations, as well as by the Bosnian Muslims'.[26]

All such debates were academic, however, until the Partisans had won the war – the war against the Četniks, that is. Both sides fought from time to time against the Axis forces, and the Partisans did so more frequently than the Četniks, partly for the reasons already stated. But it was the war against the Četniks that dominated Tito's strategy. After his flight from Serbia into the Foča region of south-eastern Bosnia at the end of 1941, Tito's main worry was that the heartlands of central Serbia and the Sandžak would now become Četnik territory, as indeed they did. Montenegro and parts of western Hercegovina soon became dominated by Četnik forces too, under regional commanders who had made a working arrangement with the Italian occupiers. (The Italians were motivated in this by a desire for a quiet life, a wish to create a bulwark against the Partisans, and a genuine willingness to let the local Serb population protect itself against Ustaša massacres.) In the summer of 1942 Tito marched north-westwards through Bosnia, along the dividing-line between the German and Italian occupation zones, and settled in an area centring on Bihać where there were no Axis troops. Here he spent several months strengthening his forces, gathering in Bosnian Serbs and some Croats too. By the autumn he claimed to control a 'liberated' area the size of Switzerland, but this was largely because neither Axis nor NDH forces had taken the trouble to attack him.

Although Tito's army contained thousands of very brave and hardy fighters, it must be said that nearly all the large-scale fighting between it and the Axis forces occurred on the initiative of Axis commanders, who decided every now and then to clear out the Partisans from particular areas. Tito's 'liberation' of areas of remote countryside did not affect the German war effort in any vital way: the Germans and Italians continued to control the large towns, the major roads and railways, and the mines. It is often said that Tito 'pinned down' large numbers of German divisions; but at the beginning of 1943 there were only four German divisions, of low calibre, in the whole of Yugoslavia. (In August of that year they were joined by two reserve divisions of trainee recruits, and one burnt-out division from Stalingrad; and a few more were brought in towards the end of the year after the surrender of Italian forces in September.)[27] As one hostile but perceptive critic of Tito has written: 'In the areas of Bosnia, Hercegovina and Croatia where these Partisan forces lumbered back and forth there were of course frequent clashes with Axis troops. Communications were sabotaged but not in accordance with any strategic plan. Rather, they were broken to protect Partisan retreats; and the movements were practically always retreats.'[28]

The main reason why the Germans decided to clear Tito's forces out of north-western Bosnia in early 1943 was that they feared an Allied landing on the Dalmatian coast, and therefore wanted to strengthen their control over the strategically important hinterland. For the same reason, the Germans also planned an offensive against the Četniks in Hercegovina and Montenegro.[29] Thoughts of an

Allied landing now dominated the strategies of all the military leaders. Mihailović also wanted to clear out the Partisans, so that there would be no obstacle to a speedy Allied advance inland to join his own forces.[30] As for Tito, he sent three of his senior officials to negotiate with the Germans in March 1943, first in the Bosnian town of Gornji Vakuf and then in Zagreb: they informed the Germans that 'Tito in the event of an Anglo-American landing was prepared to cooperate with the German divisions in Croatia in common operations against the invaders'.[31] Tito knew that an Allied occupation of Yugoslavia would mean the restoration of the King and his government, and the end of all dreams of an immediate Communist takeover. Such fears continued to plague him even after he had begun to receive direct support from the Allies in the late summer of 1943. As one senior German official in Yugoslavia noted, 'in 1944 there were moments when Partisans worried less about the Germans than about the Allied landing'.[32]

During 1943 these conflicting aims produced a succession of shifting tactical alignments between the strategies of the three different forces – or rather, four, since the Italians' policy towards the Četniks differed from that of the more distrustful Germans. Tito's Partisans were pushed down by the Germans towards Hercegovina in early 1943; he had been planning a southwards move anyway, to tackle the Četnik forces in Hercegovina and Montenegro. In March, although pursued by the Germans and opposed by the Četniks, he succeeded in crossing the river Neretva in Hercegovina and moving southwards into the Četnik stronghold of Montenegro. (It was at this point that he began his negotiations with the Germans, to persuade them that it was in their interests to let him have 'a free hand' against Mihailović.)[33] The Italians were cooperating closely with the Četniks, but the Germans still regarded the destruction of Mihailović's forces as a strategically important goal: they captured and disarmed several thousand Montenegrin Četniks in May, and sent the regional Četnik commander to a prison camp in Galicia.[34] Then, in the early summer of 1943, the Germans turned on the Partisans, almost surrounding them on Mount Durmitor in northern Montenegro. Tito's men fought with tremendous determination and finally broke through the encirclement, moving up through south-eastern Bosnia, skirting round to the east of Sarajevo and then marching westwards from Olovo to Travnik.[35] Eventually he was able to set up his headquarters in the Jajce district of west-central Bosnia.

On Mount Durmitor Tito had been joined by a British officer, William Deakin, who was profoundly impressed by the Partisans' fighting abilities. Reports from him and other British officers who visited the Partisans during the summer and autumn persuaded the Allies to transfer their backing from Mihailović to Tito. And at the same time the Partisans gained a huge advantage over the Četniks when the Italians surrendered in September 1943 and large quantities of Italian equipment fell into Partisan hands. Mihailović's regional commanders now began collaborating directly, for the first time, with the Germans.[36] During 1944 Allied support for Tito was intensified; and his forces grew in size as the general breakdown of Ustaša rule filled his ranks with disaffected Croats and Muslims as well as Serbs. In the summer of that year the Germans began their withdrawal from Yugoslavia. Large supplies of weapons were sent to Tito to enable him to impede their withdrawal; but Tito's main concern was completing his victory in the civil war. In September the Allies persuaded King Peter to appeal to all Yugoslavs to support Tito. By the end of the year, Soviet forces (Marshal Tolbukhin's Third Ukrainian Army) had occupied nearly a third of the country. Communist rule in Yugoslavia was now assured.

The position of the Bosnian Croats and the Bosnian Serbs during these four years of fighting is easily understood. The former behaved in the same way as the Croats in Croatia: a minority became active Ustaša supporters, while the majority welcomed the establishment of the NDH to begin with and became more and more disenchanted thereafter, until in 1943 and 1944 large numbers of them were joining the Partisans. The Bosnian Serbs, as we have already seen, were quickly driven into opposition to the Ustaša state and the Axis military occupation. There were three main periods when the Partisan army spent several months in one place, drawing breath and gathering in new recruits, and all three were spent on Bosnian territory (Foča in the first half of 1942, Bihać in the second half of that year and Jajce in the second half of 1943); so there were plenty of opportunities for Bosnian Serbs to enlist in the Partisans. Mihailović's Četniks also recruited Bosnian Serbs, especially in the

Drina valley region of eastern Bosnia and in the Hercegovina-Montenegro borderlands.

The position of the Bosnian Muslims was more complex. As we have seen, the general political sympathies of the Muslims had been with Zagreb rather than Belgrade throughout the inter-war period. Although the official policy of the Yugoslav Muslim Organization was for 'Yugoslavism' tempered by a degree of regional autonomy, and although Spaho had always described himself as a Yugoslav, most of his Muslim colleagues had called themselves Muslim Croats. This identification had its limits, however; when the most pro-Croat of the Muslim politicians, Hakija Hadžić, set up a Muslim branch of the Croatian Peasant Party for the elections of 1938, he was joined only by a handful of Spaho's opponents and received barely a few thousand votes.[37] And among the Islamic clergy there was a peculiarly mixed attitude to the idea of any 'Croaticization' of the Bosnian Muslims. Mehmed Spaho's brother Fehim, who was Reis ul-ulema from 1938 to 1942, was a self-identified 'Croat' who played a leading role in the pro-Croat Muslim cultural association, the Narodna Uzdanica. (The rival association, Gajret, continued to take a strongly pro-Serb line.) But Fehim Spaho was also keen to preserve the special identity of the Muslims, which he felt was under threat. And so he issued instructions against mixed marriages and against the use of non-Muslim names for children; he even advised Muslims not to enter Catholic churches, for fear of having to take off their fezes if they did so.[38]

Faced with a choice between being ruled from Belgrade or Zagreb, most of the Muslim politicians and senior clergy would have chosen Zagreb, so long as they had some guarantees that the practice of Islam would continue unmolested. And that is what Ante Pavelić took care to promise to them within days of coming to power. On 25 April 1941 he sent an emissary to assure Fehim Spaho that he wanted the Bosnian Muslims to feel 'free, contented and possessed of equal rights'. Freedom of religion, including their education system, was guaranteed to the Muslims, and eleven former Yugoslav Muslim Organization politicians were invited to join the pseudo-parliament in Zagreb.[39]

The leader of that party, Džafer Kulenović, was appointed vice-president of the NDH government in November 1941. He had always been pro-Croat in his outlook, and had become very disillusioned, as we have seen, with the political process in Belgrade in the final years before the war; but he was not an Ustaša enthusiast. As one expert on this period has put it: 'Although he stayed in the government until the end, he never gained the trust of the Ustaša, and he lost reputation among his Yugoslav Muslim Organization followers; under pressure from them he frequently stated that he was not their representative on the NDH government, and that he represented only himself.'[40] The most influential man in the Yugoslav Muslim Organization after the death of Mehmed Spaho was a businessman from Sarajevo, Uzeir-aga Hadžihasanović. He encouraged Kulenović to join the NDH government in order to obstruct illegalities and use his influence against the pro-Croat extremist Hakija Hadžić, who had now been appointed Ustaša 'Commissioner' for Bosnia. At the end of April 1941 Hadžihasanović took part in a joint Muslim-Serb delegation, together with the Bosnian Serb politician Milan Božić, to ask Hakija Hadžić for autonomy for Bosnia. The result of this initiative was that Božić and his Serb colleagues were arrested and murdered soon afterwards, and Hadžihasanović was told to abandon his 'anti-Croat' ideas.[41]

Disillusionment set in quickly among many of the Muslims. Although there was no general pogrom against them, the promise that their rights would be respected was not kept; the rule of law simply did not operate in the Ustaša NDH. A series of public resolutions and protests were issued by the Muslim clergy during the summer and autumn of 1941, beginning on 2 August. Such resolutions appeared in Sarajevo, Prijedor, Mostar, Banja Luka, Bijeljina and Tuzla. The Mostar resolution referred to 'innumerable crimes, abuses, illegalities and forced conversions which have been and are being committed against the Orthodox Serbs and other fellow-citizens'; the resolution of the Muslim clergy of Banja Luka complained of the theft and looting of property belonging to Serbs and Jews; and a petition organized by Hadžihasanović and signed by a hundred prominent Sarajevan Muslims in October denounced the violence against Jews and Serbs and demanded 'security of life, dignity, property and religion for all citizens'. By the end of the year the Germans were reporting that 'relations between the Muslims and the government have considerably deteriorated'.[42]

At the same time, the acts of violence committed by Serb villagers against Muslims, especially in Hercegovina, made it impossible for Muslims to join them in their resistance to the Ustaša. On the contrary, some Muslims were motivated to join the ranks of the Ustaša militia instead. The Bosnian Muslims were not even represented in the royal government-in-exile, and could feel little loyalty to that government's military representative, Mihailović. But in the second half of 1941, when the Partisans became more politically and militarily distinguishable from the Četniks (and when the Partisan commanders put a check to their own men's attacks on Muslim villages), Muslims did begin to join Tito's army. The first Muslim Partisan unit, the 'Mujina četa', was formed after August 1941, and by December it had grown into a battalion. A unit of Muslim youths was also formed during Tito's stay at Foča in the winter of 1941–2, and in early 1942 Muslims were also joining Partisan battalions at Zenica and in Hercegovina. Other Muslim units were formed during the course of that year, and December saw the formation of the 'Eighth Regional (Muslim) Brigade' under the command of Osman Karabegović.[43] The number of Muslim recruits was small at first. Only one prominent Muslim politician, Nurija Pozderac, joined the Communists at this early stage; and it was hard to convince the imams and muftis of Bosnia that the future of their people lay with atheistic Communism. They had probably heard something of the appalling treatment of Islam in the Soviet Union during the previous twenty-odd years, and were not convinced by the pamphlets which Tito's organization now issued, portraying Stalin's Russia as a wonderland of tolerance and Islamic religious freedom.[44]

During the same period, however, even while regional Četnik commanders were allowing their men to attack Muslim villages, the Četniks were officially appealing to Muslims for their support. As one of the Četnik leaders in Hercegovina, Dobrosav Jevdjević, wrote in July 1942, it was necessary to be tolerant towards the Muslims for tactical reasons, 'while not forgetting that there can be no true unity with them'.[45] Muslims in many parts of south-east Bosnia and Hercegovina were unlikely to forget that, since Četniks and other local Serb forces had killed many thousands of Muslims in the winter of 1941–2 and the summer of 1942. Some of the worst killings were in the Foča–Čajniće region. At least 2000 Muslims were killed there by forces under one local Četnik commander, Zaharia Ostojić, in August 1942, and in February 1943 more than 9000 were massacred, including 8000 elderly people, women and children.[46] A terrible system of mutually fuelled enmities was now at work. The more Muslims there were joining the Partisans, the more the Četniks regarded Muslims as such as their foes; and the worse the killings of Muslims by the Četniks became, the more likely local Muslims were to cooperate with Partisan, German, Italian or NDH forces against the Četniks.

Nevertheless, the pattern varied from place to place. In some areas it was even possible for Muslims and Četniks to cooperate. One such Muslim–Četnik group in the Zenica region sent a message to the Germans in May 1942: 'Remove the Ustaše from Bosnia, and we Muslims and Serbs will create order here within two weeks.'[47] The most active pro-Četnik Muslims were Dr Ismet Popovac, who had been Mayor of Konjica, and Fuad Musakadić, a former Sarajevo police chief. Popovac wrote to Mihailović suggesting that he recruit Muslims into his ranks; there were supporters of this idea among the more pro-Serb or anti-Communist Muslims in several Bosnian towns, and by December 1943 it was estimated that up to eight per cent of Mihailović's soldiers were Muslim – perhaps 4000 or more.[48] Popovac himself led an attack which 'liberated' a Muslim village in January 1943. Later that year, however, both he and Fuad Musakadić were captured by the Communists and shot.[49]

In this whirlpool of conflicting forces – every one of which, it will be noted, had its origin outside Bosnia – the most natural and popular course for Muslims to follow was to form their own local defence units and try to protect themselves against all comers. Small groups of this kind sprang up all over the country. By October 1942 there was also a 'Muslim Volunteer Legion' of roughly 4000 men, which fought more against the Partisans than against the Četniks, distrusted the Ustaša government (from which, however, it obtained supplies of weapons), and tried to deal directly with the Germans.[50] A similar but more independent force was assembled in the Cazin region of north-western Bosnia (near Bihać) in the summer of 1943: led by an ex-Partisan called Huska Miljković and composed mainly of demoralized former Partisans and deserters from local defence forces, it had eight full battalions and controlled a large area. Huska Miljković was wooed alternately by the NDH and the Partisans; he kept his distance until February 1944, when he made an agreement with the Partisans – whereupon he was assassinated by pro-Ustaša members of his army.[51]

To many of the Muslim political leaders, some kind of autonomy for Bosnia seemed the only solution. And the only way to get it was to appeal directly to the Germans, in whose gift it lay. This was not just a revival of the old dream of Muslim politicians, though it did echo the requests made by people such as Šerif Arnautović for autonomy under Hungarian rule at the end of the first world war: it was an attempt to find a practical solution to an increasingly unbearable situation. Hence the famous 'Memorandum' addressed by Bosnian Muslim leaders to Hitler in November 1942 and already mentioned in the first chapter of this book. Apart from boasting about Gothic origins, it complained bitterly about killings of Muslims by the Ustaša, and requested that all Ustaša activity on Bosnian territory should be stopped. To protect the country it asked for permission to expand the Muslim Volunteer Legion, and to reassure the Germans it suggested that the Legion be placed under direct German control.[52]

This was a carefully calculated package of proposals; but its one essential demand, Bosnian autonomy, was unacceptable to the Germans, who knew that it would cause intolerable offence in Zagreb. They were interested, however, in expanding the recruitment of soldiers from the region. In December Hitler ordered the Prinz Eugen SS division, which consisted mainly of ethnic Germans from Romania, to move to the NDH and enlist more ethnic Germans there. When in February 1943 he said that he wanted that division to supervise the raising of a whole new division in the NDH, Himmler suggested making one out of Bosnian Muslims. Over fierce objections from Zagreb, the proposal went through.[53] The principle of recruiting 'volunteer' SS divisions from occupied countries was already well established, with divisions from France, Belgium, Holland and Denmark. The Muslim division was numbered the Thirteenth SS division, and given the name 'Handžar', after the traditional weapon of the region, the Turkish curved dagger or scimitar.

Recruitment began in April 1943, and the Germans took advantage of a visit to Sarajevo by the pro-German Grand Mufti of Jerusalem to appeal for support among the Muslim clergy. (The Grand Mufti, El Huseini, had been fired by anti-British zeal for a long time: after the Balfour Declaration on Palestine in 1917 he had called on the Arabs to form an Arab-Muslim-German alliance to oppose British policy.) Some of the Bosnian muftis and imams helped in the recruitment drive, and each unit in the division was given a young mufti as a spiritual adviser; the officers, however, were nearly all ethnic Germans.[54] By the end of April 12,000 had been recruited, and the division's eventual full strength was 21,000 men. Enlistment was voluntary in most cases, though many seem to have been given a very misleading prospectus about the purposes the division would serve.[55] To the disappointment of the Bosnian Muslims generally, who had also been misled into thinking that the division would be used to protect their towns and villages, the recruits were sent off in the summer of 1943 for a long period of training in Germany and France. Two groups of Muslims, from Sarajevo and Banja Luka, were sent to join some Croatian engineers at a training centre in Villefranche-de-Rouergue, near Toulouse. There, on the night of 17 September, under the leadership of a Muslim, Ferid Džanić, and a Croat, Bozo Jelenek, they seized their ethnic German officers, put them hastily on trial, and shot them. They planned to slip away and join the French Resistance, but one officer had given the alert, and they were attacked by German troops. Jelenek got away; fifteen of the rebels died, and another 141 people were killed in the subsequent clean-up operation. The anniversary of this rebellion is still celebrated today at Villefranche-de-Rouergue, under the slightly one-sided title of 'la révolte des Croates'.[56]

While the Handžar division was sent for further training in the even more remote location of Silesia, discontent was mounting in Bosnia. There were increasing complaints from the Bosnian Muslims about attacks on their people by Ustaša units. Many Muslims started forming local defence units known as 'green cadres'; this organization acquired a political leader, Professor Nešad Topčić, who also campaigned for Bosnian autonomy. A similar move was made by a senior member of the council of the Muslim clergy in Sarajevo,

Muhamed Pandža, who called on the Muslims in November 1943 to throw off Ustaša rule and set up an autonomous Bosnian state with equal rights for all citizens, regardless of their religion. News of his appeal had a strong effect on the Handžar division, since he had been one of the original supporters of its recruitment drive.[57] At the same time, however, there was a heavy enrolment of Muslims in the ranks of the Partisans, stimulated by the formation of Tito's 'Sixteenth Muslim Brigade' in September 1943.[58]

After many requests for the return of the Handžar division, Hitler finally sent it back to Bosnia in March 1943 for 'peace-keeping' operations. It was stationed in northern and eastern Bosnia (Tuzla, Gradačac, Brčko, Bijeljina and Zvornik) where, during the spring and summer of that year, it committed indiscriminate reprisals – murders and other crimes – against the local Serb population.[59] The exact number of victims is not known, but it was certainly many hundreds, perhaps several thousand. As the year progressed, several new developments made the Muslims more willing to cast their lot with the Partisans. The increasingly open German–Četnik agreements were making the Muslims more suspicious of the Germans; they were also troubled by the breaking of relations between Germany and Turkey. Tito was enjoying new military successes, and after his capture of the town of Derventa in September he issued an ultimatum demanding that all Croatian and Bosnian forces should join the Partisans: up to 2000 members of the Handžar division did so. Anti-NDH feeling was growing ever stronger among the Muslim soldiers, as the Ustaša became reckless in their attempts to intimidate the Muslim population with summary executions. The Handžar division rapidly disintegrated, and in October the German authorities in Zagreb reported to Berlin that it was no longer operationally capable. Absurdly, the suggestion was now made to set up a second division; but nothing came of it. At the end of 1944 all the SS units from the NDH were disbanded.[60]

Sarajevo was liberated by the Partisans on 6 April 1945; within a few weeks the whole territory of Bosnia was under their full control. A 'People's Government' for Bosnia was appointed on 28 April. Many of the Muslims were now reconciled to the prospect of Communist rule: instead of absorption in Croatia (the Ustaša solution) or absorption in Serbia (the Četnik plan), they were offered a vaguely federal solution in which Bosnia would continue to exist. But above all they looked forward to a time when there would be no more killing. Altogether 75,000 Bosnian Muslims are thought to have died in the war: at 8.1 per cent of their total population, this was a higher proportion than that suffered by the Serbs (7.3 per cent), or by any other people except the Jews and the Gypsies.[61] Muslims had fought on all sides – Ustaša, German, Četnik, Partisan – and had been killed by all sides. Many had been killed in Croatian and German death-camps, including Jasenovac, Buchenwald, Dachau and Auschwitz.[62] They had not started this war, and had fought above all to defend themselves. But the killing was not yet over.

14

Bosnia in Titoist Yugoslavia, 1945–1989

Tito is often given great credit for having brought internal peace and reconciliation to Yugoslavia after the second world war. It is true that peace came, and that the wounds of the war gradually healed; it is true also that Tito gave some thought to balancing the conflicting claims of Yugoslavia's peoples and regions. But power was more important to Tito than reconciliation, and Communist power was imposed on Yugoslavia at a very heavy price. What has now become the best-known instance of this was the treatment meted out to the remnants of various anti-Partisan forces (and associated civilians) who had taken refuge in Allied-controlled Austria in April and May 1945: Slovene 'home guards', Ustaša soldiers, and Serb and Muslim Četniks. Bosnian Croats, Serbs and Muslims were thus all present in this great mass of defeated soldiers. More than 18,000 were sent back to Yugoslavia by the British at Tito's insistence; most were massacred within hours of their arrival on Yugoslav soil.

Altogether it has been estimated that up to 250,000 people were killed by Tito's mass shootings, forced death marches and concentration camps in the period 1945–6.[1] One report on the situation in Yugoslavia sent by an American official in February 1945 observed: 'Propaganda and organized "spontaneous" demonstrations, forced labour, high-handed and summary requisitioning, arrests and punishment [and] a sense of intimidation are all too reminiscent of occupation.'[2] Tito's secret police, the 'Department for the Protection of the People' (OZNa), was zealous in rounding up real or imagined political enemies. In Tito's own words, the purpose of OZNa was 'to strike terror into the bones of those who do not like this kind of Yugoslavia' – and there were many of them.[3] The lucky ones became a source of labour on the country's many new construction projects; and their work was complemented by the efforts of the foreign volunteers who came to work on the 'youth railways', the first of which was built in 1947 from Sarajevo to Šamac (on the Bosnian-Croatian border). As one observer has noted: 'The paved highway from Belgrade to Zagreb, one of the proud accomplishments of the period, was built not only by volunteer youth brigades, as advertised, but also with extensive use of prison labour, especially that of "class enemies" from the bourgeoisie, which may be one reason why it is so badly built.'[4]

Once Stalin had expelled Yugoslavia from Cominform (the successor-organization to Comintern) in 1948, Yugoslav history was soon being rewritten to show that Tito had always pursued an independent, liberal-minded and anti-Stalinist line. The truth is that before the break with the Soviet Union, and for several years after it, Tito's policies were closely modelled on those of Stalin.[5] Even the Yugoslav federal constitution, proclaimed in January 1946, was simply a direct imitation of the Soviet constitution promulgated ten years earlier. It contained the usual mixture of fine-sounding declarations and logical black holes, proclaiming, for example, that each constituent republic was 'sovereign', but also eliminating the right to secede by declaring that the peoples of Yugoslavia had chosen to live together for ever.[6] Needless to say, the constitution made no mention of the Communist Party, from which all power actually flowed. Tito followed the method, similar to that used in other East European countries, of camouflaging the Party in a 'Popular Front' to begin with, until all political pluralism could finally be eliminated.[7] An excessively ambitious Five Year Plan was announced in 1947; and in 1949, after the break with Stalin, a rapid collectivization of agriculture was forced through, with the consequence that grain production plummeted and the major cities were threatened with starvation in the following year.[8]

One of the most typical features of this period of Stalinist policies was the campaign against religion. The Catholic Church was treated with special harshness, in view of the collaboration of some of its clergy with the Ustaša in Croatia and Bosnia. Some churches were destroyed, and monasteries, convents and seminaries were closed down. The Orthodox Church fared a little better, even though its institutions came under strong pressure during the first three or four years. Some of its senior clergy had cooperated with the quisling régime in Serbia, but there were also several 'progressive' young priests who had served as chaplains in Tito's army. So-called associations of such priests were encouraged within the Church, as a way of allowing the Communist Party to exercise indirect control.[9] As for Islam, it seems to have suffered a double disadvantage in the eyes of the new Yugoslav rulers: first, it was seen (correctly) as a type of religion which involved not only private beliefs but also social practices, and secondly it was viewed as backward and Asiatic. There was also a sense of old scores being settled at the end of the war, as Muslim activists were later to recall: 'The most severe losses were inflicted at the time by the Communists when military units entered villages. All potential opponents, mainly people of higher social standing and intellectuals known to be believers, were simply put to death without any judicial proceedings or investigation.'[10] The 1946 constitution did of course contain the usual clauses proclaiming that Yugoslavia would maintain the freedom of belief and the separation of Church and state; events were to suggest otherwise.

The courts of Islamic sacred law were suppressed in 1946; a law forbidding women to wear the veil was issued in 1950; in the same year the last of the mektebs, elementary schools where children acquired a basic knowledge of the Koran, were closed down, and the teaching of children in mosques was made a criminal offence. In 1952 all the tekkes in Bosnia were shut down, and the dervish orders were banned. According to some reports, Muslims doing military service or working in so-called volunteer labour brigades were forced to eat pork, and Communist officials were warned not to have their sons circumcised. The Muslim cultural and educational societies, Gajret, Narodna Uzdanica and others, were abolished; only one official (and, from 1947, state-controlled) Islamic association was permitted, together with its one carefully supervised medresa for the training of Muslim clergy. The Muslim printing-house in Sarajevo was also closed down, and no Islamic textbook was allowed to be issued in Yugoslavia until 1964. Some of these measures were covertly resisted, however: Islamic texts continued to circulate, children were taught in mosques, the dervish orders kept up their practices in private houses, and one students' organization, the 'Young Muslims', resisted the campaign against Islam until several hundred of its members were imprisoned in 1949–50.

The Muslim community had already suffered severe material damage during the war: it has been calculated that in the whole of Yugoslavia 756 mosques had been destroyed or badly damaged. Many were rebuilt by local initiative, but by 1950 there were still 199 disused mosques in Bosnia, some of them awaiting repair, others converted by the Communist authorities into museums, warehouses or even stables. The body which administered the vakufs was put in effect under state control, and instructed to hand over many of its most valuable properties (including the first modern office-block in Sarajevo) to the local authorities. Many Muslim graveyards were turned into parks or building-sites for offices and houses; true, the Reis ul-ulema Čaušević had suggested something similar before the war, but he had not imagined that it would be done without the consent of the Muslim community. And the final blow to the vakufs, whose properties had already been whittled down by the expropriation of agricultural land, came with the nationalization of rental property in 1958. The great charitable foundations which had operated for 400 years or more, such as that founded by Gazi Husrev-beg in the 1530s, were now defunct.[11]

The general conditions of religious life in Yugoslavia improved after 1954, when a new law was passed guaranteeing freedom of religion (again) and placing the Churches under direct state control. There was a vigorous programme of restoring Orthodox monasteries from 1956 onwards, partly for touristic purposes, and partly because a slightly more cosy relationship had now been established between the senior Orthodox clergy and the state.[12] But the general treatment of Islam improved in the late 1950s and 1960s for a very special reason: Yugoslavia's Muslim community was now being used as a tool of Tito's self-styled 'non-aligned' foreign policy.

Like many of Tito's widely acclaimed achievements, this was a policy into which he had stumbled almost by accident. Having been ejected (to his surprise) from Cominform, and having become heavily dependent on Western loans, subsidies and diplomatic support, he needed an ideology which would make this awkward position look purposive and at the same time enable him to justify keeping the embarrassingly helpful Western democracies at arm's length. He found it on a tour of Ethiopia, India and Egypt in 1955. Soon thereafter he started making speeches decrying the division of the world into blocs, and in the following year he took up the rhetoric of the non-aligned movement during a joint visit to Yugoslavia by Nasser and Nehru.[13] Both Nasser and the Indonesian leader Sukarno were introduced to the Reis ul-ulema on their visits to Belgrade in 1956; and whereas the official body representing Yugoslav Muslims, the 'Islamic Religious Community', had been instructed to boycott the World Islamic Congress in Karachi in 1952, its members were soon being sent round the world to appear as token Muslims in all kinds of Third World and non-aligned gatherings.[14] Soon a Muslim background was a positive advantage for anyone hoping to get on in the Yugoslav diplomatic service. By the mid-1960s there were prominent Bosnian Muslim diplomats serving in several Arab states and Indonesia, including the son of a former Reis ul-ulema.[15] That these officials were Communist Party members who had largely abandoned their religion seemed not to matter, so long as they had names such as Mehmed, Ahmed and Mustafa.

The question of what it meant to be a Muslim in Bosnia – of whether it was a religious, an ethnic or a national identity – had not gone away, despite the belief of the Yugoslav Communist Party in the early Tito years that it would. In the 1940s the official position was that this problem would gradually solve itself as Muslims came to identify with Croats or Serbs. At the first Party Congress after the end of the war it was stated that 'Bosnia cannot be divided between Serbia and Croatia, not only because Serbs and Croats live mixed together on the whole territory, but also because the territory is inhabited by Muslims who have not yet decided on their national identity'.[16] What 'decided on their national identity' meant here was 'decided whether to call themselves Serbs or Croats'. Party members were put under some pressure to declare themselves as one or the other. An analysis of Party functionaries with Muslim names in the first (1956) Yugoslav *Who's Who* shows that 17 per cent declared themselves as Croats and 62 per cent as Serbs – a sign, among other things, of which way the wind was blowing in Bosnian political life at this time. In the 1948 census the Muslims had three options: they could call themselves Muslim Serbs, Muslim Croats or 'Muslims, nationally undeclared' (or 'undetermined'). This gave the Bosnian Muslims a chance to demonstrate just how reluctant they were to be either Serbified or Croaticized: 72,000 declared themselves as Serbs and 25,000 as Croats, but 778,000 registered as 'undeclared'. The next census, in 1953, produced a similar result. This time, the official policy was to promote a spirit of 'Yugoslavism': the category 'Muslim' was removed from the census altogether, but people were allowed to register as 'Yugoslav, nationally undeclared'. In Bosnia, 891,800 did so.[17]

It was in the 1960s that the official policy began to change, and it is not altogether clear why this happened. For the first fifteen to twenty years after the war, the senior official posts in Bosnia were dominated by Serbs: in the 1940s the Bosnian Communist Party membership was 20 per cent Muslim and 60 per cent Serb. The policy of the Bosnian republican government was very subservient to Belgrade, with a tendency to treat the republic as little more than an outer province of Serbia. With the stepping down of the Serb Djuro Pucar as Bosnian Party boss in 1965 this influence was weakened; and with the dismissal from the Yugoslav Central Committee of Aleksandar Ranković, Tito's brutal Serb security chief, in the following year, there was a general relaxation of policy towards the non-Serb peoples of the whole country. Yet the shift towards recognizing the Bosnian Muslims as a nation was already under way before these events. Probably it arose from a conjunction of two causes: the decision to drop the policy of 'integral Yugoslavism' and strengthen republican identities instead in the early 1960s, and the belated rise of a small élite of Muslim Communist officials within the Party machine in Bosnia.[18]

The first sign of a change came with the 1961 census, where people were allowed to call themselves 'Muslim in the ethnic sense'. Then the 1963 Bosnian constitution referred equally in its preamble to 'Serbs, Croats and Muslims allied in the past by a common life' – implying, but not stating, that they were equally to be regarded as nations.[19] This was regarded as a decisive step, and from now on it became common in Bosnia to treat the Muslims as a national grouping on a par with the others; one reflection of this change was that the documents for the election of officials of the Bosnian League of Communists in 1965 simply listed people as either 'Serb',

'Croat' or 'Muslim'.[20] But still the designation of the Muslims as a nation had not been officially made, and a number of academics and officials (under the intellectual leadership of Professor Muhamed Filipović, and with the assistance of Communist functionaries such as Atif Purivatra) continued to campaign for 'the capital M' – in other words, for 'Musliman' as the term for a member of a nation, rather than 'musliman' as the word for a religious believer. There was residual resistance to this in the Party, which expelled Professor Filipović in 1967. But success finally came at a meeting of the Bosnian Central Committee in May 1968, where a communiqué was issued containing the following statement: 'Practice has shown the harm of different forms of pressure . . . from the earlier period when Muslims were designated as Serbs or Croats from the national viewpoint. It has been shown, and present socialist practice confirms, that the Muslims are a distinct nation.'[21] Despite fierce objections in Belgrade from Serbian nationalist Communists such as Dobrica Ćosić, this policy was accepted by the central government. And so, on the 1971 census form, for the first time, the phrase appeared: 'Muslim, in the sense of a nation'.[22]

The other source of opposition to this policy was the Communist Party hierarchy in Macedonia. The Macedonians themselves had only been recognized, belatedly, as a nation in 1945, and did not like the idea that their own sizeable Slav Muslim minority might now detach itself in a similar way from Macedonian nationality.[23] But the comparison with Bosnia in fact enables us to see why the Bosnian policy, though strange-sounding, made sense. In the case of a Macedonian Slav Muslim, it is possible to talk about religion as a kind of surface layer which can be peeled back to reveal the ethnic or national substratum underneath. Remove the layer of Islam, and you are left with a Slav who can be identified as 'Macedonian' by criteria of language and history. But in the case of a Bosnian Muslim, what is one to call the substratum? One can call it 'Slav' or 'Bosnian', and one might call it 'Serbo-Croat'; but to call it *either* Serb *or* Croat would be wrong, for two reasons. First, because no such distinct 'Serb' or 'Croat' identities existed in Bosnia in the period before Islamicization; so it would be false to talk about a 'Muslim Serb' as if to imply that his ancestors were Serbs before they became Muslims. And the second reason is that when Bosnian

Christians began, at a very late stage, to identify themselves as Serbs or Croats, they did so purely on grounds of religion. (Thus the descendants of Catholic Hungarian or German settlers who came to Bosnia in the Austro-Hungarian period have come to identify themselves as 'Croats', and the descendants of Orthodox Romanian Gypsies have identified themselves as 'Serbs'.)[24] Many of the Orthodox Bosnians may have been descended from Serb immigrants or Vlachs, as we have seen; but there had been so many influxes and effluxes of populations, as well as conversions, that few individuals can have been certain of their precise ethnic genealogy. For centuries the language, history and geographical location of these two sorts of Bosnian Christians had been the same – which means that in most important respects the substratum which lay beneath their own religious identities was one and the same.

The artificial move, in other words, was the move made by Orthodox or Catholic Bosnians in the late nineteenth and early twentieth centuries when they started to call themselves by the ethnic labels of Serbs and Croats. That they did so is historically understandable, as we have seen. But once they had made that move, it became impossible for the Muslims to take the logical course, which would have been to describe their religion as Muslim and their ethnic substratum as Bosnian. That would have had the effect of setting up 'Bosnian' as a third term in contradistinction to 'Serb' and 'Croat' – which would be like the use of 'Muslim' as a third term, only even more divisive, since at least the three groups can now still be referred to as Bosnian Muslims, Bosnian Serbs and Bosnian Croats.

The drive for recognition of the Muslims as a nation in the late 1960s and early 1970s was not an Islamic religious movement. On the contrary, it was led by Communists and other secularized Muslims who wanted the Muslim identity in Bosnia to develop into something more definitely non-religious. Two quite distinct trends can be seen in Bosnia during this period: this movement of secular 'Muslim nationalism', and a separate revival of Islamic religious belief.[25] What later became the best-known product of the latter revival was a short treatise written (but not published) in the late 1960s by Alija Izetbegović, the *Islamic Declaration*.[26] The arguments of Izetbegović's treatise (which will be discussed in the next chapter) were not merely distinct from those of politicians such as Purivatra, but positively contrary to them: concerned not with the problems of Bosnia but with the situation of Islam in the whole world, Izetbegović wrote of nationalism as a divisive force and of Communism as an inadequate system. This anti-Communist religious revival was a small phenomenon at first, though the effects of Tito's 'non-aligned' policy made it easier for Bosnian Muslims to make contact with the wider Muslim world and thereby stimulate the study of Islamic theology in Bosnia. More Bosnians were allowed to study at Arab universities in the 1970s, and in 1977 a Faculty of Islamic Theology was even set up (with Saudi Arabian money) at Sarajevo University.[27]

Such developments were far from what campaigners such as Purivatra had been striving for. Their concerns were that the Muslims of Bosnia were under-represented politically in the Communist administration of the republic, and that the republic as a whole was regarded as somehow lower in status than the other republics of Yugoslavia. This inferior treatment had come about, they felt, because Bosnia was seen as containing not a distinctive nation but merely fragments of two other nations (Serbs and Croats) and a non-nation. It was an analysis which contained a great deal of truth. Bosnia did punch below its weight in the Yugoslav federal system, and its economic development lagged far behind those of its more powerful neighbours. There had been a brief spurt of development after the break with Cominform in 1948, when Tito, preoccupied with thoughts of a Soviet invasion, had decided to locate armaments factories and other strategically important industries in the more inaccessible parts of Bosnia. This phase of planning had quickly passed, and Bosnia had been left with what one analyst has described as 'new (and often unfinished) factories established in splendid isolation from markets, roads or skilled manpower'.[28]

Relatively to the rest of Yugoslavia, Bosnia stagnated and declined during the 1950s and 1960s, with its per capita social product falling from 79 per cent of the Yugoslav average in 1953 to 75 per cent in 1957 and 69 per cent in 1965. In 1961 much of Bosnia was officially declared an under-developed region. Out of all the Yugoslav republics, Bosnia had the lowest rate of economic growth over the entire period 1952–68; Bosnia's national income, which was 20 per cent below the national average in 1947, had fallen to 38 per cent below average by 1967.[29] The social statistics tell a similar story, revealing problems which were partly symptoms of economic backwardness and partly causes. By the early 1970s Bosnia had the highest infant mortality rate of any part of Yugoslavia except Kosovo; the highest illiteracy rate (except Kosovo again); the highest proportion of people whose only education was three years of primary school (except Kosovo); and the smallest proportion of people living in towns (except Kosovo). It also had by far the largest rate of net intra-Yugoslav emigration – roughly 16,000 people every year throughout the 1950s and 1960s. Most of these emigrants were Serbs going to live in Serbia.[30] It was partly as a result of this that the Muslims overtook the Serbs in Bosnia as the largest component of the population in the mid-1960s.

The establishment of Muslim nationhood in the late 1960s played some part in the revival of republican pride which helped to turn the Bosnian economy around. Several changes to the federal constitution during this whole period, starting with the new constitution of 1963 and ending with another rewriting of the constitution in 1974, also gave more scope for the pursuit of development policies by the individual republics; during the 1970s the Bosnian authorities were promoting some grandiose industrial projects and adding large new tower-block suburbs to their major towns. By 1980 one observer could report that Sarajevo 'appeared to be a huge public works project. The city plumbing system was being redone, main streets down-town were being dug up and repaired, tram lines were being torn up to be replaced by wider tracks', and so on.[31] The immediate cause of all such activity in the Bosnian capital was of course the scheduling of the Winter Olympics there for 1984. But this new development was merely the most dramatic example of a type of work being carried out in many other parts of the republic, mainly on borrowed money.

The trend towards the decentralization of Yugoslavia, which reached its high point in the constitution of 1974, was nevertheless creating more problems than it was solving. Just enough of a principle of separate national political identities was conceded to whet the appetite for more. History suggests that federations of different national entities can work successfully only if they are based on a genuinely democratic political system; but this was not the case in Communist Yugoslavia, where any striving for greater national autonomy was bound to absorb like blotting-paper all the bitter political dissatisfaction which was flowing through the whole system. It is easy to persuade one nation that it is being oppressed or connived against by another, when the whole political system in which both nations are locked is undemocratic and intrinsically oppressive. And the natural breeding-ground for all kinds of discontent is a weak and malfunctioning economy – something which was also guaranteed under the Yugoslav Communist system. Indeed, the malfunctioning grew generally worse as a result of the decentralizing measures of the 1960s and 1970s, since there were now redundant duplications of industries and infrastructure projects between the republics. The very worst kind of competition is the sort which happens when the competitors are operating on politically arranged loans and subsidies, and the competition itself is not made subject to the real discipline of a market.

There were many revivals of resentful national feeling during the period from the mid-1960s to the late 1980s, some brandishing better justifications than others. The most important were those in Croatia and Serbia. In the late 1960s a number of different Croatian complaints and discontents began to coalesce: complaints about the development of an official version of the Serbo-Croat language which was dominated by the Serbian forms of words, about the hold which Belgrade-based banks had on the tourist economy of Dalmatia, and about a range of other economic and demographic problems.[32] This movement to insist on the rights of Croatia, which became combined with a campaign for greater liberalization of the Yugoslav political system, was known in the West as the 'Croatian spring'. It was essentially directed against the Serbs, but it carried over the fight onto Bosnian territory too.

By 1971 a Croatian journal published an analysis of the ethnic identities of all the officials in the Bosnian administration, which demonstrated that the Croats were thoroughly under-represented. Although they were more than 20 per cent of the population, they hardly featured in important media posts such as the directorships of Sarajevo Radio and Television; all presiding judges were Serbs, and none of the directors of the various republican agencies was a

Croat. Senior Bosnian politicians such as Hamdija Pozderac replied that it should not matter what nationality an official was, provided that he worked for the benefit of the whole of Bosnia.[33] But the competition between Croatian and Serbian nationalist concerns over Bosnia was already too strong to be fobbed off with such arguments. Already in 1969 a Serbian writer, Josip Potkozorac, had published a book arguing that the entire population of Bosnia (and of Dalmatia too) was 'really' Serb. As these arguments sputtered on through the 1970s, Croatian and Serbian nationalists started to talk openly of carving pieces of 'ethnic' territory off Bosnia and incorporating them in Croatia and Serbia respectively.[34] No attempt was made to show that the policies of the Bosnian authorities were actively anti-Croat or anti-Serb during this period; purely statistical oppression on the one hand, and bogus ethnic history on the other, were sufficient. The only effect of these statistical arguments on the way things were done in Bosnia was that a cumbersome quota system developed of proportional or 'one-of-each' appointments to public jobs – a small further contribution to economic and administrative sclerosis.

The growth of Serbian nationalism was, in the end, to prove more destructive. On the face of it, Serbia had fewer reasons for discontent than any other Yugoslav republic during the first twenty years of Communist rule. The country was governed from Belgrade again; Serbs dominated the Party and the armed forces; and for those who had lived through the war there was a strong sense that Serbia's record was morally superior to Croatia's. But Tito's post-1945 settlement had not given Serbia the sort of territorial rewards which were the customary gains of war. The whole territory of Yugoslav Macedonia was turned into a separate republic; although it had a non-Serb population, it had been conquered by Serbian armies in 1912–13 and incorporated into the Serbian kingdom under the made-up title of 'Southern Serbia'. So the change in 1945 was seen by nationalist Serbs as a theft of Serbian territory. The northern region of Vojvodina, where Serbs were less than 50 per cent of the population, had become part of the Yugoslav kingdom in 1918; Tito gave it the status of an 'autonomous province' within Serbia. This was also seen as an anti-Serbian act by some Serbs, even though Vojvodina had never been part of Serbia itself. And the region of Kosovo with its Albanian majority, also conquered by Serbia in 1912–13, was declared by Tito to be an 'autonomous region' of Serbia. These changes rankled with many Serbs, and outweighed in their minds the territorial gain which Serbia had made when Tito gave it Srem, the large eastern tip of the Croatian territory. (Tito made no change whatsoever to the historic border between Serbia and Bosnia, which remained as it had been in the late Ottoman and Austro-Hungarian periods.)

Conditions were ripe for a conspiracy theory which argued that Tito, the half-Croat, half-Slovene, had plotted against Serbia's historic interests. And such feelings grew stronger during the 1960s and early 1970s, as the frequent alterations to the constitution gave more and more administrative autonomy to Vojvodina and Kosovo – until, in the 1974 constitution, they had some (but not all) of the powers of full republics, including their own representation on the main federal bodies. After the fall in 1966 of Tito's security chief, Aleksandar Ranković, who had ruled Kosovo with a rod of iron and a large number of Serb officials, the situation there changed dramatically. First there was a backlash of local Albanians against local Serbs, with anti-Serb riots in 1968 and other reported incidents of violence, and then there was a rapid 'Albanianization' of the province, during which the Serbs in Kosovo became uncomfortably aware of their own status as a small minority of the province's population. Thousands of Serbs left the province for Serbia proper; some were fleeing because they felt threatened, but many were looking for work and/or taking part in that general drift of outlying populations towards their national heartlands which, as we have seen, was affecting Bosnian Serbs too during the same period.[35]

The situation in Kosovo, which by the early 1980s had reached a state of permanent crisis and military occupation, became the main focus for the revival of Serbian nationalism. As early as 1968, Serbian nationalist Communists such as Dobrica Ćosić were complaining about the reversal of policy in Kosovo after Ranković's fall. 'One could witness even among the Serbian people a reignition of the old historic goal and national idea – the unification of the Serbian people into a single state', he said.[36] This statement, phrased as a warning but issued in the spirit of a threat, caused Ćosić to be expelled from the Central Committee. The fact that Ćosić also bitterly opposed the granting of national status to the Bosnian Muslims is not coincidental. Because the Kosovo Albanians were predominantly Muslim, anti-Islamic sentiment became an ever more important feature of Serbian nationalism; it had long been part of the baggage of Serbian literary culture, but was now expressed in much stronger forms, as in the fiercely anti-Muslim novel *Nož* ('The Knife'), published by the radical nationalist Vuk Drašković in the early 1980s.[37] The Serbian Orthodox Church also saw its opportunity to revive the sense of religious identity in the literary and political culture of the country; and the Serbs' obsessively possessive claims about Kosovo were indeed partly based on the fact that some of the Serbian Orthodox Church's oldest monasteries and church buildings, including the patriarchate itself, were located in the province.

Together with a revival of Orthodoxy, there was also a revival of interest in the forbidden topic of the Četniks during the second world war. And just as – indeed, because – the Communist policy had been to damn all the Četniks uncritically as fascist collaborators, so now the reaction of Serb nationalists was to praise them almost equally uncritically. The régime would have reason to regret its long-lasting suppression of objective historical studies of the war. Dobrica Ćosić published a novel in 1985 which featured a sympathetic portrait of the Četnik ideologist, Dragiša Vasić; and in the same year a book about the Četniks by the historian Veselin Djuretić was launched at a party hosted by the Serbian Academy of Sciences. This event was an important turning-point, a signal that Serbian nationalism could now be openly embraced by the intellectual establishment in Belgrade. In January of the following year two hundred prominent Belgrade academics and writers signed a petition which referred in hysterical terms to the 'Albanian aggression' and 'genocide' in Kosovo. All the old Serbian resentments now came to the surface: 'a rigged political trial of the Serb nation and its history has been going on for decades', it complained.[38]

Later in 1986 a 'Memorandum' was drawn up by the Serbian Academy of Sciences (or at least, by a committee of it, whose membership is known to have included Ćosić), in which grievances about Kosovo were combined with the open accusation that Tito's policies had aimed at the weakening of Serbia. 'Nationalism', it complained, had been 'created from above'. This was a reference not to Serbian nationalism, of course, which these writers were busily helping to create from their own vantage-point, but to the national identities of Croats, Slovenes, Macedonians, Montenegrins and Bosnian Muslims. The Memorandum claimed that a sinister programme of assimilation was under way in Croatia, designed to turn the Serbs there into Croats, and it also complained that ethnic Serb writers in places such as Montenegro and Bosnia were being described as writing not Serbian literature but 'Montenegrin' or 'Bosnian' literature instead. The fundamental argument of the Memorandum was that the 'Serb people' throughout Yugoslavia was a kind of primary entity, possessing a unitary set of rights and claims which transcended any mere political or geographical divisions: 'The question of the integrity of the Serb people and its culture in the whole of Yugoslavia poses itself as a crucial question for that people's survival and development.'[39] It was the pursuit of that 'integrity' which would eventually destroy Yugoslavia, and bring about the destruction of Bosnia too.

With this climate of opinion developing in Serbia during the 1970s and early 1980s, there was an increasing sensitivity on the part of the authorities in Bosnia towards any expressions of the Muslim religious revival which might seem to have political implications. The Bosnian republican government was not acting, it must be said, in the new spirit of anti-Muslim Serbian nationalism. On the contrary, it was trying to preserve the official Communist policy which aimed at the eventual withering away of any religious element in national identity. It was therefore as much alarmed by any signs of religiously-motivated politics among the Muslims as it was by the new alliance of nationalism and Orthodoxy among the Serbs, and could see that any growth in the former would supply ammunition to the latter. Members of the Muslim clergy in Bosnia were becoming more outspoken in their criticisms of the Communist system; and after the Iranian revolution of 1979 there were stories of pictures of the Ayatollah Khomeini being seen posted in Bosnian windows, which caused an extra frisson of alarm. Although it was their own 'non-aligned' policy which had lifted Islam out of the doldrums in Bosnia and increased its contacts with the rest of the Muslim world, the authorities now decided to act against any further growth in popularity of the Islamic faith. In 1979 one Muslim Communist, Derviš Šušić, was encouraged to publish in the Sarajevo newspaper *Oslobodjenje* a series of extracts from a book he was writing which exposed the collaboration of senior members of the Muslim clergy with the Ustaša and the Germans during the second world war. When Šušić was attacked for this by the official publication of the Islamic community, *Preporod*, he was publicly defended by one of the leading spokesmen of official policy on religion, Professor Fuad Muhić of Sarajevo University. The most senior Muslim Communist politician, Hamdija Pozderac, also joined the fray, launching several public attacks on what he called 'Pan-Islamism'.[40]

It was against this background that the most famous clampdown on Muslim activists in Bosnia took place: the trial in Sarajevo in 1983 of thirteen people charged with 'hostile and counter-revolutionary acts derived from Muslim nationalism'. The leading defendant was Dr Alija Izetbegović, a lawyer and retired director of a building company, who had completed his *Islamic Declaration* thirteen years previously. He and three others of the accused had all been members of the 'Young Muslims' organization which had opposed the Communist attack on Islam at the end of the second world war. This was raked up against them, and they were accused of reviving the aims of a 'terrorist' organization. Izetbegović was also accused, for good measure, of advocating the introduction of Western-style parliamentary democracy. The main piece of evidence was the text of the *Islamic Declaration*, which according to the prosecution was a manifesto for the creation of an ethnically pure Muslim Bosnian state. Izetbegović pointed out that the text said nothing about making Bosnia ethnically pure, and indeed that it contained no reference to Bosnia at all; but such details did not detain the court, which sentenced him to fourteen years' imprisonment, reduced on appeal to eleven years.[41]

This crackdown had an intimidating effect on Muslim religious activists in Bosnia, and for a while strengthened the position of the senior Muslim Communists, such as Hamdija Pozderac, who could be content with the idea of Muslim national identity so long as it remained essentially secular. But it was not long before this form of Muslim politics was also undermined, by a spectacular business scandal which brought about Pozderac's own downfall. The scandal involved an enterprise in the north-western corner of Bosnia, called Agrokomerc, which started off as a poultry-farming business in the 1960s and grew from there. Indeed, under its charismatic director, Fikret Abdić, it grew so much that by 1987 it was employing 13,000 people in the region and was one of the thirty largest enterprises in Yugoslavia. The secret of its growth was that it had issued promissory notes, at high rates of interest, without the backing of any collateral – something which was possible so long as the notes were endorsed by the official stamp of the local bank. (The stamp had apparently been handed over to Agrokomerc, to save the bother of having to take the notes to the bank.) This was not an untypical story of the way things were done in Yugoslavia: the only unusual thing about it was the sheer scale of the operation, involving as it did promissory notes worth as much as $500 million. As one senior Belgrade banker put it, 'All the top bankers and politicians must have known that Agrokomerc was overspending. What Abdić did is done everywhere. His only mistake was in going too far.' Equally, everyone knew that senior members of the Bosnian government were connected with the enterprise, including Pozderac, whose brother Hakija was on the Agrokomerc payroll as a consultant. Abdić himself was a member of the Bosnian Central Committee; he was now dismissed. Pozderac held a far more prestigious post, that of Vice-President of Yugoslavia; he eventually resigned, though still protesting his innocence.[42]

Abdić in particular remained a very popular figure among ordinary Muslims, who felt that he had tried hard to bring employment and prosperity to a very poor area of Bosnia. Many were convinced that the whole affair had been manipulated from Belgrade as a way of cutting down some of the most prominent Muslim politicians. Pozderac himself had been in line to become President of Yugoslavia; he had also been chairing the Constitutional Committee, working on a new revision to the constitution which, it was believed in Belgrade, would be 'anti-Serbian' in the changes it made. Certainly it was pressure from Serbian newspapers, notably *Borba*, that had forced Pozderac to resign. The consequences of the affair were devastating for the economy of the whole north-western region of Bosnia, with its mainly Muslim population.

In two ways this whole episode symbolized the malaise which was afflicting Bosnia and the whole of Yugoslavia by the middle of the 1980s. First there was the general breakdown of a ramshackle economic system which had only been able to boom on borrowed money. The country was littered with giant factories which would have run at a loss even without the interest payments on the loans which had financed their creation. At Zvornik in eastern Bosnia, for example, there was the largest alumina plant in Europe, employing 4000 workers. It was built there, financed by foreign loans, to process the local bauxite; once it was in operation the managers discovered that the local bauxite was not of good enough quality, and by 1987 they were having to import bauxite from Africa instead.[43] The whole Titoist economic system – which has been aptly described as 'Self-Mismanagement' – was in a state of terminal decline, with a steep and steady fall in real wages and a rise in absenteeism and strikes. When the Bosnian Croat leader Branko Mikulić was appointed Prime Minister of the federal government in 1986, he promised to implement far-reaching economic reforms and to bring the inflation rate down to 20 per cent. Some austerity measures were introduced, which contributed to the general unpopularity of the government and the federal system, but the major structural reforms never materialized, and the government spent months instead on deciding such matters as whether it could raise the limit for private employment to ten employees per enterprise. Meanwhile inflation rose to 120 per cent in 1987 and 250 per cent in 1988. By the end of that year, Yugoslavia's total foreign debt came to $33 billion, of which $20 billion was repayable in hard currencies to the West.[44] In this way, the long-term legacy of Tito's economic policies had been to create an increasingly discontented and impoverished population – the perfect place for demagogues to get to work, stirring up the politics of resentment.

The second way in which the Agrokomerc affair symbolized the state of Yugoslavia generally was in what it revealed about the entire class of senior Communist politicians. For decades most of the country had been ruled by local dynasties, political families which had done well out of the war and had been promoted early on to positions where they could develop networks of personal patronage. Those who had fought with the Partisans could expect to share the fruits of power with Tito for the rest of their lifetimes. (As one Yugoslav joke put it: 'What is the difference between Yugoslavia and the USA?' Answer: 'In the USA you work for forty years and then become President for four; in Yugoslavia you fight for four years and then become President for forty.') The Pozderac family was the most prominent example of this in Bosnia: since the eldest brother, Nurija, had joined Tito in 1941, the political future of the entire family was assured. The leading Bosnian Serb politician during the 1970s and 1980s, Milanko Renovica, was also trading on his war record, having been one of the few pro-Partisan Serbs in a predominantly pro-Četnik area.

This system worked as an overlapping set of medieval dukedoms, with networks of influence and patronage extending outwards from these privileged individuals through all areas of life. At its most benign, like any system of patronage, it could give assistance and promotion to deserving individuals; but the whole system was intrinsically corrupt. It was also stagnating, as the generation which had fought in the war passed its retirement age. A new generation of people who had worked their way up through the post-war Communist hierarchy was now manoeuvring for power, and the general political stagnation and economic decline made it easy for them to find levers with which to remove those who stood above them. The disillusionment of ordinary Yugoslavs was almost universal. For many, this took the form of a withdrawal from any kind of political life. At the 1987 conference of the Bosnian League of Communists the main complaint – somewhat primly phrased – was that 'there is an increasing tendency for young people to exhibit passivity, indifference and neutrality, reflecting their dissatisfaction with current conditions'.[45] But elsewhere in Yugoslavia, as the economy collapsed, stronger emotions were aroused.

In July 1988 thousands of factory workers demonstrated in Belgrade against the Mikulić government's austerity measures. Later that summer, mass demonstrations took place against the local Party bosses in Vojvodina and Montenegro, eventually forcing the resignation of the entire Politburos in both places in October 1988 and January 1989 respectively. This popular pressure had been carefully organized and promoted by the new leader of the Serbian Communists, Slobodan Milošević, who was now able to replace those

Politburos with his own supporters. What Milošević had done was to hijack the genuine discontentments of ordinary Vojvodinans and Montenegrins – including some frustration with the whole Communist system as such – and put it to his own uses. At the same time he was putting strong pressure on the Communist hierarchy in Kosovo, aiming at a similar transformation there from opposition to client status; and the fact that the local Albanians resisted this pressure from Belgrade made it easy for him to portray the operation in nationalist terms as a defence of Serbian national interests against the perfidious Albanians. In March 1989 the Serbian Assembly passed, at his request, constitutional amendments which abolished the political autonomy of Kosovo and Vojvodina: this provoked mass demonstrations and a general strike in Kosovo, which were crushed by the Serbian security forces.[46] All the pieces of the jigsaw were now in place. There was an ambitious politician in Belgrade who had learnt the methods of Communist power-politics as he worked his way up the system; there was general economic malaise and discontent, which made people yearn for decisive leadership; and the ideology of Serb nationalism, so long frustrated, was now finding an expression in a policy which 'restored' Vojvodina and Kosovo to Serbian control. Two processes seemed fused into one: the gathering of power into Milošević's hands, and the gathering of the Serbs into a single political unit which could either dominate Yugoslavia or break it apart.

15

Bosnia and the death of Yugoslavia: 1989–1992

On 28 June 1989 several hundred thousand Serbs assembled at the battlefield site of Gazimestan, outside the Kosovar capital, Priština, to celebrate the six-hundredth anniversary of the Battle of Kosovo.[1] For many weeks a ferment of national feeling had been created inside Serbia; the bones of Prince Lazar, who died at the battle, had been taken on a tour of the country, becoming an object of pilgrimage wherever they were. In the courtyard of the monastery at Gračanica (south of Priština), while people queued to pay their devotions to the Prince's bones inside, stalls sold icon-style posters of Jesus Christ, Prince Lazar and Slobodan Milošević side by side. At the ceremony on the battlefield Milošević was accompanied by black-robed metropolitans of the Orthodox Church, singers in traditional Serbian folk costumes, and members of the security police in their traditional dress of dark suits and sunglasses. 'After six centuries', Milošević told the crowd, 'we are again engaged in battles and quarrels. They are not armed battles, but this cannot be excluded yet.'[2] The crowd roared its approval.

This was a symbolic turning-point in the history of the Yugoslav lands. Milošević now had much of what he wanted. He had acquired an unchallengeable personal standing in Serbia, by a combination of Communist methods and nationalist rhetoric. Out of the eight votes in the federal government, he now controlled four: Serbia, Vojvodina, Kosovo and Montenegro. He had only to reduce Macedonia to client status as well to be able to do what he wanted with the federal government; and the federal constitution could then be rewritten to entrench the dominance of Serbia.

However, the very process which had brought him to this point had made it unlikely that the parts of Yugoslavia which he did not control would ever submit to any such reordering of their country. The Croatian nationalist feelings which had been simmering discontentedly ever since the suppression of the 'Croatian spring' in the early 1970s had been stung into action by the revival of Serbian nationalism in the mid-1980s. Milošević had not merely ended the taboo on certain forms of anti-Croat rhetoric, he had positively encouraged them – so that by now the official Serbian media were commonly referring to the head of the Croatian Communists, Ivica Račan, as an 'Ustaša'.[3] All the old Croatian grievances came to the surface again, and in the new atmosphere of breaking taboos about the second world war many were beginning to resent both the automatic linking of Croats and the Ustaša, and the official histories which had crudely exaggerated the total numbers killed in Croatia during the war. The result was an upsurge not of Ustaša apologists (though there would be some of those later) but of Croatian nationalists, such as the former Partisan and Yugoslav army general, Franjo Tudjman, who wanted to distinguish the long-standing national aspirations of Croatia for independence of Belgrade from the Ustaša history with which they had become entangled. And apart from all the historical debates, there were real fears for the future too, such as those sparked off by Dobrica Ćosić in July 1989 when he told an interviewer that large parts of Croatia should be 're-assigned' to another republic.[4]

Meanwhile the most Westernized and independent-minded of the republics, Slovenia, was making arrangements to protect itself from the next stages of Milošević's slow-moving constitutional coup. In September and October 1989 it drafted and passed a new Slovenian constitution, giving itself legislative sovereignty – in other words, saying that its own laws would take precedence over those of the federal state – and explicitly declaring its right to secede.[5] While this was happening, the dramatic collapse of Communist power in Eastern Europe was filling the television screens night after night. The trickle of independent political parties which had been started up in Yugoslavia in 1988 now became a flood. In January 1990 the Slovenian Communists walked out of the Yugoslav Communist Party Congress; two weeks later they renamed themselves the Party of Democratic Renewal. Both Slovenia and Croatia made arrangements for multi-party elections in the spring of 1990: these were won in the former republic by a liberal-nationalist coalition and in the latter by the new Croatian nationalist party, the 'Croatian Democratic Union' (HDZ), led by Franjo Tudjman.

Milošević too renamed his party (as the 'Serbian Socialist Party'), and began talking of multi-party elections in Serbia. These were postponed until the end of the year; Milošević may have been unsettled by a period of relative unpopularity which he underwent in the first half of 1990, and perhaps wanted to wait for something more like a situation of national crisis to develop in which he could resume his role as Serbia's saviour. Since he had Serbian radio and television under close control, there was little risk of him losing a properly planned election. But there was a need during the first half of 1990 for him to rethink his strategy. Up till now he had pursued his first preference, which was to gain control over Yugoslavia through the existing structures of the Communist Party and the federal government. But this option had slipped from his grasp, with the disintegration of the Communist Party and the 'vertical' division of Yugoslav politics into a set of national parties in the various republics. That left him with his second option: if Yugoslavia could not be controlled as a single entity, then he would carve out of it a new entity, an extended Serbian territory, which would be his and his alone. Slovene and Croatian politicians spent much of 1990 pleading for a peaceful and negotiated transformation of Yugoslavia from a federal into a confederal state – that is, from one in which federal law and institutions are primary to one in which it is the republics which hold the real authority, and the federal bodies simply act as their joint agencies. But Milošević showed no interest in any such schemes.

The first clear sign of Milošević's new strategy came in the Knin region of Croatia – part of the old Military Frontier or 'Krajina' zone on Bosnia's north-western border which had a majority population of Serbs. For the Croatian elections in April 1990 these Serbs had organized themselves into a 'Serbian Democratic Party' (SDS); Milošević had probably taken an interest from the start in this development, but it seems to have been essentially a local initiative, expressing the fears of the local Serbs that they would lose their cultural identity in the new nationalist Croatia. Some of the party's more extreme members, echoing the propaganda from Belgrade, declared that they had to defend themselves against an 'Ustaša state' – a reference in the first place to the revival of the Croatian chequerboard flag, which had indeed been an Ustaša symbol, but had also been the Croatian national flag for hundreds of years. After the election, when the new government began dismissing Communist functionaries, it was also claimed that Serbs were being dismissed *en masse* from their jobs. Since the Serbs were heavily overrepresented in the state apparatus in Croatia (making up nearly 40 per cent of the Communist Party members and 67 per cent of the police force), they were bound to figure disproportionately in the dismissals; and no doubt there were some unjust settlings of old scores too.

In the summer of 1990, however, the Knin SDS was taken over by an extremist leader who seems to have been in close contact with Milošević. A local referendum was held in August on 'autonomy' for the Serbs, in defiance of the Croatian government, which declared it illegal; an armed Serb militia began to appear on the streets of Knin, apparently aided by officers of the federal army garrison (whose commanding officer was General Ratko Mladić); the Croatian authorities tried to confiscate the arms supplies of the local police reserve units; and the Serbs, told by their leaders and by the Belgrade media that the 'Ustaša' were planning to massacre them, asked the federal army for protection. Riots occurred, and Croatian policemen were shot. By January 1991 the local Serb leaders were describing the area as the 'Serb Autonomous Region of the Krajina', and forming their own 'parliament'. Two months later armed men from the Krajina tried to take over the nearby Plitvice National Park, the most important tourist resort in inland Croatia: this was a direct and deliberate challenge to the Croatian government. A shoot-out occurred with Croatian police, and the Federal presidency ordered the army (over Croatia's strong objections) to occupy the park to 'restore peace'.[6]

These events occurring on the other side of Bosnia's north-western border are worth looking at in some detail, because they constitute the blueprint for what was later done in Bosnia itself. Three techniques were at work, one general and two particular. The general method was to radicalize the Serb population with a non-stop bombardment of misinformation and fear-mongering through the media and the local politicians: every action of Tudjman's government was presented as an act of 'Ustaša' terror. (It must be pointed out that some of the Croatian government's measures were crassly insensitive, such as ordering the removal of street-signs in the Cyrillic alphabet; whereas the Bosnian government was to lean over backwards to placate its own Serb population.) The second method was a standard technique which could be found in textbooks on guerrilla warfare: the technique of 'compromising the villages', as employed by the French Resistance, the Viet-Cong and innumerable other guerrilla movements. This technique involves staging an incident – for example, shooting a carload of Croatian policemen outside a particular village – to invite a crackdown or reprisal, and then distributing arms to the villagers, telling them that the police are planning to attack them. When armed police do arrive, it is easy to spark off a gun battle; and suddenly a whole village, previously uncommitted, is now on the side of the insurgents. And the third technique was a simple trick and a very transparent one: creating violent incidents and then asking the army to intervene as an impartial arbiter, when it was perfectly clear that the army, with its loyalty to Belgrade and its Serb-dominated officer corps, was acting on behalf of Milošević and the Serbs.

This carve-up of Croatian territory, which had thus begun a year before the Croatian declaration of independence of July 1991, relied quite heavily on the allegation that Serbs in Croatia were threatened by an 'Ustaša' régime. In Bosnia there was no possibility of making such a claim seem plausible; so a different threat to the Serbs had to be devised. Instead of 'Ustaša hordes', the Bosnian Serbs were told that they were threatened by 'Islamic fundamentalists'. It is necessary to look briefly at how the possibility of making this claim arose, and why it was false.

In Bosnia, as in most of the other republics, the Communist Party had disintegrated in early 1990 and a set of nationalist or national parties had been formed. From 1989 onwards the neighbouring nationalisms of Serbia and Croatia had become intimidating presences, with the ultimate ambitions of Milošević and Tudjman barely concealed. Milošević was openly associated with the pan-Serb political projects of Ćosić and the Serbian Academy; Tudjman was on record as believing that most of the Bosnian Muslims were 'incontrovertibly of Croatian origin' and that Bosnia and Croatia form 'an indivisible geographic and economic entity'.[7] In the autumn and winter of 1989 senior Bosnian officials were expressing fears that both Serbia and Croatia would seek to redraw the map, and in March 1990 the chambers of the Bosnian assembly met in a special joint session to denounce the idea of making any changes to Bosnia's borders. The situation was not altogether symmetrical between the Serbs and the Croats, however: there was a clear sense that it was Milošević who was making the running, and the official policy of Tudjman's party, the HDZ, was against the idea of any alterations to borders – since it knew that if any such idea were admitted, Croatia's own borders would be the first to suffer. The bombardment of propaganda from Belgrade about the 'imperilment' of the Serbs in Bosnia, which had already begun by the summer of 1989, had the effect of bringing Bosnian Croats and Muslims together on one side of the argument and putting the Serbs on the other. When a Croat party was founded in Bosnia in early 1990 it was an offshoot of Tudjman's HDZ, and its official policy was to keep the borders of Bosnia inviolate. But when a Serb party was founded in Bosnia in July, it called itself the SDS – the same as the party which was already agitating for 'autonomy' in the Croatian Krajina and would soon be in open revolt.[8]

The main Bosnian Muslim party, which called itself the 'Party of Democratic Action' (SDA), was founded in May 1990. Its leader was Alija Izetbegović, who had been released from prison in 1988; as the chief defendant in the most famous trial of the decade, he was a natural choice for Bosnia's first post-Communist and non-Communist Muslim party. (Indeed, when he eventually became head of the Bosnian government he was the only head of government in any of the post-Communist Yugoslav republics who had not himself been a Communist official.) Placed between the hammer and the anvil of Serbian and Croatian nationalism, the Bosnian Muslims reacted in two different ways: they strengthened their own Muslim nationalism by giving greater emphasis to the most distinctive thing about it, its religious component, and they also emphasized that they stood for the preservation of Bosnia's unique character as a multi-national, multi-religious republic. The religious element was expressed in the public symbolism of the SDA, with its green banners and crescents; and the pluralist element was expressed in its programme. That there was some real tension between these two elements was shown in September 1990, three months before the Bosnian elections, when one of the leaders of the SDA, the returned émigré millionaire Adil Zulfikarpašić, broke away to found his own party, the 'Bosnian Muslim Organization' (MBO), with an explicitly non-religious programme. Despite the very name of his new party, Zulfikarpašić was trying to lay the foundations of a non-sectional politics, in which people would vote on their choice of political programmes (liberal, socialist or whatever) rather than voting simply to assert their national identity. As Izetbegović himself pointed out, this was an unrealistic ambition at the time. He told one journalist:

> By their oppression the Communists created this longing among people to express their religious or national identity. Perhaps in four or five years we shall have passed through the minefield to the horizon of civil society. For now, unfortunately, our party *must* be sectional. The parties that try to represent everyone are small and weak. There is a real risk of civil war here; our main aim as a party is to keep Bosnia-Hercegovina together.[9]

But Izetbegović himself, of course, was personally identified with the religious element of the 'religious or national identity'. The treatise which had been used as the basis of the charges against him in 1983, the *Islamic Declaration*, was republished in Sarajevo in 1990. Some readers may have thought that it was a kind of personal manifesto for the Bosnian elections, and it has often been represented by Serbian propagandists as a blueprint for the transformation of Bosnia into a fundamentalist Islamic state. But no such plans were contained either in the programme of the SDA, or in the text of the *Islamic Declaration* itself.

This treatise, written in the late 1960s, is a general treatise on politics and Islam, addressed to the whole Muslim world; it is not about Bosnia and does not even mention Bosnia. Izetbegović starts with two basic elements: Islamic society and Islamic government. Islamic government, he says, cannot be introduced unless there is already an Islamic society, and the latter exists only when the absolute majority of the people are sincere and practising Muslims. 'Without this majority, the Islamic order is reduced to mere power (because the second element, Islamic society, is lacking), and can turn into tyranny.'[10] This provision ruled out the creation of an Islamic government in Bosnia, where Muslims – even nominal Muslims, let alone practising and devout ones – were in a minority. The entire discussion of the nature of an Islamic political system, which occupies most of the book, is thus inapplicable to Bosnia too. When Izetbegović says, for example (in a sentence frequently quoted in isolation by Serbian propagandists) that 'there is no peace or coexistence between the Islamic faith and non-Islamic social and political institutions', he is referring to countries which, unlike Bosnia, have Islamic societies, and arguing that where the majority of the people are practising Muslims they cannot accept the imposition of non-Muslim institutions.[11] There is only one passage in the entire treatise which applies directly to the political status of the Bosnian Muslims: 'Muslim minorities comprised in non-Muslim communities, so long as there is a guarantee of religious freedom and normal life and development, are loyal and are obliged to carry out all obligations towards that community, except those which harm Islam and Muslims.'[12]

Some of the arguments in this treatise which have been described as 'fundamentalist' are simple statements of orthodox belief with which any sincere Muslim would agree: thus Izetbegović writes that an Islamic state should try to stamp out alcoholism, pornography and prostitution; he argues that Islam is not simply a set of private beliefs but a whole way of life with a social and political dimension too; and he insists that the brotherhood of the entire world of Islamic believers, the *umma*, transcends national boundaries.[13] None of these points can be described as fundamentalist. The very term 'fundamentalism' is, admittedly, loose and impressionistic: it is not much used by scholars of Islam, who would want to distinguish carefully between different kinds of neo-conservative, radical or anti-modernist Islamic movements, ranging from the Wahhabi doctrine of the traditionalist Saudi Arabian state to the revolutionary ideology of Ayatollah Khomeini's Iran.[14] Instead, the term 'fundamentalism' is used mainly by politicians and journalists to lump together a number of characteristics. One of these is political extremism, the belief that the end of establishing Islamic power justifies any and every means. Izetbegović explicitly rejects this belief, attacking the idea of seizing power in order to create an Islamic society from above. His central argument is that an Islamic society can be created (in a population the majority of which are at least nominal Muslims) only by a long process of religious education and moral suasion.[15]

Another characteristic of what is loosely called fundamentalism is a fierce political and cultural hostility to the West. Izetbegović does criticize the rapid and coercive secularization of Turkey under Atatürk, which, he suggests, was based on the assumption that everything Islamic was culturally backward and primitive; and he inveighs against those 'so-called progressives, Westernizers and modernizers' who apply a similar policy elsewhere in the Muslim world.[16] But his general position in this treatise certainly does not involve the rejection of Western civilization. 'From its first foundation,' he writes, 'Islam undertook, without prejudice, the study and collection of the sum of knowledge bequeathed to it by earlier civilizations. We do not see why Islam today should take a different approach to the achievements of the Euro-American civilization with which it is in such broad contact.'[17] Izetbegović's views on these matters were set out much more fully in a longer and more important book written in the early 1980s, *Islam Between East and West*, in which he tried to present Islam as a kind of spiritual and intellectual synthesis which included the values of Western Europe. The book contained some eloquent pages in praise of Renaissance art (including portraiture) and European literature; it described Christianity as 'a near-union of supreme religion and supreme ethics'; and it also had a special chapter praising Anglo-Saxon philosophy and culture, and the social-democratic tradition.[18] No fundamentalist could have written that.

Talk of a fundamentalist threat in Bosnia was in any case particularly inappropriate, because the Bosnian Muslims were by now among the most secularized Muslim populations in the world. Small-scale and occasional attempts at fundamentalist agitation in Bosnia were undoubtedly made in the 1980s: one report in a London-based Muslim extremist publication proudly declared that such agitation had 'lit the fire of Islam by inspiring hundreds of

Bosnian Muslims'.[19] But even 'hundreds' of militants could have little effect on a population of two million Muslims, the absolute majority of whom did not think of themselves as religious believers and only followed some of the practices of Islam as a matter of culture and tradition. One survey in 1985 put the proportion of religious believers in Bosnia at 17 per cent.[20] Decades of secular education and Communist political culture had been reinforced, in this respect, by an ever-increasing Westernization of society too. The growing urbanization of Bosnia, though slow at first, had also had an effect; by the late 1980s 30 per cent of marriages in urban districts were 'mixed' marriages. For many rural Muslims and the vast majority of urban ones, being a Muslim was reduced to a set of cultural traditions: 'Muslim names, circumcision, baklava and the celebration of Ramazan Bajram [the feast which marks the end of the fasting month of Ramadan], getting a godparent to cut a one-year-old child's hair, a preference for tiny coffee cups without handles, a sympathy for spiders and various other traditional practices, the origins of which are frequently unknown to those who practise them.'[21] No 'fundamentalist' programme could ever have been pursued by a party which had first to gain the votes of these secularized Muslims, and then to function in government as part of an alliance with at least one of the other two national parties.

When the votes were counted in the elections of December 1990, Izetbegović's party gained 86 seats out of the 240 in the assembly, and other Muslims, including Zulfikarpašić's MBO, gained another 13. The Serbian party, the SDS, led by the Sarajevo psychiatrist (of Montenegrin origin) Radovan Karadžić, gained 72. It had campaigned in vague terms for the defence of Serb rights, but had not said anything about dividing Bosnia even by peaceful methods, let alone by war; so the idea can be excluded that this election, which broadly entitled Dr Karadžić to call himself the 'leader' of the Bosnian Serbs, gave him any democratic mandate for his subsequent actions. (Many Serbs had not in fact voted for him, and there were 13 other elected Serbs in the assembly who did not belong to his party.) The Croatian HDZ gained 44 seats. Altogether there were 99 Muslims, 85 Serbs, 49 Croats and seven 'Yugoslavs'. These proportions (41 per cent Muslim, 35 per cent Serb, 20 per cent Croat) roughly matched those of the population as a whole

(44, 31 and 17 per cent respectively).[22] Izetbegović formed what was in effect a government of national unity, constructed out of a formal coalition between all three major parties, and the government posts were shared out between them. That Izetbegović acted in this way, when he could have governed the country simply through a Muslim-Croat alliance, was a token of good faith. But from an early stage in the life of this government, it became clear that the Serb party had a very different agenda.

The general situation in Yugoslav politics when Izetbegović's government took office at the end of 1990 was very tense. The struggle between Serbia on the one hand and Slovenia and Croatia on the other had intensified in the second half of the year, to the point where Serbia had slapped import duties in October on goods from those two republics. It also became clear that Milošević had simply seized a large part of the Yugoslav federal budget and spent it on Serbia, thus torpedoing the economic reform plan with which the federal Prime Minister, Ante Marković, was attempting to control the country's rocketing inflation. In December 1990 the Slovenes held a referendum on whether their republic should become an independent and autonomous state; over 90 per cent of the electorate voted, and the vote in favour was 89 per cent.[23] In the hazy retrospective view of some Western politicians in 1991–3, Slovenia's move towards independence was regarded as the result of German 'pressure'. But to all serious observers in Slovenia and Yugoslavia at the time, it was quite clear that the pressure which was making economic and political life within Yugoslavia impossible for the Slovenians in late 1990 was coming directly from Belgrade.

By early 1991 Milošević was saying publicly that if there were any attempt to replace the federal structure of Yugoslavia with some looser, confederal arrangement, he would seek to annex whole areas of Croatia and Bosnia. Yet at the same time, far from defending the federal status quo, he was actively demolishing the federal constitution. In June 1990 he had unilaterally abolished the provincial assembly in Kosovo, reducing the status of the province to something less than a municipality; but he continued to field a representative of Kosovo's now non-existent local government in the federal Yugoslav presidency. In March 1991, rattled by student demonstrations against him in Belgrade, he tried to force the federal

President, Borisav Jović, to declare a state of emergency throughout the country; when Jović refused, Milošević engineered his resignation, and also forced out the representatives of Montenegro, Vojvodina and Kosovo. Milošević now went on television to announce that Serbia would no longer obey the federal presidency. For a couple of days it looked as if his constitutional coup had entered its final phase. But then Jović simply returned to his post. Milošević stepped back from the brink; he also appointed, illegally, a new 'representative' for Kosovo on the presidency. As Branka Magaš noted at the time: 'The new man, Sejdo Bajramović, is an oddity even for recent Serbian politics: elected by 0.03 per cent of votes in his Kosovo constituency . . . this retired army sergeant is renowned only for his addiction to tombola.'[24]

The position of the Bosnian government was logical but awkward. In any debate about changing the federal structure into a looser confederation, Bosnia would be on the side of Slovenia and Croatia as they pressed for change, since it too wanted to reduce the scope for the domination and manipulation of Yugoslavia by Belgrade. But at the same time Bosnia could not support Slovenia and Croatia all the way in these arguments. The prospect of those two republics actually carrying out their threat to leave Yugoslavia was deeply alarming to most Bosnians, since they would then be left, together with another weak republic, Macedonia, entirely under Serbia's thumb.

While Izetbegović tried to perform this difficult balancing act during the first half of 1991, the future of both Croatia and Bosnia was being openly challenged by the Serbs. The 'Autonomous Region of the Krajina' set up by the SDS in Croatia was becoming more militant in its demands, as it became more heavily armed by Serbia. In May the SDS in Bosnia began demanding the secession of large parts of northern and western Bosnia, which would then join up with the Croatian 'Krajina' to form a new republic. Three areas of Bosnia with predominantly Serb populations were declared 'Serb Autonomous Regions' by the SDS, following exactly the same method that had been used in the previous summer in Croatia. Not long after this a minor party in Croatia, the extreme nationalist Party of Rights, demanded the annexation by Croatia of the whole of Bosnia. More alarmingly, by July 1991 there was evidence that regular secret deliveries of arms to the Bosnian Serbs were being arranged by Milošević, the Serbian Minister of the Interior, Mihalj Kertes, and the Bosnian SDS leader, Radovan Karadžić.[25] Confirmation of this came in August, when the outgoing federal Prime Minister, Ante Marković, released a tape recording of a telephone conversation in which Milošević could be heard informing Karadžić that his next delivery of arms would be supplied to him by General Nikola Uzelac, the federal army commander in Banja Luka.[26] There could be little doubt by now that Karadžić's actions were being directed, step by step, by the Serbian President: he even boasted to one British journalist in August that he and Milošević 'speak several times a week on the phone'.[27]

By then, full-scale war had begun in Yugoslavia. The final straw for Slovenia and Croatia had been Serbia's refusal in May to accept a Croatian, Štipe Mesić, as the next holder of the automatically rotating federal presidency. The federal system, which Serbia claimed to be defending, was once again paralysed. Croatia then held a referendum (on 19 May) on full independence: 92 per cent voted in favour. On 25 June both Croatia and Slovenia declared independence; a column of federal army tanks entered Slovenia the next morning. Encouraged both by the EEC, which had stated in April that it was committed to the 'unity and territorial integrity of Yugoslavia', and by America's Secretary of State James Baker, who had made a similar pledge in Belgrade on 20 June, Milošević felt that he could quickly make an example of Slovenia *pour encourager les autres*.[28] The Serb-dominated federal army leadership, which broadly shared Milošević's aims (it depended on a continuing Yugoslavia for its privileges, its finances – more than 55 per cent of the federal budget – and its whole system of military industries), thought it could quickly intimidate both Slovenia and Croatia back into line. But Slovenia mounted a well-planned resistance, and was soon dropped from Milošević's and the army's strategic plans. In Croatia there was a two-track policy: general military intimidation (rather than conquest, to begin with) directed at Croatia as a whole, and at the same time a consolidation of the pockets of Serb-populated territory which were already controlled by armed Serbs.

By late August both of these operations had escalated to the point of full-scale war: towns were now being attacked in Slavonia, and in September the bombardment of Dubrovnik began.[29]

A particularly ominous feature of the fighting, foreshadowing the war in Bosnia, was the use of Serbian irregular forces. 'The strategy', one commentator noted in September 1991, 'seems to be to link up various pockets of Serbian settlement by driving out the Croats in between through terror and intimidation.'[30] Small paramilitary units had been functioning since 1990 in the Serb-held regions of Croatia: they had been used in such operations as the attack on the Plitvice National Park in March 1991. Early in 1991 the Minister of the Interior in Belgrade, Mihalj Kertes, had set up a training camp for such a force, to be known as the 'Serbian Volunteer Guard', under the command of Željko Raznjatović, better known as 'Arkan'. Arkan was a mafia-style criminal wanted by Interpol for several offences and widely suspected of having worked for the Yugoslav Secret Service in the surveillance and/or assassination of Yugoslav émigrés.[31] To begin with, this force was financed by the Interior Ministry; later in the year, when it had become known as 'Arkan's Tigers', it was self-financing – indeed, highly profitable – with truckloads of looted goods sent back from Croatian towns and villages.

A similar force was the self-styled 'Četnik' army set up by the Serbian extremist Vojislav Šešelj, a man who had been prosecuted in 1985 for publishing a demand that Yugoslavia be divided into two states, Serbia and Croatia, with Bosnia shared out between them.[32] Šešelj was now leader of the extreme nationalist 'Serbian Radical Party', a position from which he could engage in a kind of competitive auction of nationalist policies with Milošević. (The competition was on a basis of mutual support, however: it was Milošević who engineered Šešelj's election to the Serbian parliament in July 1991.)[33] In an interview with *Der Spiegel* in early August 1991, he presented the latest version of his plan, which involved transferring to Serbia the whole of Bosnia, Macedonia, Montenegro and most of Croatia, leaving the Croats with 'what you can see from the top of Zagreb Cathedral'. Asked by the interviewer about Bosnia, he replied: 'The Muslims of Bosnia are in fact Islamicized Serbs, and part of the population of so-called Croats consists in fact of Catholic Serbs.' The interviewer continued: 'What if the Muslims resist the suppression of their status as a nation?' Šešelj: 'In that case, we will kick them out of Bosnia.' 'Where to?' 'To Anatolia.'[34]

With such views being openly expressed by Bosnian Serbs too, the possibility of any political solution to the crisis within Bosnia was utterly remote. One well-intentioned but doomed attempt was made in early August by the minor Muslim party, the MBO, whose leader, Zulfikarpašić, tried to establish a 'historic agreement' with Karadžić guaranteeing the integrity of the Bosnian republic. As the deputy leader of the MBO, Professor Muhamed Filipović, explained: 'The Serbs are armed to the teeth, they have created a state within a state in Bosnia . . . It is possible that a conflict between Serbs and Muslims will break out any day. To prevent this, an attempt is being made to sign an agreement on the preservation of the integrity of Bosnia.' Such an agreement could be nothing more than a political pledge between one large party and one small one; it could have no constitutional status, and President Izetbegović, who was trying to hold together a tri-national government, objected to it on the grounds that the Croats had not even been consulted. But in any case it was hard to see what such a pledge from Karadžić could mean, when his own party was declaring large parts of the country 'Serb Autonomous Regions' and demanding their secession from Bosnia. A few days after Izetbegović had expressed his criticisms, the SDS representatives on the republican presidency took their opportunity to declare that they would boycott the presidency meetings from now on.[35]

In September 1991 the Bosnian Serbs – or rather, that tiny proportion of them which was active in the local SDS leadership – took their next step. The 'Serb Autonomous Regions', of which there were now four, asked the federal army to intervene to 'protect' them, after a number of minor local incidents and shootings. (They were by now, thanks to the help of the federal army and the Ministry of the Interior, extremely well armed.) Federal troops were immediately deployed: a column of one hundred vehicles was sent to western Hercegovina, another column moved to the communications centre in Nevesinje, and 5000 troops were sent into Hercegovina from Sarajevo. By the end of September these forces had established the 'borders' of the 'Serb Autonomous Region of

Hercegovina'; they had also created a heavily manned military launching-point for their operations against Dubrovnik, just over the Bosnian-Croatian border.[36] (As a *quid pro quo*, the Serbs of Hercegovina sent hundreds of their own men, led by the mayor of Trebinje, to assist in the bombardment of the Croatian city.) These were not the only federal army operations on Bosnian soil; the tank-training centre at Banja Luka had been one of the bases of operations against Croatia from mid-August. A federal armoured column, heading for Vukovar, tried to pass through the Višegrad area at the end of September and was stopped by Muslim and Croat civilians: it opened fire on them.[37]

The situation was becoming intolerable for the Bosnian government. President Izetbegović, who had once remarked that choosing between Tudjman and Milošević was like having to choose between leukaemia and a brain tumour, declared in early October that Bosnia was neutral between Serbia and Croatia. Radovan Karadžić denounced this declaration as 'an anti-Serb act', explaining that the war in Croatia was a war against a 'vampirised fascist consciousness'. Only a sovereign government, he said, could declare neutrality.[38] On that last point he was strictly correct; and the Bosnian assembly was now beginning seriously to debate the idea of declaring Bosnian sovereignty. By this it meant not full independence but legislative sovereignty within Yugoslavia, so that it would be able, in legal theory at least, to pass laws overriding the federal army's rights to use its territory. On 14 October Karadžić marched his deputies out of the assembly, which then voted for Bosnian sovereignty. A few days later Karadžić and his party set up what they called a 'Serb National Assembly' in the federal army stronghold of Banja Luka, assuming all the trappings of a parliament, a government, and indeed a state.[39]

The steps taken by Karadžić and his party – 'Autonomous Regions', the arming of the Serb population, minor local incidents, non-stop propaganda, the request for federal army 'protection', the Serb 'parliament' – matched exactly what had been done in Croatia. Few observers could doubt that a single plan was in operation. Any lingering uncertainties about the nature of the plan were dispelled at the congress of Milošević's Serbian Socialist Party at Peć on 9 October 1991. The vice-president of the party, the former dissident philosopher Mihailo Marković, described very clearly in his speech to the congress the nature of the carve-up which he and his master were planning:

> In the new Yugoslav state there will be at least three federal units: Serbia, Montenegro and a united Bosnian and Knin region [i.e. a territory consisting of some of the Bosnian 'Serb Autonomous Regions' and the main Croatian one]. If the Bosnian Muslims wish to remain in the new Yugoslav state, they will be allowed to do so. If they try to secede, they must know that . . . the Bosnian Muslims' state will be encircled by Serbian territory.

Commenting on this speech at the time, I wrote: 'Mr Milošević's plan, then, is for a country which would be Yugoslavia in name, but Greater Serbia in reality, with the option of a sort of enfeebled Muslim Bophutatswana in the middle.'[40] Terms such as Bophutatswana and Bantustan would be heard more often during discussions of the future of the Bosnian Muslims in 1993.

Such clear declarations of Serbia's war aims were ignored, however, by most Western leaders, and by the EEC-appointed negotiator, Lord Carrington, who continued to believe that some looser version of the old federal Yugoslavia was still feasible. In September the United Nations imposed an arms embargo on the whole of the Yugoslav territory: this had little effect on the Yugoslav federal army, with its massive stockpiles and its large armaments industry, but it did weaken the Croatian forces which were just beginning to hold the federal army to a stalemate in many parts of western and north-eastern Croatia. Had they been properly armed, they might have been able to repel the attacks on cities such as Vukovar; as it was, they held on there with extraordinary tenacity, to the point where the federal army generals began to feel that the conquest of territory in Croatia was an operation with steeply diminishing returns. (When Vukovar eventually fell, with almost every building in the city destroyed, Arkan's men 'cleaned up' the city and killed hundreds of its inhabitants.) The Croatian government did manage to establish supply-lines for weaponry from ex-Warsaw Pact countries and the Middle East; and a further blow to Serbia's plans was the international recognition of Croatia and Slovenia, which was finally agreed by the EEC, at Germany's insistence, in mid-December, and came into effect on 15 January 1992. A peace settlement in Croatia, negotiated by the UN representative Cyrus Vance, was agreed a few weeks later: it placed the territory conquered by the federal and Serb irregular forces in a limbo of 'UN-protected' zones, the long-term status of which remained very unclear.

The recognition of Croatia helped to end the war in that republic. It was in any case a recognition of reality: any idea that Croatia could have been persuaded to rejoin a federal Yugoslavia, after cities such as Vukovar had been reduced to rubble, was utterly unreal. One consequence of this move, however, was that it was now necessary for Bosnia to seek independence too; otherwise it would be left in a rump Yugoslavia under Serbian control. The EEC had understood this, inviting applications for independence from the other republics and asking Bosnia, as a condition of recognition, to hold a referendum on the question. Lord Carrington complained that the EEC had shot his horse, ruining his plans for a general settlement for all six republics within the framework of Yugoslavia. But it is quite clear that his plans would never have been accepted by the Croats or the Slovenians, and would not have satisfied Serbia's ambitions either: his horse was already broken-backed.[41] The only thing that has given Lord Carrington's complaints an aura of plausibility is the fact that the move of Bosnia towards independence was used as a pretext by Milošević and Karadžić to begin the military phase of their carve-up of Bosnia.

The military planning was well advanced. Important communications centres in Bosnia had been occupied by the army in the autumn of 1991. Heavy artillery positions were constructed round major Bosnian towns, including Sarajevo, in the winter of 1991–2. As the fighting wound down in Croatia in January and February, columns of federal army tanks and artillery were 'withdrawn', with the approval of the UN, into Bosnia. Extraordinarily, President Izetbegović had even allowed the army to confiscate the weapons supplies of the local territorial defence units: it seems that he was trying thereby to assure the army commanders of his own peaceful intentions, and he may also have been misled, as was surely intended, by the army's 'confiscation' of arms from some of the Serb paramilitary forces too.[42] That the army was not impartial or unpolitical was made evident on 29 February and 1 March, when the referendum was held in Bosnia. While Karadžić's SDS forbade Serbs to vote in the referendum and erected road-blocks to prevent ballot-boxes entering the areas of Bosnia it controlled, federal army planes dropped leaflets supporting the boycott. Roughly 64 per cent of the electorate did vote, however, including many thousands of Serbs in the major cities, on a ballot-paper which asked: 'Are you in favour of a sovereign and independent Bosnia-Hercegovina, a state of equal citizens and nations of Muslims, Serbs, Croats and others who live in it?'[43] Almost unanimously, they voted 'yes'.

On the morning of 2 March 1992, the day when the results of the referendum were announced, members of Serb paramilitary forces set up barricades and sniper positions near the parliament building in Sarajevo. For twenty-four hours it looked as if the military takeover of Bosnia had begun; but thousands of Sarajevo citizens came out onto the streets – in front of the snipers – to demonstrate, and for some reason the coup was aborted. The ostensible reason for the action had been the shooting of a Serb by two young Muslims at a wedding party in Sarajevo on the previous day. This killing, which seems to have arisen from a sudden flare-up of tempers with no premeditation, was taken as an excuse to denounce Muslim 'terrorism'.[44] The tactic was transparent; and of course no one had ever thought of erecting barricades in Sarajevo to protest at the numerous killings of Muslims and other such incidents in previous months, such as the shooting of Mehmed Ganibegović by members of a Serb paramilitary group in Šipovo on 7 October, or the machine-gunning of the Mehmed-aga mosque in Tuzla by federal army reservists on 13 October.[45]

Still one possible choice remained for the Serb politicians: between the carve-up of Bosnia by military means, and the carve-up of Bosnia by political means backed with the threat of armed force. This second method remained a possibility until the last week of March, and it depended very much on the attitude of the Bosnian Croats. Some degree of symmetry had been observable for a long time between the Serbian and Croatian positions on Bosnia: in March 1991 Presidents Milošević and Tudjman had met to discuss possible ways of dividing Yugoslavia, and the division of Bosnia had been on their agenda.[46] But the symmetry was only partial:

Serbia had gone much further, much earlier, and whereas the Bosnian Serbs had set up 'Autonomous Regions' in May 1991 and a 'parliament' in October 1991 (finally declaring a Bosnian 'Serb Republic' on 27 March 1992), the Croat counterpart, the 'Croatian Community of Herceg-Bosna', was not proclaimed until July 1992, after three months of Serbian military offensive in Bosnia. The leader of the Croat party in Bosnia, Stjepan Kljuić, was in favour of preserving Bosnia's borders, and his party voted in favour of Bosnian independence. Even the notion of turning Bosnia into a Swiss-style confederation of 'cantons' did not appeal to the HDZ leadership. As the General Secretary of the party, Ivan Markešić, said in October 1991: 'Even in a so-called "Serb" region such as Banja Luka, there are 120,000 Croats. We cannot divide Bosnia into national cantons. In Switzerland the cantons were there first, and Switzerland was created out of them. But in Bosnia cantons would mean dividing the country, and you could not do that without a war.'[47]

However, a lobby of Hercegovinan Croats, led by Mate Boban, had steadily increased its influence within the party, and in January 1992, in a move widely regarded as engineered by Croatia's President Tudjman, Boban replaced Kljuić as leader of the Bosnian HDZ.[48] The Croats of Hercegovina had some reason to be more hard-line, having witnessed the military build-up and the establishment of the 'Serb Autonomous Region' there. (They were also in close touch with the Croatian paramilitary force, the HOS; in late 1991 they refused to hand over the weapons of their territorial defence force to the federal army, and began making their own preparations.)[49] The general pattern of events, both military and political, was that the Croats were responding to Serb initiatives and, to some extent, imitating them. Thus when the SDS issued a map proposing the national 'cantonization' of Bosnia (with roughly 70 per cent of the territory as Serb cantons) in December 1991, the HDZ replied not long afterwards with a map of its own (with roughly 30 per cent as Croat cantons).[50] It was quite clear that what the Serbs meant by cantonization was setting up a constitutional half-way house from which they could move to the full secession that they had previously demanded; and when Radovan Karadžić went to Austria at the end of February 1992 to discuss the future of

Bosnia with Milošević and Tudjman, it was partition, not cantonal confederation, that they talked about.[51] But the EEC and Lord Carrington, keen to clutch at the straw of cantonization, chaired several negotiations on this topic between the three main Bosnian parties in Brussels and Lisbon during March. On 9 March it was the Serb delegation which refused to accept a plan for a federal Bosnian constitution in which each national group would have had a veto on any major political or economic issue.[52] Later that month the EEC pushed strongly for a 'cantonal' plan based on a modified version of the Serb map. The plan was at first accepted by all three sides as the basis for further negotiations; then the Croat HDZ rejected it on 24 March, followed by Izetbegović's party, the SDA, on the next day. That the Croats had rejected it first is not surprising, since it gave them only 17 per cent of Bosnian territory and left 59 per cent of the Croat population in non-Croat cantons.[53]

The only thing which all such plans demonstrated in the end was the impossibility of making any such divisions in a way that would not leave hundreds of thousands of Bosnian citizens unhappy with the result. The majority of Bosnians had in any case voted for a democratic and independent Bosnia of equal citizens. Leaving aside the torrent of rhetoric in the Serb media about how Bosnia was in the grip of an 'Ustaša-fundamentalist coalition', there is no sign that any intelligent observer ever believed that discriminatory laws were being introduced, or even dreamed of, by the Bosnian government against any national group in Bosnia. But a kind of political psychosis had been created by the Serb and Serbian politicians and media, in which the 'defence' of the 'rights' of the Bosnian Serbs was given such absolute status that people ceased even to wonder whether they were really under attack. Once this psychosis was fully established, the final step to military action was a small one to take.

16

The destruction of Bosnia: 1992–1993

On 6 April 1992 Bosnia was recognized as an independent state by the EC. There had been brief moments of quasi-autonomy or semi-independence during the previous two centuries – Husejn-kapetan's ascendancy in 1831, the national government in Sarajevo in July 1878, the handing of power by Baron Sarkotić to the Bosnian National Council in November 1918 – but properly speaking this was Bosnia's first appearance as an independent state since 1463. Commentators were quick to point out that Bosnia had spent the intervening 529 years as part of two empires, a kingdom and a Communist federal republic. Bosnia could never be a state, they claimed, because it contained three different nationalities; history showed that it could exist only as part of a larger whole. The first of these claims begged the question of whether only nation-states are viable states. If so, the majority of the 170-odd member-states of the United Nations must be deemed unviable. As for the lesson of history, what it indicated was not that Bosnia had to be kept in check by a larger power to prevent it from destroying itself from within, but almost the opposite: what had always endangered Bosnia was not any genuinely internal tensions but the ambitions of larger powers and neighbouring states. The history of Bosnia shows that, leaving aside the economic conflict between landowners and peasants, the 'national' animosities within the country have reached the point of inter-ethnic violence only as a result of pressures coming from outside Bosnia's borders. Even the conflict between landowners and peasants was significantly – perhaps decisively – intensified by the international political situation during the nineteenth century, with the rise of a semi-autonomous

Serbia creating a sense of embattled isolation among the Bosnian Muslim ruling class.

A long process of nationalist competition between Serbia and Croatia had, from the late nineteenth century onwards, made Bosnia's internal politics much more intractable than they would otherwise have been, by persuading the Orthodox and Catholic Bosnians that they should think of themselves as Serbs and Croats. After they had been joined in the same country with Serbia and Croatia for seventy-four years, it was natural that many of the members of these communities in Bosnia would identify with those two ethnic fatherlands. But once Yugoslavia had ceased to exist, the very same fact which made the preservation of Bosnia difficult – its nationally mixed population – also made it imperative. So kaleidoscopically intermingled were these two peoples, together with a third which had no other fatherland to look to, that their separation could only be achieved at an appalling and unjustifiable cost. The price demanded of ordinary Bosnians that would have enabled them to live together in peace, on the other hand, was a comparatively small contribution of normality and goodwill. The majority were happy to pay that contribution. A minority, acting under the direction of a neighbouring state, were not; and they had the guns.

On the day of international recognition, Serb paramilitary forces repeated the operation which they had aborted in Sarajevo one month before. This time between 50,000 and 100,000 Bosnians, of all national groups, came out onto the streets in protest. In the words of a news report, 'One speaker said, "Let all the Serb chauvinists go to Serbia and let the Croat chauvinists go to Croatia. We want to remain here together. We want to keep Bosnia as one." This moving spectacle was interrupted repeatedly by rounds of automatic weapons fire.'[1] Those bursts of gunfire were not the first fighting in the war, however. For more than a week there had been shootings and bombings in several Bosnian towns: Banja Luka, Bosanski Brod and Mostar. In the first two of these it was apparently Serb paramilitary forces which took the initiative; in Mostar the blowing up of a petrol tanker near the federal army barracks could have been either the work of Croat paramilitaries, or an attempt by Serbs to prove that the federal army was being threatened.[2] On 30 March the federal army chief, General Adžić, had announced, predictably, that his army was prepared to intervene to protect Serbs against 'open aggression'.[3]

But the most sinister development in the first days of April was the arrival of Arkan's paramilitary force in the north-eastern Bosnian town of Bijeljina. These heavily armed men, most of them Serbians, not Bosnian Serbs, had recently finished their 'clean-up' operations in Vukovar. Some of them had moved into Banja Luka at the end of March, where they took control of the city, mounting road-blocks and 'roaming the streets with rocket-propelled grenade launchers, AK-47s and Scorpion automatic pistols'.[4] They arrived in the peaceful and predominantly Muslim town of Bijeljina and began to 'liberate' parts of it, including the central mosque. Muslims were harassed and expelled; a Muslim member of the Bosnian presidency, Fikret Abdić, was turned back at gunpoint when he tried to enter the town; and by 4 April it was reported that water and electricity supplies had been cut and that bodies were lying in the streets.[5] The main aims, clearly, were first to terrify the local Muslims into flight, and secondly to radicalize the local Serb population, recruiting some of its young men into this glamorous new occupation, in order to establish Serbian control over the area. For these two purposes mass-murder was not necessary; a good number of random killings in cold blood would suffice. One later report estimated that nearly one hundred Muslims were killed.[6] As the events of the next few weeks would show, Bijeljina was chosen first because of its strategic importance. It was the axial point, close to the Serbian border, from which extended the two main swathes of territory to be taken over by Serbian forces: a broad strip of land across northern Bosnia, linking Serbia with the military base at Banja Luka, the Bosnian 'Krajina' and the occupied areas of Croatia, and a swathe on the eastern side of Bosnia, running all the way down the Bosnian-Serbian border (thus including vital entry-points for supply lines from Serbia) to the ethnically Serb areas of eastern Hercegovina.[7]

Within a few days, several more of the towns with large Muslim populations in that eastern swathe of Bosnia had been subjected to the same treatment. Apart from Arkan's Tigers, other Serbian paramilitary groups were also used, including the 'White Eagles', led by Mirko Jović, and Šešelj's Četniks. In several cases, such as the attack on Zvornik in the second week of April, artillery units of the federal army were used to bombard the town for several days; then, when it capitulated, the paramilitaries were sent in to deal with the population. The psychology of terror which the paramilitary commanders introduced into these places was not just a matter of frightening the local Muslims into flight – though in this they were successful, and it was estimated that 95 per cent of the Muslims of Zvornik, Višegrad and Foča had fled their homes by the end of April.[8] An equally important part of the psychological operation was to convince the local Serbs that they had to 'defend' themselves against their Muslim neighbours. The ground had been prepared, of course, by the broadcasts of Radio Television Belgrade, warning Serbs of Ustaša pogroms and fundamentalist jihads. And having seen genuine news footage of dead bodies and burning villages in Croatia over the previous nine months, ordinary Serb peasants and townsmen were easily persuaded that these threats were real. All that was needed was a few more local details to complete the picture. A chilling news report from Foča by the Reuters correspondent Andrej Gustinčić shows how it was done:

> 'Do you see that field?' asks a Serbian woman, pointing to a sloping meadow by the Drina river. 'The jihad was supposed to begin there. Foča was going to be the new Mecca. There were lists of Serbs who were marked for death,' the woman says, repeating a belief held by townspeople and gunmen. 'My two sons were down on the list to be slaughtered like pigs. I was listed under rape.' None of them has seen the lists but this does not prevent anyone from believing in them unquestioningly.[9]

Whether the federal army commander in eastern Bosnia, Colonel Milan Jovanović, believed such stories is altogether more doubtful. While his men were expelling Muslims from their homes in the town of Višegrad he told one British journalist that he was still on Yugoslav soil, and added: 'There was a rebellion here by the Muslims. It had been prepared for quite some time and the brunt of it was against the Serbs.'[10] But what is evident is that it was this entire joint operation of regular and paramilitary forces which had been prepared for quite some time. In the words of one leading analyst: 'In view of the speed with which they were implemented and the high level of coordination they revealed, these operations clearly had not been mounted spontaneously.'[11] Using the advantages of surprise and overwhelming superiority, the federal army and its paramilitary adjuncts carved out within the first five to six weeks an area of conquest covering more than 60 per cent of the entire Bosnian territory.

Some local Serb forces raised in the 'Serb Autonomous Regions' of Bosnia also joined these operations in several areas of the country. But it is quite clear that the conquest was mainly achieved by federal army forces (including planes, which were used to bomb the towns of Kupres, Doboj and Tuzla) directed by Belgrade, and paramilitary groups from Serbia. In other words, even though some of the soldiers serving in the federal army were Bosnian Serbs, and even though it was coordinated with elements of a Serb insurrection in some areas, this was predominantly an invasion of Bosnia planned and directed from Serbian soil. During the early weeks of the invasion, the official statements issued by Milošević and the federal army commanders consisted of two claims, both of them false: first, that the army was acting only as a peacekeeper to separate local fighters, and secondly, that no Serbian units were crossing the border into Bosnia.[12] Not only were paramilitary units crossing into the country, but also, as one eye-witness report from the border put it, 'the federal army has this week strung a massive presence of men, artillery and tanks along the road from Serbia as it surges into Bosnia'.[13]

On 27 April, however, President Milošević and the Montenegrin government declared the creation of a new federal state of Yugoslavia consisting of their two republics alone. This placed the federal army in Bosnia in a peculiar position, since it could no longer pretend even to be acting as a peacekeeper on Yugoslav soil. In early May Milošević announced that he would withdraw those soldiers in the army in Bosnia who were citizens of the new two-republic Yugoslavia; those who were Bosnian Serbs would be transferred, together with all the armaments and supplies, to the so-called 'Serb Republic', and placed under the command of General Ratko Mladić. That Mladić was appointed by Milošević, and that the entire changeover was a largely cosmetic exercise, was clear. No foreign observers had any way of checking whether all the Serbian and Montenegrin soldiers did in fact leave Bosnia; by 20 May it was claimed that 14,000 had gone, but that would have left at least 80,000.[14] Reading the testimonies of victims of war crimes from later in 1992, one comes across numerous references to soldiers from Serbia and Montenegro. It is not possible to believe that the army which was fighting in Bosnia from late May onwards consisted entirely of Bosnian Serbs. And for those soldiers in it who were from Bosnia, the change-over would have made no essential difference to what they were doing: they were fighting with the same federal army weaponry, receiving constant supplies of ammunition, food and fuel from Serbia, acting in cooperation with paramilitary forces from Serbia and pursuing the same overall strategy which the Serbian leader had established. Not until eleven months later, when General Mladić disagreed with Milošević over acceptance of the Vance-Owen plan, was there any divergence between the strategy of the 'Bosnian Serb' army leadership and the policies of Belgrade.

Nevertheless, this cosmetic exercise had the desired effect. Prominent Western politicians, such as the British Foreign Secretary, Douglas Hurd, were soon describing the fighting in Bosnia as 'a civil war'. A distinguished former editor of *The Times* published a number of articles in which the fighting was described as a typical 'civil war'. The BBC referred constantly to all sides in the conflict, including the Bosnian government, as 'warring factions'; otherwise it described the war as 'a breakdown in law and order'. (On one occasion in late April 1992 when six UN aid trucks were hijacked by Serbian paramilitary forces, the BBC reported that 'efforts to bring aid to the refugees are being hampered by a breakdown in law and order'; this must be the first recorded instance in history of a truck being driven away by a breakdown.)[15] In Britain there was one extra reason for this inability to understand what was happening, which was that in the crucial early days of April 1992 Britain was in the throes of a general election. Few commentators and no politicians could devote any attention to what was happening in Bosnia; by the time they woke up to the existence of a war there, all they could see was a number of equally fierce-looking combatants fighting one another for equally incomprehensible reasons. In the USA the presidential elections were not to happen for another seven months; but the Bush administration was already worried about making any policy commitments on Bosnia which might prove electorally damaging, and was content to accept the strangely possessive argument of EEC leaders who had claimed from the start of the Yugoslav war that this was 'a European problem'.

Starting from a state of extreme unpreparedness, the local territorial defence forces of the Bosnian government, numbering perhaps 3500 armed men altogether, did attempt to mount some resistance during April. But at this early stage the main opposition to the Serb invasion-cum-insurrection was Croat. In western Hercegovina the local Croats had made some preparations, and had been joined by men from the Croatian paramilitary force, the HOS. This force had been officially merged with the Croatian army during the 1991–2 war in Croatia, and as that war drew to a close many of its members had gone to Hercegovina as a way of moving out of Croatian army control. In April 1992 they made up roughly 5000 of the force of 15,000 Croat fighters which was assembled in that area; the local Croats had been organized under the aegis of the 'Croat Defence Council' (HVO). At the end of May they began a counter-offensive which, after more than a month of fighting, succeeded in pushing the federal army forces away from the Mostar region. In this they were joined by up to 15,000 regular army troops from inside Croatia, who brought with them a small quantity of tanks and artillery pieces; on 16 June Presidents Izetbegović and Tudjman had signed a formal military alliance between their two countries, legitimizing the use of both Croatian army troops and the local HVO forces.[16] In parts of northern Bosnia too, notably the Posavina region close to the Croatian border, the resistance by Croat forces held the Serb advance in check and in some places succeeded in repelling it.

The political intentions of the Croatian and Bosnian Croat leaderships were open to some doubt. For many weeks they had pleaded with Izetbegović to declare a confederation of Bosnia and Croatia; he had always refused to do this, either because he feared an eventual absorption of Bosnia into a Greater Croatia, or because he thought such a move would give an aura of justification to the arguments of the Serbs. His thinking seems to have been dominated by the idea that his government must represent Serbs as well as Muslims and Croats, and he did indeed maintain Serb ministers in his government throughout the war. Izetbegović's attempts to be even-handed irritated the Croats, whose strategic military thinking was clearer than his at this stage; and he also offended them by appointing to his senior command one of the few Muslims who had risen to the rank of General in the Yugoslav federal army – Šefer Halilović, who had commanded federal army units attacking Croatia during the previous war. Throughout June and July the Bosnian HDZ leader Mate Boban put pressure on Izetbegović to agree to a confederation, either by threatening to withdraw forces or by blocking arms deliveries. And in early July Boban declared the creation of the 'Croat Community of Herceg-Bosnia', a kind of Croat Autonomous Region in which the Croatian currency was introduced and the Croatian flag was flown. Later, an official statement by one of Boban's advisers would still insist that this was a temporary measure, and that the area should eventually become 'an integral part of Bosnia' once again.[17]

That Boban himself really wanted this area to join Croatia may be presumed; but President Tudjman's official pronouncements continued to recommend preserving the integrity of Bosnia's borders. Some of Tudjman's close advisers, notably his Hercegovinan-born Defence Minister, Gojko Šušak, were in favour of carving territory out of Bosnia; but many other ministers, and most of the opposition parties in Croatia, were against it. It is probably fair to say that Tudjman's own position was that of a rational opportunist. If he were given clear signs by the outside world that they would not allow the defeat and carve-up of Bosnia, then he would go along with that policy; but if the world was prepared to let the Serbs seize territory and hold it, then he would wish to have his slice of the cake too. In the event, the outside world gave him no clear signs that it would follow the former policy. And at the same time the signs it was giving about the future of the Serb-occupied areas of Croatia were extremely unclear, with a succession of merely temporizing measures designed to extend the UN mandate over them. This gave Tudjman an added reason to wish to acquire more bargaining chips in Bosnia.

The reaction of the international community had been generally confused or negative. When the fighting started in Bosnia, the UN was just in the process of setting up a headquarters in Sarajevo, and bases in some northern Bosnian towns, in order to direct its peacekeeping operations in Croatia. In early May the Secretary-General, Boutros Boutros-Ghali, ruled out the use of UN peacekeeping forces in Bosnia, and on 16 May most of the UN force already in Sarajevo was withdrawn. Two weeks later Boutros-Ghali issued a report which repeated the main line of Milošević's public relations exercise, which was that the army and paramilitary forces in Bosnia were 'independent' and had nothing to do with Belgrade. The purpose of this report was to argue against the imposition of sanctions on Serbia – a measure advocated by the American government, but resisted by the British and the French, who said they wanted Milošević to be given 'a further opportunity to halt the violence in Bosnia'.[18] (Sanctions were in fact imposed on Serbia on 30 May, but they had little effect on the Serbian war effort, and were strongly undermined by deliveries of oil and other supplies, which came overland from Greece and up the Danube from Russia and the Ukraine.)

The fundamental failure of the Western politicians was that they looked only at the symptoms of the war, not at its causes: it was as if they did not even want to understand the nature of Milošević's project. They insisted on treating the war as essentially a military problem rather than a political one. Apportioning responsibility or blame simply became a matter of pointing to people who were firing guns; and since there were two sides now firing them, the blame was apportioned to both. 'Everybody is to blame for what is happening in Bosnia and Hercegovina', declared the EEC negotiator, Lord Carrington, in one of his most revealingly uncomprehending remarks, 'and as soon as we get the cease-fire there will be no need to blame anybody.'[19] The fixation with cease-fires – of which, on some counts, more than a hundred were made and broken during the rest of the year – became the most telling symptom of this lack of political understanding.

Because the war was seen essentially as a military problem – caused by a thing called 'violence' which had 'flared up' on 'both sides' – the efforts of the West were directed at what was described as 'reducing the quantity of fighting'. Hence the biggest single contribution by the West to the destruction of Bosnia: the refusal to lift the arms embargo against the Bosnian government. This embargo had been introduced by the UN in September 1991 against the whole of Yugoslavia, which at that stage was still, formally speaking, a single country. Although the UN itself recognized Bosnia and admitted it as a member-state distinct and separate from Yugoslavia on 22 May 1992, it continued to apply the embargo as if nothing had changed. Of course it continued to apply it to Serbia too; but Serbia held most of the stockpiles of the former federal army, and had a large armaments industry of its own. (Some of the key armaments factories in Bosnia were also located in ethnically Serb areas, such as the artillery shell factory in the Serb district of Vogošća outside Sarajevo, which was seized by Serb forces at the beginning of the war.) In addition, the Yugoslav army had purchased an extra 14,000 tons of weaponry from the Middle East just before the arms embargo came into force in 1991.[20] Serb military commanders sometimes boasted that they had enough arms and ammunition to continue the war in Bosnia for another six or seven years; the embargo could have no real effect on their military capability. But to the Bosnian defence forces it was in the long term a sentence of death.

Small supplies of arms did reach the Bosnians, mostly via Croatia, despite the blockade of the Croatian coast mounted from July 1992 by NATO and WEU flotillas. A few armaments factories still lay within Bosnian government-controlled areas, and some production was kept up there despite the dislocation of supplies. Occasionally the Bosnian government forces also captured material from the Serb army: in the most spectacular such operation, north of Tuzla in May, an entire armoured column was seized. But what the Bosnians always lacked was heavy armour, artillery and anti-tank weapons. In September it was estimated that they possessed two tanks and two armoured personnel carriers (APCs), while the Serb army in Bosnia had 300 tanks, 200 APCs, 800 artillery pieces and 40 aircraft.[21] A later estimate, in June 1993, was that the arms captured by the Bosnians included up to 40 tanks and 30 APCs, together with a larger number of light artillery pieces; the Croat forces were thought to have roughly 50 tanks and more than 100 artillery pieces.[22]

Yet despite this heavy imbalance, and despite the constant flow of fuel and supplies to the Serb forces, the military history of the war during 1992 was one of virtual stalemate from the moment the

Croat and Bosnian government forces began to be properly organized in late May 1992. For the next nine months, the Serb forces were to be kept mainly in check, and in some areas they were actually pushed back: notably in Hercegovina in May and June, round Goražde in August, in the Brčko 'corridor' of north-eastern Bosnia intermittently throughout the autumn, and in parts of the Drina valley region of eastern Bosnia in January 1993. There was a difference in tactics between the two sides, expressing a difference in psychology and motivation. The main tactic of the Serb side was the one previously used in Croatia: to sit back at a prudent distance and soften up the areas it was attacking with artillery bombardments for weeks or even months on end. Many of the conscripts serving in this ex-federal army did not bring the same degree of motivation to the attack on Muslim and Croat homes that the owners of those homes brought to their defence.[23] Had the Bosnian government been able to exercise the normal right of any government to obtain arms for the defence of its people, it is quite likely that the Serb gains would have been rolled back in many parts of Bosnia, if not to the point of outright defeat for the Serb leaders, then at least to the point where they would have realized that they would not get the territory they wanted by conquest. The war might then have ended within four to six months. This did not happen, because the delivery of arms to the Bosnian government was vigorously opposed by statesmen such as Douglas Hurd, who argued that allowing the Bosnians to defend themselves would 'only prolong the fighting'.

The first sign of a possible change in Western policy came in early August 1992, after a number of journalists and a television crew had reached one of the Serb-run detention camps in northern Bosnia. For the first time ordinary Western voters – and politicians – could see with their own eyes startling evidence of what was happening to a large part of the Muslim population in that area. The facts were not, or should not have been, unknown to the UN and Western governments: a stream of reports from UN personnel in neighbouring areas of Croatia had referred to these detention camps over the previous two months, and a report issued by the International Society for Human Rights on 29 May had already listed many examples of Muslim civilians being rounded up, held in schools or other centres, and, in some cases, murdered.[24] In early

June the Bosnian government had issued a list of ninety-four known locations of Serb-run prisons and detention camps, together with an estimate of the number of people killed in them so far, amounting to 9300.[25] This was nowhere near the total number of civilians killed, of course: apart from the victims of bombardments, there were many who had been rounded up and shot in villages and towns all over Bosnia. In one particularly well-documented case, that of the Muslim village of Zaklopača, at least eighty-three villagers – nearly all the menfolk in the village – were 'summarily executed' by Serbian paramilitaries on 16 May 1992. In the words of one typical statement:

> My brother-in-law, Haso Hodžić, was outside in front of the house when the Četniks approached. They started calling him an Ustaša. My brother-in-law started to walk towards them and they told him to give up his weapons. He told them that he did not have any weapons but that they could take his cows. Then one of the Četniks opened fire and killed him.[26]

In some places there was a deliberate killing of educated Muslims and leaders of the local community: teachers, doctors, lawyers. Detailed reports which emerged later in the year showed that some of the detention camps had also been used for systematic murder. And there were also some well-documented reports of women being held in special buildings for the purpose of systematic rape.[27]

The politicians in the West reacted to the sight of the emaciated prisoners in the camps with expressions of indignation and concern. Lord Owen, writing as an individual commentator, called for air strikes against Serb forces. Douglas Hurd replied to all such calls for intervention with the statement: 'There is ample *justification* for action. If we judged that a few days of sharp military action would bring the suffering to an end, the case would be overwhelming.'[28] Here he was admitting for the first time the point of principle that it might be right to 'increase the quantity of fighting' in the short term in order to end it in the long term. But he was still resolutely opposed to the idea of applying this principle by allowing the Bosnian government to defend itself using its own forces and an adequate supply of weapons. And since he, like most other Western leaders, still viewed the fighting in terms of a civil war ('it is a war with no front line . . . village is divided against village'), he was understandably reluctant to intervene with British troops on the ground – something the Bosnian government was not, in any case, asking him to do.

It fell to the British government, as holder of the rotating presidency of the EEC, to chair a joint EEC-UN conference on the entire situation in Yugoslavia, which was held in London during the last week of August. The paralysis of the West was made only more apparent. John Major obtained what he thought were solemn pledges from the Serb leaders to lift the sieges of Bosnian towns and cities and place their heavy weaponry under UN supervision. It later emerged that 'supervision' was to be interpreted in its original, etymological sense: UN monitors were allowed to look over the artillery pieces above Sarajevo every day while they were being fired. The other measures agreed at the conference included tightening the enforcement of sanctions against Serbia on the Danube (though there was still no method for stopping barges from proceeding, apart from the use of loud-hailers), declaring a no-fly zone over Bosnia (though there was no provision for enforcing it) and appointing the belligerent Lord Owen to replace Lord Carrington as EEC negotiator (though Lord Owen then immediately dropped his support for threats of military action, and began treating the Serbs as an equal party in the negotiations with equally valid claims).

Once again the international community had failed to consider the fundamental causes of the conflict. The emphasis was now on two kinds of things: military solutions to military problems, and humanitarian solutions to humanitarian problems. Although the term 'ethnic cleansing' was now in general currency, there was still a tendency to assume that the essential problem was military, and that the flight of coerced and terrorized populations was merely a by-product of the fighting. It was then described as a humanitarian problem which could be 'solved' by moving refugees into refugee camps outside Bosnia. What was still not fully understood was that ethnic cleansing was not a by-product of the war. It was a central part of the entire political project which the war was intended to achieve, namely the creation of homogeneous Serb areas which could eventually be joined to other Serb areas, including Serbia itself, to create a greater Serbian state.

The humanitarian missions mounted by the outside world undoubtedly saved lives. They also had some undesired but not unforeseeable consequences: local militias treated them as a source of supply, regularly receiving as much as a quarter of the deliveries which passed through their checkpoints, and extorting large sums of money as well.[29] While private and public aid agencies made strenuous efforts to bring food and medicines into Bosnia during the second half of 1992, they were joined by a growing number of UN troops (nearly 8000 by the end of the year), whose role, apart from protecting aid convoys, was unclear. The political consequence of placing this small and lightly-armed UN force in Bosnia was, however, that they now functioned as hostages, making the Western governments extremely reluctant to adopt any policies which might invite retaliation by the Serbs against these vulnerable troops. Thus by December the British government, which had helped to set up the theoretical no-fly zone over Bosnia, was arguing at the United Nations against measures to enforce it, for fear of what might happen to British soldiers in Bosnia if a Serbian plane was ever shot down by RAF fighters.[30]

In late October 1992 the EEC and UN negotiators, Lord Owen and Cyrus Vance, produced the first detailed proposal for a political settlement. This was a 'solution' arrived by taking the demands of the Serbs, Croats and Muslims and trying to find some geometrical mid-way point between them. The result gave the Serbs enough to make the Muslims feel that the Serbs were being rewarded for their actions, and enough also for the Serbs to feel that if they continued their actions they could press for more. Put together originally by a Finnish diplomat, Martti Ahtisaari, the plan was for turning Bosnia into a set of 'autonomous provinces' or cantons which would exercise almost all the functions of government, including policing. The central government of Bosnia would be concerned only with national defence and foreign affairs. The Serbs pushed harder, and when the plan was issued in what was said to be its final form at Geneva in January 1993, even defence had been stripped from the powers of the central government.[31]

The merits of the Vance-Owen plan were its insistence that refugees should be allowed to return to their homes throughout Bosnia, and its provision that the cantons corresponding to Serb-occupied areas would not be connected on the map in such a way as to make it easy for them to seek to join Serbia as a single territorial block. Unfortunately these two meritorious principles were flatly contradicted both by the rest of the plan, and by reality. The rest of the plan gave full legislative, judicial and executive powers (including policing) to the cantons, making it impossible to believe that Muslim refugees could safely return to Serb-ruled cantons.[32] And the reality on the ground was that the Serb-held areas were already joined on the map; Serb military leaders would never sacrifice these links, which were a key element in their own plans.

But there was one feature of the Vance-Owen plan, as it was now set out, which was to prove not just unsuccessful but immensely harmful. In the January version, unlike the initial version proposed in October, the cantons were given 'ethnic' labels on the map, and at the same time the impression was given that the precise boundaries on the map were not yet final. This had the entirely predictable effect of inciting renewed competition for territory. And, worst of all, it incited competition between Croat and Muslim forces for parts of central Bosnia where there had been a mixed Muslim-Croat population. After the arms embargo, this was the second most important contribution of the West to the destruction of Bosnia: it stimulated the development of a genuine Bosnian civil war, and in so doing it broke down the Croat-Muslim alliance which had been the only effective barrier to the Serbs.

There had already been tensions between the Bosnian Muslim and Croat leaderships, as we have seen. In September 1992 there had been a report that the Croat leader, Mate Boban, was telling his HVO forces to cease helping the Bosnian defence force in its attempts to break the siege of Sarajevo.[33] In October there were some clashes between Muslim and Croat militias in Travnik and Prozor, and bitter recriminations between the two over the fall of Jajce to the Serbs. But still there was no large-scale fighting between them, and the overall alliance held. This situation gradually changed under the influence of the Vance-Owen plan in early 1993: in February Muslim forces in Gornji Vakuf were besieged by HVO soldiers, and in the area between Vitez and Kiseljak (a contested zone on the Vance-Owen map) both Muslim and Croat militias engaged in what one report described as 'freelance ethnic cleansing'.[34] By early April there were outbreaks of heavy fighting between Muslims and Croats in the Travnik-Vitez-Zenica area of central Bosnia.[35] The UN human rights rapporteur Tadeusz Mazowiecki issued a report in the following month clearly warning that the Vance-Owen plan was stimulating ethnic cleansing; but by then it was too late.[36]

The combined effects of the arms embargo and the Vance-Owen plan had fatally weakened the military resistance to the Serbs. As late as January 1993 there were reports of Serb forces being pushed back in several areas, especially the Bratunac region of the Drina valley.[37] But the lack of ammunition was beginning seriously to hamper the Bosnian defence force, and in the early months of 1993 Serb forces stepped up their campaign against a number of Muslim enclaves which remained within the Serb-conquered area of eastern Bosnia. Despite some well-publicized initiatives by the UN commander, General Morillon, and by the US Air Force, which dropped supplies to them by parachute, these enclaves could not hold out. Srebrenica, which, with its German miners, Ragusan merchants and Franciscan friary, had been in the late middle ages the most prosperous inland town in the whole of the western Balkans, had turned into a giant refugee camp stinking of human excrement. Žepa, when it was finally entered by foreign observers, had become a Marie Celeste township: when its defenders ran out of ammunition the people fled into the hills above the town, where they lived in caves and were kept alive by American air-drops.[38]

Bowing to this military pressure, the Bosnian government moved during March and April towards an acceptance of the Vance-Owen plan. There was by now little hope that the West would remove the main cause of the Bosnian military weakness, the arms embargo: both the American and the German governments had briefly expressed an intention to lift it, but they had been energetically persuaded by Douglas Hurd to change their minds.[39] Even the outspoken intervention of Lady Thatcher on British and American television in mid-April did not shake the policies of the governments of those countries. The British government in particular was mesmerized by the Vance-Owen 'peace process', and would not contemplate any move that could be seen as jeopardizing it – even though it required no clairvoyance at this stage to say that 'a blind man can see that the Vance-Owen plan is never going to be fulfilled'.[40]

The only way in which the Vance-Owen plan could gain even token acceptance among the Serbs was on the clear assumption that it would be a temporary resting-place on the way to the full secession of the Serb-conquered territories. On that basis Radovan Karadžić was encouraged by Slobodan Milošević to sign the plan at a special meeting convened in Athens on 2 May 1993. The basis of the Serbian approach was explained by Dragoslav Rančić, the confidant and spokesman of the nationalist ideologue Dobrica Ćosić (who was now President of the Serbian-Montenegrin rump Yugoslavia). 'It is just the first stage', he said. 'It is not going to last long. Not even Lord Owen believes in it.' He added that the Muslims would eventually be left with 'a Balkan Lesotho', and that the Serbs would get everything they wanted.[41] Many of the Bosnian Serb politicians and military commanders believed, however, that they could get what they wanted without even bothering to pass through the diversion of the Vance-Owen plan. Opposition was especially strong among those Serb politicians who had become in effect the personal rulers of larger territorial fiefdoms, and did not want their powers to be clipped by any administrative interference.[42] They rejected the plan which Karadžić had signed at Athens, and organized a 'referendum' on 15 May at which they successfully persuaded the Serb soldiers and peasants to reject it too. Their position was backed by General Mladić, who appeared to have a strong disagreement with Milošević over this tactic. For a few days Milošević insisted publicly that he would close the border between Serbia and Bosnia; but he refused to allow international observers to monitor the border, and within a couple of weeks the flow of supplies was resumed.[43]

The final death-warrant for Bosnia was written on 22 May in Washington, at a gathering of the foreign ministers of Britain, France, Russia and the USA. All talk of possible air strikes, which had been used as a threat to the Serbs in the run-up to the Athens meeting, was now dropped. Even the idea of enforcing the Vance-Owen plan was also abandoned. Instead, it was decided that the remnants of Bosnia's two million Muslims would be allowed to congregate in a number of so-called 'safe areas', where their safety would not in fact be guaranteed: they would be guarded by UN forces whose mandate entitled them to return fire not if the Muslims were shot at but only if they, the UN soldiers, came under attack.[44]

When President Izetbegović heard the news of this agreement – the foreign ministers having not even bothered to consult him in the matter – he issued the following statement: 'If the international community is not ready to defend the principles which it itself has proclaimed as its foundations, let it say so openly, both to the people of Bosnia and to the people of the world. Let it proclaim a new code of behaviour in which force will be the first and the last argument.'[45] Over the remaining summer months, those who wielded that argument – Slobodan Milošević, Franjo Tudjman and the ever-adaptable Lord Owen – would put forward a succession of cruder, more naked plans for the division of Bosnia into three states. Whether the fig-leaf of an overall Bosnian 'confederal state' was preserved or not hardly mattered. Each version of the plan would create an unviable Muslim Bantustan, a settlement which the most determined of the already uprooted Muslim soldiery would never accept. Such a prospect, with all the long-term instability which any carve-up of Bosnia would create in the region, was described by Lord Owen as 'not an ideal solution'. To be more accurate, it was not a solution at all.

Looking back at the history of this war, one sees that the real causes of Bosnia's destruction have come from outside Bosnia itself, and have done so twice over: first in the form of the political strategy of the Serbian leadership, and then in the form of the miscomprehension and fatal interference of the leaders of the West. And yet every observer who has looked at the almost unimaginable atrocities committed during this war (atrocities committed in the first place overwhelmingly against Muslims and Croats, and later against Serbs too), has sometimes wondered whether there was not some deep psychosis within the population of Bosnia as a whole which finally broke to the surface. It cannot be denied that there are some gruesome practices, such as the mutilation of corpses, the knowledge of which has been passed down in a kind of tradition from earlier wars and folk memories – stretching back at least as far as stories of the feared *martolosi* of the sixteenth century. There were old men still in Bosnia who could remember such things from the second world war. But to suppose that this Bosnian war was some sort of spontaneous continuation of the inter-ethnic fighting of the second world war is to read from the script prepared by Karadžić and Milošević.

The atrocities in Bosnia in 1992 were not committed by old men, or even by young Bosnians nursing grudges about the second world war. The pattern was set by young urban gangsters in expensive sunglasses from Serbia, members of the paramilitary forces raised by Arkan and others; and though the individuals who performed these acts may have gained some pathological pleasure from them, what they were doing was to carry out a rational strategy dictated by their political leaders – a method carefully calculated to drive out two ethnic populations and radicalize a third. Having travelled widely in Bosnia over fifteen years, and having stayed in Muslim, Croat and Serb villages, I cannot believe the claim that the country was forever seething with ethnic hatreds. But having watched Radio Television Belgrade in the period 1991–2, I can understand why simple Bosnian Serbs came to believe that they were under threat, from Ustaša hordes, fundamentalist jihads or whatever. As the independent Belgrade journalist Miloš Vasić put it to an American audience, it was as if all television in the USA had been taken over by the Ku Klux Klan: 'You must imagine a United States with every little TV station everywhere taking exactly the same editorial line – a line dictated by David Duke. You too would have war in five years.'[46] But perhaps the best comment on the tactics of Milošević and Karadžić, and on what they have achieved in Bosnia – more than 150,000 deaths, more than two million people expelled from their homes, villages and towns burnt and devastated, and several hundred mosques and churches deliberately blown up – is a judgement by another historian on another country's descent into blood:

> Like the protagonists in Dostoyevsky's *Possessed*, the Bolsheviks had to spill blood in order to bind their wavering adherents with a band of collective guilt. The more innocent victims the Bolshevik Party had on its conscience, the more the Bolshevik rank and file had to realize there was no retreating, no faltering, no compromising, that they were inextricably bound to their leaders, and could only march with them to 'total victory' regardless of the cost . . .[47]

Notes

1: Races, myths and origins: Bosnia to 1180

1 The best modern survey of the archaeological, historical and linguistic evidence is Wilkes, *Illyrians*. See also Stipčević, *Illyrians*; Russu, *Illirii*; and Stadtmüller, *Forschungen zur albanischen Frühgeschichte*.
2 Wilkes, *Illyrians*, p. 244; Stipčević, *Illyrians*, p. 137.
3 Wilkes, *Illyrians*, pp. 205–13.
4 See Wilkes, *Dalmatia*, pp. 266–80; Klaić, *Geschichte Bosniens*, pp. 48–9; Jireček, *Die Handelsstrassen*; Miller, *Essays on the Latin Orient*, p. 462.
5 Markotić, 'Archaeology', pp. 45–6.
6 Alföldy, *Bevölkerung der Provinz Dalmatien*, pp. 184–8.
7 Dio Cassius, quoted in Wilkes, *Illyrians*, p. 260.
8 Stipčević, *Illyrians*, p. 80.
9 Durham, *Some Tribal Origins*, p. 102. See also Truhelka, 'Die Tatowirung'.
10 See Stipčević, *Illyrians*, p. 241, for the theory about polyphonic music developed by the Sarajevan ethnomusicologist Cvjetko Rihtman. The classical sources say merely that the Illyrians were fond of music.
11 The use of the term 'Illyrians' for South Slavs has a long history, going back to fifteenth-century humanist writers: see Hadžijahić, 'Die Anfänge der nationalen Entwicklung', pp. 171–2.
12 Stadtmüller, *Geschichte Südosteuropas*, p. 21.
13 On the *Libellus Gothorum* see the introduction by Ferdo Šišić to his translation of the *Chronicle, Letopis popa Dukljanina*, and Jireček, *Istorija Srba*, vol. 1, pp. 166–7. The text of the *Chronicle* is printed in von Schwandner, *Scriptores rerum hungaricarum*, vol. 3, pp. 476–509; see pp. 476–7 on the migration of the Goths.
14 Orbini, *Il Regno de gli Slavi*, p. 97. On Orbini see Radojčić, *Srpska istorija Mavra Orbinija*, pp. 5–11; on the 'Gothism' in his work and that of other Ragusan writers, see Zlatar, *Our Kingdom Come*, pp. 365–71. Orbini's theory must have seemed a little far-fetched, even at the time; but it must be set in the context of other theories of

the period which ascribed a special potency or significance to the Germanic-Scandinavian races. The Dutch scholar Grotius argued that the native races of North America were originally Scandinavian; and the Flemish theorist Goropius Becanus claimed that German was the original language spoken in the Garden of Eden.

15 Redžić, *Muslimansko autonomaštvo*, p. 72. (The memorandum also claimed, for good measure, that ninety per cent of Bosnians had fair hair.) Similar claims were made on behalf of the Croats by Ante Pavelić in 1941: Dedijer *et al.*, *History of Yugoslavia*, p. 577.

16 Kovačević, *Istorija Crne Gore*, pp. 282–8.

17 Markotić, 'Archaeology', p. 49. A small Avar kingdom remained in Pannonia (southern Hungary) until it was finally destroyed by Charlemagne in the 790s.

18 Andjelić, 'Periodi u kulturnoj historiji', p. 200.

19 Malingoudis, *Slavoi stê mesaiônikê Ellada*, p. 39.

20 There are in fact two different accounts of these events in Constantine's book. See the discussion in Fine, *Early Medieval Balkans*, pp. 49–59.

21 Rostovtseff, *Iranians and Greeks*, pp. 135–46.

22 Kaulfuss, *Die Slawen*, pp. 6–9.

23 Gimbutas, *Slavs*, p. 60.

24 Fine, *Early Medieval Balkans*, p. 56.

25 Obolensky, *Byzantine Commonwealth*, p. 136; Guldescu, 'Political History', p. 86.

26 Gimbutas, *Slavs*, pp. 140–1. On the *zadruga* see Sicard, *La Zadruga sud-slave*, and Byrnes, ed., *Communal Families in the Balkans*.

27 Gimbutas, *Slavs*, pp. 165–8; Markotić, 'Archaeology', p. 52.

28 Dvornik, *Byzantine Missions to the Slavs*, pp. 9–20.

29 Ćorović, *Historija Bosne*, pp. 133–4.

30 Hadžijahić, 'Sinkretistički elementi', pp. 304–5 (mountain-tops), 309–13 (gods' names).

31 Andjelić, 'Periodi u kulturnoj historiji', pp. 202–3.

32 Fine, *Early Medieval Balkans*, pp. 159, 262–5; Obolensky, *Byzantine Commonwealth*, pp. 159–60.

33 Constantine Porphyrogenitus, *De administrando imperio*, p. 160 ('kai eis to chôrion Bosona to Katera kai to Desnêk'). Desnik is presumably modern Desnik (though Jireček thought it was Tešanj, on the river Usora), and Katera is probably the modern village of Kotor or Kotorac, near Sarajevo: see Jireček, *Die Handelsstrassen*, pp. 29–30; Skarić, *Sarajevo i njegova okolina*, p. 32; Ćorović, *Historija Bosne*, p. 112.

34 Fine, *Early Medieval Balkans*, pp. 201, 278–80; Obolensky, *Byzantine Commonwealth*, pp. 287–8.

35 Fine, *Early Medieval Balkans*, p. 288.
36 Cinnamus, *Epitome*, p. 104 (bk. 3, ch. 7).
37 Andjelić, 'Periodi u kulturnoj historiji', pp. 204–5.
38 Ćirković, 'Die bosnische Kirche', pp. 547–8.
39 Ćorović, *Historija Bosne*, p. 113; D. Mandić, *Etnička povijest Bosne*, p. 33.

2: The medieval Bosnian state, 1180–1463

1 Truhelka, 'Das mittelalterlicher Staatswesen', p. 72; Fine, *Late Medieval Balkans*, pp. 18–21.
2 Orbini mentions one abortive attempt during the reign of Stephen Kotromanić: *Regno de gli Slavi*, pp. 354–5.
3 *Essays on the Latin Orient*, p. 468; the proverbial saying, 'The times of Ban Kulin have returned', was also recorded in 1601 by Orbini: *Regno de gli Slavi*, p. 351.
4 Miller, *Essays on the Latin Orient*, p. 468; Coquelle, *Histoire du Monténégro*, p. 82.
5 See the letter from Vulcanus (Vukan) of Zeta to Innocent III, Sept. 1199, in Fermendžin, ed., *Acta Bosnae*, p. 5.
6 Fine, *Late Medieval Balkans*, pp. 18, 43–7; for a detailed analysis of the council of Bolino Polje, see Fine, *Bosnian Church*, pp. 126–34. The act of renunciation is printed in Migne, ed., *Patrologia latina*, vol. 215, cols. 153–5.
7 Fermendžin, ed., *Acta Bosnae*, pp. 8–11.
8 Fine, *Late Medieval Balkans*, pp. 144–5. Professor Fine identifies this as the town of Vrhbosna (modern Sarajevo); but the reference is surely to the region of Vrhbosna, since the town did not yet exist. A report of 1244 says that the *župa* of Vrhbosna was centred on the town of Brdo, which was the seat of the Ban and the Catholic bishop (probably the modern village of Ban-Brdo): see Jireček, *Die Handelsstrassen*, p. 31.
9 Fine, *Late Medieval Balkans*, p. 146.
10 Fine, 'Was the Bosnian Banate Subjected to Hungary?'
11 Miller, *Essays in the Latin Orient*, p. 473; Fine, *Late Medieval Balkans*, p. 148.
12 On the Šubić period see Thallóczy, *Studien zur Geschichte Bosniens*, pp. 46–8.
13 Fine, *Late Medieval Balkans*, pp. 275–9.
14 D. Mandić, *Franjevačka Bosna*, pp. 17, 39.

15 Fermendžin, ed., *Acta Bosnae*, p. 28.
16 Fine, *Late Medieval Balkans*, p. 281.
17 *Ibid.*, pp. 281–2.
18 *Ibid.*, pp. 368–70.
19 *Ibid.*, pp. 384–6; Klaić, *Geschichte Bosniens*, pp. 201–3; Ćirković, *Istorija bosanske države*, pp. 135–40.
20 Fine, *Late Medieval Balkans*, pp. 394–8; Coquelle, *Histoire du Monténégro*, pp. 113–18.
21 Fine, *Late Medieval Balkans*, pp. 408–11; Emmert, 'The Battle of Kosovo'. For a concise survey of the Kosovo tradition in oral epic poetry (Serbo-Croat and Albanian), see Lord, 'The Battle of Kosovo'.
22 Le Bouvier, *Le Livre de la description*, p. 22.
23 Fine, *Late Medieval Balkans*, pp. 453–69; Fine, *Bosnian Church*, pp. 210–41.
24 For the traditional view see Skarić, *Sarajevo i njegova okolina* pp. 35–6 (also arguing that Vrhbosna and Hodidjed were first yielded to the Turks under an agreement in 1428, then lost and later recaptured by them in 1435). For the revised view see Šabanović, 'Pitanje turske vlasti'. Šabanović describes the development of this area in 'Bosansko krajište'.
25 Thallóczy, *Studien zur Geschichte Bosniens*, pp. 146–59; Fine, *Late Medieval Balkans*, pp. 577–8.
26 Fermendžin, *Acta Bosnae*, p. 211.
27 Fine, *Bosnian Church*, pp. 332–3. Previous historians (e.g. Miller, *Essays on the Latin Orient*, p. 485) have misinterpreted this evidence, giving a figure of 40,000 refugees instead of forty.
28 Fine, *Late Medieval Balkans*, pp. 583–4 (to the Pope); Fermendžin, ed., *Acta Bosnae*, p. 252 (to Venice).
29 Lachmann, ed., *Memoiren eines Janitscharen*, pp. 139–40. The King's widow, Queen Katarina, managed to flee to Rome; she died there in 1478, and her tomb is still to be seen in the Church of S. Maria in Aracoeli, on the Capitol: see Thallóczy, *Studien zur Geschichte Bosniens*, pp. 110–20, and J. Turčinović, ed., *Povijesno-teološko simpozij*.
30 Jireček dates their arrival to the thirteenth century (*Die Handelsstrassen*, p. 43). Saxon miners had certainly reached Serbia by the second half of the thirteenth century: see Takács, 'Sächsische Bergleute im mittelalterlichen Serbien', p. 34. But the most detailed modern study of mining in medieval Bosnia can find no documentary evidence earlier than 1312 (for the mine at Trešnjica) and 1319 (at Lipnik): Dinić, *Za istoriju rudarstva*, p. 46.
31 Dinić, *Za istoriju rudarstva*, pp. 7–8.

32 For all the foregoing details, see Jireček, *Die Handelsstrassen*, pp. 41–9; Fine, *Late Medieval Balkans*, pp. 282–4.

33 Benac and Čović, *Kulturna istorija Bosne*, p. 411.

34 The term *kmet* is derived from the Latin *comitatus*, a word for the estates (possibly monastic) on which they originally worked. In Serbia it developed a different meaning, referring to the head-man of a village.

35 Verlinden, 'Patarins réduits en esclavage'.

36 On all these classes and ranks see Truhelka, 'Das mittelalterliche Staatswesen', pp. 90–105.

37 The significance of this council is emphasized by Ćirković (*Istorija srednovjekovne države*, pp. 224–5) and Andjelić ('Barones Regi i državno vijeće'), and questioned by Fine (*Late Medieval Balkans*, pp. 453–4).

38 Truhelka, 'Das mittelalterliche Staatswesen', p. 110. Truhelka also notes the presence of 'istriones' at the court of Tvrtko II in 1440, and wonders what the term meant; it was surely a reference to 'histriones', or stage-players.

39 Andjelić, 'Periodi u kulturnoj historiji', p. 209. The nature of 'bosančica' has been the subject of a complex scholarly debate; see the classic study by Truhelka, 'Die Bosančica', and the recent discussion by Lehfeldt, *Das serbokroatische Aljamiado-Schrifttum*, pp. 43–5. Tandarić presents some evidence that glagolitic (the early west Balkan alternative to Cyrillic) was also used in early medieval Bosnia ('Glagoljska pismenost', p. 43); but the evidence he gives of its use in fifteenth-century Bosnia comes from areas which were then part of Croatia-Hungary.

40 Benac and Čović, *Kulturna istorija Bosne*, pp. 422–31.

41 Ćorović, *Historija Bosne*, p. 9.

3: The Bosnian Church

1 For a good recent survey of the historians' arguments, see Džaja, *Die 'bosnische Kirche'*, pp. 1–68; an important earlier historiographical account is Šidak, 'Problem "bosanske crkve" u historiografiji'. There is a rich bibliography in Fine, *Bosnian Church*, pp. 393–434, which can be supplemented by further references in the notes to Okiç, 'Les Kristians de Bosnie'.

2 Rački, *Bogomili i patareni*.

3 The classic general accounts of the Bogomils are Runciman, *Medieval Manichee*, pp. 63–93, and Obolensky, *Bogomils*. On Bogomilism in

Serbia see Solovjev, 'Svedočanstva pravoslavnih izvora'. The classic study of Bogomilism in Bulgaria is Angelov, *Bogomilstvoto*; but his treatment of Bosnia (pp. 420–8) is slight and uncritical. On Manichaean beliefs see Lieu, *Manichaeism*: Mani was a third-century Persian whose dualist teachings combined Zoroastrianism, Greek-Jewish Gnosticism and Christianity.

4 On the Cathars see Borst, *Katharer*, and Duvernoy, *Le Catharisme*. Catharism was not just a form of Bogomilism transplanted to Western Europe: it drew on strong local traditions of quasi-Gnostic heresy (see Puech, 'Catharisme et Bogomilisme').

5 The earliest writer to make the connection with Bogomils seems to have been Chaumette-des-Fossés, in a work published in 1816 (Šamić, *Les Voyageurs français*, p. 131). On the early Catholic writers see Matasović, 'Tri humanista o patarenima', and Fine, *Bosnian Church*, pp. 63–73.

6 Petranović, *Bogomili, crkva bosanska i krstjani*.

7 The theory was supported by Glušac in 1924 ('Srednjovekovna crkva'), but attacked by Šidak in 1937 ('Problem "bosanske crkve" u historiografiji').

8 See the Bibliography; for a fuller listing of Solovjev's many publications, see Fine, *Bosnian Church*, pp. 428–9.

9 The leading exponents of this theory have been Father Leo Petrović (*Kršćani bosanske crkve*) and, although with an increasing acknowledgement of heretical tendencies in his later writings, Jaroslav Šidak (*Studije o 'crkvi bosanskoj'*).

10 See my discussion of the Islamicization of Bosnia in chapter 5.

11 For a concise summary of the statistics, geography and dating, see M. Wenzel, 'Bosnian Tombstones', pp. 102–15. Dr Wenzel has also produced a detailed geographical analysis of the different motifs employed: *Ukrasni motivi*. On the outlying areas of distribution see the references in Fine, *Bosnian Church*, p. 104, n. 119.

12 See von Asbóth, *Bosnien und die Hercegowina*, pp. 94–118; Solovjev, 'Le Symbolisme' and 'Bogumilentum und Bogumilengräber'.

13 Džaja, *Die 'bosnische Kirche'*, pp. 25–6.

14 M. Wenzel, 'Bosnian Tombstones', p. 103.

15 *Bosnien und die Herzegowina*, p. 101. Solovjev concedes that the cross does appear on at least 85 *stećci*: 'Simbolika srednjovekovnih spomenika', p. 17.

16 For the pagan designs see M. Wenzel's 'Medieval Mystery Cult'; for the armorial designs and the Vlachs, see her 'Bosnian Tombstones'. (On the identity of the Vlachs see below, chapter 6.) Other criticisms

of Solovjev's theory are made in S. Radojčić, 'Reljefi bosanskih stečaka'. Fine summarizes a wide range of objections in *Bosnian Church*, pp. 88–93.

17 Fine, *Bosnian Church*, pp. 48–62.

18 The source was a fifteenth-century Serbian manuscript cited by a Russian in 1859. The Russian scholar never published the original text, and it has since conveniently disappeared; no other surviving manuscript of the same work includes the word 'Bogomil' at that point (*ibid*., p. 44).

19 *Ibid*., pp. 212–13.

20 Matasović, 'Tri humanista o patarenima'. There may in some cases have been a deliberate play on words, referring to Bosnian 'monachi' (monks) as 'manichei' (Manichaeans): see Dragojlović, *Krstjani i jeretička crkva*, p. 154. The term 'Manichaean' had persisted, though with a very general meaning, in Byzantine writings; in one fourteenth-century summary of Justinian's laws it is used as a virtual synonym for 'heretical' (Lieu, *Manichaeism*, p. 177). It does appear in the Bolino Polje declaration (1203) as a term for the heretics to whom the Bosnian monks promised not to give shelter.

21 Fine offers one apparent example of the use of the word being attributed to Bosnians (*Bosnian Church*, p. 248), but he has misconstrued the Latin. The meaning is not 'The clergy of the Kingdom of Bosnia are called Patarins by the Bosnians themselves', but 'The Patarins are called the "religiosi" [i.e. "monks"] of the Kingdom of Bosnia by the Bosnians themselves'. For the original Latin see Miletić, *I 'Krstjani' di Bosnia*, p. 52; for the significance of 'religiosi', *ibid*., pp. 56–62.

22 For the history of the term see Thouzellier, *Hérésie et hérétiques*, pp. 204–21. Lambert writes that it was used in the anti-heresy bull of 1184 as 'a technical term for Italian heretics, most often applied to the Cathars' (*Medieval Heresy*, 1st edn., p. 84); the bull in question applied to Cathars, Waldensians and Humiliati, all of whom were found on Italian soil, so there was probably no 'technical' theological identification of 'Patarins' with the dualist doctrines which were peculiar to the Cathars.

23 Thouzellier, *Hérésie et hérétiques*, p. 216: this is a summary of the Archbishop's letter in another letter from the Pope.

24 On the historical debate about this story see Fine, 'Aristodios and Rastudije'.

25 Šidak, *Studije o 'crkvi bosanskoj'*, pp. 177–209; Fine, *Bosnian Church*, pp. 118–21; Lambert, *Medieval Heresy*, 2nd edn., pp. 128–31. Dra-

gojlović has argued that 'ecclesia sclavoniae' was the Bosnian Church, and 'ecclesia dalmatiae' referred to heretics in Serbia (*Krstjani i jeretička crkva*, pp. 124–7); but the evidence seems too confused to support such a precise correlation.

26 For the text see Migne, ed., *Patrologia latina*, vol. 215, cols. 153–5.

27 Džaja, *Die 'bosnische Kirche'*, p. 55.

28 Fine, *Bosnian Church*, p. 64; Matasović, 'Tri humanista o patarenima', pp. 237, 240.

29 Miletić, *I 'Krstjani' di Bosnia*, pp. 50–66, 117–21. Dragojlović also notes that in early Slav monasticism the term *gast* (= *gost*) is sometimes used for the igoumen or abbot (*Krstjani i jeretička crkva*, p. 157). Fine has some useful comments on the monastic character of the declaration (*Bosnian Church*, pp. 126–34), but the one major shortcoming of his book is that he was unaware of Miletić's work when he wrote it.

30 Miletić presents the evidence in *I 'Krstjani' di Bosnia*, pp. 52–3; she notes that 'christianus' is also used in this sense in some early Slav sources from Kiev and Prague (pp. 65–6). See also Dragojlović, *Krstjani i jeretička crkva*, pp. 150–1.

31 Miletić, *I 'Krstjani' di Bosnia*, p. 102; Fine adds (*Bosnian Church*, p. 155) that it was used as the title of a senior abbot in eleventh-century Croatia.

32 Kniewald, 'Hierarchie und Kultus', pp. 588–9.

33 See Miletić, *I 'Krstjani' di Bosnia*, p. 112 for the original text and a translation (preferable to the one in Fine, *Bosnian Church*, p. 262).

34 Matthew 8:11 ('many shall come from the east and west, and shall sit down with Abraham, and Isaac, and Jacob, in the kingdom of heaven'); Luke 16: 19–31 (the story of Dives and Lazarus). If I am correct, Fine's argument that this inscription in itself proves an acceptance of the Old Testament (*Bosnian Church*, p. 262) becomes less compelling.

35 Fine, *Bosnian Church*, pp. 256–60.

36 *Ibid.*, pp. 176–7.

37 For the Cathar theory see Loos, *Dualist Heresy*, pp. 298–302.

38 See Jireček, 'Die Romanen in den Städten Dalmatiens', part 1, pp. 50–7.

39 Kniewald, 'Hierarchie und Kultus', p. 600. The Church had forbidden the creation of any new 'double monasteries' in 787 (Miletić, *I 'Krstjani' di Bosnia*, p. 56), but perhaps this prohibition was seen as inoperative, given that the already existing double monasteries were allowed to continue.

40 Lambert, *Medieval Heresy*, 1st edn., pp. 377–8.

41 Džaja, *Die 'bosnische Kirche'*, p. 35. The glagolitic liturgy continued in many parts of Dalmatia and Croatia until the Counter-reformation: see Zimmermann, *Reformation bei den Kroaten*, pp. 5, 20.
42 Džaja, 'Fineova interpretacija', pp. 58–9.
43 Fine, *Bosnian Church*, pp. 137–50.
44 For the two texts, see Solovjev, 'La Messe cathare'; for an important correction to his interpretation of one phrase, see Wakefield and Evans, *Heresies*, p. 781. The manuscript refers to 'the days of *djed* Ratko', so presumably comes from within the Bosnian Church. It can be dated to the mid-fifteenth century, but the text was copied from an earlier source.
45 Dragojlović, *Krstjani i jeretička crkva*, pp. 208–13.
46 Lambert, *Medieval Heresy*, 2nd edn., p. 109 (Cathars); Orbini, *Regno de gli Slavi*, p. 354 (Bosnian Church).
47 Dragojlović, *Krstjani i jeretička crkva*, pp. 173–4.
48 All these points (and others) are discussed in Fine, *Bosnian Church*, pp. 357–61, except the evidence drawn from Gost Radin's will (for which see Lambert, *Medieval Heresy*, 1st edn., pp. 374–80) and from the Turkish registers (see Okiç, 'Les Kristians de Bosnie', p. 125). For further differences see Dragojlović, *Krstjani i jeretička crkva*, pp. 165–72, 199–201.
49 Fine, *Bosnian Church*, pp. 264–75.
50 Lambert, *Medieval Heresy*, 1st edn., pp. 375–6; King Matijaš was Matthias Corvinus of Hungary.
51 Lasić, *De vita et operibus S. Iacobi*, p. 438. This is the least benign of the four miracles performed by St Jacob in Bosnia.
52 Kniewald, 'Vjerodostojnost latinskih izvora', pp. 156–63.
53 Fermendžin, ed., *Acta Bosnae*, pp. 38, 248.
54 Loos, 'Les Derniers Cathares'.
55 Kniewald, 'Vjerodostojnost latinskih izvora', pp. 168–9.
56 See Fine's comments: *Bosnian Church*, pp. 56–8.
57 *Ibid.*, pp. 58, 308–9; and see Matasović, 'Tri humanista o patarenima'. The argument by Nicolas López Martínez that Torquemada must have had detailed information about Bosnia is very unconvincing (Torquemada, *Symbolum pro informatione manichaeorum*, 'Introducción', pp. 20–3).
58 Dragojlović, *Krstjani i jeretička crkva*, pp. 109–11.
59 Fermendžin, ed., *Acta Bosnae*, p. 225.
60 Fine, *Bosnian Church*, p. 334.
61 Okiç, 'Les Kristians de Bosnie', pp. 129–30.

62 *Ibid.*, p. 115. Some of these *kristianlar* are listed with their sons (p. 131) and we know that both Bosnian monks and the Bogomil 'elect' were meant to be celibate.

63 Draganović, 'Izvješće apostolskog vizitatora', p. 44. However, Masarechi included in his report material which he had gleaned about the Patarins from earlier written sources (Fine, *Bosnian Church*, pp. 65–8); it is not clear which of his comments about them gave first-hand or contemporary information.

4: War and the Ottoman system, 1463–1606

1 Lachmann, ed., *Memoiren eines Janitscharen*, p. 140.

2 For a dramatic account of an expedition to bring food to Jajce in 1525, see G. Wenzel, ed., *Marino Sanuto világkrónikájának tudósításai*, vol. 3 (=25), pp. 332–42.

3 Ćirković, *Herceg Stefan Vukčić-Kosača*, pp. 260–7.

4 Šabanović, *Bosanski pašaluk*, pp. 44–7; Fine, *Late Medieval Balkans*, pp. 585–9.

5 For a concise but detailed account of the Ottoman expansion, see Shaw, *History of the Ottoman Empire*, vol. 1, pp. 55–94. On the formation of the military frontier see Rothenberg, *Austrian Military Border*, pp. 17–39.

6 Shaw, *History of the Ottoman Empire*, vol. 1, pp. 184–7; Rothenberg, *Austrian Military Border*, pp. 52–61; and see chapter 6 below.

7 For a fuller summary of the military system see Shaw, *History of the Ottoman Empire*, vol. 1, pp. 122–31. On the system in Bosnia see Šabanović, 'Vojno uredjenje Bosne', especially pp. 216–19 on the auxiliary forces.

8 The best account of this system is Papoulia, *Ursprung und Wesen der 'Knabenlese'*.

9 Kunt, 'Transformation of *Zimmi* into *Askerî*', p. 62.

10 Pelletier lists the grand viziers and notes that there were sixty-five Bosnian-born governors of Bosnia between 1488 and 1858: *Sarajevo*, p. 75.

11 Sugar, *Southeastern Europe under Ottoman Rule*, p. 58; Shaw, *History of the Ottoman Empire*, vol. 1, p. 114.

12 Rycaut, *Present State of the Ottoman Empire*, p. 197. The last devşirme in Serbia was in 1638 (Tomasevich, *Peasants, Politics, and Economic Change*, p. 27). There may have been some attempt to revive it: the

sieur de la Croix, secretary to the French Embassy in Istanbul, wrote in 1684 that it was now held every ten years (*Mémoires*, pp. 201–2).

13 Sugar, *Southeastern Europe under Ottoman Rule*, p. 56.

14 Lehfeldt, *Das serbokroatische Aljamiado-Schrifttum*, p. 48; Hottinger, *Historia orientalis*, p. 463.

15 Shaw, 'Ottoman View of the Balkans', pp. 69–70.

16 For details see Sugar, *Southeastern Europe under Ottoman Rule*, pp. 37–8; Rycaut, *Present State of the Ottoman Empire*, pp. 172–3.

17 On the timar system see Tomasevich, *Peasants, Politics, and Economic Change*, pp. 28–33; Sugar, *Southeastern Europe under Ottoman Rule*, pp. 98–9, 212.

18 Fine, *Late Medieval Balkans*, p. 583.

19 Tomasevich, *Peasants, Politics, and Economic Change*, p. 24.

20 Kunt, 'Transformation of *Zimmi* into *Askerî*'.

21 A *kadiluk* could be further divided into two or more *nahije*, administered by deputy judges; in Bosnia these often followed the old *župa* boundaries. See Kreševljaković, *Kapetanije u Bosni*, pp. 9–10.

22 Except the sandžaks of Požega (in Slavonia) and Zvornik, which were in the *eyalet* of Buda from 1541 to 1580: *ibid*., p. 10.

23 For details see *ibid*., pp. 9–10, and Djurdjev, 'Bosna', p. 1263.

5: The Islamicization of Bosnia

1 Mažuranić, *Südslaven im Dienste des Islams*, pp. 21–7; Hukić, ed., *Islam i muslimani u Bosni*, pp. 20–1.

2 Balić, *Das unbekannte Bosnien*, pp. 84–9.

3 Filipović, 'Napomene o islamizaciju'; Džaja, *Die 'bosnische Kirche'*, pp. 71–3. For other evidence, from documents and gravestones, showing that Sarajevo had a Muslim population before 1463, see Hadžijahić, *Porijeklo bosanskih Muslimana*, p. 66.

4 Okiç, 'Les Kristians de Bosnie', pp. 118–19.

5 Džaja, *Die 'bosnische Kirche'*, p. 74.

6 Fine, *Bosnian Church*, p. 384. The figures given by D. Mandić (*Etnička povijest Bosne*, p. 154) are incorrect. The total population calculated from defters of the 1520s for the sandžaks of Bosnia, Zvornik and Hercegovina is 211,595 Christians and 133,295 Muslims (Hadžijahić, *Porijeklo bosanskih Muslimana*, p. 165).

7 Hadžijahić, *Porijeklo bosanskih Muslimana*, p. 78. D. Mandić also notes more rapid Islamicization in the districts of Konjić and Foča in the early sixteenth century: *Etnička povijest Bosne*, p. 161.

8 D. Mandić, *Etnička povijest Bosne*, pp. 153–8.
9 Handžić, *Tuzla i njena okolina*, pp. 118–22, 136–42. See also the discussion of this in Džaja, *Die 'bosnische Kirche'*, pp. 80–8.
10 D. Mandić, *Etnička povijest Bosne*, p. 211. The priest's name was 'Athanasio Georgiceo', variously rendered by modern historians as Grgičević (which is certainly incorrect), Georgijević and Jurjević. 'Bosnia' in these seventeenth-century reports means the whole Franciscan province of that name, corresponding roughly to the *eyalet* of Bosnia, a much larger area than the sandžak of Bosnia.
11 'De Turchi saranno tre parti, et à pena de Catholici una, Schismatici saranno per la metà di Catolici, de quali saranno cento cinquata [*sic*] milla anime in circa' (Draganović, 'Izvješće apostolskog vizitatora', p. 43). A summary placed at the beginning of the report (p. 10), by another writer, misinterpreted this as meaning 150,000 Orthodox and 300,000 Catholics (and therefore 900,000 Muslims); nearly all subsequent writers have followed him.
12 *Turkuš* is derived from *türk ušaklı*, 'son of a Turk'.
13 Kulišić, 'Razmatranja o porijeklu Muslimana', pp. 145–7; Hadžijahić, *Porijeklo bosanskih Muslimana*, pp. 128–41; Fine, *Bosnian Church*, p. 382; Džaja, *Konfessionalität und Nationalität*, p. 57. The basis of all scholarship on this subject is the research in the Istanbul archives by Ömer Lütfi Barkan, who has found no evidence of any settlement of groups of Turks or Asiatics in Bosnia; see his 'Les déportations comme méthode de peuplement'.
14 Džaja, *Die 'bosnische Kirche'*, p. 84.
15 Smailović, *Muslimanska imena*, pp. 50–4; Blau lists Muslim surnames and notes that some were also derived from place-names: *Reisen in Bosnien*, pp. 62–3.
16 See Sugar, *Southeastern Europe under Ottoman Rule*, pp. 45–6.
17 For the grant, an *ahd-name* or decree of protected status, see Batinić, *Djelovanje franjevaca u Bosni*, vol. 1, p. 132.
18 G. Wenzel, ed., *Marino Sanuto világkrónikájának tudósításai*, vol. 1 (=14), p. 155.
19 Džaja, *Konfessionalität und Nationalität*, pp. 159–64; Fermendžin, ed., *Acta Bosnae*, pp. 477–8.
20 Fermendžin, ed., *Acta Bosnae*, p.341.
21 Džaja, *Die 'bosnische Kirche'*, p. 93.
22 Balić, *Das unbekannte Bosnien*, pp. 92–4.
23 Fine, *Bosnian Church*, pp. 384–5.
24 Džaja, *Die 'bosnische Kirche'*, p. 91.
25 Wheler, *Journey into Greece*, p. 441.

26 Fine, *Bosnian Church*, p. 13.

27 Bordeaux, *La Bosnie populaire*, p. 52. For a more detailed study of the use of amulets and protective inscriptions by Muslims in Bosnia, see Kriss and Kriss-Heinrich, *Volksglaube*, vol. 2, pp. 99–103. Evans prints illustrations of some typical amulets, and notes (writing in 1876) that the sale of protective inscriptions is 'a regular source of income to the Franciscan monks': *Through Bosnia*, pp. 289, 292. For other folk practices and beliefs see Durham, *Some Tribal Origins*, pp. 248–74, and Lilek, 'Vjerske starine'.

28 Balagija, *Les Musulmans yougoslaves*, p. 31. Hadžijahić ('Sinkretistički elementi', pp. 316–22) distinguishes the different ways in which Christian festivals were used by Muslims, and notes that many had pre-Christian origins.

29 Hadžijahić, 'Sinkretistički elementi', pp. 326–7 (the icon of the Virgin at Olovo); Gibbons, *London to Sarajevo*, p. 181 (the Catholic church of St Anthony in Sarajevo: 'Orthodox and Jews and Moslems all going there to pray'); Chaumette-des-Fossés, *Voyage en Bosnie*, pp. 74–5 (on Masses for illness, and noting that Muslims have 'a sort of penchant' for Catholic rites).

30 Fermendžin, ed., *Acta Bosnae*, pp. 525–6.

31 F. W. Hasluck, *Christianity and Islam*, vol. 1, pp. 77 (dervishes), 69 (quotation). Hasluck also notes a record of Catholics, Orthodox and Muslims frequenting a picture of the Virgin for cures in 1621 (p. 66).

32 These include the distinguished scholars Safvet-beg Bašagić and Ćiro Truhelka: see Hadžijahić, *Porijeklo bosanskih Muslimana*, pp. 91–2.

33 Shaw, *History of the Ottoman Empire*, vol. 1, p. 114 (spelling it 'potor').

34 For all these Turkish sources see Hadžijahić, *Porijeklo bosanskih Muslimana*, pp. 87–90.

35 Akademia e shkencave, *Fjalor i gjuhës së sotme Shqipe*. For a picture of an Albanian *potur*, see Start and Durham, *Durham Collection of Garments*, p. 35.

36 D. Mandić, *Etnička povijest Bosne*, pp. 207–8, 225.

37 *Ibid.*, p. 211. The 'fire' here is, of course, punishment for apostasy from Islam, not treatment of Christians as such.

38 For other Ottoman examples see F. W. Hasluck, *Christianity and Islam*, vol. 2, pp. 469–74; Dawkins, 'Crypto-Christians of Turkey'; Amantos, *Scheseis Ellênôn kai Tourkôn*, pp. 193–6.

39 Rycaut, *Present State of the Ottoman Empire*, pp. 129–31 (book 2, chapter 12).

40 Solovjev, 'Le Témoignage de Paul Rycaut'.

41 Rycaut, *Present State of the Ottoman Empire*, p. 149. On the Bektashi

see F. W. Hasluck, *Christianity and Islam*, vol. 2, and Birge, *Bektashi Order*.

42 In 1676 George Wheler met a Polish Muslim convert, working as a dragoman or translator, who said he had been one of Rycaut's chief informants: *Journey into Greece*, p. 202.

43 Hadžijahić, *Porijeklo bosanskih Muslimana*, pp. 90–1.

44 Stanojević, 'Jedan pomen o kristjanima': this report of 1692, often cited in modern studies of Bosnia, does not mention Poturs, and is actually from Dalmatia.

45 Jukić, *Zemljopis i poviestica Bosne*, p. 143, quoted in Andrić, *Development of Spiritual Life in Bosnia*, p. 20.

46 Čubrilović, 'Poreklo muslimanskog plemstva'.

47 Skarić, *Sarajevo i njegova okolina*, p. 42

48 B. Zlatar, 'O nekim muslimanskim feudalnim porodicama'.

49 Skarić, *Sarajevo i njegova okolina*, p. 76.

50 Braudel, *Mediterranean*, vol. 1, pp. 420–1, 595.

51 Kuripešić, *Itinerarium der Botschaftsreise*, p. 44.

52 On the general role of the devşirme in the Islamicization process see Papoulia, *Ursprung und Wesen der 'Knabenlese'*, pp. 98–108.

53 For the text of the *kanun* see Andrić, *Development of Spiritual Life in Bosnia*, pp. 23–4; Rośkiewicz also prints it and comments that many of its provisions had fallen into disuse long before its abolition in 1839: *Studien über Bosnien*, pp. 251–2.

54 D. Mandić, *Etnička povijest Bosne*, pp. 246–7. On the seizure of Muslim children from Bosnia by Christian forces during the sixteenth and seventeenth centuries, see Klen, 'Pokrštavanje "Turske" djece'.

55 Handžić, 'O gradskom stanovništvu u Bosni', pp. 252–3.

56 Hrabak, 'Izvoz plemenitih metala iz Bosne'.

57 Skarić, *Sarajevo i njegova okolina*, pp. 36–8; Pašalić and Mišević, eds., *Sarajevo*; B. Zlatar, 'Une ville typiquement levantine'.

58 Pelletier, *Sarajevo*, p. 76.

59 Skarić, *Sarajevo i njegova okolina*, p. 51.

60 Sugar, *Southeastern Europe under Ottoman Rule*, p. 51.

61 B. Zlatar, 'Une ville typiquement levantine', p. 96.

6: Serbs and Vlachs

1 Fine, *Bosnian Church*, p. 172.

2 *Ibid.*, pp. 305–7; Džaja, *Konfessionalität und Nationalität*, p. 158; D. Mandić, *Etnička povijest Bosne*, pp. 456–67.

3 Džaja, *Konfessionalität und Nationalität*, pp. 125–6.
4 Fine, *Bosnian Church*, p. 379.
5 For a report of 1455 see Fermendžin, ed., *Acta Bosnae*, pp. 224–6.
6 Fine, *Bosnian Church*, pp. 379–80; Džaja, *Konfessionalität und Nationalität*, p. 129.
7 Džaja, *Konfessionalität und Nationalität*, pp. 126–7; Skarić, *Sarajevo i njegova okolina*, p. 56. The first certain evidence of an Orthodox Church in Sarajevo, however, is from 1616: Skarić, *Srpski pravoslavni u Sarajevu*, p. 10.
8 For evidence of conversions see D. Mandić, *Etnička povijest Bosne*, pp. 467–94. There were also some conversions from Orthodox to Catholic.
9 Džaja, *Die 'bosnische Kirche'*, pp. 75–82.
10 Vasić, 'Etnička kretanja', pp. 233–9; for a report of a serious plague in 1584, which allegedly killed 200,000 in Bosnia, Hercegovina and Serbia, see Fermendžin, ed., *Acta Bosnae*, p. 338.
11 Kuripešić, *Itinerarium der Botschaftsreise*, pp. 34–5. Smederovo is a town in northern Serbia, south-east of Belgrade. Kuripešić also found Serbs in the second part of his journey, between Sarajevo and Kosovo; these he refers to simply as Serbs (p. 43).
12 Rośkiewicz, *Studien über Bosnien*, p. 77.
13 Vasić, 'Etnička kretanja', p. 238; Šabanović, 'Vojno uredjenje Bosne', pp. 218–19.
14 Kuripešić, *Itinerarium der Botschaftsreise*, p. 43. Many Vlachs crossed over to the Austrian side after the Ottoman defeat at Sisak in 1593 (Gušić, 'Wer sind die Morlaken?', p. 461).
15 See Rothenberg, *Austrian Military Border*, and for a useful summary his *Military Border in Croatia*, pp. 6–11.
16 The literature on the Vlachs is huge and, for the most part, unsatisfactory. For an extensive bibliography see Năsturel, ed., *Bibliografie macedoromână*. The best general introductions are still Weigand, *Die Aromunen*, and Wace and Thompson, *Nomads of the Balkans*. The best modern study is Winnifrith, *Vlachs*; Nandriş, 'Aromâni', is also valuable.
17 Gyóni, 'La Transhumance des Vlaques'.
18 Bartusis, *Late Byzantine Army*, pp. 216, 256; Năsturel, 'Les Valaques balcaniques', p. 110.
19 D. Radojčić, 'Bulgaralbanitoblahos'.
20 I should say that I have not been able to consult Father Mandić's full statement of his theory, *Postanak Vlaha*, which was published in Buenos Aires; I have relied on the summary in his 'Ethnic and Religious History of Bosnia', pp. 383–6.

21 There is a large technical literature on the links between Romanian and Albanian. See especially Barić, *Lingvističke studije*; for good modern summaries see Du Nay, *Early History of Rumanian*, and Illyés, *Ethnic Continuity*, pp. 191–290.

22 See Haarmann, *Der lateinische Lehnwortschatz*. The evidence shows that the variety of late Latin which developed into Romanian was in close contact with Albanian, though some of the Albanian borrowings are from earlier Latin too.

23 The most distinguished independent (i.e. non-Balkan) scholars include Jireček, Weigand and Stadtmüller. For a useful survey (though of course emphasizing Albanian geographical origins for the Albanians), see Çabej, 'Problem of Place of Formation'. Some Romanian writers have attempted to turn the tables by arguing that the Albanians came from Romania. The most ingenious Romanian compromise was that of Marienescu, who argued that the Illyrian characteristics of the language were picked up first of all by Roman legionaries in Macedonia, who were then redeployed north of the Danube ('Ilirii, macedo-românii şi albanesii', pp. 153–4).

24 Jireček, 'Die Romanen in den Städten Dalmatiens', part 1, pp. 35–40; Gušić, 'Wer sind die Morlaken?'; Dragomir, *Vlahii şi Morlacii*, pp. 15–52. See also Valentini, 'L'elemento *vlah* nella zona scutarina', for Venetian records of Vlachs further down the coastline in southern Montenegro and northern Albania.

25 Dragomir, *Vlahii din nordul peninsulei balcanice*, pp. 49–52 and map 1.

26 I. Popović, 'Valacho-serbica', pp. 372–3 (I have corrected Popović's spelling of *tîrdzîu*); Huld, *Basic Albanian Etymologies*, p. 57. In modern Romanian *tîrziu* is 'late' and *zară* is 'whey' or 'sour milk'. For evidence of Albanian pastoralism in Dalmatia, and of groups of Albanian origin among the Vlachs of Hercegovina and Serbia, see Gušić, 'Wer sind die Morlaken?', p. 456; Jireček, 'Die Romanen in den Städten Dalmatiens', part 1, pp. 41–3; M. Filipović, 'Struktura i organizacija katuna', pp. 50–8.

27 Their descendants may survive in the form of the Islamicized transhumant shepherds, traditionally known as *balije*, in the remoter areas of Bosnia: see Balagija, *Les Musulmans yougoslaves*, pp. 82–3; Kulišić, 'Razmatranja o porijeklu Muslimana', p. 153. One family of *balije* investigated by Weigand turned out to be probably of Turcoman origin ('Rumänen und Aromunen in Bosnien', pp. 191–7); but most are clearly of Balkan stock.

28 Gušić, 'Wer sind die Morlaken?', p. 457. See for example a complaint of 1403 in Fermendžin, ed., *Acta Bosnae*, p. 85.

29 Novaković (*Selo*, p. 33) also identifies the *Crnogunjci* with the Sarakatsani, whose name may come from the Turkish *Karakaçan*, meaning 'black retreater'; but the Sarakatsani, who have evidently been Greek-speaking for a long time, are another mystery.

30 The seventeenth-century historian Ioannes Lucius of Trogir (Ivan Lukić) states that the term was used in contrast to the '*Bili-Vlahi*, id est *Albi Latini*' (white Vlachs) ('De Regno Dalmatiae', in von Schwandner, ed., *Scriptores rerum hungaricarum*, vol. 3, p. 459); but I have not seen any phrase for 'white Vlachs' quoted from any early source. Jireček thinks the Ragusans and Dalmatians made the distinction to differentiate themselves (also sometimes called Vlachs because of their Latinate language) from the inland Vlachs, and Gušić thinks they were distinguishing between their original local Vlachs (who wore white) and a wave of newcomers. Both theories are unconvincing, because there is no reason why Ragusans or other Dalmatians should have used Greek. Lucius of Trogir was at least aware of this problem; he suggested the term *Mavrovlachos* was brought back from Greece by the Venetians.

31 The word *Morovlah* occurs in Ragusan references to local Vlachs from the thirteenth century (Jireček, 'Die Romanen in den Städten Dalmatiens', part 1, p. 35), and the effect of folk-etymologizing on the pronunciation of the word had evidently occurred by the late twelfth century, when the Priest of Duklje referred to 'Morovlachi' (though he was aware that the meaning was 'nigri Latini'): von Schwandner, ed., *Scriptores rerum hungaricarum*, vol. 3, p. 478. Both these elements of the evidence conflict with the argument put forward in Gušić, 'Wer sind die Morlaken?', pp. 459–60.

32 Fortis, *Travels into Dalmatia*, pp. 53, 85. Many of Fortis's observations (but not these ones) were contested in a later and more valuable work, by a writer with much better local knowledge: Lovrich, *Osservazioni*.

33 Balić, *Das unbekannte Bosnien*, p. 175; Wilson, *Life of Vuk Karadžić*, pp. 192–4. Wilson's own translation is on pp. 361–3.

34 Beldiceanu, 'Les Valaques de Bosnie'.

35 Beldiceanu, 'Sur les valaques des balkans slaves', p. 97; Beldiceanu and Beldiceanu-Steinherr, 'Quatre actes de Mehmed II', p. 118; see also Hadžibegić, 'Džizja ili harač', part 1, p. 68. By the late eighteenth century, however, the descendants of the Vlachs in the Bosnian border region did pay the *haraç*: Lovrich, *Osservazioni*, p. 83.

36 Beldiceanu, 'Sur les valaques des balkans slaves', p. 94; Hadžijahić, *Porijeklo bosanskih Muslimana*, p. 137 n. Compare the observation by Kuripešić, above (at n. 11).

37 Džaja, *Die 'bosnische Kirche'*, p. 75.
38 Beldiceanu, 'Sur les valaques des balkans slaves', p. 91. Trifunovski dates the change towards settlement in a single village to the fifteenth century: 'Geografske karakteristike katuna', pp. 36–7.
39 Lovrich, *Osservazioni*, pp. 174, 179.
40 The founder of this interpretation was the nineteenth-century historian Stojan Novaković; see his *Selo*, pp. 29–30. The Russian historian E. P. Naumov also argues that the Vlachs were heavily Slavicized as early as the thirteenth century: 'Balkanskiye vlakhi'. Serbian writers who accept that the Vlachs had a different ethnic identity were not deterred by that mere fact; as one modern Serbian nationalist historian quaintly writes, 'Even Vlachs and their ways became so threatened that they joined the Serbs to survive, and in the process helped out the preservation and the continuation of the Serbian ethnic, religious and cultural identity' (Pavlovich, *Serbians*, p. 78).
41 Beldiceanu, 'Les valaques de Bosnie', p. 123 n.
42 M. Filipović, 'Struktura i organizacija katuna', p. 52 (names); Jireček, 'Die Romanen in den Städten Dalmatiens', part 1, p. 40 (island); Niger, *Geographiae commentariorum libri*, p. 103 (corrupt Latin); Nandriş, 'Aromâni', p. 38 (counting-words).
43 Jireček, 'Die Romanen in den Städten Dalmatiens', part 1, p. 41.
44 D. Mandić, *Etnička povijest Bosne*, p. 516.
45 The difference lies in the palatalizing of certain vowels: 'ekavian', spoken in Serbia, would say 'mleko' (milk), while 'jekavian' (spoken in most of Bosnia, Hercegovina and Croatia) would say 'mljeko' or 'mlijeko'.
46 D. Mandić cites the census as evidence of continuous Vlach-speaking (*Etnička povijest Bosne*, p. 516); Filipescu, *Coloniile române din Bosnia*.
47 Weigand, 'Rumänen und Aromunen in Bosnien'. On the 'Karavlasi' see the section on Gypsies in chapter 9, below.
48 D. Mandić, with marvellous pseudo-precision, gives the figure of 50–52 per cent (*Etnička povijest Bosne*, p. 518).
49 Džaja, *Konfessionalität und Nationalität*, p. 83.

7: War and politics in Ottoman Bosnia, 1606–1815

1 Kunt, *Sultan's Servants*, p. 82.
2 Clissold, ed., *Short History*, p. 49.
3 Fermendžin, ed., *Acta Bosnae*, pp. 479, 501.

4 Shaw, *History of the Ottoman Empire*, vol. 1, p. 212.
5 A. Popović, *L'Islam balkanique*, p. 259.
6 Džaja, *Konfessionalität und Nationalität*, p. 81; Peledija writes, however, that 130,000 is the total number of Muslim refugees from the lands reconquered by the Habsburgs, not all of whom settled in Bosnia (*Bosanski ejalet*, p. 50).
7 Djurdjev, 'Bosna', p. 1267.
8 Mraz, *Prinz Eugen*, p. 40.
9 D. Mandić, *Etnička povijest Bosne*, p. 514.
10 Some Catholics did later return, however, after an amnesty was declared by the Ottoman authorities in 1699: Peledija, *Bosanski ejalet*, p. 51.
11 Džaja, *Konfessionalität und Nationalität*, p. 98.
12 This Venetian-Bosnian border was eventually delimited during the period 1721–33: see Clissold, ed., *Short History*, pp. 45, 50. Shaw mistakenly says that the treaty established the border on the river Sava (*History of the Ottoman Empire*, vol. 1, p. 232).
13 A. Popović, *L'Islam balkanique*, p. 259.
14 Džaja, *Konfessionalität und Nationalität*, p. 96. Džaja also notes revolts before the war, in 1710 and 1711.
15 Handžić, 'Bosanski namjesnik', pp. 144–5.
16 *Ibid.*, pp. 152–63.
17 Djurdjev, 'Bosna', p. 1267.
18 Handžić, 'Bosanski namjesnik', pp. 164–80.
19 Hadžijahić, 'Die Kämpfe der Ajane', p. 130.
20 Sućeska, 'Osmanlı imparatorluğunda Bosna', p. 441.
21 Hadžijahić, 'Die priviligierten Städte', p. 156.
22 Džaja, *Konfessionalität und Nationalität*, p. 98.
23 B. Jelavich, *History of the Balkans*, vol. 1, p. 90.
24 Rothenberg, *Military Border in Croatia*, pp. 72–3.
25 Shaw, *History of the Ottoman Empire*, vol. 1, p. 259.
26 Šamić, *Les Voyageurs français*, pp. 146–9.
27 Desboeufs, *Souvenirs*, pp. 132–3.
28 Pavlowitch, 'Society in Serbia', pp. 144–5; A. Popović notes that such actions continued with renewed vigour after 1815 (*L'Islam balkanique*, p. 262).
29 Kreševljaković, *Kapetanije*, pp. 13, 22.
30 *Ibid.*, pp. 52–64.
31 Bosnia could be described as a 'pashaluk', but this was a general term covering all the types of territory which could be ruled by a pasha.

Bosnia, as an eyalet, was not on a par with the pashaluk of Belgrade, for example, which was only a sandžak. On the privileges of a three-tailed pasha see d'Ohsson, *Tableau de l'Empire othoman*, vol. 7, p. 285.

32 Šamić, *Les Voyageurs français*, pp. 186–7; Kreševljaković, *Kapetanije*, p. 17

33 Šamić, *Les Voyageurs français*, p. 188.

34 Hadžijahić, 'Die priviligierten Städte', pp. 132–4. The guilds (*esnafi*) were led by Muslims, but included Christians and Jews as members. The non-Muslims could also have their own sections within the guilds. See Kreševljaković, *Esnafi i obrti*, p. 49; Skarić, *Sarajevo i njegova okolina*, p. 134.

35 Chaumette-des-Fossés, *Voyage en Bosnie*, p. 114.

36 Hadžijahić, 'Die priviligierten Städte', p. 137.

37 *Ibid.*, pp. 156–7.

38 On the Bosnian ajans see *ibid.*; Sućeska, 'Bedeutung des Begriffes A'yân'; Hadžijahić, 'Die Kämpfe der Ajane'; for the original nature of the post see Bowen, 'Ayan'; and for the use of the term elsewhere, Sugar, *Southeastern Europe under Ottoman Rule*, p. 238.

8: Economic life, culture and society in Ottoman Bosnia, 1605–1815

1 Tomasevich analyses the special use of these terms in Bosnia: *Peasants, Politics, and Economic Change*, pp. 99–100. Sugar gives a differing and more general account: *Southeastern Europe under Ottoman Rule*, pp. 214–18.

2 The transition to čiftliks throughout the Empire is a huge subject of which many aspects remain uncertain. For a valuable survey of the issues see McGowan, *Economic Life in Ottoman Europe*, pp. 57–79. Mutafchieva describes the two traditional forms in which čiftliks were originally granted (to musselims and to 'gazis' or military heroes); she also notes a special form of čiftlik made out of the old feudal properties in Bosnia ('K'm v'prosa za chiflitsite', pp. 36–42).

3 Hottinger comments on their presence in Adrianople (Edirne) in the 1650s: *Historia orientalis*, p. 463.

4 McGowan, 'Food Supply and Taxation'.

5 Šamić, *Les Voyageurs français*, p. 248.

6 McGowan, *Economic Life in Ottoman Europe*, pp. 83–6.

7 Džaja, *Konfessionalität und Nationalität*, pp. 105–6, 151, 168. Bishop

Maravić's report on Bosnia in 1655 put the total Catholic population at 63,206 souls: Fermendžin, ed., *Acta Bosnae*, p. 476.

8 Skarić, 'Popis bosanskih spahija'.

9 B. Jelavich, *History of the Balkans*, vol. 1, p. 90.

10 The figures are for non-Muslim adult males registered in the eyalet of Bosnia for the *cizye*: 12,500 in the year 1700 (including Hercegovina and Zvornik), 39,200 in 1718 (excluding Hercegovina, including Zvornik), 63,440 in 1740 (excluding Hercegovina, including Zvornik), 98,329 for 1788 (including Hercegovina and an unidentified sandžak) and 103,883 for 1815 (including Hercegovina and an unidentified sandžak): McGowan, *Economic Life in Ottoman Europe*, p. 90. The first figure seems impossibly low; it may indicate that the Bosnian administration had not yet recovered from the war, and was unable to collect the full statistics. This was also the first figure compiled on a new basis, counting adult males rather than households.

11 Estimates by Muhamed Hadžijahić, cited in Džaja, *Konfessionalität und Nationalität*, p. 82.

12 Weigand, 'Rumänen und Aromunen', p. 178.

13 Skarić, *Srpski pravoslavni narod*, p. 10.

14 D. Mandić, *Etnička povijest Bosne*, p. 514; Hadžijahić, 'Die priviligierten Städte', p. 136.

15 Hadžijahić, 'Die priviligierten Städte', p. 135.

16 Čelebi, *Putopis*, pp. 106, 116. Čelebi's figures are thought exaggerated by one modern scholar, who compares them with a much smaller figure from a register for 1841 (Nagata, *Materials on Bosnian Notables*, p. 2). But Bishop Maravić's report from 1655 gives a figure slightly larger than Čelebi's: 20,000 Muslim households and 100 Christian (Fermendžin, ed., *Acta Bosnae*, p. 476). (It is worth noting Maravić's statement that those 100 houses contained 600 souls, thus implying a larger multiplier than the one normally used by modern historians.) Sarajevo was clearly smaller in the eighteenth century than in the seventeenth, and may have declined further in the early nineteenth.

17 Quiclet, *Voyages*, pp. 68–70, 79. Peter Masarechi had commented on the high quality of Bosnian horses in 1624: Draganović, 'Izvješće Petra Masarechija', p. 42.

18 Pelletier, *Sarajevo*, p. 69.

19 Chaumette-des-Fossés, *Voyage en Bosnie*, p. 33; Hadžijahić, 'Die priviligierten Städte', p. 135.

20 The Austrians stupidly placed an import duty on their own merchants but no corresponding duty on Ottoman subjects who brought in the

same goods: see McGowan, *Economic Life in Ottoman Europe*, pp. 23–4.

21 The Leipzig trade fair exerted a strong pull on the merchants of Bosnia and other parts of the Balkans throughout this period: see Paskaleva, 'Osmanlı balkan eyâletlerinin ticaretleri', pp. 47–9.

22 On the mining of iron ore see Sugar, *Industrialization of Bosnia*, p. 16. A report by Fourcade in 1813 does mention one mineral export to France, however: orpiment (yellow arsenic), a naturally occurring chemical used in the manufacture of pigments (Vacalopoulos, 'Tendances du commerce de la Bosnie', p. 95).

23 D'Ohsson, *Tableau général de l'Empire othoman*, vol. 7, p. 296.

24 Porter, *Observations on the Turks*, vol. 1, p. 133.

25 *Ibid*., vol. 2, pp. 47, 56. Anton Hangi, whose study of life in Bosnia was written in the 1890s, made a strikingly similar comment about the honesty and lack of theft he encountered in Sarajevo, where, he said, he lived for a year without ever locking his door (*Die Moslim's in Bosnien*, p. 7). The British traveller H. C. Thomson also noted in 1897: 'All over Bosnia a Mohammedan's word may be trusted in matters of buying and selling' (*Outgoing Turk*, p. 162).

26 Mujić, 'Prilog proučavanje uživanja alkoholni pića'.

27 Šamić, *Les Voyageurs français*, p. 243.

28 Pelletier, *Sarajevo*, p. 118.

29 Andrić, *Development of Spiritual Life in Bosnia*, pp. 62–3.

30 Džaja, *Konfessionalität und Nationalität*, p. 149; Šamić, *Les Voyageurs français*, p. 243

31 Draganović, 'Izvješće Petra Masarechija', p. 46; D. Mandić, *Etnička povijest Bosne*, p. 375.

32 Fermendžin, ed., *Acta Bosnae*, p. 526.

33 *Ibid*., p. 479.

34 Chaumette-des-Fossés, *Voyage en Bosnie*, pp. 70–4.

35 'Pisna od pakla' ('Song of Hell'), by Fra Lovro Sitović; the poem is itself in the verse-form used by folk-songs, so was presumably intended to replace them. Andrić comments that 'it differs from the real verses of folk poetry only in being frequently irregular and quite devoid of any beauty': *Development of Spiritual Life in Bosnia*, p. 50. For other Catholic publications see *ibid*., pp. 47–51.

36 *Ibid*., p. 50; Hadžijahić, *Od tradicije do identiteta*, p. 32.

37 Fermendžin, ed., *Acta Bosnae*, pp. 503–4. For later attempts to encroach on the Catholics, see Džaja, *Konfessionalität und Nationalität*, pp. 208–9.

38 Chaumette-des-Fossés, *Voyage en Bosnie*, p. 75.
39 Šamić, *Les Voyageurs français*, p. 112.
40 Chaumette-des-Fossés, *Voyage en Bosnie*, p. 75.
41 Andrić, *Development of Spiritual Life in Bosnia*, p. 38.
42 Gazić, 'Les Collections manuscrits'. Reports from Sarajevo suggest that the entire collection in the Oriental Institute has been destroyed by Serb artillery.
43 See Lehfeldt, *Das serbokroatische Aljamiado-Schrifttum*, pp. 45–52.
44 For a valuable summary see Balić, *Das unbekannte Bosnien*, pp. 271–81. The most recent study, which I have not been able to consult, is Huković, *Alhamiado književnost i njeni stvaraoci*.
45 See Balić, *Das unbekannte Bosnien*, pp. 165–90.
46 Lehfeldt, *Das serbokroatische Aljamiado-Schrifttum*, p. 50; on Bašeskija's chronicle see Gazić, 'Les Collections manuscrits'.
47 Hadžijahić, *Od tradicije do identiteta*, p. 7. For many examples of writers calling their language Bosnian, see *ibid.*, pp. 24–31.
48 Orbini, *Regno de gli Slavi*, p. 377.
49 Wilson, *Life and Times of Karadžić*, p. 389.
50 For further details on all these writers, and many others, see Balić, *Das unbekannte Bosnien*, pp. 221–64.
51 See *ibid.*, pp. 300–16; for details of two particularly fine eighteenth-century Bosnian Korans, by Ibrahim Šehović and Husein Bošnjak, see Gazić, 'Les Collections manuscrits'.
52 A valuable general study of the dervish orders in the Ottoman Empire is Mirmiroglou, *Oi Dervissai*. Useful material is contained in Rycaut, *Present State of the Ottoman Empire*, pp. 135–51; F. W. Hasluck, *Christianity and Islam*; Birge, *Bektashi Order*; and Trimingham, *Sufi Orders in Islam*.
53 Handžić, 'U ulozi derviša'.
54 Pelletier, *Sarajevo*, pp. 82–9. There is a full description of these tekkes in Sikirić, 'Derviskolostorok és szent sírok'; but Sikirić is mistaken in describing the Skender-paša tekke as the earliest (pp. 577–8).
55 Čelebi, *Putopis*, p. 110.
56 See the description in Algar, 'Notes on the Naqshbandi Tariqat', pp. 73–7.
57 Balagija, *Les Musulmans yougoslaves*, p. 103; see also F. W. Hasluck, *Christianity and Islam*, vol. 2, p. 551.
58 Balić, *Das unbekannte Bosnien*, pp. 104–5; Hadžijahić, 'Udio Hamzevija u atentatu'; Hukić, ed., *Islam i muslimani u Bosni*, pp. 91–8.
59 Čelebi, *Putopis*, p. 116.

60 See for example Chaumette-des-Fossés, *Voyage en Bosnie*, pp. 55–63. Chaumette-des-Fossés also noted, like many other observers, the virtual absence of polygamy.
61 Hadžijahić, *Od tradicije do identiteta*, p. 19.
62 Quiclet, *Les Voyages*, pp. 72–3.
63 Chaumette-des-Fossés, *Voyage en Bosnie*, pp. 49–50.
64 Pertusier, *La Bosnie*, p. 91.

9: The Jews and the Gypsies of Bosnia

1 Goldstein, ed., *Jews in Yugoslavia*, pp. 27–8.
2 *Ibid.*, pp. 75–6.
3 Levy, *Die Sephardim in Bosnien*, p. 2. Freidenreich writes that these court records refer to between ten and fifteen Jewish families (*Jews of Yugoslavia*, p. 12); but that is only Levy's guess about the size of the Jewish community at that time.
4 Shaw, *Jews of the Ottoman Empire*, p. 53.
5 Pelletier noted in 1934 that the textiles in Sarajevo were sold mainly by Jews: *Sarajevo*, pp. 48–9. Skarić argues that the Jews of Sarajevo came originally from Skopje: *Sarajevo i njegova okolina*, p. 60.
6 Shaw, *Jews of the Ottoman Empire*, p. 53.
7 Levy, *Die Sephardim in Bosnien*, pp. 6–10.
8 Goldstein, ed., *Jews in Yugoslavia*, p. 72; Freidenreich, *Jews of Yugoslavia*, pp. 12, 27. The Cortijo was burnt down in the fire of 1879, and never rebuilt. For a full description of the Jewish quarter in Sarajevo, and a street-map, see Levy, *Die Sephardim in Bosnien*, pp. 85–111.
9 Levy, *Die Sephardim in Bosnien*, p. 111; it burnt down in 1794, and was rebuilt.
10 Freidenreich, *Jews of Yugoslavia*, p. 13.
11 Čelebi, *Putopis*, pp. 105–6.
12 Levy, *Die Sephardim in Bosnien*, pp. 53–5, 66; Freidenreich, *Jews of Yugoslavia*, pp. 14–15; Goldstein, ed., *Jews in Yugoslavia*, p. 65.
13 Scholem, *Sabbatai Ṣevi*, p. 560.
14 On Ḥayyon see Levy, *Die Sephardim in Bosnien*, pp. 15–17; Scholem, *Sabbatai Ṣevi*, pp. 901–2; Scholem, *Major Trends in Jewish Mysticism*, pp. 321–4; on Ashkenazi see Freidenreich, *Jews of Yugoslavia*, p. 13.
15 Levy, *Die Sephardim in Bosnien*, p. 88.
16 *Ibid.*, pp. 19–20. The main Sephardic synagogue, together with the old library and archive which it contained, was ransacked immediately

after the arrival of German troops in Sarajevo on 15 April 1941 (Levntal, ed., *Zločini fašističkih okupatora*, p. 64).

17 Shaw, *Jews of the Ottoman Empire*, p. 53.

18 *Ibid.*, p. 53. Shaw dates Pardo's arrival to 1752; Freidenreich to 1765; Levy to 1768. All agree that he left for Palestine in 1781.

19 See the description and colour reproduction of the entire manuscript in Roth, ed., *Sarajevo Haggadah*.

20 Vacalopoulos, 'Tendances caractéristiques du commerce de la Bosnie', p. 99. Pertusier also gave the total of 2000 for Bosnia (*La Bosnie*, p. 78). Chaumette-des-Fossés put it at 1200 (*Voyage en Bosnie*, p. 30).

21 Pertusier, who visited it in 1812, said the population of Travnik was entirely Muslim apart from 'a few Jewish families' (*La Bosnie*, p. 297); Chaumette-des-Fossés, who lived there for most of seven months in 1808, said it included 1000 Orthodox, 500 Catholic, 300 Gypsies and 60 Jews. William Miller in 1898 called Travnik 'one of the purest Mohammedan towns in the country' (*Travels and Politics*, p. 155).

22 Thoemmel, *Geschichtliche Beschreibung*, p. 130.

23 Levy, *Die Sephardim in Bosnien*, pp. 62–3.

24 Freidenreich, *Jews of Yugoslavia*, pp. 15–16.

25 Baernreither, *Bosnische Eindrücke*, p. 26.

26 Freidenreich, *Jews of Yugoslavia*, p. 213.

27 Curtis, *Turk and his Lost Provinces*, p. 276.

28 Freidenreich, *Jews of Yugoslavia*, pp. 19–22.

29 Shaw, *Jews of the Ottoman Empire*, p. 35; Levntal, ed., *Zločini fašističkih okupatora*, pp. 70–1.

30 For all the foregoing details see Mujić, 'Položaj cigana', pp. 140–4, and Soulis, 'Gypsies in the Byzantine Empire'. Fraser (*Gypsies*, p. 57) notes that the term *cingarije* in a Serbian edict of 1348 probably just meant 'shoemakers'.

31 Fraser, *Gypsies*, p. 83.

32 Mujić, 'Položaj cigana', pp. 146–7.

33 Vukanović, 'Le Firman relatif aux tsiganes'.

34 Weigand, 'Rumänen und Aromunen', p. 174. *Băieşĭ* is from the Hungarian *beás*, meaning 'dig'.

35 Kuripešić, *Itinerarium*, p. 31; he also says such workers were found in many other parts of Bosnia (p. 44). The usual method was not panning but dragging a sheep's fleece across the bed of the stream.

36 M. Hasluck, 'Firman regarding Gypsies', p. 2.

37 Fraser, *Gypsies*, pp. 132–4.

38 Sugar, *Southeastern Europe under Ottoman Rule*, pp. 77, 86, 103.

39 M. Hasluck, 'Firman regarding Gypsies', pp. 10–11.

40 Fermendžin, ed., *Acta Bosnae*, p. 476.
41 Mujić, 'Položaj cigana', p. 149.
42 Chaumette-des-Fossés, *Voyage en Bosnie*, p. 30; Pertusier, *La Bosnie*, p. 78.
43 Thoemmel, *Geschichtliche Beschreibung*, pp. 76–7 (for 1865); Maurer, *Eine Reise durch Bosnien*, p. 373 n. (late 1860s); Mujić, 'Položaj cigana', p. 170 (for 1870).
44 Mujić, 'Položaj cigana', p. 157; Chaumette-des-Fossés, *Voyage en Bosnie*, p. 38. Rośkiewicz noted roughly 1000 Gypsies in Sarajevo in the 1860s (*Studien über Bosnien*, pp. 179–80).
45 The account I have put together in these two paragraphs is, I hope, an accurate analysis of some rather conflicting evidence. The best discussions I have drawn on are Gilliat-Smith, 'The Dialect of the Gypsies of Serbo-Croatia'; the comments in Glück, 'Zur physischen Anthropologie der Zigeuner in Bosnien', p. 405; and an anonymous article in the *Bosnische Post* for 1895, translated in Filipescu, *Coloniile române din Bosnia*, p. 205. Filipescu himself rejects that author's argument, and develops his own 'pure Romanian' theory on pp. 199–293. Weigand refutes Filipescu in 'Rumänen und Aromunen'; Lockwood briefly discusses the White Gypsies and the *čergaši* in *European Muslims*, pp. 30–1.
46 Fraser, *Gypsies*, p. 231.
47 Thomson, *Outgoing Turk*, pp. 170–1.
48 Fraser, *Gypsies*, pp. 58–9.
49 Uhlik, 'Serbo-Bosnian Folk-Tales, no. 8', pp. 92–3.
50 Uhlik, 'Serbo-Bosnian Folk-Tales, no. 9', pp. 116–17. Most of those exterminated were Croatian Gypsies, who were nearly all Orthodox.

10: Resistance and reform, 1815–1878

1 Šamić, *Les Voyageurs français*, pp. 193–4, 201.
2 Boué, *La Turquie d'Europe*, vol. 4, p. 374; Djurdjev, 'Bosna', p. 1268.
3 On these events see Lewis, *Emergence of Turkey*, pp. 78–83; Shaw, *History of the Ottoman Empire*, vol. 2, pp. 19–24.
4 Boué, *La Turquie d'Europe*, vol. 4, pp. 375–7.
5 Rothenberg, *Military Border in Croatia*, p. 130.
6 Boué, *La Turquie d'Europe*, vol. 4, pp. 378–83.
7 *Ibid.*, vol. 4, p. 384.
8 Tomasevich, *Peasants, Politics, and Economic Change*, p. 103.

9 Chopin and Urbicini, *Provinces danubiennes*, p. 242.
10 Kreševljaković, *Kapetanije u Bosni*, pp. 68–9; Šljivo, *Omer-Paša Latas*, p. 10; Djurdjev, 'Bosna', p. 1268.
11 On the Tanzimat see Lewis, *Emergence of Turkey*, pp. 106–28; Shaw, *History of the Ottoman Empire*, vol. 2, pp. 58–133.
12 Muir Mackenzie and Irby, *Travels in the Slavonic Provinces*, vol. 1, p. 13.
13 Boué, *La Turquie d'Europe*, vol. 3, p. 53.
14 Šišić, ed., *Bosna za vezirovanja Omer-paše*, p. 27.
15 Boué, *La Turquie d'Europe*, vol. 4, p. 119.
16 Šljivo, *Omer-Paša Latas*, pp. 13–14.
17 Tomasevich, *Peasants, Politics, and Economic Change*, p. 104; for a more detailed account of Tahir-paša's attempts at tax reforms see Šljivo, *Omer-Paša Latas*, pp. 18–24.
18 Šljivo, *Omer-Paša Latas*, pp. 50–51.
19 Šabanović, *Bosanski pašaluk*, p. 96.
20 Šišić, *Bosna za vezirovanja Omer-paše*, p. 111.
21 *Ibid.*, pp. 235, 347, 357.
22 *Ibid.*, pp. 302–3.
23 Gavranović, *Bosna 1853–1870*, p. 42.
24 Lewis, *Emergence of Turkey*, p. 116.
25 Gavranović, *Bosna 1853–1870*, respectively: pp. 43, 38–9, 84–5.
26 Šišić, *Bosna za vezirovanja Omer-paše*, p. 358; Andrić, *Development of Spiritual Life in Bosnia*, pp. 64–5; Thoemmel, *Geschichtliche Beschreibung*, pp. 114–16; Gavranović, *Bosna 1853–1870*, p. 44.
27 Thoemmel, *Geschichtliche Beschreibung*, pp. 99, 102.
28 Maurer, *Eine Reise durch Bosnien*, pp. 364–5; cf. similar comments by Atanasković in 1853: Gavranović, *Bosna 1853–1870*, p. 44.
29 From a report by Atanasković's successor, Jovanović, in 1862: Gavranović, *Bosna 1853–1870*, p. 280.
30 See Andrić, *Development of Spiritual Life in Bosnia*, pp. 53–4 (Jukić); Imamović, 'O historiji bošnjačkog pokušaja', p. 41 (Petranović – and his Catholic counterpart Klement Božić, a translator at the Prussian consulate); Koetschet, *Osman Pascha*, pp. 33–4 (Pelagić). On Pelagić's colourful later career, which involved periods of agitation among Bosnian émigré circles in Belgrade and Bucharest, see Čuprić-Amrein, *Die Opposition in Bosnien*, pp. 61–4.
31 Rothenberg, *Military Border in Croatia*, p. 166.
32 For a translation of this text see Grmek *et al.*, eds., *Le Nettoyage ethnique*, pp. 42–53.

33 *Ibid.*, pp. 64–80, especially pp. 75, 78. For other proposals by Garašanin for propagandizing in Bosnia, see Slijepčević, *Pitanje Bosne*, pp. 21–2.
34 See Banac, *National Question*, pp. 85–9.
35 Shaw confuses this military expedition by Omer-paša with his governorship of Bosnia in 1850–2: *History of the Ottoman Empire*, vol. 2, p. 149.
36 Koetschet, *Osman Pascha*, pp. 1–5, 11–12.
37 *Ibid.*, p. 7; Koetschet notes, incidentally, that the entire financial administration of the *vilayet* consisted of a director, a controller and fifteen clerks. On the Provincial Reform Law see Shaw, *History of the Ottoman Empire*, vol. 2, pp. 88–91.
38 B. Jelavich and C. Jelavich, *Establishment of the Balkan National States*, p. 143.
39 For further details of the 1859 reform, see Tomasevich, *Peasants, Politics, and Economic Change*, pp. 105–6.
40 Koetschet, *Osman Pascha*, p. 6.
41 *Ibid.*, pp. 24–5. On this type of picnicking, known as *teferić*, which was still practised every Sunday by the Catholics in the 1930s, see Pelletier, *Sarajevo*, p. 143.
42 Koetschet, *Osman Pascha*, pp. 46–9. None was found; but plenty of evidence of Russian interest (and interference) in Bosnian affairs during this period can be found in Pisarev and Ekmečić, *Osvoboditel-naya borba narodov Bosnii i Rossiya*.
43 Slijepčević, *Pitanje Bosne*, p. 25.
44 Koetschet, *Osman Pascha*, p. 55.
45 Maier, *Deutsche Siedlungen*, p. 9; Anderson, *Miss Irby*, pp. 60–7; Pelletier, *Sarajevo*, p. 138.
46 Pelletier, *Sarajevo*, p. 119.
47 Arthur Evans, though strongly anti-Muslim in his attitudes, described the cathedral as a 'swaggering edifice' when he saw it in 1875: 'the Christians were not content with the permission to build a church in the most conspicuous position in one of the main streets of the city, but must needs rear a pretentious pile which should throw into the shade the biggest of the two hundred and odd mosques . . . It was perhaps hardly to be expected that the ignorant Moslem fanatics should view with equanimity this last manifestation of Christian humility' (*Through Bosnia*, p. 247).
48 Koetschet, *Osman Pascha*, p. 55.
49 *Ibid.*, p. 76.
50 M. Mandić, *Povijest okupacije*, p. 8.

51 Evans, *Through Bosnia*, pp. 337–8; Koetschet, *Aus Bosniens letzter Türkenzeit*, pp. 6–8. This is known as the Nevesinje uprising, but the first place known to have revolted was the village of Gabela on 3 July, with Nevesinje following a week later (MacKenzie, *Serbs and Pan-Slavism*, p. 30 n.).
52 On Ottoman-Montenegrin clashes of 1857–8, 1860–1 and 1874, see Shaw, *History of the Ottoman Empire*, vol. 2, p. 150, and M. Mandić, *Povijest okupacije*, p. 8.
53 M. Mandić, *Povijest okupacije*, p. 9.
54 Čubrilović, *Bosanski ustanak*, pp. 61–7. Evans commented that 'the insurrection in the Herzegovina is mainly an agrarian war' (*Through Bosnia*, p. 334); Peter Sugar comments: 'there can be little doubt that it was the agrarian question which sparked this revolution' (*Industrialization of Bosnia*, p. 22).
55 Koetschet, *Aus Bosniens letzter Türkenzeit*, pp. 12, 23; Evans, crossing into Bosnia in early August, heard of 'many Croats and Slovenes' from Zagreb, Maribor and Ljubljana on their way there (*Through Bosnia*, p. 87).
56 Mandić, *Povijest okupacije*, p. 22 (100,000); Evans, *Illyrian Letters*, p. 4 (250,000); the official Austrian report said that there were more than 100,000 on Austrian soil alone (Abtheilung für Kriegsgeschichte, *Die Occupation Bosniens*, p. 36). By May 1878 Gustav Thoemmel estimated 150,000 on Austrian territory, 70,000 in Montenegro and 10,000 in Serbia (Kapidžić, *Hercegovački ustanak*, p. 29 n.).
57 From a letter written by a Bosnian refugee in Slavonia in March 1877, quoted in Muir Mackenzie and Irby, *Travels in the Slavonic Provinces*, vol. 1, p. 36.
58 Evans, *Through Bosnia*, p. 337.
59 Abtheilung für Kriegsgeschichte, *Die Occupation Bosniens*, p. 41.
60 Evans, *Illyrian Letters*, p. 55.
61 Koetschet, *Aus Bosniens letzter Türkenzeit*, pp. 78–9.
62 *Ibid.*, pp. 86–8; M. Mandić, *Povijest okupacije*, pp. 28–30.
63 Koetschet, *Aus Bosniens letzter Türkenzeit*, pp. 90, 96, 102; M. Mandić, *Povijest okupacije*, pp. 30–1.
64 For the troop numbers see Abtheilung für Kriegsgeschichte, *Die Occupation Bosniens*, appendix, Beilag 8 (82,113 men and 1313 horses); the surveyor, Sterneck, printed some of his findings in 1877 (*Geografische Verhältnisse*).
65 Koetschet, *Aus Bosniens letzter Türkenzeit*, pp. 102–9; Abtheilung für Kriegsgeschichte, *Die Occupation Bosniens*, p. 450 (quotation); M. Mandić, *Povijest okupacije*, pp. 64–71, 97–9.

11: Bosnia under Austro-Hungarian rule, 1878–1914

1 Seton Watson, *Role of Bosnia*, p. 19.
2 Sugar, *Industrialization of Bosnia*, p. 20. The Hungarian minister Burián later recalled: 'When Andrássy accepted the mandate for occupying Bosnia-Herzegovina at the Congress of Berlin, he had the public opinion of practically the whole monarchy against him' (*Austria in Dissolution*, p. 291).
3 Schmitt, *Annexation of Bosnia*, p. 2; Shaw, *History of the Ottoman Empire*, vol. 2, p. 192.
4 Schmitt, *Annexation of Bosnia*, p. 3.
5 For a useful summary see Sugar, *Industrialization of Bosnia*, pp. 8, 26–32; on the shariat courts see also A. Popović, *L'Islam balkanique*, pp. 276–7. For a full account of the administrative structure see Schmid, *Bosnien*, pp. 54–60.
6 Abtheilung für Kriegsgeschichte, *Der Aufstand in Hercegovina*, pp. 9–11.
7 Kapidžić, *Hercegovački ustanak*, pp. 34–5.
8 Abtheilung für Kriegsgeschichte, *Der Aufstand in Hercegovina*, pp. 42–8; Kapidžić, *Hercegovački ustanak*, pp. 109–20.
9 Abtheilung für Kriegsgeschichte, *Der Aufstand in Hercegovina*, p. 102; Kapidžić, *Hercegovački ustanak*, pp. 110.
10 Abtheilung für Kriegsgeschichte, *Der Aufstand in Hercegovina*, p. 139.
11 Donia, *Islam under the Eagle*, pp. 72–6.
12 Schmid, *Bosnien*, pp. 249–50. Schmid, who was head of the statistical office in Sarajevo, boasts that Bosnia's Muslim emigration was smaller than that of other ex-Ottoman lands such as Bulgaria. If true, this is easily explained: the Muslims of Bosnia were much less likely to want to go to Turkey, because they were not Turkish-speakers.
13 Hadžijahić, 'Uz prilog Bogićevića', p. 191 (insisting on 300,000); Balić, *Das unbekannte Bosnien*, p. 51 (on the findings of the geographer Sulejman Smlatić).
14 Bogićević, 'Emigracije muslimana'; A. Popović, *L'Islam balkanique*, p. 272. This estimate of 8000 is certainly too low. Ferdinand Schmid, who was keen not to overestimate the numbers of émigrés, thought that roughly 8000 had left between the declaration of the army law in November 1882 and the introduction of exit permits in October 1883 (*Bosnien*, p. 249).
15 Kapidžić, 'Pokret za iseljavanje'.
16 Durham, *Twenty Years*, p. 163.

17 Donia, *Islam under the Eagle*, pp. 25–7; Tomasevich, *Peasants, Politics, and Economic Change*, pp. 108–9.
18 Miller, *Travels and Politics*, p. 7.
19 Sugar, *Industrialization of Bosnia*, pp. 43–50. Topal Osman-paša had previously built a short length of railway track from Banja Luka to the border; but by 1878 'grass had grown on the track, and Bosnia was still without a single train' (Miller, *Travel and Politics*, p. 108).
20 Schmid, *Bosnien*, pp. 579, 586.
21 Durham, *Twenty Years*, p. 160. For a description of the appalling state of the roads during the final decade of Ottoman rule, see Sterneck, *Geografische Verhältnisse*, pp. 21–2.
22 Sugar, *Industrialization of Bosnia*, pp. 102–13, 129–43, 167.
23 *Ibid.*, pp. 182–5; Čuprić-Amrein notes that by 1912 10 per cent of Bosnian workers were in trade unions, and 43 per cent of workers in Sarajevo (*Die Opposition in Bosnien*, pp. 153–7).
24 See for example Dedijer, *Road to Sarajevo*, p. 202, where it is called a 'major social upheaval'.
25 Miller, *Travel and Politics*, pp. 101–3.
26 Thomson, *Outgoing Turk*, p. 110. The practice was stopped because of the number of severe injuries it caused to the jockeys.
27 Durham, *Twenty Years*, p. 154.
28 Maier, *Die deutschen Siedlungen*; Schmid, *Bosnien*, pp. 246–8.
29 Schmid, *Bosnien*, p. 245. The number of soldiers in each case was roughly 7000 at the turn of the century (Curtis, *Turk and his Lost Provinces*, p. 281).
30 Miller, *Travels and Politics*, p. 97; for details of the education system see *ibid.*, p. 98; A. Popović, *L'Islam balkanique*, pp. 280–3; and Schmid, *Bosnien*, pp. 695–740.
31 For all the foregoing details see Pelletier, *Sarajevo*, pp. 137–40.
32 Miller, *Travels and Politics*, p. 91.
33 Curtis, *Turk and his Lost Provinces*, p. 275.
34 Donia, *Islam under the Eagle*, pp. 27–9, 55–9, 63–7, 93–4.
35 *Ibid.*, p. 189.
36 *Ibid.*, pp. 22–4; A. Popović, *L'Islam balkanique*, p. 275.
37 Donia, *Islam under the Eagle*, pp. 120–4.
38 *Ibid.*, pp. 124–66. The most detailed account is Hauptmann, *Borba muslimana za autonomiju*.
39 Imamović, 'O historiji bošnjačkog pokušaja', pp. 35–6.
40 Donia, *Islam under the Eagle*, pp. 52–4; Banac, *National Question*, p. 361; Imamović, 'O historiji bošnjačkog pokušaja', p. 41.

41 Thomson, *Outgoing Turk*, pp. 180–1.
42 Baernreither, *Bosnische Eindrücke*, p. 25.
43 Schmitt, *Annexation of Bosnia*, p. 12; Durham, *Twenty Years*, p. 164.
44 B. Jelavich, *History of the Balkans*, p. 111; Dedijer, *Road to Sarajevo*, p. 180.
45 Schmitt, *Annexation of Bosnia*, p. 71.
46 For the terms of the agreement see *ibid.*, p. 119; for the crisis, *ibid.*, pp. 144–229.
47 Donia, *Islam under the Eagle*, pp. 169–75.
48 Figures from Naval Intelligence Division, *Jugoslavia*, vol. 2, p. 57. The population in 1910 (1,897,962) was 43.5 per cent Orthodox, 32.4 per cent Muslim, 22.8 per cent Catholic and 0.6 per cent Jewish.
49 Banac, *National Question*, p. 366. Gajret became pro-Serb in 1909 (A. Popović, *L'Islam balkanique*, p. 285).
50 Čuprić-Amrein, *Die Opposition in Bosnien*, pp. 66–7, 75–6, 102.
51 Donia, *Islam under the Eagle*, p. 177. Ivo Banac makes a similar judgement, concluding that 'the overwhelming majority of ordinary Muslims shunned any process of "nationalization"' (*National Question*, p. 366).
52 Čuprić-Amrein, *Die Opposition in Bosnien*, p. 392. Andrić was born to a Catholic family in Travnik; he took a strongly pro-Yugoslav stance which was in effect pro-Serb. A friend described him revealingly as 'a Catholic . . . a Serb from Bosnia' (Hawkesworth, *Ivo Andrić*, p. 18).
53 Most scholars now agree that the classic account by Veselin Masleša misrepresents Mlada Bosna when it portrays it as an essentially Serb nationalist grouping (*Mlada Bosna*, e.g. p. 116).
54 Dedijer, *Road to Sarajevo*, p. 341.
55 *Ibid.*, pp. 236–45.
56 *Ibid.*, pp. 262–5.
57 *Ibid.*, p. 277.
58 Carnegie Endowment, *Report on the Balkan Wars*, pp. 148–58.
59 Dedijer, *Road to Sarajevo*, p. 278; Donia, *Islam under the Eagle*, p. 180.
60 Dedijer, *Road to Sarajevo*, pp. 206–7.
61 *Ibid.*, pp. 319–21.

12: War and the kingdom: Bosnia 1914–1941

1 Purivatra, *Nacionalni i politički razvitak*, p. 134.
2 Dedijer, *Road to Sarajevo*, p. 328.
3 *Ibid.*, pp. 289–94, 388–90.
4 *Ibid.*, pp. 418–9.

5 For a good summary of the more recent historical view, see Stone, *Europe Transformed*, pp. 326–39.
6 Skarić *et al., Bosna pod austro-ugarskom upravom*, pp. 160–1.
7 *Ibid*., pp. 157–8.
8 Hawkesworth, *Ivo Andrić*, pp. 15–17.
9 Skarić *et al., Bosna pod austro-ugarskom upravom*, pp. 157–8; Kapidžić, 'Austro-ugarska politika', p. 17.
10 On the Muslim volunteers see Balagija, *Les Musulmans yougoslaves*, p. 125.
11 Kapidžić, 'Austro-ugarska politika', p. 9 n.
12 The best account of all these arguments is Banac, *National Question*, pp. 115–25.
13 Kapidžić, 'Austro-ugarska politika', pp. 24–6, 35.
14 Krizman, *Hrvatska u prvom svjetskom ratu*, p. 255.
15 Purivatra, *Nacionalni i politički razvitak*, p. 134.
16 Krizman, *Hrvatska u prvom svjetskom ratu*, pp. 246–8.
17 *Ibid*., pp. 255–7.
18 *Ibid*., p. 316–17.
19 *Ibid*., pp. 317–20.
20 The journalist, Charles Rivet, republished the interview in his *Chez les slaves libérés*, pp. 169–74; and see Purivatra, *Nacionalni i politički razvitak*, pp. 150–1. There were also some reports in late 1918 of Muslims from north-western Bosnia raiding Serb villages in neighbouring Croatia (Banac, *National Question*, p. 130).
21 Tomasevich, *Peasants, Politics, and Economic Change*, p. 225.
22 Banac, *National Question*, p. 367 n.
23 A. Popović, *L'Islam balkanique*, p. 329.
24 On Gajret see *ibid*., p. 285; Balagija, *Les Musulmans yougoslaves*, pp. 126–7. On the pro-Serb group in the Yugoslav Muslim Organization, see Purivatra, *Nacionalni i politički razvitak*, p. 165.
25 Protić's comments are recorded in the memoirs of the sculptor Ivan Meštrović: 'When our army crosses the Drina, it will give the Turks 24 or 48 hours to return to the faith of their ancestors. Anyone who refuses is to be massacred, the way we did it before in Serbia' (Grmek *et al*., eds., *Le Nettoyage ethnique*, p. 126).
26 Rivet, *Chez les slaves libérés*, pp. 154–61, 177.
27 Purivatra, *Nacionalni i politički razvitak*, p. 181; for details of voting patterns within Bosnia, and of the extreme weakness of the other Muslim parties, see Banac, *National Question*, pp. 370–1.
28 Tomasevich, *Peasants, Politics, and Economic Change*, pp. 347–55.
29 Banac, *National Question*, p. 370.

30 For a useful summary of the Vidovdan constitution, and a map of the oblasts, see Naval Intelligence Division, *Jugoslavia*, vol. 2, pp. 322–8.
31 Maček, *Struggle for Freedom*, p. 94.
32 Banac, *National Question*, pp. 374–5.
33 Evans, *Through Bosnia*, p. 191.
34 A. Popović, *L'Islam balkanique*, pp. 279, 283; Yelavitch, 'Les Musulmans de Bosnie', p. 128.
35 Balić, *Das unbekannte Bosnien*, p. 342.
36 Lewis, *Emergence of Modern Turkey*, p. 101. It replaced the turban.
37 Balić, *Das unbekannte Bosnien*, pp. 342–5.
38 Curtis, *Turk and his Lost Provinces*, p. 287. Arthur Evans had been similarly struck by the 'thoroughly Mahometan appearance' of the Christians, with their veiled women and pig-tailed men: *Through Bosnia*, p. 133.
39 Gibbons, *London to Sarajevo*, p. 180.
40 Hornby, *Balkan Sketches*, p. 153. The *gusle* is a simple bowed string instrument, used as an accompaniment to songs and epic ballads.
41 Dragnich, *First Yugoslavia*, pp. 30, 48–9.
42 Dedijer *et al.*, *History of Yugoslavia*, pp. 543–4 n.
43 B. Jelavich, *History of the Balkans*, vol. 2, pp. 200–1.
44 Dragnich, *First Yugoslavia*, p. 94; Clissold, ed., *Short History of Yugoslavia*, pp. 183–4.
45 A. Popović, *L'Islam balkanique*, pp. 318–19.
46 *Ibid.*, p. 323; Djordjević, 'Yugoslav Phenomenon', p. 319.
47 'Statuto della comunità musulmana'.
48 Stojadinović, *Ni rat ni pakt*, pp. 344–6.
49 Hoptner, *Yugoslavia in Crisis*, pp. 128–9.
50 Maček, *Struggle for Freedom*, p. 188.
51 *Ibid.*, pp. 190–2; Clissold, ed., *Short History of Yugoslavia*, pp. 198–200.
52 Dragnich, *First Yugoslavia*, pp. 116, 127.
53 Hoptner, *Yugoslavia in Crisis*, pp. 198–9.
54 For a summary of these events emphasizing the continuity of the post-coup government's policies, see B. Jelavich, *History of the Balkans*, vol. 2, pp. 235–7.

13: Bosnia and the Second World War, 1941–1945

1 The Serbian historian Bogoljub Kočović has calculated that there were 1,014,000 deaths in Yugoslavia (*Žrtve u Jugoslaviji*, p. 124). The

Croatian scholar Vladimir Žerjavić has arrived independently at a similar figure of 1,027,000 (Balić, *Das unbekannte Bosnien*, p. 7).

2 Hory and Broszat, *Der kroatische Ustascha-Staat*, pp. 89, 91.
3 Levntal, ed., *Zločini fašističkih okupatora*, p. 64.
4 Roth, ed., *Sarajevo Haggadah*, p. 8.
5 Levntal, ed., *Zločini fašističkih okupatora*, pp. 15, 61–70.
6 B. Jelavich, *History of the Balkans*, vol. 2, p. 263.
7 Hory and Broszat, *Der kroatische Ustascha-Staat*, pp. 99, 102. Grmek *et al.* claim that the first killings after the German invasion were of Croats and Muslims, and that the massacres of Serbs came later (*Le Nettoyage ethnique*, p. 187 n.). Since they do not give the dates of these events, the matter is difficult to judge; but it is quite evident that the killing and/or expulsion of Serbs was a major aim of the Ustaša, not a casual response to other events.
8 Dedijer *et al., History of Yugoslavia*, pp. 591–2; Dedijer and Miletić, *Genocid nad Muslimana*, pp. 6–8. In Dedijer and Miletić's account these massacres by local Serbs are attributed, improbably, to 'Četniks'.
9 Dedijer *et al.*, *History of Yugoslavia*, p. 596.
10 The best accounts of Mihailović's organization are in Roberts, *Tito, Mihailović and the Allies*; Tomasevich, *Chetniks*; Milazzo, *Chetnik Movement*; and Karchmar, *Draža Mihailović*.
11 For the instructions see Roberts, *Tito, Mihailović and the Allies*, p. 26, and Deroc, *British Special Operations*, p. 210.
12 Pavlowitch, *Tito*, p. 26.
13 *Ibid.*, p. 34; Djilas, *Wartime*, p. 4.
14 See the map in Tomasevich, *Chetniks*, p. 169 (also including territory to be taken from Hungary, Romania and Bulgaria).
15 The text is printed in Dedijer and Miletić, *Genocid nad Muslimana*, pp. 8–16 (with a sketch-map on p. 15), and translated in Grmek *et al.*, *Le Nettoyage ethnique*, pp. 191–7.
16 Dedijer and Miletić, *Genocid nad Muslimana*, pp. 33–4.
17 For the document see *ibid.*, pp. 25–30 (where it is presented as genuine). For photo-reproductions of two pages see Država komisija, *Dokumenti*, vol. 1, pp. 11–12. Tomasevich accepts it as genuine (*Chetniks*, p. 170); but Lucien Karchmar has presented detailed and convincing reasons for thinking it a forgery, contrived by the two commanders to give themselves stronger authorization for their actions (*Draža Mihailović*, pp. 397, 428–30).
18 *Zbornik*, vol. 1, book 2, p. 377; the dating of this document is uncertain, and the possibility should not be excluded that it has been either forged or misattributed.

19 Martin, *Web of Disinformation*, p. 51.
20 Karchmar, *Draža Mihailović*, p. 575.
21 Deroc, *British Special Operations*, p. 226; Pavlowitch, *Tito*, pp. 17–22.
22 Höpken, 'Die Kommunisten und die Muslime', p. 187.
23 *Ibid.*, pp. 188–9.
24 Irwin, 'Islamic Revival', p. 439.
25 Purivatra, *Nacionalni i politički razvitak*, pp. 52–5; Höpken, 'Die Kommunisten und die Muslime', p. 189.
26 Höpken, 'Die Kommunisten und die Muslime', pp. 192–4.
27 See the letters to the *Times Literary Supplement* by Albert Seaton (19 May 1972) and Norman Stone (28 May 1993).
28 Lees, *Rape of Serbia*, pp. 84–5.
29 Roberts, *Tito, Mihailović and the Allies*, p. 100.
30 Tomasevich, *Chetniks*, pp. 233–4.
31 Höttl, *Secret Front*, p. 171. Höttl (also known as 'Walter Hagen') was the senior German Intelligence officer for Yugoslavia. He also noted a captured message to Tito from Stalin, instructing him to cooperate with the Germans against an Allied landing. These Partisan-German negotiations had been hushed up until the appearance of Höttl's account in the 1950s; thereafter they were discussed by Roberts (*Tito, Mihailović and the Allies*, pp. 108–9) and finally admitted by one of the participants, Djilas (*Wartime*, pp. 231–7).
32 Neubacher, *Sonderauftrag Südost*, pp. 179–80.
33 Milazzo, *Chetnik Movement*, p. 133.
34 Tomasevich, *Chetniks*, pp. 252–3, 349. On the severe tensions between Italian and German policy towards the Četniks at this time, see Milazzo, *Chetnik Movement*, p. 127.
35 Deakin, *Embattled Mountain*, pp. 1–60.
36 Direct collaboration is to be distinguished from 'parallel actions'. As recently as the summer of 1943, decrypts of German signals had shown 'no evidence of Četnik collaboration with the Germans'; the first signs of such collaboration in the signals intelligence came in October and November (Hinsley *et al.*, *British Intelligence*, vol. 3, part 1, pp. 146, 154–5). Deakin's main report in August 1943, which influenced Allied policy, said that Četnik collaboration with Germany had been 'close, constant and increasing' over the past two years (*ibid.*, p. 150). It must be doubted whether the so-called Bosnian Četniks seen by Deakin in August 1943 had anything to do with Mihailović's forces (Roberts, *Tito, Mihailović and the Allies*, p. 120).
37 Zulfikarpašić, *Bosanski Muslimani*, p. 14.

38 Balić, *Das unbekannte Bosnien*, p. 345; on the cultural societies see Zulfikarpašić, *Bosanski Muslimani*, p. 14.
39 Höpken, 'Die Kommunisten und die Muslime', p. 190.
40 Redžić, *Muslimansko autonomaštvo*, p. 14.
41 *Ibid*., p. 15.
42 Höpken, 'Die Kommunisten und die Muslime', p. 190; Zulfikarpašić, *Bosanski Muslimani*, pp. 21–2; Redžić, *Muslimansko autonomaštvo*, pp. 16, 30.
43 Purivatra, *Nacionalni i politički razvitak*, pp. 112–14; Redžić, *Muslimansko autonomaštvo*, p. 52.
44 Höpken, 'Die Kommunisten und die Muslime', p. 191; A. Popović, *L'Islam balkanique*, p. 342.
45 Redžić, *Muslimansko autonomaštvo*, p. 59.
46 Dedijer and Miletić, *Genocid nad Muslimana*, pp. xxvi–xxviii, 383.
47 Redžić, *Muslimansko autonomaštvo*, p. 55.
48 *Ibid*., pp. 60–1; Avakumović, *Mihailović prema nemačkim dokumentima*, pp. 71–2. The numerical estimate is based on Mihailović's claim that 74 per cent of his men were Orthodox and 84 per cent were 'Serbs' (pp. 71–2 n.). He probably counted some 'Catholic Serbs'; but there may have been some Orthodox non-Serbs too.
49 Avakumović, *Mihailović prema nemačkim dokumentima*, p. 71 n. Redžić notes that the Muslim village 'liberated' by Popovac was defended by a large Muslim volunteer force (*Muslimansko autonomaštvo*, pp. 105–6).
50 Redžić, *Muslimansko autonomaštvo*, p. 68.
51 *Ibid*., pp. 131, 160.
52 *Ibid*., pp. 71–4.
53 Sundhaussen, 'Zur Geschichte der Waffen-SS in Kroatien', pp. 191–3.
54 Redžić, *Muslimansko autonomaštvo*, pp. 87, 119–20, 155. There were nine Muslim officers in the entire division (p. 189 n.).
55 *Ibid*., p. 89; Sundhaussen, 'Zur Geschichte der Waffen-SS in Kroatien', p. 193.
56 Redžić, *Muslimansko autonomaštvo*, p. 136; Erignac, *La Révolte des Croates*.
57 Redžić, *Muslimansko autonomaštvo*, pp. 140, 147, 177–8.
58 *Ibid*., pp. 138–9; Purivatra, *Nacionalni i politički razvitak*, p. 114.
59 Redžić, *Muslimansko autonomaštvo*, pp. 166–7, 183.
60 *Ibid*., pp. 190–206; Sundhaussen, 'Zur Geschichte der Waffen-SS in Kroatien', p. 193.
61 Balić, *Das unbekannte Bosnien*, p. 7.

62 Dedijer and Miletić, *Genocid nad Muslimana*, pp. xxx–xxxi; Zulfikarpašić, *Bosanski Muslimani*, pp. 19–20.

14: Bosnia in Titoist Yugoslavia, 1945–1989

1 Karapandzich, *Bloodiest Yugoslav Spring*, p. 20.
2 Quoted in Beloff, *Tito's Flawed Legacy*, p. 131.
3 Djordjević, 'Yugoslav Phenomenon', p. 329.
4 Rusinow, *Yugoslav Experiment*, p. 38. On the 'youth railway' project see Thompson, *Paper House*, pp. 118–20.
5 For a lucid summary account of Tito's Stalinism, see Pavlowitch, *Tito*, pp. 50–61.
6 Lapenna, 'Suverenitet i federalizam', pp. 17–18.
7 This process is fully described in Koštunica and Čavoški, *Party Pluralism or Monism*.
8 Rusinow, *Yugoslav Experiment*, pp. 35–6.
9 Chadwick, *Christian Church in the Cold War*, p. 37.
10 Poulton, *Balkans*, p. 43.
11 For all these changes see Balić, 'Der bosnisch-herzegowinische Islam', pp. 120, 128–34, and A. Popović, *L'Islam balkanique*, pp. 347–53.
12 McFarlane, *Yugoslavia*, p. 79.
13 The movement had begun with the Chinese-sponsored conference at Bandung in Indonesia in 1955; Tito placed himself at the head of the movement in the UN in 1960, and declared its principles official Yugoslav policy in 1961. The real nature of the movement was apparent to most observers even before Fidel Castro became chairman of it in 1979. See Pavlowitch, *Tito*, pp. 61–5; Milivojević, *Descent into Chaos*, pp. 20–1; Ivanović, 'Reforma vanjske politike'.
14 Irwin, 'Islamic Revival', pp. 441–2; A. Popović, *L'Islam balkanique*, pp. 353–4.
15 Balić, 'Der bosnisch-herzegowinische Islam', p. 125.
16 Höpken, 'Die Kommunisten und die Muslime', p. 194.
17 *Ibid.*, p. 195; I have used the detailed breakdown of the 1948 figures in Purivatra, *Nacionalni i politički razvitak*, pp. 32–3; Höpken gives a total figure for the 'Serb' and 'Croat' Muslims (170,000), which is incorrect; it is possibly a misprint for the total of such Muslims in the whole of Yugoslavia (190,000).
18 Höpken, 'Die Kommunisten und die Muslime', pp. 199–201. S. Ramet treats the fall of Ranković as decisive: *Nationalism and Federal-*

ism, pp. 178–9. On the dominance of Serbs in Bosnia in the period 1945–65 see Peroche, *Histoire de la Croatie*, p. 367.

19 Höpken, 'Die Kommunisten und die Muslime', pp. 196–7; Irwin, 'Islamic Revival', p. 443.

20 Balić, 'Der bosnisch-herzegowinische Islam', p. 124.

21 Höpken, 'Die Kommunisten und die Muslime', pp. 198–200; Irwin, 'Islamic Revival', p. 444. (I have substituted 'designated as' for the unfortunately ambiguous translation 'determined to be'.)

22 Höpken, 'Die Kommunisten und die Muslime', p. 200.

23 On the lengthy quarrel with Macedonia over this issue see S. Ramet, *Nationalism and Federalism*, pp. 182–4.

24 Hadžijahić, *Od tradicije do identiteta*, pp. 67–8.

25 On this point see A. Popović, 'Islamische Bewegungen', p. 281, and Irwin, 'Islamic Revival', pp. 445–6.

26 Izetbegović began to prepare it in 1966–7, and finished writing it in the first half of 1970 (Zulfikarpašić, ed., *Sarajevski proces*, p. 239).

27 P. Ramet, 'Die Muslime Bosniens', p. 111; A. Popović, *L'Islam balkanique*, p. 351; information from Majo Topolovac.

28 Rusinow, *Yugoslav Experiment*, p. 100.

29 *Ibid.*, pp. 99–100, 119; S. Ramet, *Nationalism and Federalism*, pp. 138–44.

30 All these statistics (mainly drawn from the 1971 census) can be found in Breznik, ed., *Population of Yugoslavia*. The area with the largest net inflow was Vojvodina: the policy was not only to replace the more than 300,000 ethnic Germans who had been killed or expelled, but also to ensure a Serb absolute majority.

31 S. Ramet, *Nationalism and Federalism*, p. 144.

32 *Ibid.*, pp. 98–115.

33 *Ibid.*, p. 124.

34 *Ibid.*, pp. 105, 125.

35 See Magaš, *Destruction of Yugoslavia*, pp. 37, 47 n. The claim that 'over 100,000' Serbs left Kosovo in the period 1968–78 (Beloff, *Tito's Flawed Legacy*, p. 212) is false. The censuses recorded 227,016 Serbs in Kosovo in 1961, 228,261 in 1971 and 209,497 in 1981 (Islami, *Fshati i Kosovës*, p. 176).

36 Tomashevich, 'The Serbian Question', p. 39.

37 Sirc, 'The National Question', p. 88.

38 Magaš, *Destruction of Yugoslavia*, p. 50.

39 Grmek *et al.*, eds., *Le Nettoyage ethnique*, pp. 236–69; quotations from pp. 256, 265.

40 A. Popović, *L'Islam balkanique*, p. 355; Irwin, 'Islamic Revival', pp. 448–51.
41 Zulfikarpašić, *Sarajevski proces*, esp. pp. 240–1, 249; Poulton, *Balkans*, pp. 42–3.
42 The best account of this affair, which I have used here, is Lydall, *Yugoslavia in Crisis*, pp. 168–71 (quotation on p. 171); see also McFarlane, *Yugoslavia*, pp. 171–2, and Magaš, *Destruction of Yugoslavia*, pp. 111–12.
43 Lydall, *Yugoslavia in Crisis*, pp. 85–6.
44 *Ibid*., pp. 91–2, 220–2; Milivojević, *Descent into Chaos*, pp. 11–12.
45 Lydall, *Yugoslavia in Crisis*, p. 217.
46 Milivojević, *Descent into Chaos*, p. 10; S. Ramet, *Nationalism and Federalism*, pp. 226–34; Thompson, *Paper House*, pp. 163–5; Magaš, *Destruction of Yugoslavia*, pp. 197–213, 227–34.

15: Bosnia and the death of Yugoslavia: 1989–1992

1 The official media reported, absurdly, that 3 million people were present. I attended the rally, and estimated that between 300,000 and 500,000 people were there.
2 Glenny, *Fall of Yugoslavia*, p. 35.
3 Magaš, *Destruction of Yugoslavia*, p. 241. As Branka Magaš points out, Račan's family had in fact been murdered by the Ustaša during the war.
4 S. Ramet, *Nationalism and Federalism*, p. 244.
5 *Ibid*., pp. 240–2; Magaš, *Destruction of Yugoslavia*, pp. 224–6; Gow, *Legitimacy and the Military*, pp. 78–94.
6 On all these events see Poulton, *Balkans*, pp. 24–7; Magaš, *Destruction of Yugoslavia*, pp. 293, 313; Glenny, *Fall of Yugoslavia*, pp. 13–19.
7 Irwin, 'Fate of Islam in the Balkans', p. 392.
8 S. Ramet, *Nationalism and Federalism*, pp. 233, 243.
9 Thompson, *Paper House*, p. 99.
10 Izetbegović, *Islamska deklaracija*, p. 37.
11 *Ibid*., p. 22.
12 *Ibid*., pp. 37–8.
13 *Ibid*., pp. 21–4, 30.
14 For a lucid analysis by one of the leading scholars, see Esposito, *Islam and Politics*, esp. pp. 269–301.
15 Izetbegović, *Islamska deklaracija*, pp. 37–42.
16 *Ibid*., p. 7.

17 *Ibid.*, p. 31.
18 Izetbegović, *Islam izmedju Istoka i Zapada*, pp. 107–9, 132, 251–64.
19 Hussein, 'Communist Yugoslavia's Fear of Islam', p. 34.
20 Poulton, *Balkans*, p. 43.
21 Sorabji, *Bosnia's Muslims*, pp. 5–6.
22 Poulton, *Balkans*, p. 44.
23 *Ibid.*, pp. 37–8.
24 Magaš, *Destruction of Yugoslavia*, pp. 276, 283–93 (quotation from p. 293). Branka Magaš gives an extremely lucid account of these events.
25 S. Ramet, *Nationalism and Federalism*, p. 259.
26 Mazower, *War in Bosnia*, p. 4.
27 Frei, 'Bully of the Balkans', p. 12.
28 Almond, *Blundering in the Balkans*, pp. 4, 21. One EEC Commissioner announced, after the declarations of independence, that the EEC would 'refuse all high level contacts' with the two republics. As Mark Almond points out, the EEC had more than mere principles at stake: it had just given the federal government in Belgrade credits worth 730 million ecus (pp. 20–1).
29 The best summary and analysis of these events is Gow, 'One Year of War', pp. 1–7.
30 Moore, 'Question of all Questions', p. 38.
31 Mazower, *War in Bosnia*, pp. 5–6.
32 Sirc, 'National Question', pp. 88–9.
33 Report by Dusko Doder, *European*, 7 January 1993.
34 Grmek *et al.*, *Le Nettoyage ethnique*, pp. 304–5.
35 S. Ramet, *Nationalism and Federalism*, p. 260.
36 Gow, 'One Year of War', pp. 7–8.
37 *Ibid.*, p. 8; S. Ramet, *Nationalism and Federalism*, p. 261.
38 Malcolm, 'Waiting for a War', pp. 15–16.
39 Magaš, *Destruction of Yugoslavia*, p. xv.
40 Malcolm, 'Waiting for a War', p. 16. I took the quotation of Marković's speech from reports in *Borba* and *Politika*.
41 See for example the report of Slovenian and Croatian objections to the Carrington plan by Roger Boyes in *The Times*, 8 November 1991. Boyes concluded: 'there are cracks in the foundation of the plan'.
42 Gow, 'One Year of War', p. 8. It has been suggested (falsely) that the Bosnian Minister of Internal Affairs, Alija Delimustafić, was working for federal military counter-intelligence at the time.
43 Mazower, *War in Bosnia*, p. 7; Magaš, *Destruction of Yugoslavia*, p. xviii.

44 The fullest account of this incident is in Rojo, *Holocausto en los Balcanes*, pp. 145–6.
45 *Mina informativni bilten*, 4 November 1991.
46 Hayden, 'Partition of Bosnia', pp. 2–4.
47 Interviewed by me, Sarajevo, 11 October 1991.
48 Report by Judy Dempsey, *Financial Times*, 8 July 1992.
49 Gow, 'One Year of War', pp. 8–9.
50 Hayden, 'Partition of Bosnia', pp. 4–6.
51 Report by Michael Montgomery, *Daily Telegraph*, 29 February 1992.
52 Report by John Palmer, *Guardian*, 10 March 1992.
53 Hayden, 'Partition of Bosnia', p. 7.

16: The Destruction of Bosnia: 1992–1993

1 Report by Michael Montgomery, *Daily Telegraph*, 7 April 1992.
2 Reports by Yigal Chazan, *Guardian*, 27 March 1992; Tim Judah and Dessa Trevisan, *The Times*, 4 April 1992.
3 Report by staff correspondent, *Daily Telegraph*, 30 March 1992.
4 Helsinki Watch, *War Crimes in Bosnia*, p. 149. The Helsinki Watch team which encountered these gunmen later found the local UNPROFOR commander in the Hotel Bosna: he said he was unaware that the town had been sealed off by road-blocks, and that anyway it was nothing to do with him.
5 Report by Tim Judah and Dessa Trevisan, *The Times*, 4 April 1992.
6 Report by Anne McElvoy, *The Times*, 20 April 1992.
7 See the analysis in Mazower, *War in Bosnia*, pp. 10–11.
8 *Ibid.*, p. 13.
9 Quoted in Glenny, *Fall of Yugoslavia*, p. 166.
10 Report by Philip Sherwell, *Daily Telegraph*, 16 April 1992.
11 Gow, 'One Year of War', p. 8.
12 See for example the reports by Ian Traynor, *Guardian*, 17 April 1992, and Anne McElvoy, *The Times*, 20 April 1992.
13 Report by Philip Sherwell, *Daily Telegraph*, 16 April 1992.
14 Mazower, *War in Bosnia*, p. 15.
15 See my quotation of this report in *The Spectator*, 2 May 1992.
16 For all the foregoing details of military forces see Gow, 'One Year of War', pp. 8–9; on the 16 June agreement see the forthcoming volume edited by Daniel Bethlehem and Marc Weller, *The 'Yugoslav' Crisis in International Law* (Cambridge, 1993 or 1994).

17 For the foregoing details see Helsinki Watch, *War Crimes in Bosnia*, pp. 43–5, and the typescript statement 'Why the Croatian Community of Herzeg-Bosna was founded', issued by Vlado Pogarčić, foreign affairs adviser to Mate Boban, in June or July 1993.
18 Helsinki Watch, *War Crimes in Bosnia*, pp. 150–3.
19 See my report in *The Spectator*, 2 May 1992.
20 Helsinki Watch, *War Crimes in Bosnia*, p. 159.
21 US Congressional Record, 30 September 1992.
22 Gow, 'One Year of War', pp. 2–3.
23 Of course, as the war developed, there were many cases of Muslims and Croats attacking Serb homes too; but the overall imbalance, in strategy as well as tactics, remained.
24 Helsinki Watch, *War Crimes in Bosnia*, pp. 168–9; ISHR (British Section), *Human Rights and Serbia* (typescript report, 1992).
25 Bosnian Government Information Office, 'List of Concentration Camps and Prisons at the Territory of the Republic of Bosnia and Hercegovina' (typescript).
26 Helsinki Watch, *War Crimes in Bosnia*, pp. 50–5; here pp. 52–3. The term 'Četnik' was by now being used as a general term for all Serb irregular forces.
27 See the reports by Tadeusz Mazowiecki, Médecins sans frontières and Amnesty International collected in Bouchet, ed., *Le Livre noir*. For the detailed and harrowing testimony of one woman who was held at a rape camp in Foča see the report by Victoria Clark, *Observer*, 21 February 1993. The question of organized rape is viewed by some commentators as contentious. The Bosnian government has assembled details of 13,000 rape victims; the EEC mission offered the very rough estimate of 20,000 in January 1993 (*ibid.*, p. 460). What is clear is that rape was being used in many places as part of the general policy of the Serb forces against the civilian population, and was not simply a matter of individual acts by disorderly soldiers.
28 Article by Douglas Hurd, *Mail on Sunday*, 9 August 1992.
29 'A report by Thomas O'Brien to the US AID agency in January 1993 noted that . . . Serbian warlords were allocated 23 per cent of UN relief supplies' (Sharp, *Bankrupt in the Balkans*, p. 14).
30 The no-fly zone was agreed in principle in August 1992 and proclaimed by the UN in October; provisions for its enforcement were finally made in April 1993, but it continued to be routinely violated thereafter.
31 Sharp, *Bankrupt in the Balkans*, pp. 16–17; Hayden, 'Partition of Bosnia', pp. 9–10.

32 International Conference on the Former Yugoslavia, 'Agreement for Peace in Bosnia and Herzegovina' (typescript), articles I and II.
33 Report in *East European Reporter*, vol. 5, no. 6 (November–December 1992), p. 64.
34 Report by Robert Fox, *Daily Telegraph*, 2 March 1993.
35 Moore, 'Endgame in Bosnia?', p. 20.
36 Report by Michael Binyon, *The Times*, 20 May 1993.
37 Report by Tim Judah, *The Times*, 7 January 1993.
38 Report by Joel Brand, *The Times*, 11 May 1993.
39 Report by Robin Gedye, *Daily Telegraph*, 18 February 1993: 'Mr Hurd said he had made it clear that a balance had to be struck between the German view that a supply of arms to the Muslims was the only fair way of allowing them to defend themselves, and the danger of escalating the fighting.' Mr Hurd did not explain why persuading Germany to conform with the second of these two contradictory interpretations should be described as striking a balance between them.
40 I hope I may be forgiven this quotation from an article I wrote in the *Daily Telegraph* (2 April 1993). The Foreign Secretary replied with a letter published in the *Daily Telegraph* on 5 April, in which he coined the term 'level killing field' to describe the consequences of lifting the arms embargo. The phrase 'The Killing Fields' had in fact been invented to describe a situation similar to that which already obtained, thanks to the policy supported by Mr Hurd, in many areas of Bosnia.
41 Report by Tim Judah, *The Times*, 3 May 1993.
42 This point was emphasized to me in a conversation with Kemal Kurspahić, the editor of *Oslobodjenje*.
43 Report by Michael Montgomery, *Daily Telegraph*, 8 May 1993.
44 Foreign Office News Department, communiqué.
45 Bosnian Government Information Centre, statement.
46 Report in *New Yorker*, 15 March 1993.
47 Richard Pipes, quoted in Lieven, *Nicholas II*, p. 246.

Glossary

This glossary lists terms which recur in the text. Where more than one form of the same word has been mentioned, the abbreviations 'T' and 'S-C' are used here to indicate 'Turkish' and 'Serbo-Croat' respectively.

aga: original meaning: lord or senior janissary officer. Normal meaning in Bosnian history: landowning 'lord', belonging to the lower of the two categories of landowner.

agaluk: normal meaning in Bosnian history: property held by an 'aga' (where landlord-peasant relations were governed by traditional feudal law). Special meaning: territorial division of Bosnia, governed by an 'aga'.

ahd-name: grant of privilege by the Sultan.

ajan: elected local official and administrator.

asper: Ottoman unit of currency, a coin originally containing three grams of silver, but subject to frequent devaluation and debasement (to less than two grams in the mid-sixteenth century, and less than one by 1600).

ban: Croatian term, used also in medieval Bosnia, for ruler. Revived in 1929 when Yugoslavia was divided into 'banovinas', each governed by a 'ban'.

banovina: territory ruled or governed by a 'ban'.

beg: lord or landowner, belonging to the higher of the two categories of landowner.

beglerbeg (S-C), beylerbeyi (T): the highest category of pasha, the vizier or governor of Bosnia.

beglik: property held by a 'beg' (where landlord-peasant relations were not governed by traditional feudal law).

bezistan: cloth-market, covered market.

Bogomil: medieval Bulgarian dualist heretic.

bosančica: script used in medieval Bosnia, related to Cyrillic but differing from it.

Cathar: medieval French dualist heretic.

Četnik: traditional Serbian term for an irregular fighter, applied to forces under Draža Mihailović in the second world war. Also commonly used to refer to all Serb irregulars fighting in Croatia and Bosnia in 1992–3 (and specifically used for Serb irregulars under Vojislav Šešelj).

čiftlik: private estate.

cizye: poll-tax, paid by non-Muslims.

defter: tax-register.

devşirme: boy-tribute, the gathering of Christian male children to be converted to Islam and trained as janissaries and imperial officials.

djed: head of the Bosnian Church (literally, 'grandfather').

eyalet: province of the Ottoman Empire (the largest administrative division, corresponding to one or more modern countries).

gost: member of the hierarchy of the Bosnian Church (literally, 'host').

Grenzer: Austro-Hungarian frontier soldier, an inhabitant of the frontier-zone bordering the Ottoman Empire.

Groschen: Austrian unit of currency.

hajduk: bandit or guerrilla.

hamam: Turkish baths.

haraç (T), harač (S-C): poll-tax paid by non-Muslims (originally a land-tax, but merged with the 'cizye' to form a graduated poll-tax).

hass: large feudal estate.

HDZ: Croatian Democratic Union, the Croatian nationalist party led by Franjo Tudjman in Croatia, of which an off-shoot in Bosnia was led first by Stjepan Kljuić, then by Mate Boban.

hiža: monastic house of the Bosnian Church.

HOS: Croatian Defence Union, a Croatian paramilitary force.

HVO: Croatian Defence Council, the military organization set up by the 'HDZ' in Bosnia.

imam: Muslim prayer-leader.

janissary: Ottoman soldier, originally recruited as a slave of the Sultan through the 'devşirme', but from mid-seventeenth century recruited from ordinary Muslims.

kadi: judge.

kadiluk: area administered by a 'kadi'.

Kadizâdeler: members of a seventeenth-century ultra-orthodox Muslim sect.

kajmak: administrator acting as the governor's military representative.

kanun-i raya: traditional code of laws applied to 'raya'.

kapetan: originally, a military administrator in a frontier zone. Normal meaning in Bosnian history: an administrator of a territorial division of Bosnia, with wide-ranging powers, whose office was hereditary.

kapetanija: area administered by a 'kapetan'.

Karavlah: Gypsy of Romanian origin in Bosnia.

kaza: see 'kadiluk'.

kmet: serf or peasant.

krajina: frontier-zone.

kristian: term used in Ottoman records for an ordinary member of the Bosnian Church.

krstjanin: monastic member of the Bosnian Church (literally, 'Christian').

mahala: small division of a town.

Manichaean, Manichee: originally, a follower of Mani, teacher of non-Christian dualist beliefs in the third century. Later used as a general term for dualist heretics within Christianity.

martolos: local Christian (Vlach or Serb) free-booter infantryman.

MBO: Bosnian Muslim Organization, the party led by Adil Zulfikarpašić.

medresa: Muslim theological school.

mekteb: Muslim primary school.

Morlach: type of Vlach in Dalmatia and (especially) the Croatian 'krajina'.

musselim: administrator, acting as a representative of the governor.

NDH: 'Independent State of Croatia', the puppet-state which comprised most of Croatia and Bosnia from 1941 to 1945.

pandur: gendarme, local militia-man.

pasha: general term for territorial governor.

pashaluk: territory governed by a pasha.

Patarin: term used by Ragusans and Italians to refer to members of the Bosnian Church (also used in Italy for Italian Cathars).

Potur: ordinary Islamicized Slav peasant in Bosnia (probably from the Turkish word 'potur', meaning a type of trousers worn by such peasants).

raya: originally, non-Ottoman subject-people (Muslim as well as

Christian); by the nineteenth century it generally meant non-Muslim subjects only.

Reis ul-ulema: head of the Muslim religious community.

sandžak (S-C), sancak (T): the largest territorial subdivision of an 'eyalet', originally a military district.

sandžak-beg: governor of a 'sandžak'.

SDA: Party of Democratic Action, the party led by Alija Izetbegović.

SDS: Serbian Democratic Party, first formed in the Knin region of Croatia, then formed in Bosnia, where it was led by Radovan Karadžić, under the supervision of Slobodan Milošević in Belgrade.

şeriat (T), shariat: Islamic sacred law.

spahi: cavalryman.

starac: member of the hierarchy of the Bosnian Church (literally, 'elder').

stečak (plural: stećci): Bosnian medieval gravestone.

strojnik: member of the hierarchy of the Bosnian Church (literally, 'steward').

tekke: dervish lodge.

tımar (T), timar: feudal estate.

timariot: holder of a 'timar'.

tretina: payment by serf to landowner of one third of the crop.

Ustaša: Croatian extreme nationalist and terrorist movement led by Ante Pavelić, installed in power in the 'NDH'.

vakıf (T), vakuf (S-C): religious-charitable foundation, holding property in perpetuity.

vilayet: province of Ottoman Empire (replacing the 'eyalet' in 1864).

vizier: the highest rank of administrator in the Ottoman Empire.

Vlach: descendant of romanized pre-Slav Balkan population.

vojnuk: Christian (Serb or Vlach) free-booter infantryman.

župa: territorial division in early Slav period.

župan: ruler of a 'župa'.

Bibliography

This bibliography is confined to listing works cited in the text or notes of this book (excluding news reports and statements or communiqués, for which full references have been given in the notes). The alphabetical order is English, not Serbo-Croat.

Abteilung für Kriegsgeschichte des k. k. Kriegs-Archivs, *Die Occupation Bosniens und der Hercegovina durch k. k. Truppen im Jahre 1878* (Vienna, 1879)

Der Aufstand in der Hercegovina, Süd-Bosnien und Süd-Dalmatien 1881–1882 (Vienna, 1883)

Akademia e shkencave e R.P.S. të Shqiperisë: Instituti i gjuhësisë dhe i letërsisë, *Fjalor i gjuhës së sotme Shqipe* (Tirana, 1980)

Alföldy, G., *Bevölkerung und Gesellschaft der römischen Provinz Dalmatien* (Budapest, 1965)

Algar, H., 'Some Notes on the Naqshbandi Tariqat in Bosnia', *Studies in Comparative Religion*, vol. 9 (1975), pp. 69–96

Almond, M., *Blundering in the Balkans: the European Community and the Yugoslav Crisis* (Oxford, 1991)

Amantos, K., *Scheseis Ellênôn kai Tourkôn apo tou endekatou aiônos mechri tou 1821* (Athens, 1955)

Anderson, D., *Miss Irby and Her Friends* (London, 1966)

Andjelić, P., 'Periodi u kulturnoj historiji Bosne i Hercegovine u srednjem vijeku', *Glasnik zemaljskog muzeja Bosne i Hercegovine u Sarajevu*, n.s., vol. 25 (1970), pp. 119–212

'Barones Regni i državno vijeće srednjovjekovne Bosne', *Prilozi za istoriju*, vols. 11–12 (1975–6), pp. 29–48

Andrić, I., *The Development of Spiritual Life in Bosnia under the Influence of Turkish Rule* (Durham, North Carolina, 1990)

Angelov, D., *Bogomilstvoto v B'lgariya* (Sofia, 1969)

von Asbóth, J., *Bosnien und die Hercegowina: Reisebilder und Studien* (Vienna, 1888)

Avakumović, I., *Mihailović prema nemačkim dokumentima* (London, 1969)

Baernreither, J. M., *Bosnische Eindrücke* (Vienna, 1908)

Balagija, A., *Les Musulmans yougoslaves (étude sociologique)* (Algiers, 1940)

Balić, S., 'Der bosnisch-herzegowinische Islam', *Der Islam*, vol. 44 (1968), pp. 115–37

Das unbekannte Bosnien: Europas Brücke zur islamischen Welt (Cologne, 1992)

Banac, I., *The National Question in Yugoslavia: Origins, History, Politics* (Ithaca, New York, 1984)

Barić, H., *Lingvističke studije*, Naučno društvo n.r. Bosne i Hercegovine, djela, vol. 1 (Sarajevo, 1954)

Barkan, Ö. L., 'Les déportations comme méthode de peuplement et de colonisation dans l'Empire ottoman', *Revue de la faculté des sciences économiques de l'Université d'Istanbul*, vol. 11 (1949–50), pp. 67–131

Bartusis, M. C., *The Late Byzantine Army: Arms and Society, 1204–1453* (Philadelphia, 1992)

Batinić, M. V., *Djelovanje franjevaca u Bosni i Hercegovini sa prvih šest viekova njihova boravka*, 3 vols. (Zagreb, 1881–7)

Beldiceanu, N., 'Sur les valaques des balkans slaves à l'époque ottomane (1450–1550)', *Revue des études islamiques*, vol. 34 (1966), pp. 83–132

'Les Valaques de Bosnie à la fin du XVe siècle et leurs institutions', *Turcica*, vol. 7 (1975), pp. 122–34

and I. Beldiceanu-Steinherr, 'Quatre actes de Mehmed II concernant les valaques des balkans slaves', *Südostforschungen*, vol. 24 (1965), pp. 103–18

Beloff, N., *Tito's Flawed Legacy: Yugoslavia and the West, 1939 to 1984* (London, 1985)

Benac, A., Čović, B., *et al*, *Kulturna istorija Bosne i Hercegovine od najstarijih vremena do početka turske vladavine* (Sarajevo, 1966)

Birge, J. K., *The Bektashi Order of Dervishes* (London, 1937)

Blau, O., *Reisen in Bosnien und der Herzegowina: topographische und pflanzengeographische Aufzeichnungen* (Berlin, 1877)

Bogićević, V., 'Emigracije muslimana Bosne i Hercegovine u Tursku u doba Austro-Ugarske vladavine 1878–1918 godine', *Historijski zbornik*, vol. 3 (1950), pp. 175–88

Bordeaux, A., *La Bosnie populaire: paysages, moeurs et coutumes, légendes, chants populaires, mines* (Paris, 1904)

Borst, A., *Die Katharer* (Stuttgart, 1953)

Bouchet, P., ed., *Le Livre noir de l'ex-Yougoslavie: purification ethnique et crimes de guerre* (Paris, 1993)

Boué, A., *La Turquie d'Europe*, 4 vols. (Paris, 1840)

Bowen, H., 'Ayan', in *The Encyclopaedia of Islam*, 2nd edn., ed. H. A. R.

Gibbs, J. H. Kramers, E. Lévi-Provençal and J. Schacht, 6 vols. (Leiden, 1960–), vol. 1, p. 778
Braude, B., 'Foundation Myths of the *Millet* System', in B. Braude and B. Lewis, eds., *Christians and Jews in the Ottoman Empire: The Functioning of a Plural Society*, 2 vols. (New York, 1982), vol. 1, pp. 69–88
Braudel, F., *The Mediterranean and the Mediterranean World in the Age of Philip II*, tr. S. Reynolds, 2 vols. (London, 1972)
Breznik, D., ed., *The Population of Yugoslavia*, publication of the Demographic Research Centre, Institute of Social Sciences (Belgrade, 1974)
Burián, S., *Austria in Dissolution*, tr. B. Lunn (London, 1925)
Byrnes, R., ed., *Communal Families in the Balkans: The Zadruga: Essays by Philip Mosely and Essays in his Honor* (Notre Dame, 1976)
Çabej, E., 'The Problem of the Place of Formation of the Albanian Language', in A. Buda, E. Çabej, *et al, The Albanians and their Territories* (Tirana, 1985), pp. 63–99
Carnegie Endowment for International Peace, *Report of the International Commission to Inquire into the Causes and Conduct of the Balkan Wars* (Washington, DC, 1914)
Čelebi, Evlija, *see* Evlija
Chadwick, O., *The Christian Church in the Cold War* (London, 1992)
Chaumette-des-Fossés, A., *Voyage en Bosnie dans les années 1807 et 1808* (Berlin, 1812)
Chopin, J., and A. Urbicini, *Provinces danubiennes et roumaines* (Paris, 1856)
Cinnamus, *Epitome rerum ab Ioanne et Alexio Comnenis gestarum*, ed. A. Meinecke (Bonn, 1836)
Ćirković, S. M., 'Die bosnische Kirche', in *L'Oriente cristiano nella storia della civiltà*, Accademia nazionale dei Lincei, quaderno 62 (Rome, 1964), pp. 547–75
Herceg Stefan Vukčić-Kosača i njegovo doba, Srpska akademija nauka i umetnosti, posebna izdanja, vol. 376 (Belgrade, 1964)
Istorija srednjovekovne bosanske države (Belgrade, 1964)
Clissold, S., ed., *A Short History of Yugoslavia from Early Times to 1966* (Cambridge, 1968)
Constantine Porphyrogenitus, *De administrando imperio*, ed. G. Moravscik, tr. R. J. H. Jenkins (Washington, DC, 1967)
Coquelle, P., *Histoire du Monténégro et de la Bosnie depuis les origines* (Paris, 1895)
Ćorović, V., *Historija Bosne*, Srpska kraljevska akademija, posebna izdanja, vol. 129 (Belgrade, 1940)
Croix, Sieur de la, *Mémoires* (Paris, 1684)

Čubrilović, V., 'Poreklo muslimanskog plemstva u Bosni i Hercegovini', *Jugoslovenski istoriski časopis*, vol. 1 (1935), pp. 368–403
Bosanski ustanak 1875–1878, Srpska kraljeva akademija, posebna izdanja, vol. 83 (Belgrade, 1936)
Čuprić-Amrein, M. M., *Die Opposition gegen die österreichisch-ungarische Herrschaft in Bosnien-Hercegovina (1878–1914)* (Bern, 1987)
Curtis, W. E., *The Turk and his Lost Provinces* (Chicago, 1903)
Dawkins, R. M., 'The Crypto-Christians of Turkey', *Byzantion*, vol. 8 (1933), pp. 247–75
Deakin, F. W. D., *The Embattled Mountain* (London, 1971)
Dedijer, V., *The Road to Sarajevo* (London, 1966)
Dedijer, V., and A. Miletić, *Genocid nad Muslimana, 1941–1945: zbornik dokumenata i svjedočenja* (Sarajevo, 1990)
Dedijer, V., Božić, I., Ćirković, S., and M. Ekmečić, *History of Yugoslavia* (New York, 1974)
Deroc, M., *British Special Operations Explored: Yugoslavia in Turmoil, 1941–1943, and the British Response* (Boulder, Colorado, 1988)
Desboeufs, Capitaine, *Souvenirs*, ed. C. Desboeufs (Paris, 1901)
Dinić, M. J., *Za istoriju rudarstva u srednjevekovnoj Srbiji i Bosni*, Srpska akademija nauka, posrebna izdanja, vol. 240 (Belgrade, 1955)
Djilas, M., *Wartime*, tr. M. B. Petrovich (London, 1977)
Djordjević, D., 'The Yugoslav Phenomenon', in J. Held, ed., *The Columbia History of Eastern Europe in the Twentieth Century* (New York, 1992), pp. 306–44
Djurdjev, B., 'Bosna', in *The Encyclopaedia of Islam*, 2nd edn., ed. H. A. R. Gibbs, J. H. Kramers, E. Lévi-Provençal and J. Schacht, 6 vols. (Leiden, 1960–), vol. 1, p. 1261–75
Donia, R. J., *Islam under the Double Eagle: The Muslims of Bosnia and Hercegovina 1878–1914* (Boulder, Colorado, 1981)
Draganović, K, 'Izvješće apostolskog vizitatora Petra Masarechija o prilikama katoličkog naroda u Bugarskoj, Srbiji, Srijemu, Slavoniji i Bosni g. 1623 i 1624', *Starine jugoslavenske adademije znanosti i umjetnosti*, vol. 39 (1938), pp. 1–48.
Dragnich, A. N., *The First Yugoslavia: The Search for a Viable Political System* (Stanford, California, 1983)
Dragojlović, D., *Krstjani i jeretička crkva bosanska*, Srpska akademija nauka i umetnosti: balkanološki institut, posebna izdanja, vol. 30 (Belgrade, 1987)
Dragomir, S., *Vlahii şi Morlacii: studiu din istoria românismului balcanic* (Cluj, 1924)
Vlahii din nordul peninsulei balcanice în evul mediu (Bucharest, 1959)

Država komisija za utvrdjivanje zločina okupatora i njihovih pomagača, *Dokumenti o izdajstvu Draže Mihailovića*, vol. 1 (Belgrade, 1945)

Du Nay, A., [pseudonym] *The Early History of the Rumanian Language*, Edward Sapir monograph series in Language, Culture and Cognition, vol. 3 (supplement to *Forum Linguisticum*, vol. 2, no. 1, August 1977) (Lake Bluff, Illinois, 1977)

Durham, M. E., *Twenty Years of Balkan Tangle* (London, 1920)

Some Tribal Origins, Laws, and Customs of the Balkans (London, 1928)

Duvernoy, J., *Le Catharisme*, 2 vols. (Toulouse, 1976–9)

Dvornik, F., *Byzantine Missions among the Slavs* (New Brunswick, New Jersey, 1970)

Džaja, S., *Die 'bosnische Kirche' und das Islamisierungsproblem Bosniens und der Herzegowina in den Forschungen nach dem zweiten Weltkrieg* (Munich, 1978)

'Fineova interpretacija bosanske srednjovjekovne konfesionalne poviesti', in J. Turčinović, ed., *Povijesno-teološko simpozij u povodu 500. obljetnice smrti bosanske kraljice Katarine* (Sarajevo, 1979), pp. 52–9

Konfessionalität und Nationalität Bosniens und der Hercegowina: voremanzipatorische Phase 1463–1804, Südosteuropäische Arbeiten, vol. 80 (Munich, 1984)

Emmert, T. A., 'The Battle of Kosovo: Early Reports of Victory and Defeat', in W. S. Vucinich and T. A. Emmert, eds., *Kosovo: Legacy of a Medieval Battle* (Minneapolis, Minnesota, 1991), pp. 19–40

Érignac, L., *La Révolte des Croates de Villefranche-de-Rouergue* (Villefranche-de-Rouergue, 1980)

Esposito, J. L., *Islam and Politics*, 3rd edn. (New York, 1984)

Evans, A. J., *Through Bosnia and the Herzegovina on Foot during the Insurrection, August and September 1875*, 2nd edn. (London, 1877)

Illyrian Letters: A Revised Selection of Correspondence from the Illyrian Provinces of Bosnia, Herzegovina, Montenegro, Albania, Dalmatia, Croatia, and Slavonia, addressed to the 'Manchester Guardian' during the Year 1877 (London, 1878)

Evlija Čelebi, *Putopis odlomci o jugoslovenskim zemljama*, ed. and tr. H. Šabanović (Sarajevo, 1973)

Fermendžin, E., ed., *Acta Bosnae potissimum ecclesiastica cum insertis editorum documentorum regestis ab anno 925 usque ad annum 1752*, Monumenta spectantia historiam slavorum meridionalium, vol. 23 (Zagreb, 1892)

Filipescu, T., *Coloniile române din Bosnia: studiu etnografic şi antropogeografic* (Bucharest, 1906)

Filipović, M., 'Struktura i organizacija srednjovekovnog katuna', in Filipović, M., ed., *Simpozijum o srednjovjekovnom katunu održan 24 i 25 novembra 1961 g.* (Sarajevo, 1963), pp. 45–108

Filipović, N., 'Napomene o islamizaciju u Bosni i Hercegovini u 15. vijeku', *Godišnjak akademije nauka i umjetnosti Bosne i Hercegovine* vol. 7 (= Centar za balkanološka ispitivanja, vol. 5) (1970), pp. 141–67

Fine, J. V. A., 'Aristodios and Rastudije – A Re-examination of the Question', *Godišnjak društva istoričara Bosne i Hercegovine*, vol. 16 (1965), pp. 223–9

'Was the Bosnian Banate Subjected to Hungary in the Second Half of the Thirteenth Century?', *East European Quarterly*, vol. 3 (1969), pp. 167–77

The Bosnian Church: A New Interpretation. A Study of the Bosnian Church and its Place in State and Society from the Thirteenth to the Fifteenth Centuries (Boulder, Colorado, 1975)

The Early Medieval Balkans: A Critical Survey from the Sixth to the Late Twelfth Century (Ann Arbor, Michigan, 1983)

The Late Medieval Balkans: A Critical Survey from the Late Twelfth Century to the Ottoman Conquest (Ann Arbor, Michigan, 1987)

Fortis, A., *Travels into Dalmatia* (London, 1778)

Fraser., A., *The Gypsies* (London, 1992)

Frei, M., 'The Bully of the Balkans', *The Spectator*, 17 August 1991, pp. 11–13

Freidenreich, H. P., *The Jews of Yugoslavia: A Quest for Community* (Philadelphia, 1979)

Gavranović, B., *Bosna i Hercegovina od 1853–1870 godine* (Sarajevo, 1956)

Gazić, L., 'Les Collections des manuscrits orientaux à Sarajevo', *Prilozi za orijentalnu filologiju*, vol. 30 (1980), pp. 153–7

Gibbons, J., *London to Sarajevo* (London, 1930)

Gilliat-Smith, B., 'The Dialect of the Gypsies of Serbo-Croatia', *Journal of the Gypsy Lore Society*, 3rd series, vol. 27 (1948), pp. 139–44

Gimbutas, M., *The Slavs* (London, 1971)

Glenny, M., *The Fall of Yugoslavia: The Third Balkan War* (London, 1992)

Glück, L., 'Zur physischen Anthropologie der Zigeuner in Bosnien und der Hercegovina', *Wissenschaftliche Mittheilungen aus Bosnien und der Herzegowina*, vol. 5 (1897), pp. 403–33

Glušac, V., 'Srednjovekovna "bosanska crkva"', *Prilozi za književnost, jezik, istoriju i folklor*, vol. 4 (1924), pp. 1–55

Goldstein, S., ed., *Jews in Yugoslavia* (Zagreb, 1989)

Gow, J., *Legitimacy and the Military: The Yugoslav Crisis* (London, 1992)
'One Year of War in Bosnia and Herzegovina', *Radio Free Europe/Radio Liberty Research Report*, vol. 2, no. 23 (4 June 1993), pp. 1–13
Grmek, M., Gjidara, M., and N. Simac, eds., *Le Nettoyage ethnique: documents historiques sur une idéologie serbe* (Paris, 1993)
Guldescu, S., 'Political History to 1526', in F. M. Eterovich and C. Spalatin, eds., *Croatia: Land, People, Culture*, 2 vols. (Toronto, 1964), vol. 1, pp. 76–130
Gušić, B., 'Wer sind die Morlachen im adriatischen Raum?', *Balcanica*, vol. 4 (1973), pp. 453–64
Gyóni, M., 'La Transhumance des Vlaques balkaniques au moyen age', *Byzantinoslavica*, vol. 12 (1951), pp. 29–42
Haarmann, H., *Der lateinische Lehnwortschatz im Albanischen*, Hamburger philologische Studien, vol. 19 (Hamburg, 1972)
Hadžibegić, H., 'Džizja ili harač', *Prilozi za orijentalnu filologiju i istoriju jugoslovanskih naroda pod turskom vladavinom*, part 1: vols. 3–4 (1952–3), pp. 55–135; part 2: vol. 5 (1954–5), pp. 43–102
Hadžijahić, M., 'Uz prilog profesora Vojislava Bogićevića', *Historijski zbornik*, vol. 3 (1950), pp. 189–92
'Udio Hamzevija u atentatu na Mehmed-pašu Sokolovića', *Prilozi za orijentalnu filologiju i istoriju jugoslovanskih naroda pod turskom vladavinom*, vol. 5 (1954–5), pp. 325–30
'Die priviligierten Städte zur Zeit des osmanischen Feudalismus', *Südostforschungen*, vol. 20 (1961), pp. 130–58
'Die Anfänge der nationalen Entwicklung in Bosnien und in der Herzegowina', *Südostforschungen*, vol. 21 (1962), pp. 168–92
'Die Kämpfe der Ajane in Mostar bis zum Jahre 1833', *Südostforschungen*, vol. 28 (1969), pp. 123–81
Od tradicije do identiteta: geneza nacionalnog pitanja bosanskih muslimana (Sarajevo, 1974)
'Sinkretistički elementi u Islamu u Bosni i Hercegovini', *Prilozi za orijentalnu filologiju*, vols. 28–9 (1978–9), pp. 301–28
Porijeklo bosanskih Muslimana (Sarajevo, 1990)
Handžić, A., 'Bosanski namjesnik Hekim-oglu Ali-paša', *Prilozi za orijentalnu filologiju i istoriju jugoslovanskih naroda pod turskom vladavinom*, vol. 5 (1954–5), pp. 135–80
Tuzla i njena okolina u 16. vijeku (Sarajevo, 1975)
'O gradskom stanovništvu u Bosni u XVI stoljeću', *Prilozi za orijentalnu filologiju*, vols. 28–9 (1978–9), pp. 247–56
'U ulozi derviša u formiranju gradskih naselja u Bosni u XV stoljeću',

Prilozi za orijentalnu filologiju, vol. 31 (1981), pp. 169–78

Hangi, A., *Die Moslim's in Bosnien-Herzegowina: ihre Lebensweise, Sitten und Gebräuche* (Sarajevo, 1907)

Hasluck, F. W., *Christianity and Islam under the Sultans*, ed. M. M. Hasluck, 2 vols. (Oxford, 1929)

Hasluck, M. M., 'Firman of A.H. 1013–14 (A.D. 1604–5) Regarding Gypsies in the Western Balkans', *Journal of the Gypsy Lore Society*, 3rd series, vol. 27 (1948), pp. 1–12

Hauptmann, F., *Borba muslimana Bosne i Hercegovine za vjersku vakufsko-mearifsku autonomiju* (Sarajevo, 1967)

Hawkesworth, C., *Ivo Andrić: Bridge between East and West* (London, 1984)

Hayden, R. M., 'The Partition of Bosnia and Herzegovina, 1990–1993', *Radio Free Europe/Radio Liberty Research Report*, vol. 2, no. 22 (28 May 1993), pp. 1–14

Helsinki Watch, *War Crimes in Bosnia-Hercegovina* (New York, 1992)

Hinsley, F. W., *et al.*, *British Intelligence in the Second World War*, 5 vols. (London, 1979–90)

Höpken, W., 'Die jugoslawischen Kommunisten und die bosnischen Muslime', in A. Kappeler, G. Simon and G. Brunner, eds., *Die Muslime in der Sowjetunion und in Jugoslawien: Identität, Politik, Widerstand* (Cologne, 1989), pp. 181–210

Hoptner, J. B., *Yugoslavia in Crisis, 1934–1941* (New York, 1962)

Hornby, L. G., *Balkan Sketches: An Artist's Wanderings in the Kingdom of the Serbs* (Boston, 1927)

Hory, L. and M. Broszat, *Der kroatische Ustascha-Staat* (Stuttgart, 1964)

Hottinger, J. H., *Historia orientalis* (Zurich, 1660)

Höttl, W., *The Secret Front* (London, 1953)

Hrabak, B., 'Izvoz plemenih metala iz Bosne u Dubrovnik u vreme osmanlijske vlasti', *Godišnjak društva istoričara Bosne i Hercegovine*, vols. 28–30 (1977–9), pp. 75–85

Hukić, A., ed., *Islam i muslimani u Bosni i Hercegovini* (Sarajevo, 1977)

Huković, M., *Alhamadio književnost i njeni stvaraoci* (Sarajevo, 1986)

Huld, M. E., *Basic Albanian Etymologies* (Columbus, Ohio, 1983)

Hussein, A., 'Communist Yugoslavia's Fear of Islam', *Issues in the Islamic Movement*, vol. 4 (1983–4), pp. 34–5

Illyés, E., *Ethnic Continuity in the Carpatho-Danubian Area* (Boulder, Colorado, 1988)

Imamović, M., 'O historiji bošnjačkog pokušaja', in A. Purivatra, M. Imamović and R. Mahmutćehajić, *Muslimani i Bošnjaštvo* (Sarajevo, 1991), pp. 31–70

Irwin, Z. T., 'The Islamic Revival and the Muslims of Bosnia-Hercegovina', *East European Quarterly*, vol. 17 (1984), pp. 437–58

'The Fate of Islam in the Balkans: A Comparison of Four State Policies', in P. Ramet, ed., *Religion and Nationalism in Soviet and East European Politics*, revised edn. (Durham, North Carolina, 1989), pp. 378–407

Islami, H., *Fshati i Kosovës: kontribut për studimin sociologjiko-demografik të evolucionit rural* (Priština, 1985)

Ivanović, V., 'Reforma vanjske politike', in V. Ivanović and A. Djilas, eds., *Demokratske reforme* (London, 1982), pp. 40–50

Izetbegović, A., *Islam izmedju Istoka i Zapada* (Sarajevo, 1988)

Islamska deklaracija (Sarajevo, 1990)

Jelavich, B., *History of the Balkans*, 2 vols. (Cambridge, 1983)

and C. Jelavich, *The Establishment of the Balkan National States, 1804–1920*, A History of East Central Europe, ed. P. F. Sugar and D. Treadgold, vol. 8 (Seattle, Washington, 1977)

Jireček, K., *Die Handelsstrassen und Bergwerke von Serbien und Bosnien während des Mittelalters: historisch-geographische Studien* (Prague, 1879)

'Die Romanen in den Städten Dalmatiens während des Mittelalters', *Denkschriften der kaiserlichen Akademie der Wissenschaften: philosophisch-historische Classe*; part 1: vol. 48, no. 3 (1902); parts 2 and 3: vol. 49, nos. 1 and 2 (1904)

Istorija Srba, 4 vols. (Belgrade, 1922–3)

Jukić, I. F. ('Slavoljub Bošnjak'), *Zemljopis i poviestnica Bosne* (Zagreb, 1851)

Kapidžić, H., 'Austro-ugarska politika u Bosni i Hercegovini i jugoslovensko pitanje za vrijeme prvog svjetskog rata', *Godišnjak istoriskog društva Bosne i Hercegovine*, vol. 9 (1957), pp. 7–53

Hercegovački ustanak 1882 godine (Sarajevo, 1958)

'Pokret za iseljavanje srpskog seljaštva iz Hercegovine u Srbiju 1902 godine', *Godišnjak društva istoričara Bosne i Hercegovine*, vol. 11 (1960), pp. 23–54

Karapandzich, *The Bloodiest Yugoslav Spring, 1945 – Tito's Katyns and Gulags* (New York, 1980)

Karchmar, L., *Draža Mihailović and the Rise of the Četnik Movement, 1941–1942*, 2 vols. (New York, 1987)

Kaulfuss, R. S., *Die Slawen in den ältesten Zeiten bis Samo (623)* (Berlin, 1842)

Klaić, V., *Geschichte Bosniens von den ältesten Zeiten bis zum Verfalle des Königreiches*, tr. I. von Bojničić (Leipzig, 1885)

Klen, D., 'Pokrštavanje "Turske" djece u Rijeci u XVI i XVII stoljeću', *Historijski zbornik – Šidakov zbornik*, vols. 29–30 (1976–7), pp. 203–7

Kniewald, D., 'Vjerodostojnost latinskih izvora o bosanskim krstjanima', *Rad jugoslavenske akademije znanosti i umjetnosti*, vol. 270 (1949), pp. 115–276

'Hierarchie und Kultus bosnischer Christen', in *L'Oriente cristiano nella storia della civiltà*, Accademia nazionale dei Lincei, quaderno 62 (Rome, 1964), pp. 579–605

Kočović, B., *Žrtve drugog svetskog rata u Jugoslaviji* (London, 1985)

Koetschet, J., *Aus Bosniens letzter Türkenzeit*, ed. G. Grassl (Vienna, 1905)

Osman Pascha, der letzte grosse Wesier Bosniens, und seine Nachfolger, ed. G. Grassl (Sarajevo, 1909)

Koštunica, V., and K. Čavoški, *Party Pluralism or Monism: Social Movements and the Political System in Yugoslavia, 1944–1949* (Boulder, Colorado, 1985)

Kovačević, J., *Istorija Crne Gore* (Titograd, 1967)

Kreševljaković, H., *Kapetanije u Bosni i Hercegovini*, Naučno društvo n.r. Bosne i Hercegovine, djela vol. 5 (Sarajevo, 1954)

Esnafi i obrti u Bosni i Hercegovini, Naučno društvo n.r. Bosne i Hercegovine, djela vol. 17 (Sarajevo, 1961)

Kriss, R., and H. Kriss-Heinrich, *Volksglaube im Bereich des Islam*, 2 vols. (Wiesbaden, 1960–2)

Krizman, B., *Hrvatska u prvom svjetskom ratu i hrvatsko-srpski politički odnosi* (Zagreb, 1989)

Kulišić, Š., 'Razmatranja o porijeklu Muslimana u Bosni i Hercegovini', *Glasnik zemaljskog muzeja u Sarajevu*, n.s., vol. 8 (1953), pp. 145–58

Kunt, I. M., 'Transformation of *Zimmi* into *Askerî*', in B. Braude and B. Lewis, eds., *Christians and Jews in the Ottoman Empire: The Functioning of a Plural Society*, 2 vols. (New York, 1982), vol. 1, pp. 55–67

The Sultan's Servants: The Transformation of Ottoman Provincial Government, 1550–1650 (New York, 1983)

Kuripešić, B., *Itinerarium der Botschaftsreise des Josef von Lamberg und Niclas Jurischitz durch Bosnien, Serbien, Bulgarien nach Konstantinopel 1530*, ed. E. Lamberg-Schwarzenberg (Innsbruck, 1910)

Lachmann, R., ed. and tr., *Memoiren eines Janitscharen oder Türkische Chronik*, Slavische Geschichtsschreiber, vol. 8 (Graz, 1975)

Lambert, M. D., *Medieval Heresy: Popular Movements from Bogomil to Hus* (1st edn., London, 1977; 2nd edn., London, 1992)

Lapenna, I., 'Suverenitet i federalizam u ustavu Jugoslavije', in V. Ivanović and A. Djilas, eds., *Demokratske reforme* (London, 1982), pp. 9–30

Lasić, D., *De vita et operibus S. Iacobi de Marchia: studium et recensio quorundam textuum* (Ancona, 1974)

Laštrić, F. ['Philippus ab Occhievia'], *Epitome vetustatum bosnensis provinciae* (Venice, 1765)

Le Bouvier, G., *Le Livre de la description des pays* (Paris, 1908)

Lees, M., *The Rape of Serbia: The British Role in Tito's Grab for Power 1943–1944* (San Diego, California, 1990)

Lehfeldt, W., *Das serbokroatische Aljamiado-Schrifttum der bosnisch-hercegovinischen Muslime: Transkriptionsprobleme*, Beiträge zur Kenntnis Südosteuropas und des Nahen Orients, vol. 9 (Munich, 1969)

Levntal, Z., ed., *Zločini fašističkih okupatora i njihovih pomogača protiv jevreja u Jugoslaviji* (Belgrade, 1952)

Levy, M., *Die Sephardim in Bosnien: ein Beitrag zur Geschichte der Juden auf der Balkan-Halbinsel* (Sarajevo, 1911)

Lewis, B., *The Emergence of Modern Turkey*, 2nd edn. (Oxford, 1968)

Lieu, S. N. C., *Manichaeism in the Later Roman Empire and Medieval China: A Historical Survey* (Manchester, 1985)

Lieven, D., *Nicholas II: Emperor of All the Russias* (London, 1993)

Lilek, E., 'Vjerske starine iz Bosne i Hercegovine', *Glasnik zemaljskog muzeja*, vol. 6 (1894), pp. 141–66, 259–81, 365–88, 631–74

Lockwood, W. G., *European Muslims: Economy and Ethnicity in Western Bosnia* (New York, 1975)

Loos, M., *Dualist Heresy in the Middle Ages* (Prague, 1974)

'Les Derniers Cathares de l'occident et leurs relations avec l'église patarine de Bosnie', *Historijski zbornik – Šidakov zbornik*, vols. 29–30 (1976–7), pp. 113–26

Lord, A. B., 'The Battle of Kosovo in Albanian and Serbocroatian Oral Epic Songs', in A. Pipa and S. Repishti, eds., *Studies on Kosova* (Boulder, Colorado, 1984), pp. 65–83

Lovrich, G., *Osservazioni sopra diversi pezzi del viaggio in Dalmazia del signor Alberto Fortis* (Venice, 1776)

Lydall, H., *Yugoslavia in Crisis* (Oxford, 1989)

Maček, V., *In the Struggle for Freedom*, tr. E. and S. Gazi (London, 1957)

McFarlane, B., *Yugoslavia: Politics, Economics and Society* (London, 1988)

McGowan, B., 'Food Supply and Taxation on the Middle Danube (1568–1579)', *Archivum Ottomanicum*, vol. 1 (1969), pp. 138–96

Economic Life in Ottoman Europe: Taxation, Trade and the Struggle for Land, 1600–1800 (Cambridge, 1981)

MacKenzie, D., *The Serbs and Russian Pan-Slavism 1875–1878* (Ithaca, New York, 1967)

Magaš, B., *The Destruction of Yugoslavia: Tracking the Break-up, 1980–1992* (London, 1993)

Maier, H., *Die deutschen Siedlungen in Bosnien* (Stuttgart, 1924)
Malcolm, N. R., 'Waiting for a War', *The Spectator*, 19 October 1991, pp. 14–15
Malingoudis, F., *Slavoi stê mesaiônikê Ellada* (Salonica, 1991)
Mandić, D., *Postanak Vlaha prema novim poviesnim iztraživanjima* (Buenos Aires, 1956)
'The Ethnic and Religious History of Bosnia and Hercegovina', in F. M. Eterovich and C. Spalatin, eds., *Croatia: Land, People, Culture*, 2 vols. (Toronto, 1964), vol. 2, pp. 362–93
Etnička povijest Bosne i Hercegovine (Rome, 1967)
Franjevačka Bosna: razvoj i uprava bosanske vikarije i provincije 1340–1735 (Rome, 1968)
Mandić, M., *Povijest okupacije Bosne i Hercegovine (1878)* (Zagreb, 1910)
Marienescu, A. M., 'Ilirii, macedo-românii şi albanesii: dissertaţiune istorică', *Analele Academiei române*, series 2, vol. 26 (1903–4), pp. 117–69
Markotić, V., 'Archaeology', in F. M. Eterovich and C. Spalatin, eds., *Croatia: Land, People, Culture*, 2 vols. (Toronto, 1964), vol. 1, pp. 20–75
Martin, D., *The Web of Disinformation: Churchill's Yugoslav Blunder* (San Diego, California, 1990)
Masleša, V., *Mlada Bosna* (Belgrade, 1945)
Matasović, J., 'Tri humanista o patarenima', *Godišnjak Skopskog filozofskog fakulteta*, vol. 1 (1930), pp. 235–51
Maurer, F., *Eine Reise durch Bosnien, die Saveländer und Ungarn* (Berlin, 1870)
Mazower, M., *The War in Bosnia: An Analysis* (London, 1992)
Mažuranić, V., *Südslaven im Dienste des Islams (vom X. bis XVI. Jahrhundert): ein Forschungsbericht*, ed. and tr. C. Lucerna (Zagreb, 1928)
Migne, J.–P., ed., *Patrologiae cursus completus*, series latina prima, 221 vols. (Paris, 1844–64)
Milazzo, M. J., *The Chetnik Movement and the Yugoslav Resistance* (Baltimore, 1975)
Miletić, M., *I 'Krstjani' di Bosnia alla luce dei loro monumenti di pietra*, Orientalia christiana analecta, vol. 149 (Rome, 1957)
Milivojević, M., *Descent into Chaos: Yugoslavia's Worsening Crisis* (London, 1989)
Miller, W., *Travels and Politics in the Near East* (London, 1898)
Essays on the Latin Orient (Cambridge, 1921)
Mirmiroglou, V., *Oi Dervissai* (Athens, 1940)
Moore, P., 'The "Question of all Questions": Internal Borders', *Radio Free*

Europe/Radio Liberty Report on Eastern Europe, vol. 2, no. 38 (20 September 1991), pp. 34–9

'Endgame in Bosnia and Herzegovina?', *Radio Free Europe/Radio Liberty Report on Eastern Europe*, vol. 2, no. 32 (13 August 1993), pp. 17–23

Mraz, G., *Prinz Eugen: sein Leben, sein Wirken, seine Zeit* (Vienna, 1985)

Muir Mackenzie, G., and A. P. Irby, *Travels in the Slavonic Provinces of Europe*, 3rd edn., 2 vols. (London, 1877)

Mujić, M., 'Položaj cigana u jugoslovenskim zemjlama pod osmanskom vlašću', *Prilozi za orijentalnu filologiju i istoriju jugoslovenskih naroda pod turskom vladavinom*, vols. 3–4 (1952–3), pp. 137–91

'Prilog proučavanju uživanja alkoholni pića u Bosni i Hercegovini pod osmanskom vlašću', *Prilozi za orijentalnu filologiju i istoriju jugoslovanskih naroda pod turskom vladavinom*, vol. 5 (1954–5), pp. 286–98

Mutafchieva, V., 'K'm v'prosa za chiflitsite v osmanskata imperiya prez XIV–XVII v.', *Istoricheski pregled*, vol. 14 (1958), pp. 34–57

Nagata, Y., *Materials on the Bosnian Notables*, Studia culturae islamicae, no. 11 (Tokyo, 1979)

Nandriş, J. G., 'The Aromâni: Approaches to the Evidence', in R. Rohr, ed., *Die Aromunen: Sprache–Geschichte–Geographie* (Hamburg, 1987), pp. 15–71

Năsturel, P. Ş., 'Les Valaques balcaniques aux Xe–XIIe siècles (mouvements de population et colonisation dans la Romanie grecque et latine)', *Byzantinische Forschungen*, vol. 7 (1979), pp. 89–112

ed., *Bibliografie macedo-română* (Freiburg, 1984)

Naumov, E., 'Balkanskiye vlakhi i formirovanye drevneserbskoi narodnosti', in Ivanov, V. V., Korolyuk, V. D., and E. P. Naumov, eds., *Etnicheskaya istoriya vostochnikh romantsev: drevnost'i sredniye vyeka* (Moscow, 1979), pp. 18–61

Naval Intelligence Division, British Admiralty, *Jugoslavia*, Geographical Handbook series, B.R. 393, 3 vols. (London, 1944)

Neubacher, H., *Sonderauftrag Südost 1940–1945*, 2nd edn. (Göttingen, 1957)

Niger, D. M., *Geographiae commentariorum libri XI (Basel, 1557)*

Novaković, S., *Selo* (Belgrade, 1965)

Obolensky, D., *The Bogomils: A Study in Balkan Neo-Manichaeism* (Cambridge, 1948)

The Byzantine Commonwealth: Eastern Europe, 500–1453 (London, 1974)

d'Ohsson, M., *Tableau général de l'Empire othoman*, 7 vols., Paris, 1788–1824

Okiç, T., 'Les Kristians (Bogomiles Parfaits) de Bosnie d'après des documents turcs inédits', *Südostforschungen*, vol. 19 (1960), pp. 108–33

Orbini, M., *Il Regno de gli slavi hoggi corrottamente detti Schiavoni* (Pesaro, 1601)

Papoulia, B. D., *Ursprung und Wesen der 'Knabenlese' im osmanischen Reich*, Südosteuropäische Arbeiten, vol. 59 (Munich, 1963)

Pašalić, E., and R. Mišević, eds., *Sarajevo* (Sarajevo, 1954)

Paskaleva, V., 'Osmanlı balkan eyâletlerinin avrupalı devletlerle ticaretleri tarihine katki (1700–1850)', *Istanbul üniversitesi iktisat fakültesi mecmuası*, vol. 27 (1967–8), pp. 37–74

Pavlovich, P., *The Serbians: The Story of a People* (Toronto, 1983)

Pavlowitch, S. K., 'Society in Serbia, 1791–1830', in R. Clogg, ed., *Balkan Society in the Age of Greek Independence* (London, 1981), pp. 137–56

Tito, Yugoslavia's Great Dictator: A Reassessment (London, 1992)

Peledija, E., *Bosanski ejalet od karlovačkog do požarevačkog mira 1699–1718* (Sarajevo, 1989)

Pelletier, R., *Sarajevo et sa région: chez les Yougoslaves de la Save à l'Adriatique* (Paris, 1934)

Peroche, G., *Histoire de la Croatie et des nations slaves du sud, 395–1992* (Paris, 1992)

Pertusier, C., *La Bosnie considérée dans ses rapports avec l'Empire Ottoman* (Paris, 1822)

Petranović, B., *Bogomili, crkva bosanska i krstjani* (Zadar, 1867)

Petrović, L., *Kršćani bosanske crkve* (Sarajevo, 1953)

Pisarev, Y. A., and M. Ekmečić, *Osvoboditelnaya borba narodov Bosnii i Gertsegovini i Rossiya*, 2 vols. (Moscow, 1985–8)

Popović, A., *L'Islam balkanique: les musulmans du sud-est européen dans la période post-ottomane*, Osteuropa-Institut an der freien Universität Berlin: balkanologische Veröffentlichungen, vol. 11 (Berlin, 1986)

'Islamische Bewegungen in Jugoslawien', in A. Kappeler, G. Simon and G. Brunner, eds., *Die Muslime in der Sowjetunion und in Jugoslavien: Identität, Politik, Widerstand* (Cologne, 1989), pp. 273–86

Popović, I., 'Valacho-serbica: der rumänische Spracheinfluss auf das Serbokroatische und dessen Geographie', *Südostforschungen*, vol. 21 (1962), pp. 370–93

Porphyrogenitus: *see* Constantine Porphyrogenitus

Porter, Sir James, *Observations on the Religion, Law, Government, and Manners, of the Turks* (London, 1768)

Poulton, H., *The Balkans: Minorities and States in Conflict* (London, 1991)

Puech, H. C., 'Catharisme médiévale et Bogomilisme', in *Oriente ed occidente nel medio evo* (Rome, 1957), pp. 84–104

Purivatra, A., *Nacionalni i politički razvitak muslimana* (Sarajevo, 1972)
Quiclet, Monsieur, *Les Voyages de M. Quiclet à Constantinople par Terre* (Paris, 1664)
Rački, F., *Bogomili i patareni*, Srpska kraljeva akademija, posebna izdanja, vol. 87 (Belgrade, 1931)
Radojčić, N., *Srpska istorija Mavra Orbinija*, Srpska akademija nauka, posebna izdanje, vol. 152 (Belgrade, 1950)
Radojčić, S., 'Reljefi bosanskih i hercegovačkih stečaka', *Letopis Matice Srpske*, year 137, vol. 287 (1961), pp. 1–15
Radojičić, D., '"Bulgaralbanitoblahos" et "Serbalbanitobulgaroblahos" – deux caractéristiques ethniques du sud-est européen des XIVe et XVe siècles. Nicodim de Tismana et Grégoire Camblak', *Romanoslavica*, vol. 13 (1966), pp. 77–9
Ramet, P., 'Die Muslime Bosniens als Nation', in A. Kappeler, G. Simon and G. Brunner, eds., *Die Muslime in der Sowjetunion und in Jugoslavien: Identität, Politik, Widerstand* (Cologne, 1989), pp. 107–14
Ramet, S. P., *Nationalism and Federalism in Yugoslavia, 1962–1991*, 2nd edn. (Bloomington, Indiana, 1992)
Redžić, E., *Muslimansko autonomaštvo i 13. SS divizija: autonomija Bosne i Hercegovine i Hitlerov treći rajh* (Sarajevo, 1987)
Rivet, C., *Chez les slaves libérés: en Yougoslavie* (Paris, 1919)
Roberts, W. R., *Tito, Mihailović and the Allies, 1941–1945*, 2nd edn. (Durham, North Carolina, 1987)
Rojo, A., *Yugoslavia, Holocausto en los Balcanes: la agonia de un estado y por qué se matan entre si sus habitantes* (Barcelona, 1992)
Rośkiewicz, J., *Studien über Bosnien und die Herzegowina* (Leipzig, 1868)
Rostovtseff, M., *Iranians and Greeks in Southern Russia* (Oxford, 1922)
Roth, C., ed., *The Sarajevo Haggadah* (London, 1963)
Rothenberg, *The Austrian Military Border in Croatia, 1522–1747*, Illinois Studies in the Social Sciences, vol. 48 (Urbana, Illinois, 1960)
The Military Border in Croatia 1740–1881 (Chicago, 1966)
Runciman, S., *The Medieval Manichee: A Study of the Christian Dualist Heresy* (Cambridge, 1947)
Rusinow, D., *The Yugoslav Experiment, 1948–1974* (Berkeley, California, 1978)
Russu, I. I., *Illirii: istoria, limba şi onomastica, romanizarea* (Bucharest, 1969)
Rycaut, P., *The Present State of the Ottoman Empire* (London, 1668)
Šabanović, H., 'Pitanje turske vlasti u Bosni do pohoda Mehmeda II 1463 godine', *Godišnjak društva istoričara Bosne i Hercegovine*, vol. 7 (1955), pp. 37–51

'Bosansko krajište 1448–1463', *Godišnjak istoriskog društva Bosne i Hercegovine*, vol. 9 (1957), pp. 177–219

Bosanski pašaluk: postanak i upravna podjela, Naučno društvo n.r. Bosne i Hercegovine, djela, vol. 14 (Sarajevo, 1959)

'Vojno uredjenje Bosne od 1463. g. do kraja XVI stoljeća', *Godišnjak istoriskog društva Bosne i Hercegovine*, vol. 11 (1960), pp. 173–223

Šamić, M., *Les Voyageurs français en Bosnie à la fin du XVIIIe siècle et au début du XIXe et le pays tel qu'ils l'ont vu* (Paris, 1960)

Schmid, F., *Bosnien und die Herzegovina unter der Verwaltung Österreich-Ungarns* (Leipzig, 1914)

Schmitt, B., *The Annexation of Bosnia 1908–1909* (Cambridge, 1937)

Scholem, G., *Major Trends in Jewish Mysticism* (London, 1955)

Sabbatai Ṣevi: The Mystical Messiah, 1626–1676 (London, 1973)

von Schwandner, J. G., ed., *Scriptores rerum hungaricarum, dalmaticarum, croaticarum, et sclavonicarum veteres ac genuini*, 3 vols. (Vienna, 1746–8)

Seton Watson, R. W., *The Role of Bosnia in International Politics (1875–1914)* (London, 1933)

Sharp, J. M. O., *Bankrupt in the Balkans: British Policy in Bosnia* (London, 1993)

Shaw, S. J., 'The Ottoman View of the Balkans', in C. Jelavich and B. Jelavich, eds., *The Balkans in Transition: Essays on the Development of Balkan Life and Politics since the Eighteenth Century* (Berkeley, California, 1963)

History of the Ottoman Empire and Modern Turkey, 2 vols. (Cambridge, 1976–7)

The Jews of the Ottoman Empire and the Turkish Republic (London, 1991)

Sicard, E., *La Zadruga sud-slave dans l'évolution du groupe domestique* (Paris, 1943)

Šidak, J., 'Problem "bosanske crkve" u našoj historiografiji od Petranovića do Glušca', *Rad jugoslavenske akademije znanosti i umjetnosti*, vol. 259 (1937), pp. 147–67

Studije o 'crkvu bosanskoj' i bogomilstvu (Zagreb, 1975)

Sikirić, S., 'Derviskolostorok és szent sírok Boszniában', *Túrán*, nos. 9–10 (November–December 1918), pp. 574–607

Sirc, L., 'The National Question in Yugoslavia', *The South Slav Journal*, vol. 9, nos. 1–2 (1986), pp. 80–93

Šišić, F., ed. and tr., *Letopis popa Dukljanina* (Belgrade, 1928)

Bosna i Hercegovina za vezirovanja Omer-paše Latasa (1850–1852) (Subotica, 1938)

Skarić, V., *Srpski pravoslavni narod i crkva u Sarajevu u 17. i 18. vijeku* (Sarajevo, 1928)

'Popis bosanskih spahija iz 1123 (1711) godine', *Glasnik zemaljskog muzeja*, vol. 42 (1930), pp. 1–99

Sarajevo i njegova okolina od najstarijih vremena do austro-ugarske okupacije (Sarajevo, 1937)

Skarić, V., Nuri-Hadžić, O., and N. Stojanović, *Bosna i Hercegovina pod austro-ugarskom upravnom* (Belgrade, *c.* 1918)

Slijepčević, D., *Pitanje Bosne i Hercegovine u XIX veku* (Cologne, 1981)

Šljivo, G., *Omer-Paša Latas u Bosni i Hercegovini 1850–1852* (Sarajevo, 1977)

Smailović, I., *Muslimanska imena orijentalnog porijekla u Bosni i Hercegovini* (Sarajevo, 1977)

Solovjev, A., 'La Messe cathare', *Cahiers d'études cathares*, vol. 3, no. 12 (1951–2), pp. 199–206

'Le Témoignage de Paul Rycaut sur les restes des Bogomiles en Bosnie', *Byzantion*, vol. 23 (1953), pp. 73–86

'Svedočanstva pravoslavnih izvora o bogomilstvu na Balkani', *Godišnjak istoriskog društva Bosne i Hercegovine*, vol. 5 (1953), pp. 1–103

'Le Symbolisme des monuments funéraires bogomiles', *Cahiers d'études cathares*, vol. 5, no. 18 (1954), pp. 92–114

'Le Tatouage symbolique en Bosnie', *Cahiers d'études cathares*, vol. 5, no. 19 (1954), pp. 157–62

'Simbolika srednjovekovnih spomenika u Bosni i Hercegovini', *Godišnjak istoriskog društva Bosne i Hercegovine*, vol. 8 (1956), pp. 5–65

'Bogumilentum und Bogumilengräber in den südslawischen Ländern', in W. Gülich, ed., *Völker und Kulturen Südosteuropas* (Munich, 1959), pp. 182–6

Sorabji, C., *Bosnia's Muslims: Challenging Past and Present Misconceptions* (London, 1992)

Soulis, G. C., 'The Gypsies in the Byzantine Empire and the Balkans in the late Middle Ages', *Dumbarton Oaks Papers*, no. 15 (1961), pp. 142–65

Stadtmüller, G., *Geschichte Südosteuropas* (Munich, 1950)

Forschungen zur albanischen Frühgeschichte, 2nd edn. (Wiesbaden, 1966)

Stanojević, G., 'Jedan pomen o kristjanima u Dalmaciji iz 1692 godine', *Godišnjak istoriskog društva Bosne i Hercegovine*, vol. 11 (1960), pp. 273–4

Start, L. E., and M. E. Durham, *The Durham Collection of Garments and Embroideries from Albania and Yugoslavia* (Halifax, 1939)

'Statuto della comunità musulmana della ex Jugoslavia (24 ottobre 1936)', *Oriente moderno*, vol. 22 (1936), pp. 44–54

Sterneck, H., *Geografische Verhältnisse, Communicationen und das Reisen in Bosnien, der Herzegovina und Nord-Montenegro* (Vienna, 1877)

Stipčević, A., *The Illyrians*, tr. S. Čulić Burton (Park Ridge, New Jersey, 1977)

Stojadinović, M., *Ni rat ni pakt: Jugoslavija izmedju dva rata* (Buenos Aires, 1963)

Stone, N., *Europe Transformed: 1878–1919* (London, 1983)

Sućeska, A., 'Bedeutung und Entwicklung des Begriffes A'yân im Osmanischen Reich', *Südostforschungen*, vol. 25 (1966), pp. 3–26

'Osmanlı imparatorluğunda Bosna', *Prilozi za orijentalnu filologiju*, vol. 30 (1980), pp. 431–47

Sugar, P. F., *The Industrialization of Bosnia-Hercegovina 1878–1918* (Seattle, Washington, 1963)

Southeastern Europe under Ottoman Rule, 1354–1804, A History of East Central Europe, ed. P. F. Sugar and D. W. Treadgold, vol. 5 (Seattle, Washington, 1977)

Sundhaussen, H., 'Zur Geschichte der Waffen-SS in Kroatien 1941–1945', *Südostforschungen*, vol. 30 (1971), pp. 176–96

Takács, M., 'Sächsische Bergleute im mittelalterlichen Serbien und die "sächsische Kirche" von Novo Brdo', *Südostforschungen*, vol. 50 (1991), pp. 31–60

Tandarić, J., 'Glagoljska pismenost u srednjevjekovnoj Bosni', in J. Turčinović, ed., *Povijesno-teološko simpozij u povodu 500. obljetnice smrti bosanske kraljice Katarine* (Sarajevo, 1979), pp. 47–51

Thallóczy, L., *Studien zur Geschichte Bosniens und Serbiens im Mittelalter*, tr. F. Eckhart (Munich, 1914)

Thoemmel, G., *Geschichtliche, politische und topographisch-statistische Beschreibung des Vilayet Bosnien das ist das eigentliche Bosnien, nebst türkisch Croatien, der Hercegovina und Rascien* (Vienna, 1867)

Thompson, M., *A Paper House: The Ending of Yugoslavia* (London, 1992)

Thomson, H. E., *The Outgoing Turk: Impressions of a Journey through the Western Balkans* (London, 1897)

Thouzellier, C., *Hérésie et hérétiques: Vaudois, Cathares, Patarins, Albigeois*, Storia e letteratura: raccolta di studi e testi, vol. 116 (Rome, 1969)

Tomasevich, J., *Peasants, Politics, and Economic Change in Yugoslavia* (Stanford, California, 1955)

The Chetniks: War and Revolution in Yugoslavia, 1941–1945 (Stanford, California, 1975)

Tomashevich, G. V., 'The Serbian Question in Current Yugoslav Press and Literature', *The South Slav Journal*, vol. 8, nos. 3–4 (1985), pp. 32–41

de Torquemada, J., *Symbolum pro informatione manichaeorum (El Bogomilismo en Bosnia)*, ed. N. López Martínez and V. Proaño Gil, Publicaciones del seminario metropolitana de Burgos, series B, vol. 3 (Burgos, 1958)

Trifunovski, J., 'Geografske karakteristike srednjovekovnih katuna', in Filipovic, M., ed., *Simpozijum o srednjovjekovnom katunu održan 24 i 25 novembra 1961 g.* (Sarajevo, 1963), pp. 19–38

Trimingham, J. S., *The Sufi Orders in Islam* (Oxford, 1971)

Truhelka, Ć., 'Bosančica', *Glasnik zemaljskog muzeja*, vol. 1 (1889), pp. 65–83

'Die Tatowirung bei der Katholiken Bosniens und der Hercegovina', *Wissenschaftliche Mittheilungen aus Bosnien und der Herzegowina*, vol. 4 (1896), pp. 493–508

'Das mittelalterliche Staats- und Gerichtswesen in Bosnien', *Wissenschaftliche Mittheilungen aus Bosnien und der Herzegowina*, vol. 10 (1907), pp. 71–155

Turčinović, J., ed., *Povijesno-teološko simpozij u povodu 500. obljetnice smrti bosanske kraljice Katarine* (Sarajevo, 1979)

Uhlik, R., 'Serbo-Bosnian Gypsy Folk-Tales, no. 8', tr. F. G. Ackerley, *Journal of the Gypsy Lore Society*, 3rd series, vol. 25 (1946), pp. 92–104

'Serbo-Bosnian Gypsy Folk-Tales, no. 9', tr. D. E. Yates, *Journal of the Gypsy Lore Society*, 3rd series, vol. 26 (1947), pp. 116–27

Vacalopoulos, C., 'Tendances caractéristiques du commerce de la Bosnie et le rôle économique des commerçants grecs au début du XIXe siècle', *Balkan Studies*, vol. 20 (1979), pp. 91–110

Valentini, G., 'L'elemento *vlah* nella zona scutarina nel secolo XV', in P. Bartl and H. Glassl, eds., *Südosteuropa unter dem Halbmond: Untersuchungen über Geschichte und Kultur der Südosteuropäischen Völker während der Türkenzeit*, Beiträge zur Kenntnis Südosteuropas und des Nahen Orients, vol. 16 (Munich, 1975), pp. 269–74

Vasić, M., 'Etnička kretanja u bosanskoj krajini u XVI vijeku', *Godišnjak istoriskog društva Bosne i Hercegovine*, vol. 11 (1960), pp. 233–49

Verlinden, C., 'Patarins ou Bogomiles réduits en esclavage', in *Studi in onore di Alberto Pincherle*, Studi e materiali di storia delle religioni, vol. 38 (Rome, 1967), pp. 683–700

Vukanović, T. P., 'Le Firman du sultan Sélim II relatif aux tsiganes, ouvriers dans les mines de Bosnie (1574)', *Études tsiganes*, vol. 15, no. 3 (1969), pp. 8–10

Wace, A., and M. A. Thompson, *The Nomads of the Balkans: An Account of Life and Customs among the Vlachs of Northern Pindus* (London, 1914)

Wakefield, W. L., and A. P. Evans, eds., *Heresies of the High Middle Ages* (New York, 1969)

Weigand, G., *Die Aromunen: ethnographisch-philologisch-historische Untersuchungen über das Volk der sogenannten Makedo-Romänen oder Zinzaren*, 2 vols., Leipzig, 1894–5

'Rumänen und Aromunen in Bosnien', *Jahresbericht des Instituts für rumänische Sprache (rumänisches Seminar) zu Leipzig*, vol. 14 (1908), pp. 171–97

Wenzel, G., ed., *Marino Sanuto világkrónikájának Magyarországot illetö tudósításai*, Magyar történelmi tár, vols. 14 (1869), 24 (1877), 25 (1878)

Wenzel, M., 'A Medieval Mystery Cult in Bosnia and Herzegovina', *Journal of the Warburg and Courtauld Institutes*, vol. 24 (1961), pp. 89–107

'Bosnian Tombstones – who made them and why', *Südostforschungen*, vol. 21 (1962), pp. 102–43

Ukrasni motivi na stećcima (Sarajevo, 1965)

Wheler, G., *A Journey into Greece* (London, 1682)

Wilkes, J., *Dalmatia (History of the Roman Provinces)* (London, 1969)

The Illyrians (Oxford, 1992)

Wilson, D., *The Life and Times of Vuk Stefanović Karadžić, 1787–1864: Literacy, Literature, and National Independence in Serbia* (Oxford, 1970)

Winnifrith, T. J., *The Vlachs: The History of a Balkan People* (London, 1987)

Yelavitch, L., 'Les Musulmans de Bosnie-Herzégovine', *Revue du monde musulman*, vol. 39 (1920), pp. 119–33

Zbornik dokumenata i podataka o narodnooslobodilačkom ratu jugoslavenskih naroda, 14 vols. (Belgrade, 1950–60)

Zimmermann, *Reformation und Gegenreformation bei den Kroaten im österreichisch-ungarischen Grenzraum* (Eisenstadt, 1950)

Zlatar, B., 'O nekim muslimanskim feudalnim porodicama u Bosni', *Prilozi Instituta za istoriju*, vols. 14–15 (1978), pp. 81–139

'Une ville typiquement levantine: Sarajevo au XVIe siècle', in V. Han and M. Adamović, eds., *La Culture urbaine des Balkans (XVe–XIXe siècles): la ville dans les Balkans depuis la fin du moyen age jusqu'au début du XXe siècle. Recueil d'études* (Belgrade, 1991), pp. 95–9

Zlatar, Z., *Our Kingdom Come: The Counter-Reformation, the Republic of Dubrovnik, and the Liberation of the Balkan Slavs* (Boulder, Colorado, 1992)

Zulfikarpašić, A., *Bosanski Muslimani: čimbenik mira izmedju Srba i Hrvata* (Zurich, 1986)

Sarajevski proces: sudjenje muslimanskim intelektualcima 1983 godine (Zurich, 1987)

Index